Popular Music in the Post-Digital Age

Popular Music in the Post-Digital Age

Politics, Economy, Culture and Technology

Edited by Ewa Mazierska, Les Gillon and Tony Rigg

BLOOMSBURY ACADEMIC
NEW YORK • LONDON • OXFORD • NEW DELHI • SYDNEY

BLOOMSBURY ACADEMIC
Bloomsbury Publishing Inc
1385 Broadway, New York, NY 10018, USA
50 Bedford Square, London, WC1B 3DP, UK

BLOOMSBURY, BLOOMSBURY ACADEMIC and the Diana logo are trademarks of
Bloomsbury Publishing Plc

First published in the United States of America 2019

Library of Congress Cataloging-in-Publication Data
Names: Mazierska, Ewa. | Gillon, Les. | Rigg, Tony.
Title: Popular music in the post-digital age : politics, economy, culture and
technology / edited by Ewa Mazierska, Les Gillon and Tony Rigg.
Description: New York, NY : Bloomsbury Academic, 2019. | Includes
bibliographical references and index.
Identifiers: LCCN 2018039972| ISBN 9781501338373 (hardback : alk. paper) |
ISBN 9781501338397 (epdf)
Subjects: LCSH: Music trade. | Music and the Internet. | Popular
music—Social aspects. | Streaming audio—Social aspects.
Classification: LCC ML3790 .P667 2019 | DDC 781.6309/051—dc23 LC record
available at https://lccn.loc.gov/2018039972

ISBN: HB: 978-1-5013-3837-3
       ePDF: 978-1-5013-3839-7
       eBook: 978-1-5013-3838-0

Typeset by RefineCatch Limited, Bungay, Suffolk

To find out more about our authors and books visit www.bloomsbury.com
and sign up for our newsletters.

Contents

List of Contributors   vii

Introduction: The Future of and Through Music
Ewa Mazierska, Les Gillon and Tony Rigg   1

Part One   The Music Industry

1   Rethinking Independence: What Does 'Independent Record Label'
Mean Today? *Patryk Galuszka and Katarzyna M. Wyrzykowska*   33

2   The Future of Digital Music Infrastructures: Expectations and
Promises of the Blockchain 'Revolution' *Paolo Magaudda*   51

3   'The Sound of the Future Is Here Today': The Market for
Post-rock within the Traditional Small Music Festival
Landscape *Kenny Forbes*   69

4   'They Sold the Festival Out!' Axionormativity as the Future of
Festivals *Waldemar Kuligowski*   93

5   The Hidden Worker Bees: Advanced Neoliberalism and
Manchester's Underground Club Scene *Kamila Rymajdo*   111

Part Two   The Musicians and their Music

6   The Adaptive Musician: The Case of Peter Hook and Graham
Massey *Ewa Mazierska and Tony Rigg*   135

7   Where Do We Go From Here? The Future of Composers in the
Post-digital Era *Lars Bröndum*   155

8   Searching for International Success in Europe's Periphery:
The Case of Gin Ga and Fran Palermo *Ewa Mazierska*   171

9   Electro Swing: Re-introduction of the Sounds of the Past
into the Music of the Future *Chris Inglis*   191

Part Three Music Consumption

10 Back to the Future: Proposing a Heuristic for Predicting the Future
    of Recorded Music Use *Mathew Flynn*   211

11 Current Music and Media Use of Young People in Austria:
    The Musical Practice of the Future? *Michael Huber*   235

12 Curators as Taste Entrepreneurs in the Digital Music
    Industries *Emília Barna*   253

13 An Echoic Chamber: Algorithmic Curation and Personalized
    Listening *Andrew Fry*   269

Index   291

List of Contributors

Emília Barna, PhD, is Assistant Professor at the Department of Sociology and Communication, Budapest University of Technology and Economics. Her doctoral thesis (University of Liverpool, 2011) examined the relationship between music scenes, networks and the internet through a case study of contemporary Liverpool indie rock bands. Her main areas of research include the study of popular music scenes and genres, the digital music industries, and popular music, gender and technology. Together with Tamás Tófalvy, she recently co-edited the book *Made in Hungary: Studies in Popular Music* (Routledge, 2017). She is a member of the International Association for the Study of Popular Music (IASPM), former Chair of IASPM Hungary, and an Advisory Board Member for *IASPM@Journal*.

Lars Bröndum, PhD, is a Senior Lecturer in Music at the University of Skövde at the Department of Media, Aesthetics and Narration (School of Informatics). He is also a professional musician and composer, and has performed all around the world. Bröndum's music often explores the interaction between acoustic and electronic instruments and integration of improvization into through-composed music. He performs live as a solo artist and in several ensemble configurations using analogue modular synthesizers, theremin and effect pedals. His album *Fallout* (2015) was awarded 'Best Experimental Music Album' at the SOM (Independent Music Labels of Sweden) Manifest Awards. Bröndum completed his PhD in Music Theory and Composition at University of Pittsburgh in 1992. He also has a masters degree in Composition and Music Theory (1989) and a Bachelors of Music degree in Guitar Performance (1987) from the Dana School of Music at Youngstown State University. Bröndum runs an independent record label, Antennae Media (www.antennaemedia.se).

Mathew Flynn is a lecturer in Music Industry Studies at the University of Liverpool. Before moving into higher education, Mat was a self-employed practitioner in the music industries, owning rehearsal rooms and an independent record label. His research on the music industries was first published in the edited collection *Music Entrepreneurship* (Bloomsbury Academic, 2016). His other primary area of research is on listening attention paid to music. He has published articles in the journals *Kinephanos* and *The Listening Experience Database* exploring the impact of music streaming on listening. In 2017, Mat coordinated the Liverpool section of the UK Live Music Census project. His other research interests include musicians' decision-making processes and the digitization of the music industries.

Kenny Forbes is a Lecturer in Commercial Music at the University of the West of Scotland, where he teaches on live music, the digital economy, cultural studies, copyright and creativity. He achieved his doctorate in 2015 at the University of Glasgow, and his thesis reflected on the 'legendary' reputation of the Glasgow Apollo Theatre (1973–85). Kenny's current research projects involve separate studies that focus on playlist recommendations, remix technology and copyright, and Scotland's hidden music heritage.

Andrew Fry runs Sounds et al, a record label and publisher exploring sound, collaboration and curation, based in Portland, OR, and New York, NY. The label has released work from artists including Grasscut, manabu shimada, Ben Glas, Kaori Suzuki, Ant'lrd and Benoît Pioulard, and has organized and promoted events, exhibitions and performances in the USA, Canada, Germany and the UK, including as part of Design Week Portland, and PICA's TBA festival. He worked in the London music industry for nearly a decade, completed his BSc in Music Technology (Audio Systems) at London Metropolitan University, and his MA at London South Bank University, with a final dissertation on Cage's 4'33".

Patryk Galuszka holds a PhD in Management from the University of Lodz, Poland, and an LLM in Law and Economics from Erasmus University Rotterdam, the Netherlands. Currently, he is an Assistant Professor in the Faculty of Economics and Sociology at the University of Lodz. His articles have been published in journals such as *International Journal of Communication*, *International Journal of Cultural Studies*, *Popular Music*, *Popular Music and Society*, *Media, Culture and Society*, and *Continuum: Journal of Media and Cultural Studies*. His research interests include creative industries, popular music studies, and media economics.

Les Gillon, PhD, is a musician and academic based within the School of Journalism Media and Performance at the University of Central Lancashire. In addition to his teaching and practice-based research in music composition and performance, he also writes on visual art and aesthetics. His book on the Turner Prize, *The Uses of Reason in the Evaluation of Artworks* (Palgrave Macmillan, 2017), explores the rational basis for value judgements in the arts.

Michael Huber is an Associate Professor for Music Sociology at the University of Music and Performing Arts Vienna. His doctoral thesis (Vienna University, 2006) was on the benefits and challenges of sociographical research in urban and rural areas. He is a board member for the Austrian Music Council and the Austrian Music Business Research Association. His research is focused on music reception in the digital age and musical socialization. He has published in German, English, French and Czech, for example, in the *Encyclopedia of Music in the Social and Behavioral Sciences*.

Chris Inglis is a musicologist based in Cardiff, whose research explores the emergence and development of the electro swing genre. After graduating from the BA (Hons) Music, Technology and Innovation programme at De Montfort University, he has recently completed the MA Musicology programme at the University of Sheffield. As of 2018, he is working on his PhD at the University of South Wales. He was published in *Continental Drift, 50 Years of Jazz from Europe*, the proceedings of the 2016 'Continental Drift' conference, held at Edinburgh Napier University. His other research interests include punk and the art of live performance.

Waldemar Kuligowski is Professor at the Department of Ethnology and Cultural Anthropology at Adam Mickiewicz University in Poznań, Poland. He is also an editor-in-chief of *Czas Kultury* (Time of Culture), a Polish socio-cultural quarterly. He has conducted fieldwork in Poland, Germany, Uzbekistan, Spain, Serbia, Hungary and Albania. His research interests focus on the theory of culture, reflexive ethnography, globalization, and the anthropology of motorway and festivals. He has published in English in *Art in Contemporary Cultural Systems. Central and Eastern Europe* (Wydawnictwo Nauka i Innowacje, 2014); *Sterile and Isolated? An Anthropology Today in Hungary and Poland* (Wydawnictwo TIPI, 2015, co-edited with A. Stanisz); and *Cultures of Motorway. Localities through Mobility as an Anthropological Issue* (Wydawnictwo TIPI, 2016).

Paolo Magaudda is Lecturer in Cultural Sociology at the University of Padova (Italy), where he works with the PaSTIS Research Unit, and Adjunct Lecturer in

Sociology of Consumption at the IUSVE University in Venice. His main research interest is the relationship between society, culture and technology, with a specific focus on the history of digital media, the evolution of media consumption practices, and the role of digital music technologies. His most recent books include *A History of Digital Media. An Intermedia and Global Perspective* (with G. Balbi, Routledge, 2018) and *Fallimenti Digitali. Un'archeologia dei 'nuovi' media*, an edited collection on digital media failures (in Italian, co-edited with G. Balbi, 2018). Amongst other activities, he is co-founder of the open access journal *Tecnoscienza: the Italian Journal of Science and Technology Studies* and secretary of STS Italia, the Italian society for the study of science and technology.

Ewa Mazierska is Professor of Film Studies, at the University of Central Lancashire. She has published more than twenty monographs and edited collections on film and popular music. These include *Contemporary Cinema and Neoliberal Ideology* (Routledge, 2018; co-edited with Lars Kristensen), *Sounds Northern: Popular Music, Culture and Place in England's North* (Equinox, 2018), *Popular Music in Eastern Europe: Breaking the Cold War Paradigm* (Palgrave, 2016), *Relocating Popular Music* (Palgrave, 2015; co-edited with Georgina Gregory), and *Falco and Beyond: Neo Nothing Post of All* (Equinox, 2014). Her recent monograph on popular electronic music in Vienna is forthcoming from Routledge in 2019. Mazierska's work has been translated into over twenty languages. She is also principal editor of the Routledge journal *Studies in Eastern European Cinema*.

Tony Rigg leads the Master of Arts programme in Music Industry Management and Promotion at the University of Central Lancashire. He also has thirty years of experience as an active music industry professional. He has occupied senior management positions in market leading, FTSE 250, and privately held organizations, including as Operations Director for Ministry of Sound. He has extensive experience in areas relating to the social consumption of live and recorded music, having overseen the management of more than 100 music venues and thousands of events. He is also a musician, artist and producer with a chart pedigree.

Kamila Rymajdo received a Creative Writing PhD from Kingston University. Previously she studied English Language and Literature at the University of

Manchester, where she also completed an MA. She has published on music, literature and cinema in journals such as *Popular Music History* and edited collections *Contemporary Cinema and Neoliberal Ideology* (edited by Ewa Mazierska and Lars Kristensen, Routledge, 2018) and *Sounds Northern: Popular Music, Culture and Place in England's North* (edited by Ewa Mazierska, Equinox, 2018), as well as writing for magazines such as *Vice, Mixmag, Dazed* and *Interview Magazine*.

Katarzyna M. Wyrzykowska holds a PhD in sociology from the Institute of Philosophy and Sociology of the Polish Academy of Sciences, where she is working as Assistant Professor in the Social Structure Research Department. Her interests include the sociology of music, musical distinctions, and the economic sociology of music. She has published on music in journals such as *Popular Music* and *Media Industries* and the edited collection *Understanding Society through Popular Music* (edited by Joseph A. Kotarba, Routledge, 2017). Her current research project, 'Musical distinctions. Musical tastes and social stratification in the process of Poles' lifestyles formation', examines to what extent lifestyle is a factor of social stratification in Poland and how musical taste is treated as the key indicator of this phenomenon.

Introduction: The Future of and Through Music

Ewa Mazierska, Les Gillon and Tony Rigg

Researchers in all disciplines are interested in the future of their art, but the 'future of music' plays a greater role in music studies than the 'future of plastic art' in art history, and the 'future of film' in film studies, as testified by the large volume of articles and books devoted to this topic. This significance reflects the widespread perception that music is at the forefront of technological, political, economic and cultural change, and therefore what happens in music should be of interest to everyone. This idea was captured by Jacques Attali, who pronounced that music 'is prophetic. It has always been in its essence a herald of things to come' (Attali 2014: 4). 'It runs parallel to human society, is structured like it, and changes when it does. It does not evolve in a linear fashion, but is caught up in the complexity and circularity of the movements of history' (ibid.: 10).

Consequently, philosophers and sociologists frequently borrow from the language of music to capture changes in society and culture. For example, Nicolas Bourriaud, the French philosopher and art critic, relates contemporary art and cultural work to that of a DJ. He wishes to emulate the DJ who remixes existing materials, using 'culture as a toolbox', refashioning the supposedly finished product, even though – or for the very reason that – for Bourriaud 'today it is said that nothing is finished' (Bourriaud, quoted in Barham 2014: 133). In a similar way, Lev Manovich observes that remixing was originally used only in relation to music, but gradually the term became increasingly broad, and today refers to any reworking of already existing cultural work(s) (Manovich 2007).

The prophetic character of music and especially contemporary music can be explained by several factors. One such factor is the close link between people's taste in music and their other preferences and identity. As Pierre Bourdieu states, 'nothing more clearly affirms one's "class", nothing more infallibly classifies, than tastes in music' (Bourdieu 2010: 10; see also Born 2011). This means that by

[handwritten margin notes: 2 logics. Interesting. Predictive preferences. based to music preferences. This also in Hobsbawm.]

knowing the choices individuals and societies make in music, one can predict, for example, their economic and political decisions. Certain companies are already built around this idea, for example The Echo Nest, which promises to make accurate political predictions using computer algorithms based on listeners' musical preferences (Vanderbilt 2014). Another factor is the speed of change in music and its entanglement with technology, as well as its highly competitive character. These are also the characteristics of economic activity pertaining to capitalism, and especially its late form: neoliberalism. For example, music, much more than other forms of art, encapsulates the concepts of the post-object economy (Anderson 2014: 175) and 'immaterial labour', which is labour 'that produces an immaterial good, such as a service, a cultural product, knowledge or communication' (Hardt and Negri 2000: 289–90; see also Attali 2014: 4). The importance of immaterial labour for the development of neoliberalism lies not in the fact that it dominates the production of goods – most people are still employed in material production – but that the rest of the economy has to adapt to its rules. Hence, by looking at the development of music, and especially popular music, we can make conjectures about where the world is heading. This is what this collection tries to achieve: it aims to examine the present of popular music and offer some predictions on the future state of music and a wider social reality.

[handwritten: Objective of the edition.]

When did the present begin?

The future of (mostly) popular music has attracted much academic and popular interest in the last twenty or so years, with the majority of studies focusing on the recording industry (Kusek and Leonhard 2006; Knopper 2009; Rogers 2013; Wikström 2009, 2013; Anderson 2014; Collins and Young 2014; Leyshon 2014; Mulligan 2015; Nowak 2016; Nowak and Whelan 2016; Strachan 2017). This interest can be attributed to the significant changes in production, dissemination and consumption of music, which began in the early 1990s and are predominantly linked to digitization. However, in our opinion the changes pertaining to politics and economy, most importantly the global triumph of neoliberalism, are equally important.

[handwritten margin notes: Technological and Political change has sparked industry reflection.]

'Digitisation' comprises various dimensions and stages. Of specific interest for this collection is the period captured by terms such as 'post-digital' and 'post-internet'. Other terms used in this context are 'Great Disruption' and 'post-Web.2.0'.

Periodizing / post-digital

Significantly, terms such as 'post-digital' and 'post-internet' do not refer to the period when digital technologies or the internet ceased to operate or matter but, on the contrary, when they became ubiquitous. Kim Cascone, who was probably the first to use the term 'post-digital' in the context of music in an article published in 2000, explains coining this term as 'the revolutionary period of the digital information age has surely passed. The tendrils of digital technology have in some way touched everyone' (Cascone 2000: 12; see also Alexenberg 2014). 'Post-internet' art is defined by authors such as Archey and Peckham as art that is

> consciously created in a milieu that assumes the centrality of the network, [embracing] everything from the physical bits to the social ramifications of the Internet … This understanding of the Post-Internet refers not to a time "after" the Internet, but rather to an Internet state of mind – to thinking in the fashion of the network.
>
> Archey and Peckham 2014: 8

'Post-digital', as Florian Cramer suggests, might also refer to disenchantment with 'digital' and an attempt to revive analogue technologies and objects, such as, in the case of music, vinyl records and audio cassettes (Cramer 2015: 13).

Michael Waugh, alluding to such opinions, argues that 'post-internet' is marked by blurring the distinction between digital and analogue, online and offline, virtual and physical, because the digital, virtual, and online have dominated our lives (Waugh 2017: 234–35). For Fred Botting, such frequent use of the prefix 'post', which we can also find in earlier terms such as 'post-industrial', 'post-modern' and 'post-real', is a sign of living in a transitional age (Botting 1999: 1). It is at such times when, to quote from Leonard Cohen's song *The Future*, 'things are going to slide, slide in all directions'. Obviously, such a period of instability is more conducive to speculations about the future than the time of stability.

This post-digital/post-internet present can be regarded as the most recent phase in the period Robert Strachan describes as 'convergent digitization', which arrived when a 'number of different strains coming from earlier patterns of digitization converged upon the singular site of the personal computer' (Strachan 2017: 6). Strachan identifies the mid-1990s as the start of this phase. In relation to music, convergent digitization can be seen through a prism of dematerialization of objects containing recorded music, from the object, through the file, to the stream. The key distinctions between the three are defined by

A kind of 'nostalgia' vinyl, typewriters etc

1   Post-digital
Convergent digitization in music

how and where the sounds are stored. 1985 to 1999 saw the rise of the CD, which required the user to have physical space in which to store the object. 2000 to 2014 was marked by the emergence and increasing illegal and then legal dominance of digital audio files, such as MP3, AAC and FLAC. Although such files are physically intangible, the user had to have sufficient digital storage capacity on devices, hard drives or within cloud storage systems. 2015 onwards heralded the emergence and dominance of the stream category, which includes audio streaming services such as Spotify, Deezer, Apple Music and YouTube. This category does not require the user to store the music. In relation to the two latter formats Jeremy Wade Morris uses the term 'digital music commodity' (Morris 2015: 21), emphasising the difference from a CD due to the immateriality and specific type of packaging. The domination of streaming also equates to the subsuming of recorded music to large media platforms such as Google, Amazon, Facebook and Apple, which act as intermediaries between producers and consumers of music and exert great power over the music community.

The period of 'convergent digitization' coincides with the hegemony of neoliberalism, whose birth is associated with the ascent to power in the early 1980s of Margaret Thatcher in the UK and Ronald Reagan in the United States. David Harvey, its leading analyst and critic, defines neoliberalism as a version of capitalism, in which accumulation of capital is achieved by ruthless dispossession consisting of: (1) privatization and commodification of public assets; (2) financialization, so that any commodity can become an instrument of economic speculation; (3) management and manipulation of crises; and (4) state redistribution, by which wealth and income are distributed upwards, from lower to upper classes and from poorer to wealthier countries and regions (Harvey 2005: 160–62). Neoliberalism is an extreme version of capitalism, marked by a high degree of what Karl Marx describes as 'primitive accumulation'. Numerous statistics confirm Harvey's assessment of how neoliberalism works: in a nutshell, under this system the rich get richer, the poor get poorer and the wages of the middle stratum stagnate or deteriorate (Storper 2001: 89–90; Frank 2013: 28–34). As Timothy Taylor observes, the same rule of profit going upwards also applies to the popular music industry. For example, under neoliberalism musicians working in advertising are pressurized to produce music ever more quickly and the former practice of labels subsidising moderately profitable musicians through their most successful musicians became replaced by a system of seeking to market only the bestselling musicians (Taylor 2016: 51).

There is no essential link between the dominance of neoliberalism and the technological changes captured by the terms 'convergent digitization', 'post-digital' and 'post-internet', but they support each other. 'Convergent digitization', widely perceived as a cause of a crisis in the music industry, helps to create a borderless world where capital flows uninterrupted by national regulations and it is easier to achieve a monopolist position by controlling access to specific means of production; in this case the internet. Neoliberalism, on the other hand, strengthens the importance of the 'virtual world', because in this world wealth accumulation is at its fastest, in part thanks to the subtle and widespread exploitation of 'free' digital labour (Terranova 2004: 73–97). Let's now have a closer look at the effect of convergent digitization and neoliberalism on the popular music industry.

Breaking and consolidating: the music industry under conditions of convergent digitization

Globally, the 1990s, when CD sales dominated global revenues, was a very prosperous period for what is regarded as a privileged sector of the music industry – the recording industry. In 1999, the trade value of physical recorded music had reached a record level, however, this is also the year when the file-sharing site Napster was launched, marking the beginning of the end of the golden years for the record industry. According to the IFPI Report, 'world sales of recorded music for the year 2000 fell by 1.3 per cent in value and by 1.2 per cent in units compared with 1999', and the global music market was worth US$36.9 billion in 2000 (IFPI 2000). Since then we have observed a steady decline, which halted only in 2012 when the value of global recording music revenues grew for the first time since 1999, reaching $16.5 billion (over $10 billion less than a decade previously) (IFPI Digital Music Report 2013; Smirke 2013). By 2014, the value of records in physical form had fallen to $6.8 billion, and although digital revenues increased to $6.9 billion that year, marking the first time that digital music revenues (roughly) matched physical format sales, MP3 sales combined with streaming revenues was no panacea to the overall decline (IFPI Digital Music Report 2015). A resurgence in the popularity of vinyl made a modest yet positive contribution to physical music sales, affording music producers and record shops a new lease of life, but most likely the new vinyl market will not make up for the losses resulting from the dominance of the internet, given that in 2014 vinyl records accounted for only 2 per cent of global revenues (IFPI Digital Music Report 2015; Savage 2016).

The phase after 2005, when platforms such as YouTube and Spotify were launched in 2005 and 2008, respectively, is of special interest here. We label this the phase of 'advanced convergent digitization'. In this period streaming supplanted other types of music consumption as consumers needed to pay nothing or very little to access their favourite music. Authors such as Matthew David argue that this period represents a 'triumph of free sharing' rather than moving away from this model (David 2016). The term 'triumph', however, should be qualified, because it refers at best to the position of the consumer, who receives music seemingly for free or almost free. However, it ignores the fact that this music takes great labour to produce, disseminate and promote. It is not free for those who make it available, and in a sense the consumer of such music also pays for it by providing their data to corporations such as Google or Amazon that use it to create profit (Coté, Gerbaudo and Pybus 2016). The growing importance of streaming as a means of disseminating, obtaining and consuming recorded music is reflected in the list of the most powerful people in the music business, published by *Billboard*. In 2017, Daniel Ek, the CEO of Spotify, replaced Lucian Grainge, the CEO of Universal Music Group, at the top of the list (Guardian, Music 2017). The additional effect of the displacement of brick-and-mortar record shops by iTunes and other digital retailers has been the 'unbundling' of the album and the return of the single. As Steve Gordon says, referring to iTunes, 'Steve Jobs' insistence on offering to sell individual tracks encouraged those people who continued to actually buy records to "cherry pick" their favorite songs rather than pay for an entire album' (Gordon 2015: xxix). This is reflected in the rise of playlists offered to listeners on the streaming platforms, which include collections of tracks from different sources. The shift away from an album inevitably exacerbated the fragmentation of recording revenues (Klein, Meier and Powers 2017: 225–26).

How did the music industry react to these changes, given that every industry's priority is maximizing profit and minimizing risk?

We can list here several strategies, some of which specifically concern the recording industry, which in the twentieth century constituted the core of the music business. One strategy consists of an increased concentration of the ownership and control of the market for recorded music. By the early 1990s, five major record companies already controlled over 70 per cent of the market, and currently the sector is reduced to just Universal, Sony and Warner (Gordon 2015: xxix). Another strategy is focusing on the most profitable artists at the expense of the rest. As Andrew Leyshon observes, during the period of the most acute crisis (in the early 2000s), 'rosters of artists and repertoire were reduced, and turned over more rapidly' (Leyshon 2014: 81). Another, and connected, strategy consists of shifting the costs of producing records to musicians and other actors involved in the creation of music. This is reflected, for example, in offering recording contracts only to those musicians who can prove their potential by having a significant following on social media or winning amateur competitions. Not surprisingly, amongst the most successful performers are those who won such competitions (Fairchild 2008; Stahl 2013: 36–63), for example Camila Cabello, who was a finalist on *The X Factor* in the United States. Such competitions nowadays cover practically all genres of music and are targeted not only to performers, but also other music professionals, such as Red Bull Grime-A-Side for MCs and Riddim Rally for producers. In contrast, the old practice of sending a demo to a record company went out of fashion. In 2011, an article published in the *Guardian* announced that 'These days major labels increasingly demand that artists already have a "momentum" going before they get involved' and asked, somewhat rhetorically, 'Is the A&R era over?' (Lindvall 2011). Indeed, the size of A&R at the major labels is shrinking, although arguably it is retained in the independent companies and this role is in part taken by Spotify and similar platforms (Wikström 2013: 130–34; Rogers 2013: 7–8).

Another way of minimizing risk is to rely on a tried and tested formula. This means, for example, seeking artists who are similar to already successful ones. The previously mentioned competitions for amateurs illustrate this trend well, as examined in Charles Fairchild's caustic take on the 'Idol' phenomenon, especially *World Idol*:

> Despite their diverse geographical origins, *World Idol's* contestants offered a marked uniformity in their performance styles, repertoire choices, and the general impression they were trying to convey. All of the contestants except for the 'Pan Arabian Idol' sang in English. Few chose anything other than familiar international pop standards to perform. It was an odd, enlightening spectacle to see contestants barely fluent in spoken English belt out pitch perfect impersonations of Robbie Williams, Elton John, and Christina Aguilera. Each moved around the stage with confidence, smiling at the cameras, using a familiar array of standard pop gestures known the world over ... The gestures, the songs

through which they were expressed, and the vehicles for their expression were not German, Canadian or South American in origin or form, but embodied the generic, low-risk aesthetics of the international branch of the contemporary popular music industry.

Fairchild 2008: 95–96

Recycling and improving on existing music, by producing remixes and cover versions as well as sampling, is another aspect of this strategy. It has also been suggested that contemporary songs get simpler and more predictable, as they need to appeal to the listener's attention instantenously and facilitate their engagement (Lowder 2012). Arguably, this phenomenon is not new, as in 1941 Theodor Adorno wrote 'The whole structure of popular music is standarized, even where the attempt is made to circumvent standarization' (Adorno 1990: 302). However, current technology encourages and facilitates meeting consumers' demands for 'more of the same' by collecting intelligence about their preferences and habits and on this basis choosing or creating music that would suit them (Darer 2012; Prey 2016); a point to which we will return later. Obviously, such an approach is hostile to music revolution: even evolution in these circumstances needs to be very limited.

The industry is also unwilling to invest in 'unproven goods' and nurture a talent that needs a longer period to transform from a chrysalis to a musical butterfly. The speed with which the industry acts can be deduced from the young age of the greatest stars of today, such as Ed Sheeran, Adele, Charlie Puth, Dua Lipa, Post-Malone or the previously mentioned Camila Cabello, who sold hundreds of millions of records before the age of twenty-three. Their success is not only a measure of their talent, but also of the discarding of those musicians who needed more time to blossom. However, this remains hidden from the eyes and ears of the audience, according to the rule that under capitalism failure is rendered invisible.

Another effect of the triumph of free sharing is the increasing importance of live events as a way to recoup lost income (Kusek and Leonhard 2006: 114–17; Laing 2012; Marshall 2012; Wikström 2013: 58–60; Gordon 2015: xxxix–xliii; Mulligan 2015: 179–86). This phenomenon manifests itself in the sheer number of live concerts available to the public, both in the form of single-artist events and of festivals where many performers present their works in one place, over several days, often around a specific genre and theme. Recent years have seen a rapid expansion of both large and 'niche' festivals, as discussed here in the chapters by Ken Forbes and Waldemar Kuligowski. Tickets for live events have also increased in price, because they now provide the main source of income for touring artists, unlike in the 'golden age' of the recording industry when ticket prices were usually rather low because their main function was to promote the artists' records. The relationship between touring and recording has also changed, with recording regarded as a means to new material for new performances and a reason to return to the same places. Because touring and its associated revenue opportunities are now such an important stream of revenue, we observe attempts to integrate recording with touring, by offering successful artists 360-degree contracts (Marshall 2012).

An additional way to make up for losses from recording is seeking income from licensing rights and the 'branding business' – which includes tour and festival sponsorships, endorsement deals and synchronization revenues for the use of music in television, advertising, films and games – is proportionally growing (Wikström 2013: 94–102; Taylor 2016: 54–62), generating roughly US$2 billion for the music industries in 2016 (Meier 2017: 4). On the whole, we can see two opposite reactions by the music industry to the aforementioned changes: towards greater fragmentation and consolidation. The latter is epitomized by mergers of the record companies, as mentioned earlier, and even more by large streaming services, which make available millions of records and serve hundreds of millions, or in the case of YouTube billions, of customers.

Many of these aforementioned strategies adopted by the music industry can be seen in the wider context of a changing work environment and practices under neoliberalism, as mentioned earlier. Neoliberalization is marked by a desire to make a quicker profit than traditional capitalism and make it from immaterial goods, rather than material ones, as such goods travel faster. It is telling that the most powerful people in the music industry are no longer those who control the production of music, but those who mediate between its producers and consumers. In this sense, the music industry is not very different from retailing material goods or car transportation, where the richest are not those who own any actual goods but those who bring together the sellers and buyers online, such as the CEOs of Amazon and Uber. In addition, in the pursuit of profit neoliberal capitalists seek potential in labour that was previously not monetized. This trend is exemplified by the previously mentioned method of gaining profit from the search for new talent via talent competitions – hence from a process rather than its end-product – and insisting that the aspiring artist has significantly developed their talent before they receive a contract from the record company.

We can discuss not only consolidation of the music industry, but also its integration into different sectors of the economy. The best-known examples of such a relationship include software companies such as Apple and Google, and the venture into music by soft drinks company Red Bull and luxury clothes brand Burberry, which have their own music departments organizing competitions and releasing records by their stars. On this occasion, corporate brands become patrons of music, whilst the music and musicians they endorse become ambassadors of their products (Carah 2010; Barton 2013; Taylor 2016: 54–62; Meier 2017). To some extent this type of integration was present before, with electronics companies such as Sony establishing record labels, but the current situation is different as it is more widespread and the new patrons typically have nothing to do with music. This relationship is often presented as beneficial to both sides, allowing lesser-known artists greater space for their creativity and exposure than that offered by traditional music companies, and plugging the gaps in the economically weakened music industry (Beltrone 2012; Barton 2013). However, inevitably, the result is strengthening the link between music and neoliberalism and weakening the autonomy of music, music companies and musicians. Leslie Meier expresses it in these words:

> Music companies' and artists' increasing dependence on music licensing and brand partnership for marketing exposure and revenue has paved the way for ... popular music's *colonization* by new industry gatekeepers: brands. ... In seeking to avoid the Scylla of the major music companies ... recording artists have fallen into the Charybdis of brands.
>
> Meier 2017: 86–7; see also Taylor 2016: 54–62

By and large, the period of an 'advanced convergent digitization' has been marked by what is seen as the fundamental flaw in today's music market, known as the 'value gap'. The value gap describes the growing mismatch between the value that user upload services such as YouTube extract from music and the revenue returned to the music community – those who are creating and investing in music. As discussed in 'Rewarding creativity – fixing the value gap', a 2017 article on this topic: 'the value gap is now the industry's single highest legislative priority as it seeks to create a level playing field for the digital market and secure the future of the industry' (IFPI 2017). Its existence can be explained in part by the fact that streaming is a 'new frontier' in the consumption of music and occurred during the period of a contraction in the record industry. As a result, there are issues around transparency and the bias towards the majors getting a larger share of income (Resnikoff 2017).

The value gap exists in many other sectors of the economy, as has already been indicated; this is a defining characteristic of neoliberalism, namely the upward distribution of wealth. However, if we are to believe that music is prophetic, then we should also assume that if the music industry fails to demonstrate how to move away from the neoliberal logic, it is unlikely that other sectors of industry or other disciplines of art will liberate us from this unfortunate position either. *Can music find the wider economy a way through the neoliberal fog?*

Invest in yourself or perish: the careers of contemporary musicians

The most obvious victims of the value gap are the musicians themselves, therefore it is worth devoting the next part of this introduction to their situation. However, not all seems to go badly for musicians. One advantage is their greater exposure to music from different places and periods of history. Unlike their predecessors, who typically knew music only from a relatively narrow cultural environment, thanks to platforms such as YouTube and Spotify, musicians can now access music from every epoch and place. Consequently, there is more scope for influence from a wide variety of sources, including music created on the peripheries of the industry, taking issues from the history of music, resurrecting past phenomena and transforming them through new instruments and approaches. Two chapters included here on electro swing and post-rock examine this phenomenon in detail.

Another, albeit linked, effect of digitization is the increased potential for self-education. Whilst in the past aspiring musicians had to learn their skills in music schools or from fellow musicians, today they can do this by using the relevant tools from the internet. For example, there are numerous sites where one can download guitar chords or samples to produce electronic music, which significantly reduces the cost and difficulty of music production. In a sense, anyone with access to the internet can become a musician. Not only has the production of music become easier and cheaper, but also its dissemination. Contemporary musicians can access billions of potential listeners using platforms such as YouTube and Spotify. Moreover, social media platforms such as Facebook, Twitter and Instagram allow networking with fellow musicians,

positives of digitalization

intermediaries such as music journalists, and directly with fans. Artists can use these platforms to ask for support with their music by co-creating it or supporting it financially, buying records directly from the artist's website or organizing crowdfunding campaigns (Morris 2014; Haynes and Marshall 2017). However, this new closeness between musicians and their potential consumers can be regarded as a step back in the process of musicians gaining autonomy. Attali discusses that before the advent of capitalism, musicians adopted two principal roles, vagabond and domestic, in which they were completely dependent on their patrons (Attali 1985: 14–18). Since then they have gained a certain distance from their patrons, renamed as their fans. An important step in this direction, pioneered in Vienna by Richard Strauss, was collecting a fixed entrance fee from patrons of the ballroom or performances in parks and gardens, instead of the old practice of passing around a collection plate where income was reliant on the goodwill of the audience (Scott 2008: 122). We have reached a point where musicians' income, except in the case of the greatest stars, depends again on the goodwill of their patrons who decide how much they want to pay.

The increased access to creative tools and means of communication has been predominantly seen – at least until recently – as a mark of the diversification and democratization of popular music (McLeod 2005; Anderson 2006; Rogers 2013: 1–5). In journalistic accounts and also on occasion in academic publications, we find numerous stories of the success of unknown artists who achieved global success thanks to their talent and enterpreneurial spirit, as opposed to being backed by powerful institutions such as record labels and monetary investments. For example, Amanda Palmer secured substantial funding directly from her fans, by mastering the 'art of asking', as the title of her book declares (Palmer 2014). However, such accounts have been subsequently refuted as simplifying or twisting a complex situation.

The easy access to the tools of production and dissemination brings to mind the ideal of amateurism, heralded by Marx, who in *The German Ideology* mused on a possible society of the future, where the rounded individual will 'hunt in the morning, fish in the afternoon, rear cattle in the evening, criticize after dinner' (Marx and Engels 1947: 22). Yet, Marx saw it only as an ideal in the communist world, in which everybody is an amateur. Being an amateur in the capitalist reality, where professionalism brings distinct advantages, is a much less beneficial position. Indeed, whilst there are many musicians who are content with their status as amateurs, producing music merely for their enjoyment and that of a modest circle of their friends, others dream about becoming professionals, able to support themselves financially from making music. Since a widening of access to the tools of music production and dissemination, we observe greater competition between amateurs to become professionals.

What has been the effect of these changes on the career strategies and positions of aspiring musicians? Like their predecessors, they are trying to gain a competitive edge by writing more attractive music than their peers, as well as promoting their music more effectively. Whilst the first strategy is still very important, it is widely agreed that the burden on independent musicians shifted from production to promotion and developing strategies to 'stand out in the crowd' (Hracs et al. 2013); a term which borrows from the neoliberal jargon. Such strategies might include investing in greater or even fake exposure by paying for sponsored posts on internet platforms. This burden of moving from invisibility to visibility can be carried by the musician themselves or shared with somebody who agrees to act as the artist's promoter, typically for financial gain. As Matt Stahl puts it, 'The common dynamic is that . . . employers – often with the support of the state and popular discourse – pursue strategies for shifting burdens of cost and risk onto employees of all kinds: newcomers, established stars and everyone in between' (Stahl 2013: 227–28). However, the burden for newcomers is the greatest, as they need to prove their value for potential investors.

Whilst the lack of financial capital is not an absolute obstacle to achieving success in music, having some helps immensely and indeed helps contemporary musicians more than their predecessors. This can be deduced from statistics about the class background of people achieving success in creative industries. For example, the results of a 2015 survey on the financial situation of those working in the creative industries in the UK, conducted by Goldsmiths University and the arts organization Create, revealed that almost 90 per cent of the 2,539 respondents had been required to work for free at some point in their career, creating an environment that is unaffordable for those who do not have other means of financial support. Of those who did get paid, more than a quarter said they earned less than £5,000 a year. A further 18 per cent earned between £5,000 and £15,000, and 38 per cent did not have a contract that provided job security. Three-quarters of industry respondents came from a middle-class background, with parents who worked in a managerial or professional job. A summary of the findings, published in the *Guardian*, said that 'Middle class people dominate arts' (Ellis-Petersen 2015). Such a result can be deduced from the previously mentioned 'value gap' – the gap has to be filled somehow, and currently it is filled largely by the extra work of musicians and their families.

The difficulty of making a career in popular music can also be seen from the high numbers of contestants on programmes such as *Pop Idol* and *The X Factor* (and by the same token the ratio between the winners and losers). For example, the sixth series of *The X Factor* (UK) attracted around 200,000 contestants (Thomas 2009; see also Stahl 2013: 36–63). According to this and similar statistics, there are more unsuccessful musicians than ever before and their failure is made public, because they have to endure scornful remarks of music competition judges and see their songs failing to attract more than a few hits on YouTube. Yet, at the same time, if their records or music videos are self-produced, there is nobody on the side of the music industry to tell them to stop trying, such as a record company that would just drop them from the roster. On the contrary, the media and politicians[1] tell them not to give up, just try harder, again reflecting the rhetoric of neoliberalism. The situation can be compared to that of playing the lottery; when one ticket turns out to be unlucky, those selling the tickets suggest buying more.

The struggle to 'stand out in the crowd' for those trying to make money from music can also be deduced from the rule presented by Gustavo Azenha. This highlights the relationship between the overall size of the music market and the diversification and decentralization of the music industry, of which the difficulties of opening to new 'voices' is a good indicator. As the author puts it, under conditions of growth there are more opportunities for new actors and those on the margins of the industry to exploit; without growth it is more difficult for new actors to displace established players, regardless of the availability of potentially decentralizing technologies (Azenha 2006). Given that until recently the recording industry was contracting or stagnating, we can gather that this had a particularly negative effect on newcomers and those working at the periphery.

But even if the aspiring musician manages to produce a record that sells well, their earnings from the streaming services (where the majority of listeners access music today) are tiny, unless they have millions of hits. In an article ironically titled 'Love Streams', Damon Krukowski, a musician in a band called Galaxie 500, explained that his track 'Tugboat' was played 7,800 times on Pandora in the first quarter of 2012, for which the royalties amounted to 21 cents. Spotify paid the band £1.05 for playing 'Tugboat' 5,960 times (Krukowski 2016: 113). Krukowski concluded that 'immaterial goods turn out to generate equally immaterial income' (ibid.: 115) and services such as Pandora and Spotify are 'divorced from music'; they 'exist to attract speculative capital' (ibid.: 115–16), as opposed to working for the community of musicians.

Contemporary musicians, both young and old, also experience types of competition from which their predecessors were spared: dead musicians and virtual performers. In relation to the first of these, we can argue that living musicians always competed with the dead ones, but not in the live environment. Nowadays, the dead or rather their holograms can still tour. A 3D hologram of Roy Orbison, who died in 1988, started his world tour, alongside the Royal Philharmonic Orchestra, on 8 April 2018 in Cardiff, UK. Hatsune Miku, one of Japan's biggest pop stars, is not a real person but a virtual creation (Glynn 2017). Most likely she will soon be surrounded by similar stars, whose obvious advantage over real musicians is that they do not get addicted to (real) drugs, do not have unreasonable financial demands or die at the tender age of twenty-seven. In the virtual space, the musicians of today also compete with new types of performers, such as professional YouTubers, who might lack any specific talents, be it acting, singing or having specialized knowledge, but are more skilled in engaging the audience regarding their views or lifestyle.

The rational response to such statistics from a person from a modest background who dreams about becoming a rock star or at least able to support themself by making music, would be to abandon this dream, just as the rational approach is not to spend money on buying lottery tickets. However, aspiring artists rarely follow statistics – and even if they do, they ignore them. This is partly because for many people the need for self-expression is as great as (or greater than) the need for a sustainable income. Moreover, as we already indicated, the media is filled with the stories of individual success rather than collective failure. Furthermore, the choice of a career in art, or the creative industries in a wider sense, is less risky if we take into account that many middle-class career paths previously seen as sound (such as academia), have become much more difficult to follow or pay less than they used to. This is because the 'value gap' concerns practically all fields of the economy under neoliberalism, as exemplified by the gap between fat-cat salaries of university senior managers and those of ordinary lecturers.

Music like water or a drug: the new modes of consumption of music

Under the regime we examine here, music in certain formats – for which one previously had to pay and hence was only accessible to a more affluent sector of society – became free, easy to access and available in great abundance. As far back as 2006, Chris Anderson argued that the distribution cost of music which can be digitized approaches zero, and whereas the largest offline music store typically offers 15,000 albums, Apple's iTunes Store lists millions (Anderson 2006: 6–13). Since then, these numbers have increased, reaching 40 billion in 2013 (Leyshon 2014: 2), as well as the number of providers who offer consumers their music for free or for a very small fee. Some authors noted that music became like water (Kusek and Leonhard 2006), or even less precious than water, as water is scarce in many places whilst there is nobody complaining about a deficit of music. The consumption of music also shifts away from the material form towards consumption via the internet, principally streaming, although the speed of this shift has varied depending on geographical region (Krause, North and Hewitt 2013; IFPI Digital Music Report 2013, 2015; Flynn 2016; Huber's chapter in this collection). The abundance of music is a consequence of a series of technical innovations aimed at increasing portability of music (see Chapter 10).

What is the effect of such an abundance and democratization of access to music on the attitudes and consumption patterns of its listeners? It is impossible to describe them with precision, because fans of music from different categories tend to have different habits. Nevertheless, we can list several commonalities.

First, as several authors in this collection note, faithfulness to a specific music genre was replaced by omnivorousness. This, however, as Emília Barna argues in her chapter, does not necessarily obliterate class differences amongst fans, as omnivorous habits themselves became a marker of high cultural capital, signifying social and geographical mobility.

Second, the wealth of music choice goes hand-in-hand with the need to learn which music will best suit one's taste. In the past, the role of informers and trend-setters was largely taken up by label employees, radio and music press, as well as record stores. Under current circumstances, these trend-setters did not disappear but they have been joined by new gatekeepers, principally those operating on social media (Haynes and Marshall 2017; Meier 2017). Barna mentions bloggers, online magazines, YouTube, events such as Boiler Room, as well as festivals and well-known musicians, who often curate these festivals and whose opinions about fellow musicians might make or break their careers.

Another specificity of influencing listening choices is the importance of algorithmic curation, typically by offering customers lists of tracks based on the algorithm's assessment of what will appeal to them. Algorithmic curation appears to be non-personal, hence objective, but in reality, as Andy Fry argues in

[handwritten: Algorithmic curation reinforces the echo chamber]

Chapter 13, it is governed by rules constructed by humans. One of these rules is reinforcing what the consumer likes, rather than challenging them into learning about music completely new to them. Hence Fry uses the term the 'echo chamber', suggesting that the listener is more likely to be trapped in the narrow parameters of their taste. Another specificity of algorithmic curation is the financial incentive at the core of its design. The algorithms are primarily designed to generate more revenue, through both maintaining corporate relationships and gaining and retaining customers. Aside from their customer relationships, services also need to retain strong relationships with content suppliers (artists, labels, distributors), advertisers, and in some cases, shareholders. It appears that the current trends in consumption of music confirms Gustavo Azenha's thesis:

> The development and popularization of new technologies ultimately tends to reinforce existing social hierarchies and relations. Although increasingly accessible technologies typically destabilize established social relations, vast inequalities in access to technologies, capital and social networks inhibit a more far-reaching and lasting destabilization. Furthermore, this persistence of concentration within the music industry and the specific ways in which it is organized tend to limit the possibilities of diversification of music genres and the ethnic and national diversification of participation in the industry.
>
> Azenha 2006

[handwritten: Echo chamber]

Such insight might explain why certain genres and artists are more popular than others. In particular, the global dominance of hip-hop over other genres of popular music is linked to the supremacy of streaming over other types of music consumption, with the Nielson report claiming that the growth in popularity of the hip-hop/R&B genre was 'powered by a 72 per cent increase in on-demand audio streaming' (Nielsen 2018). In an article on this topic published in the *Independent*, Christopher Hooton explains this:

[handwritten margin note: Material reasons for sure, drowns out other certain ?]

> There are all kinds of factors besides just the popularity of hip hop that could be at work here – including the relationship of hip hop labels with Spotify, the inclusivity of the genre, the playlisting of it, the use of Spotify in social settings (where, let's face it, the trap bangers are going to come out) and the strong sense of narrative arc on hip hop releases that lead to longer listening sessions.
>
> Hooton 2015

One can gather that the first factor, the relationship of hip-hop labels with Spotify, is particularly important, yet difficult to examine due to the secrecy surrounding the deals between the music labels and streaming platforms.

An important question is whether the new channels of consumption also change the way we listen to music. In the famous conceptualization by Adorno, listening to popular music is distracting and inattentive: 'Listeners are distracted from the demands of reality by entertainment which does not demand attention either' (Adorno 1990: 310). Many authors tried to subsequently refute this claim, but questions remain whether accessing music through MP3 is more distracting than listening to a vinyl or a CD, and whether following playlists prepared for us by Spotify algorithms is more distracting than relying on the opinion of the music press? Jonathan Sterne, in his well-known study, gave a positive answer to the first question, writing that the 'anticipated praxeology of listening encoded in each MP3 emphasizes distraction over attention and exchange over use' (Sterne 2006: 828). We are also likely to answer 'yes' to the second question, arguing that what we know, or what is similar to our favourite music, does not require the same level of concentration as experiencing music that is completely new and unexpected. Moreover, the very abundance of music and its increased virtuality leads to the loss of part of its old aura. This aura came from fans possessing music in the physical form or even having an original artefact such as the vinyl record, even if this original itself was mass-produced. The vinyl revival, and such practices as numbering copies to make them appear even less accessible, can be seen as a backlash against this trend resulting from a desire to retrieve the old aura of 'authentic music'. It is worth mentioning in this context that Walter Benjamin, the author who introduced us to the idea of the aura of an object of art, was happy to see this aura disappearing, as he regarded it as a barrier to the masses participating in consumption of art on the same level as elites (Benjamin 1992: 299). What Benjamin did not envisage were the attempts to create 'mini-auras', bestowing authenticity on mass-produced objects such as records or photographs. Digitization inevitably destroyed such 'mini-aura'.

Another factor in 'de-aurization' of music can be linked to the popular musicians losing their 'romantic glow' through exposing the apparatus of music production: for example such phenomena as the ease of making music with the assistance of the internet and the tendency for engaging fans in the production of work of their favourite musicians, captured by the term 'prosumer' (producer-consumer), introduced by Alvin Toffler in 1980, yet gaining currency in the period of advanced digitization. It can be suggested that the artist who openly draws on the work of their fans comes across as less appealing than one who seeks other forms of inspiration, most importantly their inner life. Moreover, as

Matthew Stahl notes, programmes such as *X Factor* or *American Idol* 'make visible a whole process of production that would otherwise be obscured: a highly rationalized process of selection, construction, and marketing' (Stahl 2013: 46). The romantic aura is further eroded by the growing dependence of the artists on income from non-musical activities, most importantly serving brands (Meier 2017). As a result of this shift, music became subjugated to the goals of neoliberalism and was 'valued less for its own qualities than for its associations with other phenomena' (Leyshon 2014: 86). Of course, popular music was never free from commercial pressures and even the most romantic of rockers tended to follow the orders of record company executives and looked for ways to increase their income. However, in the past the link of music to capitalist production was less visible and it can be argued that selling records is a more autonomous and romantic activity than acting as an incentive to watch an advert or allow a digital platform to collect data, which can be monetized and sold to advertisers.

With the loss of aura comes the loss of political power. A telling example from this perspective is the 2016 American presidential election, when an unprecedented group of pop stars publicly endorsed Hillary Clinton's candidacy, often fundraising on her behalf. Subsequently it was suggested that this support was not only insufficient for Clinton to win, but contributed to her loss (Bryant 2016); this inability of celebrities to convince the electorate, including their fans, to vote for Clinton, gives the sense that such stars epitomize the capitalist order of what Mark Fisher describes as 'capitalist realism' (Fisher 2009).

It is worth asking is whether developments in the distribution and consumption of music will allow a restoration of the old aura of mechanically reproduced objects or whether companies such as Spotify will be able to compensate consumers for this loss through other benefits such as accessibility and convenience.

The material, structure and chapter description

It would be impossible to cover the present and speculate about the future of music on all continents and in all countries. For this reason, the authors of this collection limited themselves to the United States, the UK and continental Europe. We believe that such an approach allows us to uncover global trends, which are typically located in or extrapolated from situations in the

Wide enough to perceive global trends.

Anglo-American world, and account for the dynamics between the geographic centre and the periphery of the popular music industry. However, irrespective of the geographical region the authors cover, the vast majority adopt the position of those actors (musicians, music businesses) who compete with others in a similar position for employment and the attention of consumers, in what can be described as a 'bottom-up approach'. We believe that such a perspective provides a more balanced view of the music business than focusing on stars whose labour is in high demand and dominant companies who can dictate their conditions to the rest.

The first part of this collection is devoted to what is known as the 'music business', which covers the recording industry, live music and publishing rights. Chapter 1, by Patryk Galuszka and Katarzyna M. Wyrzykowska, is 'Rethinking independence: what does "independent record label" mean today?' True to its title, the authors compare the contemporary understanding of an 'independent record label' with that functioning in the past, and speculate how it may evolve in the future. They observe that independent labels were believed to offer an alternative to the oligopolistic practices of the major labels, but with the passage of time the term 'independent' became overused, referring to all music styles and music production located outside the mainstream. Galuszka and Wyrzykowska search for new factors that could serve to differentiate independent record labels from 'dependent' ones by drawing from empirical data collected from record labels operating in Poland. Their analysis of the respondents' motivations and attitudes indicates that profit-based and non-profit-based activity could constitute the aforementioned criterion. The authors also note that their respondents were, to a large extent, satisfied with the possibilities offered by digital technologies and show no willingness to engage in a battle for a more equitable digital music market. This makes the authors believe that current inequalities in the digital music market will be more likely addressed by artists than record labels, at least in Poland.

In Chapter 2, Paolo Magaudda discusses blockchain technology as the new digital music infrastructure, posing the question of whether it will revolutionize the distribution of recorded music and, especially, address the previously mentioned value gap, hitting independent musicians particularly hard. He observes that blockchain tends to be presented as the upcoming 'revolution' in the music industry, able to change the shape of the music business and especially gives artists the chance to regain control over their musical works, in a music environment increasingly dominated by large digital corporations. However,

[handwritten margin note at top: Skeptical of Blockchain, not every advance in tech is positive cf Adorno]

Magaudda's analysis not only helps to map the adoption paths of this technology in the music sector, but also demonstrates scepticism about the ability of blockchain to democratize the music industry.

Chapter 3, by Kenny Forbes, also deals with the concept of independence, by examining one type of independent music: post-rock. The term 'post-rock' was coined by Reynolds in 1994 to project the sound of the future. Forbes offers an analysis, arguing that it looks into both the future and the past, and then discusses the festival dedicated to this genre, ArcTanGent (ATG), as operating within the 'Alternative Alternative' environment, embracing notions of non-mainstream inclusiveness and performance virtuosity. His main question is how the organizers ensure the economic viability of such events, given that it belongs to the Long Tail of festivals, where risk of failure is particularly high. Forbes suggests that this is due to a large amount of unpaid work by the festival organizers and volunteers.

[handwritten margin note: Post-rock as independent? what about Squid Post? etc]

The topic of music festivals is continued by Waldemar Kuligowski in Chapter 4, which emphasizes the importance of values informing festivals. Using the term the 'axio-normative order', borrowed from Florian Znaniecki, he examines how different axio-normative orders are internalized by participants in three music festivals: Guča Trumpet Festival in Serbia, Jarocin Rock Festival in Poland, and the O.Z.O.R.A. Festival in Hungary. He suggests that the future of music festivals will be so-called 'festivals with the message', and that their proliferation might be seen as a response to the apoliticization and placelessness of mainstream music and a backlash against the conditions imposed by new technologies.

Part One concludes with Kamila Rymajdo, who discusses in Chapter 5 the strategies used recently by managers of the most successful of Manchester's underground music clubs, such as Hidden and The White Hotel, who succeeded in finding a way of 'standing out in the crowd' by attracting enough customers to make their operations viable and achieving critical recognition. Their strategies include playing up the niche or alternative character of the club experience (not unlike the festival discussed in the chapter by Forbes), reliance on local talent and offering their customers more than just a typical club experience, by becoming a cultural centre. However, Rymajdo also underscores the fact that probably the most important factor in these clubs' success is relying on labour which is voluntary or unpaid, as well as accepting a high risk of failure. She draws a parallel between the way these clubs operate and the exploitative methods of neoliberal companies, with their reliance on free labour and the gift economy.

[handwritten margin note: Managerial savyness of small venue owners (UK)]

[handwritten note at bottom: Exploitative methods of neoliberal ism]

Indies adopting neoliberal

What Part One shows is that the main response of the independent sector of the music industry to the current difficulties – the overcrowding of the market and diminished revenue – is putting in extra labour and lowering financial expectations, namely expecting a higher risk. In short, the response is accommodating the rules of neoliberal capitalism, rather than rebelling against them.

Part Two of the collection focuses on musicians, in particular those who can be described as 'independent' or 'working' and the work they produce. The authors looked at musicians working in different countries, such as Sweden, Austria, Hungary and the UK, and different genres, such as pop, rock, experimental music and electro swing.

This begins with Chapter 6, by Ewa Mazierska and Tony Rigg, who examine two musicians from the north-west of England whose music careers spans over forty years: Peter Hook, known best from his work in Joy Division and New Order, and Graham Massey, co-founder of 808 State. The authors try to establish how these musicians sustained such long careers, given the changing fashions in music and the crisis in the recording industry that began in the late 1990s. They pay particular attention to the context in which the subjects started their musical lives: the late 1970s and early 1980s in the North of England, the time of punk explosion and Manchester becoming a centre of music production, largely thanks to Tony Wilson. They draw attention to the skill with which both artists and especially Hook exploit their musical legacy, which allows them to have more than one stream of income. They point to the fact that whilst Hook and Massey have a competitive edge thanks to their cultural as well as monetary capital, they have to conform to the current 'rules of the game'; this is reflected, for example, in long concert tours undertaken by Hook in recent years.

Musicians can marketers

In Chapter 7, Lars Bröndum looks at the situation of independent musicians from Sweden, based on interviews with four composers from different generations. His interviewees acknowledge that the internet has opened up new possibilities for creating and marketing music, but these make it harder than ever to live on music. This leads to the artists devoting much of their time and effort to marketing their music, and finding additional ways of supporting themselves, most importantly through grants. He notes that, paradoxically, whilst in the past recording used to be the main source of revenue for Swedish composers, nowadays it is more often a means to show the grant providers that their work deserves support. Bröndum suggests that one way of overcoming the problems that might lead to making a living from music becoming

call for UBI

impossible, is by introducing a universal income, which is currently being piloted in Finland.

From Sweden we move to Central Europe in Chapter 8. Ewa Mazierska considers the careers of two young indie bands, Gin Ga and Fran Palermo, operating on the peripheries of the pop music industry in Austria and Hungary, respectively. She discusses how wider circumstances, pertaining to the period of 'advanced convergent digitalization', when they began their career, the places in which they have operated and their specific career choices, have affected their current standing and perspectives, in relation to domestic and international careers. She points to the difficulty of making an international career from such a position and the greater advantage to exploit a local market and building one's fan base there; something which Fran Palermo started to become aware of when Mazierska was finishing her research.

What these three chapters show, in common with those included in Part One, is the high level of insecurity and hardship endured by musicians trying to become or remain as professionals. This is accompanied by an awareness of the unfairness of the system, largely resulting from low royalties paid to the artists by streaming companies, and the music business favouring celebrity artists at the expense of independent and young artists. Yet, the dominant reaction to this situation is to work harder, either in the music industry or outside it, which allows the artist to maintain semi-professional status, rather than trying to break or subvert the system. Meaningfully, the conversations with the artists show little desire for joining the production of music with political activism, in parties or trade unions.

Chapter 9 concludes Part Two. Chris Inglis focuses less on the careers of musicians and more on music itself, by investigating the phenomenon of electro swing, a genre that has seen increasing popularity throughout Europe over the past decade by combining the sounds of the swing era with electronic dance music. Inglis underscores the importance of sampling, specifically the sampling of records with 'vintage' connotations in electro swing productions, and questions the meanings associated with such a practice. He also interrogates the genre's relation to jazz, and the degree to which electro swing can be called an authentic jazz style. This chapter demonstrates how the influence of the past is, in fact, having a major impact on the future of popular music. *Retro historism*

Part Three of the collection concerns the consumption of music. It begins with Chapter 10 by Mat Flynn, who points to the unwillingness of scholars to make predictions (largely motivated by a fear of being seen as unscholarly) and advocates taking a heuristic perspective of the music industries. To demonstrate this approach, Flynn uses examples of the parlour piano, phonograph and early radio to establish the importance of music consumers' active participation in determining the success of mediums for music playback. These historic trends and themes are then presented as a 'rule of thumb' for how music users will likely adapt to new music playback devices and services in the future. The author argues that future market dominant playback technologies will increasingly improve situational control and personalize choice, but continually reduce the demands of knowledge, skill, labour and time on the part of consumers.

Flynn's observations are confirmed by Michael Huber in Chapter 11. Huber uses findings from two surveys (of more than 1,000 interviewees each from 2010 and 2015) on the musical attitudes and behaviour of the Austrian population, to show how a strong music listening behaviour of young people hinges on the internet and how they use it for information, communication, and receiving music. It demonstrates that young people in Austria are predominantly influenced by the internet, rather than TV, CDs or their parents. At the same time, listening to music via older, slower, more awkward, and more expensive media survives under the circumstances of music streaming over-supply. This mode of listening to music not only applies to older people, but to the population at large.

The final two chapters are devoted to intermediation and music curation. In Chapter 12, Emília Barna explores intermediation and taste within the context of the digital music industries, analysing the role of music curators, online DJs and creators of playlists on streaming platforms, as taste entrepreneurs, primarily through the example of the former online music platform 22tracks. She asks how we should conceptualize the relationship between 'curating' and the displaying of taste, and how the current debates around gatekeeping, representation, diversity, and competition are related to the restructuring of the music industries along with digitization, in particular to the emergence of new intermediaries between producers and consumers. She argues for treating online music curators as a group of new music professionals carving out positions in the expanding intermediary space between producers and consumers. She thus undermines the idea that the conditions of advanced convergent digitization decrease the distance between producer and consumer. If anything, rather the opposite is the case.

Andrew Fry, finishing the third part of the collection with Chapter 13, discusses a seemingly different type of curation: one based on algorithms. He

Algorithmic curation
facilitating Listener Isolation

argues that the changes in music technology, especially the dominance of streaming, facilitate and encourage listener's isolation. This is because the listener's behaviour is recorded and used to adapt future music suggestions through algorithms: if rejected, a track, artist or entire genre may never be suggested again. Consequently, the listeners inhabit their own sound bubble, a controlled and structured soundscape. There is thus a contrast between the almost infinite size of the 'record shop', in which we can browse and shop, paying very little, and the small size of virtual shelves, on which we put our favourite records. By the same token, Fry points out that the democratization of music production, which leads to the wealth of music we can choose, goes hand-in-hand with limiting this choice. Echo chamber

Part Three of the collections dicusses that the mode of listening to music is affected most by convenience, including the consumer's ability to access music everywhere and with as little effort as possible. This is a more important consideration than the quality of the listening experience, as long as the loss of quality is not excessive. As a consequence, streaming is seen as the natural outcome of the development of tools for accessing music. At the same time, the old modes of accessing music are unlikely to disappear, both due to the fact that it will be a long time until those who were socialized to music in the analogue times die out, and because post-digital times are marked by a tendency amongst listeners to be omnivorous in their consumption of music, as well as nostalgia.

Detriment to quality does not matter too much (as long as loss of quality is not too much)

The majority of authors of this collection try not to ponder too much on the musical 'crystal ball', perhaps anxious that they might be caught out for offering wrong predictions. Nevertheless, their work points to a future of widening gaps: between the strength of the internet platform giants, such as Google and Facebook, and the weakness of the music industry; between the number of people engaged in producing music and working in the music industry and the small amount of money extracted from their activities; between the wealth of music available to consumers and the narrow choices made by consumers locked in their 'bubbles'; and, possibly, between the opportunities of producing an innovative, new music and what is actually produced. They also suggest that currently there is no appetite to bridge the gaps by drastic means. The prevailing order of the day is accommodating the situation, rather than resisting it, as is also the case in other branches of the economy such as manufacture, transport or education. The question is whether the music business will be at the forefront of slashing this status quo that we find unfortunate, or whether it will be the first to show how to make it workable for the foreseeable future.

Note

1   A good example is the rhetoric of New Labour under Tony Blair, with its edification of the 'creative industries' as the privileged sector of British industry.

References

Adorno, Theodor W. (1990 [1941]), 'On Popular Music', in Simon Frith and Andrew Goodwin (eds), *On Record: Rock, Pop, and the Written Word*, 301–14. London: Routledge.

Alexenberg, Mel (2011), *The Future of Art in a Postdigital Age: From Hellenistic to Hebraic Consciousness*. Bristol: Intellect.

Anderson, Chris (2006), *The Long Tail: Why the Future of Business is Selling Less of More*. New York: Hyperion.

Anderson, Tim J. (2014), *Popular Music in a Digital Music Economy: Problems and Practices for an Emerging Service Industry*. London: Routledge.

Archey, Karen and Robin Peckham (2014), 'Art Post-Internet'. Available online: http://www.karenarchey.com/artpostinternet/ (accessed 27 January 2018).

Attali, Jacques (2014 [1977]), *Noise: The Political Economy of Music*, trans. Brian Massumi. Minneapolis: University of Minnesota Press.

Azenha, Gustavo (2006), 'The Internet and the Decentralization of the Popular Music Industry: Critical Reflections on Technology, Concentration and Diversification', *Radical Musicology 1*. Available online: http://www.radical-musicology.org.uk/2006/Azenha.htm (accessed 29 November 2017).

Barham, Jeremy (2014), '"Not Necessarily Mahler": Remix, Samples and Borrowing in the Age of Wiki', *Contemporary Music Review*, 2: 128–47.

Barton, Laura (2013), 'Burberry's Christopher Bailey on his Obsession with Music', *Guardian*, 4 September. Available online: https://www.theguardian.com/fashion/2013/sep/04/christopher-bailey-music-burberry-fashion (accessed 17 January 2018).

Beltrone, Gabriel (2012), 'Behind the Music: Call it borrowed authenticity or just plain good marketing, but brands are reaching out to indie bands, and both are coming out ahead', *Adweek*, 19 March. Available online: http://www.adweek.com/brand-marketing/behind-music-138995/ (accessed 17 January 2018).

Benjamin, Walter (1992 [1936]), 'The Work of Art in the Age of Mechanical Reproduction', in Francis Frascina and Jonathan Harris (eds), *Art in Modern Culture: An Anthology of Critical Texts*, 297–307. London: Phaidon.

Born, Georgina (2011), 'Music and the Materialization of Identities', *Journal of Material Culture*, 4: 376–88.

Botting, Fred (1999), *Sex, Machines and Navels: Fiction, Fantasy and History in the Future Present*. Manchester: Manchester University Press.

Bourdieu, Pierre (2010 [1984]), *Distinction: A Social Critique of the Judgement of Taste*. London: Routledge.

Bryant, Kenzie (2016), 'Did Celebrity Endorsements Contribute to Hillary Clinton's Presidential Upset?', *Vanity Fair*, 21 November. Available online: https://www.vanityfair.com/style/2016/11/celebrity-endorsements-donald-trump-hillary-clinton (accessed 9 January 2018).

Carah, Nicholas (2010), *Pop Brands: Branding, Popular Music, and Young People*. New York: Peter Lang.

Cascone, Kim (2000), 'The Aesthetic of Failure: "Post-Digital" Tendencies in Contemporary Computer Music', *Computer Music Journal*, 12–18.

Collins, Steve and Sherman Young (2014), *Beyond 2.0: The Future of Music*. Sheffield: Equinox.

Coté, Mark, Paolo Gerbaudo and Jennifer Pybus (2016), 'Introduction: Politics of Big Data', *Digital Culture and Society*, 2: 1–12.

Cramer, Florian (2015), 'What Is "Post-digital"?', in David M. Berry and Michael Dieter (eds), *Postdigital Aesthetics: Art, Computation and Design*, 12–26. London: Palgrave.

David, Matthew (2016), 'The Legacy of Napster', in Raphael Nowak and Andrew Whelan (eds), *Networked Music Cultures: Contemporary Approaches, Emerging Issues*, 49–65. London: Palgrave.

Fairchild, Charles (2008), *Pop Idols and Pirates: Mechanisms of Consumption and the Global Circulation of Popular Music*. Aldershot: Ashgate.

Fisher, Mark (2009), *Capitalist Realism: Is There No Alternative?* Winchester: Zero Books.

Flynn, Mathew (2016), 'Accounting for Listening: How music streaming has changed what it means to listen', *Kinephanos*, 6: 35–59.

Frank, Robert H. (2013), *Falling Behind: How Rising Inequality Harms the Middle Class*. Berkeley: University of California Press.

Glynn, Paul (2017), 'Five visions for the future of music', *BBC News*, 29 December. Available online: http://www.bbc.com/news/entertainment-arts-42359324 (accessed 29 December 2017).

Gordon, Steve (2005), *The Future of the Music Business*, 4th edn. Milwaukee, WI: Hal Leonard Books.

Guardian (2017), 'Spotify's Daniel Ek named most powerful person in the music business'. *Guardian*, 10 February. Available online: https://www.theguardian.com/music/2017/feb/10/spotify-daniel-ek-most-powerful-person-music-business, accessed 29 December 2017.

Hardt, Michael and Antonio Negri (2000), *Empire*. Cambridge, MA: Harvard University Press.

Harvey, David (2005), *A Brief History of Neoliberalism*. Oxford: Oxford University Press.

Haynes, Jo and Lee Marshal (2017), 'Beats and Tweets: Social media in the careers of independent musicians', *New Media and Society*, 20 (5): 1973–93.

Hooton, Christopher (2015), 'Hip-hop is the most listened to genre in the world, according to Spotify analysis of 20 billion tracks', *Independent*, 14 July. Available online: http://www.independent.co.uk/arts-entertainment/music/news/hip-hop-is-the-most-listened-to-genre-in-the-world-according-to-spotify-analysis-of-20-billion-10388091.html (accessed 14 January 2018).

Hracs, Brian J., Doreen Jakob and Atle Hauge (2013), 'Standing Out in the Crowd: The rise of exclusivity-based strategies to compete in the contemporary marketplace for music and fashion', *Environment and Planning A*, 45: 1144–61.

IFPI (2017), 'Rewarding creativity – fixing the value gap'. IFPI. Available online: http://www.ifpi.org/value_gap.php, accessed 29 December 2017.

IFPI Digital Music Report (2013). Available at: http://www.ifpi.org/downloads/dmr2013-full-report_english.pdf (accessed 17 November 2017).

IFPI Digital Music Report (2015). Available at: http://www.ifpi.org/downloads/Digital-Music-Report-2015.pdf (accessed 18 November 2017).

IFPI Report (2000). Available at: http://www.ifpi.org/content/library/worldsales2000.pdf (accessed 17 November 2017).

Klein, Bethany, Leslie M. Meier and Devon Powers (2017), 'Selling Out: Musicians, Autonomy, and Compromise in the Digital Age', *Popular Music and Society*, 2: 222–38.

Knopper, Steve (2009), *Appetite for Self-Destruction: The Spectacular Crash of the Record Industry in the Digital Age*. London: Simon & Schuster.

Krause, Amanda E., Adrian C. North and Lauren Y. Hewitt (2015), 'Music-listening in Everyday Life: Devices and choice', *Psychology of Music*, 2: 155–70.

Krukowski, Damon (2016), 'Love Streams', in Richard Purcell and Richard Randall (eds), *21st Century Perspectives on Music, Technology, and Culture*, 113–19. London: Palgrave Macmillan.

Kusek, David and Gerd Leonhard (2006), *The Future of Music: Manifesto for the Digital Music Revolution*. Boston, MA: Berklee Press.

Laing, Dave (2012), 'What's it Worth? Calculating the economic value of live music', *Live Music Exchange Blog*, 11 June. Available online: http://livemusicexchange.org/blog/whats-it-worth-calculating-the-economic-value-of-live-music-dave-laing/ (accessed 15 December 2015).

Leyshon, Andrew (2014), *Reformatted: Code, Networks, and the Transformation of the Music Industry*. Oxford: Oxford University Press.

Lindvall, Helienne (2011), 'Behind the Music: Is the A&R era over?', *Guardian*, 27 January. Available online: https://www.theguardian.com/music/musicblog/2011/jan/27/behind-music-industry-a-r (accessed 12 January 2018).

Lowder, J. Bryan (2012), 'Does Pop Sound Louder, Dumber, and More and More the Same? One Study Says So', *Browbeat*, 27 July. Available online: http://www.slate.com/blogs/browbeat/2012/07/27/pop_music_is_getting_louder_and_dumber_says_one_study_here_s_what_they_miss_.html (accessed 29 December 2017).

Manovich, Lev (2007), 'What Comes after Remix?', *Remix Theory*. Available at: http://remixtheory.net/?p=169 (accessed 12 April 2017).

Marshall, Lee (2012), 'The 360 Deal and the "New" Music Industry', *European Journal of Cultural Studies*, 1: 77–99.

Marx, Karl and Frederick Engels (1947), *The German Ideology, Parts I and III*. New York: International Publishers.

McLeod, Kembrew (2005), 'MP3s are Killing Home Taping: The rise of Internet distribution and its challenge to the major label music monopoly', *Popular Music and Society*, 4: 521–31.

Meier, Leslie (2017), *Popular Music as Promotion: Music and Branding in the Digital Age*. Cambridge: Polity Press.

Morris, Jeremy Wade (2014), 'Artists as Entrepreneurs, Fans as Workers', *Popular Music and Society*, 3: 273–90.

Morris, Jeremy Wade (2015), *Selling Digital Music: Formatting Culture*. Oakland: University of California Press.

Mulligan, Mark (2015), *Awakening: The Music Industry in the Digital Age*. Music Trade.

Nielsen (2017), '2017 U.S/ Music Year-End Report', *Nielsen.com*. Available online: http://www.nielsen.com/us/en/insights/reports/2018/2017-music-us-year-end-report.html, accessed 14 January 2018.

Nowak, Raphael (2016), *Consuming Music in the Digital Age: Technologies, Roles and Everyday Life*. London: Palgrave.

Nowak, Raphael and Andrew Whelan (eds) (2016), *Networked Music Cultures: Contemporary Approaches, Emerging Issues*. London: Palgrave.

Palmer, Amanda (2014), *The Art of Asking or How I Learned to Stop Worrying and Let People Help*. New York: Piatkus.

Prey, Robert (2016), 'Musica Analytica: The Datafication of Listening', in Raphael Nowak and Andrew Whelan (eds), *Networked Music Cultures: Contemporary Approaches, Emerging Issues*, 31–48. London: Palgrave.

Resnikoff, Paul (2017), 'Welcome to the "Royalty Black Box"' the Music Industry's $2.5 Billion Underground Economy', *Digital Music News*, 3 August. Available online: https://www.digitalmusicnews.com/2017/08/03/music-industry-royalty-black-box/ (accessed 15 January 2018).

Rogers, Jim (2013), *The Death and Life of the Music Industry in the Digital Age*. London: Bloomsbury.

Savage, Mark (2016), 'Music streaming boosts sales of vinyl', *BBC*, 14 April. Available online: http://www.bbc.com/news/entertainment-arts-36027867 (accessed 11 January 2017).

Scott, Derek B. (2008), *Sounds of the Metropolis: The Nineteenth-Century Popular Music Revolution in London, Paris, and Vienna*. Oxford: Oxford University Press.

Smirke, Richard (2013), 'FPI Digital Music Report 2013: Global Recorded Music Revenues Climb for First Time Since 1999', *Billboard*, 26 February. Available online: https://www.billboard.com/biz/articles/news/digital-and-mobile/1549915/ifpi-digital-music-report-2013-global-recorded-music (accessed 20 November 2017).

Stahl, Matt (2013), *Unfree Masters: Recording Artists and the Politics of Work*. Durham, NC, and London: Duke University Press.

Sterne, Jonathan (2006), 'The MP3 as Cultural Artifact', *New Media & Society*, 5: 825–42.

Storper, Michael (2001), 'Livid Effects of the Contemporary Economy: Globalization, Inequality, and Consumer Society', in Jean Comaroff and John L. Comaroff (eds), *Millennial Capitalism and the Culture of Neoliberalism*, 88–124. Durham, NC, and London: Duke University Press.

Strachan, Robert (2017), *Sonic Technologies: Popular Music, Digital Culture and the Creative Process*. New York: Bloomsbury.

Taylor, Timothy D. (2016), *Music and Capitalism: A History of the Present*. Chicago, IL: The University of Chicago Press.

Terranova, Tiziana (2004), *Network Culture: Politics for the Information Age*. London: Pluto Press.

Thomas, Liz (2009), 'The X Factor: Essex Cheryl Cole lookalike with an Estuary drawl makes judges drool as she starts to sing', *Mail Online*, 21 August. Available online: http://www.dailymail.co.uk/tvshowbiz/article-1207888/The-X-Factor-Wailing-Lithuanians-Cheryl-Cole-lookalike-heartthrob-twins-appear-show.html (accessed 28 December 2017).

Vanderbilt, Tom (2014), 'Echo Nest Knows Your Music, Your Voting Choice', *Wired*. Available at: http://www.wired.co.uk/article/echo-nest (accessed 28 December 2017).

Waugh, Michael (2017), '"My Laptop is an Extension of My Memory and Self": Post-Internet identity, virtual intimacy and digital queering in online popular music', *Popular Music*, 2: 233–51.

Wikström, Patrik (2013), *The Music Industry: Music in the Cloud*, 2nd edn. Cambridge: Polity.

Williamson, John and Martin Cloonan (2013), 'Contextualizing the Contemporary Recording Industry', in Lee Marshall (ed.), *The International Recording Industries*, 11–29. London: Routledge.

Part One

The Music Industry

Rethinking Independence: What Does 'Independent Record Label' Mean Today?

Patryk Galuszka and Katarzyna M. Wyrzykowska

Until the 1990s, the term independence had a certain descriptive value. It had been regularly employed by artists, journalists, and listeners to distinguish between different products of culture. This distinction was essential in the music industry, as the independents were believed to bring an alternative to the oligopolistic practices of major record labels. Today, however, its meaning is very broad (perhaps too broad): it is widely used to name and classify artists as 'independent artists' (Brown 2012), labels as 'independent labels' (Lee 1995a, 1995b), or music genres as 'indie rock' or 'indie pop' (Hibbett 2005). Because of its extensive application, the term *artistic independence* used today has lost its semantic value. The diminishing precision of the term *independence* manifests itself in 'the uncritical grouping of a wide variety of bands, soloists and other combinations of musicians and songwriters under the heading "successful independent artists"' (Brown 2012: 520). As a result, both Radiohead (a band that cooperated with a major record label for many years) and a little-known singer-songwriter, who gathered funds for the release of their first album through the Kickstarter platform, are classified as independent. This confusion is the reason why we believe it necessary to reconsider the notion of independence in music.

Authors have indicated many different reasons for the overuse of the term *independence*, from the partial burn-out of the ethos of 'post-punk independent record labels', through the appropriation and co-optation of independent labels by major companies, to the triumph of the neoliberal attitude towards economic activity (Hesmondhalgh and Meier 2015). Problems with today's understanding of the term *independence* also stem from the economic and technological changes that the entire music industry is undergoing as a result of the digitization and spread of online methods for the distribution of recordings. Because of these methods, the distributor of a given record label is no longer a valid criterion for the distinction between dependent and independent labels (Fonarow 2006). In other words, does the fact that the catalogue of a given record label is available on Spotify or iTunes make the label dependent or independent? The difficulties with answering even a basic question such as this one show that the criterion of distribution has lost its key importance. In this context, we share the view of Hesmondhalgh and Meier that 'the current moment calls for a revisiting and perhaps redefinition of what independence means and could mean for popular music' (2015: 111). Consequently, the general goal of this chapter is to discuss what the term *independent record label* (or, more broadly, *music label*) means today. Since giving a full answer to this broad question would require much more than the space here affords, our goal in this chapter is narrower: drawing from empirical data gathered within a particular recording market, Poland, to find a new criterion to distinguish independent record labels from 'mainstream' or 'dependent' ones. In-depth interviews conducted with representatives of fifty-two record labels operating in the same economic and legal conditions allow us to compare the answers provided by our respondents. We believe that analysing the development of independent record labels in a country located away from the centre of the music industry may enrich the global debate on the issue, and that our conclusions will prove interesting to scholars working in other countries. In other words, we do not aim to present a complete picture of the Polish music market (see Galuszka and Wyrzykowska 2016 for an analysis of this type); rather, we try to look for more universal ways of distinguishing between various types of record labels. Before we move on to analysing the data collected, we provide an overview of literature on the subject of independence in music.

Independence in popular music

A definition of *independents* reads: '[t]he true independents distribute their records through independent distributors' (i.e., distributors not affiliated with major record companies) (Passman 2009: 67). The emphasis on the ability to distribute records independently results from the economic importance of distribution in the music industry before the internet became widely popular. This ability meant that a label could reach its listeners on its own (or through independent distributors). A lack thereof meant that a label was either unable to sell their records or had to use a major record label distribution network and, consequently, share profits with the music establishment, which (in light of the definition quoted above) made the label 'dependent'. It is for this reason that punk record labels active in the 1970s and 1980s put so much emphasis on building their own distribution networks (Gosling 2004). Controlling a label's own means of production (including distribution) meant being autonomous from the mainstream music industry. The establishment of the British indie record chart exemplified this logic: only records distributed without the mediation of major record companies could be listed (Fonarow 2006).

However, it should be noted that a definition of *independence* based purely on the distribution criterion does not give weight to the way in which a given label treats its artists and how it approaches artistic concerns. Hesmondhalgh pointed out the importance of these aspects:

> The discourses of fans, musicians and journalists during the counter cultural heyday of rock and soul in the 1960s and 1970s saw 'independents', or minor record companies with no ties to vertically integrated corporations, as preferable to the large corporations because they were less bureaucratic and supposedly more in touch with the rapid turnover of styles and sounds characteristic of popular music at its best. Such companies were often, in fact, even more exploitative of their musicians than the major corporations.
>
> Hesmondhalgh 1999: 35

This leads to the conclusion that the ability to distribute records independently is only one of the determinants of independence. Ethical and aesthetic factors are equally important. As the citation above shows, this was not entirely obvious until the advent of punk rock in the second half of the 1970s and the emergence of do-it-yourself (DIY) record labels releasing punk music. These labels opposed the mainstream music industry not only through building alternative distribution networks, but also through political engagement, the employment of different business practices, and more democratic, community-oriented repertoire choices (Dale 2008). Hesmondhalgh notes that the development of '[a]n aesthetic based on mobilization and access' (1999: 37) was one of the determinants crucial to the success of independent labels in the 1980s. It was this aesthetic that allowed independent labels to be perceived as more than just 'minor' record labels or merely smaller-size copies of 'major' record companies (Negus 1992).

Cammaerts recapitulates the philosophy of independent record labels:

> A more equal sharing of profit among the whole work force involved in the creative process, a shared ideological culture between artist and record label, the

participation of artists in the running and functioning of the record label, the development of alternative and genuinely independent distribution channels and the adoption of a distinct aesthetic mirroring this different attitude and ideology to music production and distribution.

Cammaerts 2010: 7

Lee (1995a, 1995b) shows that the attainment of these ideals should go hand in hand with an adherence to the elementary rules of management and economy. Otherwise, a label may be confronted with substantial financial problems. However, the need to adjust to market requirements may mean compromise. An independent record label that treats its artists fairly by paying them higher royalties, for instance, needs to compete with companies that act differently and can therefore potentially make a greater profit, which in turn allows for greater market expansion. The literature on this subject provides examples of independent record labels that managed, at least for a time, to reconcile their ideals with the difficult economic reality of the music industry (Hesmondhalgh 1997; Webb 2007). This could usually be attributed to the great success of an artist who signed a contract with a particular label (for instance, The Smiths signing a contract with Rough Trade). Such success, however, brought another type of risk: if a label somehow managed to succeed, it would very often have to resist the temptation of being 'bought out' by a major record company, resulting in what Negus describes as follows:

> The absorption of independent labels was a significant feature of the music business throughout the twentieth century and has become increasingly institutionalized through a series of joint ventures, production, licensing, marketing and distribution deals, which have led to the blurring of 'indie'/'major' organizational distinctions and mindsets.

Negus 1999: 35

This absorption was particularly visible in the 1990s, when many record companies that emerged from post-punk independent record labels created in the 1980s either went bankrupt or started a close cooperation with major record companies (Hesmondhalgh 1999; Hesmondhalgh and Meier 2014). Such a state of affairs was far removed from the ideals of independence developed in the 1980s. The meaning of *independence* was diluted by the different forms of cooperation between major record labels and independent labels (e.g., the establishment of quasi-independent labels controlled by major labels) and the evolution of the term *indie*, which began to primarily denote a musical genre

(Dale 2008). In effect, some labels, especially the smallest ones (which could be called 'micro-labels' or 'DIY labels'), have focused on putting a strong emphasis on their autonomy in order to stress the 'symbolic resistance to the totalizing discourses of capitalism' (Strachan 2007: 248). In their case, to use Bourdieu's terms (2005), economic assets (which are not likely to be obtained due to the niche appeal of their repertoire) are replaced by symbolic assets (which, in the owners' opinion, legitimizes the non-profit activity). It is worth noting at this point that, even though the subject literature is especially interested in DIY record labels originating from punk rock (Dale 2008; Dunn 2012; O'Connor 2008), some independent record labels that operated in the 1990s onwards had different origins. Such labels, despite a number of commonalities such as size, did not always share the ideology of punk rock labels, as Hesmondhalgh (1998) showed, based on the record labels that specialized in electronic music.

Apart from the tightening of cooperation between some independent labels and major record companies, the second half of the 1990s and the 2000s also brought far-reaching technological changes: the universalization of the internet and digitalization. Many authors saw these changes as a chance to equalize the opportunities for small and major labels (see the overview in Rogers 2013). Even though writers in the 2000s demonstrated excessive optimism about the democratizing impact of the internet (for example, Fox 2004; McLeod 2005), it is difficult to deny that independent record labels can now more easily reach listeners scattered across the world. In other words, the development of distribution networks is not as challenging now as it was when the post-punk independent record labels were emerging. What remains a challenge is the financing of production and promotion costs (Hesmondhalgh and Meier 2014) and the precarization of working conditions for musicians (Stahl 2013; Morris 2014).

The aforementioned phenomena (the decreased importance of distribution as a classifying criterion for record labels and the blurring of the term *independence*) necessitate a discussion about what makes an independent record label today. The blurring of *independence* does not mean that the term has lost its political potential and analytical usefulness. First, DIY record labels operate throughout the world, also as significant actors on virtual music scenes (Bennett and Peterson 2004), performing an important function within genre niches (Dunn 2012; O'Connor 2008). Some DIY labels maintain the political engagement that was characteristic for independents three decades ago. Second, as Hesmondhalgh and Meier note, labels that follow the ideals of independence from the end of the 1970s and the beginning of the 1980s constantly face new challenges, including the unequal treatment of independent artists by digital music stores and the precarization of musicians' work. Whilst our research did not aim to explore the possibility of carrying out these proposals (the former proposal would require coordinative action on a global, rather than domestic, scale), it has indicated a new aspect of the functioning of independent record labels under a constant decrease in sales.

Overview of the Polish recording market and methodology

The value of the Polish recording market was estimated at 350 million złoty in 2016 (according to wholesale prices), or US$97 million (exchange rate as of 15 December 2017) (ZPAV 2017). In recent years, the Polish recording market has climbed to around twentieth in the world in terms of value. In the first half of 2017, digital formats constituted 35 per cent of all recording sales and physical formats constituted 65 per cent. Within physical formats, the share of vinyl records amounted to 18.9 per cent (or 12.3 million złoty), a 71.2 per cent increase compared with the first half of 2016. In 2016, major record labels held a market share of 61.6 per cent and independents 38.4 per cent (Hojda and Pluta 2017). Recordings by Polish artists are highly popular, with a 37 per cent share of all sales in 2016 (for comparison, non-Polish recordings amounted to 44 per cent, compilations to 14 per cent, and classical music to 5 per cent; ZPAV 2017).

The subsequent part of this chapter is based on data gathered during two research projects. The first was carried out in 2013 and comprised fifty semi-structured in-depth interviews with representatives of record labels.[1] The second was carried out in 2017 and involved interviews with representatives of ten record labels (the same eight labels were interviewed both in 2013 and 2017). Two main criteria were applied in the selection of participants (purposeful selection): the diversity of music specialization and of entity sizes. This measure allowed for the inclusion of diverse subjects, and therefore mirrored the character and dynamics of the music industry in Poland. Consequently, although this study concentrates on independent labels, representatives of the Polish divisions of major record companies were also interviewed for the sake of comparison.

A two-tiered music industry

Christopher May (2007) notes the existence of 'a two-tiered market for music: one casual, the relatively uncommitted and volatile tier, served by the established companies, and a smaller, although lively tier of enthusiasts and artist led enterprise'. The empirical data gathered during the study confirms the existence of such a two-tiered division of the Polish music market. In a sense, this is nothing new; this chapter illustrates that record companies have existed within the major/independent dichotomy for a long time. However, the dividing line between the two parts of the music industry in Poland does not go straight between major record companies and other labels. What seems to be the right criterion for determining the division is the attitude of a given company towards the mass market and earning profits. On the one hand, some labels can, following May (2007), be considered 'established companies', or major record companies and mid-sized labels that compete with majors for the same 'mass client'. Such labels focus on profit and define their target market in broad terms. We may use the former criterion of distribution to state that this group includes both quasi-independent labels that cooperate with majors and true independents that distribute their recordings through independent distributors. This can be treated as another symptom of the fact that distribution is no longer a criterion for the distinction between independent and dependent labels.

May also mentions a different type of record label: 'enthusiasts and artist led enterprises.' These labels do not focus on profit, or frequently do not even take it into account as a motivation and see their listeners (they rarely use the word 'market') as a niche separate from the mass market. If they do criticize mainstream music, they do so mostly in terms of image (they want to stand out from the mainstream) or aesthetics (they disapprove of the music that dominates the media, for instance), rather than major record labels taking their customers. The group is also uneven, comprising both mid-sized labels and micro-labels that specialize in very different music genres. The following is a description of both types of record labels.

Minor record labels

The record labels studied here include a group that declares profit is their main objective. According to former criteria, and in particular the use of an independent distribution network, some of these labels could be classified as independent. However, because from a business point of view they function as small versions of major record companies, we consider them 'minors', after Negus (1992). A label's attitude towards the mass market and the priority of profit over other aspects of activity can be seen in statements made by the label's representatives as well as in the language they use to describe the recording market. Consider the following examples of statements made by respondents from two different labels:

> The product is our business. Music is a product, a commodity, or a service. Naturally, if we didn't run a business, we'd never move forward. And that's a bad deal for both the artist and us. We do this to make money, and when we make money, then the artist's name appears automatically everywhere we sell our product.

> Working in the music industry, I mean, running a business, a recording company or wholesaling music or something, that has little to do with music as such, right? If I wanted to have a career in music, I'd probably start a band, right? Or maybe I'd become a musician myself, right? And this, this is business, you see? I think of myself as someone who runs a business, and selling an album, right, is really the same as selling shoes. Both an album and a pair of shoes needs to meet some criteria of quality, and people need to like it, right? That's it.

This approach towards its own activity translates into a label's decisions concerning its cooperation with the artists, such as signing long-term contracts, taking over copyright for the recordings, or a positive attitude towards 360-degree contracts (although these are not signed with every artist). Some of these labels specialize in a single music genre. However, in most cases, they compete with the majors over the same mass client by releasing recordings from different music genres that the mass client finds attractive. This state of affairs is well-illustrated by a statement from a representative of a mid-size record label:

> There used to be five majors, then four majors, and now there are three majors, and they decide about the market ... In fact, these three companies set the rules for cooperation with sales networks and with the media ... What I think is, these companies have terribly spoiled the market. They fight among themselves over their market shares, over, like, the number of records sold, over position, it has terribly spoiled the market. Especially [*name of the company removed*], they totally spoiled the market here with their agreements for rebates, for deferred payments, for the right to return and other such actions. It'll pay off to those few guys up there who'll be getting their bonuses for a couple of years. But for the whole industry, it's a terrible thing.

This statement clearly shows that the company competes with majors for the market. The respondent uses economic categories ('rebates' and 'deferred payments') because they compete with major record companies on an economic level: they compete over the same mass consumer, the attention of the traditional media, shelf-space in record stores, and other factors. Minors do, in fact, resemble major record companies in their approach to the market (focus on mass audiences) and in mirroring certain business practices (e.g., promoting their artists in the tabloid press or offering 360-degree contracts). This occurs despite a lack of any connections with major record labels in terms of company capital and use of independent distribution chains. They are market-driven entities that copy the business practices and attitudes of major companies, which makes it difficult to classify them as 'independents'.

Independent record labels

The group of labels that cannot be classified as majors or minors is diversified and involves both labels that claim to follow some of the ideals of independence developed in the 1980s and those that avoid making such references. What both groups of labels have in common is their approach to profit, which is seen as a fairly unimportant factor. This may seem idealistic but in fact is rather pragmatic and stems from both the awareness that selling recordings is becoming more and more difficult:

> We are aware that the music we release won't bring us any profit, or even a quick return on the investment.

and from the goals their creators wish to achieve:

> We're a rather unusual company ... because financial gain has always been less important for us. We wanted most of all to release a very particular type of music, the one we like.

An analysis of the motivations of those who establish independent record labels shows that profit is only a secondary consideration. The respondents' statements allow us to distinguish three types of motivations that are more important than gaining profit. First, those who run independent record labels find it crucial to form friendships with the artists and others engaged in a particular musical scene and to build communities centred around the released recordings (i.e., communities that would include artists, listeners, journalists, fans, and others).

The following statements made by respondents from two different labels underline the significance of this type of motivation:

> For me, it's very important to let it all play out in an atmosphere of agreement and musical understanding, but also in one of everyday life, because I personally hate, and this has happened to us before, I hate working with people who expect too much and overestimate their value on the market, because then our work gets stressful. We take efforts to be friendly with our artists.

> I think that what makes our label fairly unique is the enterprise itself, which is created by a group of friends. We're not just working together, we're also very good friends. Right now, persons who are close to me form the core of the label. This is a great feature. You could say that we run a family business.

Interestingly, this motivation translates in a very particular manner into creative decisions. For instance, a label may choose the producers for a given project based on friendship, rather than business relations. This can be interpreted as a sign of building a community, which was an inseparable part of DIY scenes (Dunn 2012).

Second, the conviction that artistically significant music must be released and archived constitutes an important motivation, as exemplified by the following statement:

> Our aims are highly idealistic: archiving and preserving for posterity those musical pieces of art that we can preserve. We think that too much notable art, or too much notable music, is lost somewhere out there. No-one gets registered, and we try our best to follow such artistic actions and register them ... so that they can be archived and preserved for posterity.

The third factor affecting the decision to run an independent record label includes fan motivations. Fan motivations explain how a given person entered the musical market, why they have established a record label, and why they continue to run it despite the lack of profit. Consider the following statement:

> I've listened to music for as long as I can remember. It was my passion. I was a fan of various genres of music. Then I started playing myself. Yes, music has always been with me, and so the next natural stage was to enter this, excuse me, recording market and to pursue my passion there as a producer, distributor, and promoter. It's like adding your own value to it, or adding some extra energy to all this. . . . I identify very strongly with the albums I release. I approach them as a fan, I'm a fan of each of the albums we've produced.

The above statement corresponds to Strachan's conclusions: '[o]ften, running a label is seen as in keeping with a label owner's day-to-day consumption of popular music as a direct extension of their fandom' (2007: 254).

These motivations translate into the business practices of independent labels: the use of short-term contracts (usually in the form of profit-sharing deals, whereby the profit is shared equally between the label and the artist), close relationships with the artists, and basing decisions related to the repertoire on aesthetic criteria. From an economic viewpoint, the most appropriate term for such labels is *non-profit institutions*, as their mission results from the aforementioned motivations. In this context, *non-profit* means that the owners of a label deliberately ignore the compulsion to gain profit.[2] In other words, earning more than it is necessary to pay wages and overheads is not the label's ultimate goal. However, this does not mean that such labels ignore the business aspects of their activity by, for instance, exposing the company to a risk of illiquidity due to excessive spending. In a vast majority of cases, these labels are professionally managed, and their owners are pragmatic and well aware of how the music market operates, and they try to avoid disappearing from the market due to financial reasons. This distinguishes them from some independent labels from the 1980s and 1990s, which, as Lee (1995a, 1995b) shows, seemed to lack basic business knowledge. Our respondents, despite being aware that they cannot earn significant profits from their business, approached the management of a record label in a professional manner:

> It's an enterprise I treat very seriously, very seriously, 100 per cent professionally. I don't think I can do a half-baked job and think of it as a hobby simply because it's not my only activity. It is a hobby of sorts, but a hobby I treat very seriously. . . . I don't think that because it's an independent label, I can just dismiss it. Absolutely not!

Undoubtedly, thanks to today's easy access to knowledge, even about such hermetic subjects as copyright or cooperation with collecting societies, the professional management of a record label is much easier now than it was in the 1980s. Nevertheless, it should be noted that knowledge about managing a label company is not enough in itself to stay on the market, i.e., to avoid losses that could make the label go bankrupt. In addition to knowledge, discipline is required to regulate what the label can engage in and what it should never do. Dale (2008) suggests that enforcing discipline to limit one's recording ambition could have allowed some of the British independent record labels that went bankrupt at the beginning of the 1990s to survive.

Our respondents are able to stay on the market thanks to such factors as:

– Avoiding expensive investments into promotion (e.g., music videos). Investments into promotion are considered superfluous, as interested listeners will learn about the label's offers through social media and the mass client cannot be convinced anyway.
– Not trying to make physical copies of recordings available at every retail outlet. This helps to reduce distribution costs. In extreme cases, physical copies can only be purchased on the label's website or during an artist's concerts.
– Accepting the fact that recording activity generates losses, and that different labels cover these losses in different manners. Sometimes, the owner of a label supports the company with their own funds (e.g., the 'micro-independents' described by Strachan 2007) or through sponsorship. Some labels are funded from other types of activities than selling recordings (e.g., concerts or running a recording studio) or from grants provided by the government or other institutions. Interviews conducted in 2017 suggest that the role of these auxiliary revenues has increased compared to 2013.

It is worth noting at this point that whilst the falling sales of recordings, especially physical copies, make it difficult to earn a profit, the costs of running a record label have also decreased over the last decade. As a result, the owners of record labels are at a much lower risk than only over a decade ago. This means that our respondents have not had to go into debt to run their labels, and should the need arise, they can support their labels with their daytime jobs. It also means that our respondents were in a better situation than Moore's respondents, some of which were forced to declare bankruptcy and were 'still trying to get the label out of debt' (2007: 459) at the time Moore conducted the study.

The expansion of digital distribution channels for recordings allows nearly all of the labels analysed here to take advantage of multi-channel distribution. Consequently, in contrast to the independent labels from the 1980s, these labels cooperate with many distributors, rather than just one, selling their recording in a variety of formats and locations. Some focus more on physical copies: vinyl recordings and collector's editions in addition to CDs. Others actively embrace digital distribution channels, including those that can be considered mainstream (e.g., Spotify or iTunes) and those closer to the twentieth-century independence ideals (e.g., Bandcamp). Because small record labels are unable to offer their catalogues directly on Spotify, they do so through music aggregators (Galuszka 2015). In the opinion of their owners, this does not contravene 'being independent'. It should be noted, however, that there are various types of aggregators – some are independently owned companies whilst others are controlled by major record labels. Cooperation with an aggregator owned by a major record label means sharing profits with the music establishment, and this is precisely what independent labels from the 1980s struggled against. This makes discussion about preserving a label's independence in the digital realm more complex.

Thanks to a combination of the above factors (in different proportions for each label), the labels are able to operate mostly independently from the recording market. The aforementioned independence from the market is relative to some extent; it should be understood as a lack of obligation to make a profit above any other criteria, rather than the possibility to operate as though money was unimportant. This relativity corresponds well to King's definition of *independence*: 'it is also often a *relative* quality rather than one that entails absolute or clear-cut distinctions between one thing and another' (King 2015: 52).

Conclusions

The independent labels that participated in our study differ from major and minor record companies in terms of the motivations behind their engagement in phonographic activity and the use of different business practices. Because such differences also existed 30 years ago, the question arises whether anything has actually changed, apart from the obvious fact that the internet facilitates the distribution of recordings. Thus, in our analysis of what constitutes independence in today's music, it is worth considering what differentiates our respondents from the labels of the 'golden age of independence' (i.e., the post-punk independent record labels from the 1980s). The basic difference seems to lie in the fact that political and ideological motivations play a secondary role for our respondents, who do not aim to challenge the mainstream music industry. Rather, they pragmatically accept their position as niche players, and focus on the subjective quality of the recordings they release and on good relationships with artists, rather than on increasing their share on the market or taking over the mass client. This may, to some extent, result from the specificity of the Polish

Localized to Poland due to data

music market, however, verifying this hypothesis exceeds the scope of our study. In our opinion, the above attitude can be primarily attributed to the impact of the internet on the economic basis of the functioning of record labels. This has resulted in the multiplication of niches, i.e., the low costs of online communication have made it easier to reach and provide for small segments of the market, which in the past used to be inaccessible due to cost barriers. This means that small, music-oriented labels that cannot compete over the mass client are able to function despite the relatively small number of buyers. It should be noted that in some cases, this functioning is consistent with the predictions of digital optimists (the concepts of the 'long tail' and the '1,000 true fans') or, in the case of labels that occupy 'something like a permanent state of crisis and instability' (King 2015: 66), with a project-to-project mode of operation. However, because the costs of running such a label are lower today than in the 1980s, so is the risk that the owner will face significant financial problems. As a result, many owners of independent record labels seem satisfied about their situation: by letting the bigger players fight for the market, they can focus on carrying out their own, smaller projects, such as releasing what music they consider as worthwhile, building a community, and cultivating fandom. The satisfaction from carrying out these goals is at least as high as in the case of independent labels that operated before the age of the internet, while the time-consumption and financial risk related to a potential lack of profit are incomparably lower.

Continuing this train of thought, we could come to the conclusion that the sector of independent labels, which used to be defined according to the criterion of distribution, has been divided (according to May's suggestion above) into profit-oriented companies that compete over the mass client (minors) and companies that forego this competition and, as a result, have become similar to Strachan's 'micro-independent record labels'. This conclusion seems partially correct. Nonetheless, we should not ignore the differences between the independent labels analysed in this study and Strachan's 'micro-independents' that stem from different economic conditions: the use of the internet decreases our respondents' expenditures, provides a much greater range, and allows many of the labels to operate in other areas (such as organization of live performances), in addition to phonography. As a result, many of the respondents do not feel as if they are operating in a forgotten niche. Even though the segment they provide for is small, internationalization gives their activity an additional meaning.

The satisfaction with (or acceptance of) one's situation reported by our respondents leaves pertinent questions about the contemporary challenges faced by independents. Hesmondhalgh and Meier (2014) mention two challenges: the precarization of musical activity and the unequal treatment of small record labels by large entities, such as YouTube or Spotify. Our respondents almost never mentioned these challenges. This, however, does not mean that this state of affairs will continue. Nonetheless, at the moment it seems that any future change will be spurred by the artists, rather than record labels, at least on the Polish market.

Acknowledgements

This work was granted financial support from the Institute of Music and Dance, the Polish Music Information Centre, ZAiKS, ZPAV and the Ministry of Culture and National Heritage of the Republic of Poland.

Notes

1   In order to guarantee the privacy of the interviewees, the quotations used in the chapter are anonymous.
2   It should be noted that in economics two types of profits are distinguished: normal profit and economic profit. The former is a profit that is necessary for any business to be sustainable – it includes, among other things, wages which are high enough to discourage an entrepreneur from looking for other jobs. The latter is excess profit that can be, for example, paid out to shareholders in the form of dividend. Our respondents deliberately ignore the compulsion to gain *economic* profit.

References

Anderson, C. (2008), *The Long Tail: Why the Future of Business Is Selling Less of More*. New York: Hyperion Books.
Bennett, A. and R.A. Peterson (2004), *Music Scenes: Local, Translocal and Virtual*. Nashville, TN: Vanderbilt University Press.
Bourdieu, P. (2005), 'Principles of Economic Anthropology', in N.J. Smelser and R. Swedberg (eds), *The Handbook of Economic Sociology*, 75–89. Princeton, NJ: Princeton University Press.
Brown, H. (2012), 'Valuing Independence: Esteem Value and its role in the independent music Scene', *Popular Music and Society*, 35(4): 519–39.

Cammaerts, B. (2010), 'From Vinyl to One/Zero and Back to Scratch: Independent Belgian micro labels in search of an ever more elusive fan base', *Media@LSE Electronic Working Paper Series 20*, 1–25. London: London School of Economics and Political Science.

Dale, P. (2008), 'It Was Easy, It Was Cheap, So What? Reconsidering the DIY principle of punk and indie music', *Popular Music History*, 3(2): 171–93.

Dunn, K. (2012), '"If it ain't cheap, it ain't punk": Walter Benjamin's Progressive Cultural Production and DIY Punk Record Labels', *Journal of Popular Music Studies*, 24(2): 217–37.

Fonarow, W. (2006), *Empire of Dirt. The Aesthetic and Rituals of British Indie Music.* Middletown, CT: Wesleyan University Press.

Fox, M. (2004), 'E-commerce Business Models for the Music Industry', *Popular Music and Society*, 27(2): 201–20.

Galuszka, P. (2015), 'Music Aggregators and Intermediation of the Digital Music Market', *International Journal of Communication*, 9: 254–73.

Galuszka, P and K.M. Wyrzykowska (2016), 'Running a Record Label when Records Don't Sell Anymore: Empirical evidence From Poland', *Popular Music*, 35(1): 23–40.

Gosling, T. (2004), '"Not for Sale": The Underground Network of Anarcho-Punk', in A. Bennett and R.A. Peterson (eds), *Music Scenes: Local, Translocal and Virtual*, 168–83. Nashville, TN: Vanderbilt University Press.

Hesmondhalgh, D. (1997), 'Post-Punk's Attempt to Democratise the Music Industry: The success and failure of rough trade', *Popular Music*, 16(3): 255–74.

Hesmondhalgh, D. (1998), 'The British Dance Music Industry: A case study of independent cultural production', *The British Journal of Sociology*, 49(2): 234–51.

Hesmondhalgh, D. (1999), 'Indie: The institutional politics and aesthetics of a popular music genre', *Cultural Studies*, 13(1): 34–61.

Hesmondhalgh, D. and L.M. Meier (2014), 'Popular Music, Independence and the Concept of the Alternative in Contemporary Capitalism', in J. Bennett and N. Strange (eds), *Independence: Working with Freedom or Working for Free?*, 94–112. New York and London: Routledge.

Hojda, M and P. Bogusław (2017), 'Polski rynek muzyczny a wartość eksportu'. Presented during the Music Export Conference, Warsaw, 5 October.

Hibbett, R. (2005), 'What is Indie Rock?', *Popular Music and Society*, 28(1): 55–77.

Kelly, K. (2008), *1,000 true fans*. Available online: http://kk.org/thetechnium/1000-true-fans/ (accessed 14 December 2017).

King, G. (2015), 'Differences of Kind and Degree. Articulations of independence in American cinema', in J. Bennett and N. Strange (eds), *Independence: Working with Freedom or Working for Free?*, 52–70. New York and London: Routledge.

Lee, S. (1995a), 'Independent Record Companies and Conflicting Models of Industrial Practice', *Journal of Media Economics*, 8(4): 47–61.

Lee, S. (1995b), 'Re-examining the Concept of the "Independent" Record Company: The case of Wax Trax! Records', *Popular Music*, 14(1): 13–31.

May, C. (2007), 'A Multi-tiered Music Industry? Intellectual property rights, open access and the audience for music', *Journal on the Art of Record Production*, 2. Available online: http://arpjournal.com/570/a-multi-tiered-music-industry-intellectual-property-rights-open-access-and-the-audience-for-music/ (accessed 14 December 2017).

McLeod, K. (2005), 'MP3s are Killing Home Taping: The rise of Internet distribution and its challenge to the major label music monopoly', *Popular Music and Society*, 28(4): 521–31.

Moore, R. (2007), 'Friends Don't Let Friends Listen to Corporate Rock', *Journal of Contemporary Ethnography*, 36(4): 438–74.

Morris, J.W. (2014), 'Artists as Entrepreneurs, Fans as Workers', *Popular Music and Society*, 37(3): 273–90.

Negus, K. (1992), *Producing Pop*. London: Edward Arnold.

Negus, K. (1999), *Music Genres and Corporate Cultures*. New York and London: Routledge.

O'Connor, A. (2008), *Punk Record Labels and the Struggle for Autonomy: The Emergence of DIY*. Lanham, MD: Lexington Books.

Passman, D.S. (2012), *All You Need to Know about the Music Business*, 8th edn. New York: Simon & Schuster.

Rogers, J. (2013), *The Death and Life of the Music Industry in the Digital Age*. New York and London: Bloomsbury Academic.

Stahl, M. (2013), *Unfree Masters: Recording Artists and the Politics of Work*. Durham, NC: Duke University Press.

Strachan, R. (2007), 'Micro-independent Record Labels in the UK Discourse, DIY Cultural Production and the Music Industry', *European Journal of Cultural Studies*, 10(2): 245–65.

Webb, P. (2007), *Exploring the Networked Worlds of Popular Music*. London and New York: Routledge.

ZPAV (2017), 'Wzrost sprzedaży muzyki w Polsce i na świecie!' Available online: http://zpav.pl/aktualnosc.php?idaktualnosci=1520 (accessed 14 December 2017).

2

The Future of Digital Music Infrastructures: Expectations and Promises of the Blockchain 'Revolution'

Paolo Magaudda

When exploring the future of music, it is crucial to take into consideration the emerging forms of technology, infrastructures and innovations that are expected to reconfigure music content and practices in the next decade. There is no doubt that in the last 20 years major changes in music practices have been moulded around new 'affordances' (Gibson 1966) coming from digital technologies and infrastructures, such as the MP3 format, peer-to-peer networks and streaming platforms. The social and economic life of today's music can largely be considered as the consequence of ideas, visions and scripts embodied into those digital infrastructures, which reflect distinctive modes of music circulation and consumption.

In this chapter, I consider the emergence of so-called *blockchain technology* in the context of the music industry and, most specifically, the impact it is expected to have on the circulation of recorded music. I will take into account how these emerging innovations in digital music are being technically shaped as well as discursively envisioned in our present. Blockchain is a cryptographic decentralized technology at the core of the increasingly debated Bitcoin phenomenon. Its application in music has been anticipated since 2015; however, at the beginning of 2018 this technology has yet to become an actual solution for digital music circulation. Blockchain is increasingly heralded by journalists, start-ups and research reports as the upcoming 'revolution' in the music industry and is often acclaimed as a new 'disruptive technology' able to change the music business, especially in giving artists a chance to regain control over their musical works in a music environment increasingly dominated by large digital corporations.

Not to be a technological determinist.

The recent adoption of blockchain technology in several fields of our society will likely be a driver of several (possibly radical) changes in the digital capitalism of tomorrow. Still, only a blind 'technological determinism' (Williams 1974; MacKenzie and Wajcman 1985; Wyatt 2008) would trust those who see, in the application of blockchain technology to music, an automatic solution to the distortions of today's digital music political economy, increasingly dominated as it is by companies such as Apple, YouTube and Spotify. The promises about blockchain's ability to revolutionize music are today sustained by very intense and enthusiastic efforts and activities, which equate the decentralized nature of this technology with the re-appropriation of control by artists and musicians over their work, rights and economic revenues. As we will see, a critical analysis of discourses, promises and expectations generated around blockchain technology will help not only to balance the contemporary euphoria about the future consequences of music blockchain, but also to start excavating some of the eventual political, economic and also cultural implications that will drive, in the next few years, the shaping and adoption of this new music technology.

Before taking into account the application of blockchain technology in music and the discourses supporting it, I will briefly outline some of the theoretical standpoints from which I begin both my analysis on digital music infrastructures and my approach to the promises that fuel new technology development. These standpoints rely on the field of science and technology studies (STS), on the analysis of media infrastructures and data circulation (Gitelman 2013; Parks and Starosielki 2015; Balbi and Magaudda 2018), and on the history of music-related formats, standards and software (Sterne 2012; Morris 2015). Addressing my theoretical standpoints will help to situate the empirical issues that will be addressed here. I will also discuss some of the reasons why we should locate the promises supporting the development of new digital infrastructures as privileged entry points to understanding the evolution of the future of music circulation.

Technology, infrastructures and the shaping of digital music

The relevance of the notion of 'infrastructure' in social science was initially developed in the interdisciplinary field of STS in the 1990s, where infrastructures were recognized as crucial in the shaping of social arrangements, collective practices and human activities. STS scholars invite us to consider infrastructures not just as neutral carriers, or facilitators of activities or content circulation, but as distinctive sociotechnical entities, able to create relationships between human activities and technical artefacts. Infrastructures are imbued with conventions, organizational arrangements and other invisible features and, for these reasons, are able to underpin the social order (Star and Ruhleder 1996; Bowker and Star 2000). Thus, from this perspective, a dense notion of infrastructure does not refer to a static technical artefact, but to the processual qualities carried by it, and especially its ability to build up new configurations between people, technical artefacts, embodied values, and practical activities.

This relational and processual scale characterizing infrastructure has been increasingly recognized in media and communication studies as a useful entry-point to disentangle the increasingly complex intersection between media materiality, dematerialized digital content, data organization and collective media practices (Parks and Starosielski 2015; Peters 2015; Balbi and Magaudda 2018). As sociologist David Beer states, 'by bringing to the fore the material dimensions of everyday life, embodied in these infrastructures and data circulations, we are able to see how culture and media combine and fold into ordinary routine life' (Beer 2013: 2). If for a long time the relationship between music and technology has been understood in terms of 'devices', 'players' or 'supports', today cloud-based digital content, distributed through networked platforms, has displaced the *locus* of music consumption on a radically different scale: the scale of infrastructures.

On top of this, to understand the crucial role of infrastructures, we also need to outline the relevance of the discourses and representations supporting the emergence of new technological innovations. As with other emerging technologies, the early stage of infrastructures requires the mobilization of visions able to sustain the collective efforts required to establish them as viable solutions to existing problems. This is the reason why a specific line of inquiry in STS has been devoted to the analysis of expectations, imaginaries and promises that future technologies generate in the present (Van Lente 1993; Jasanoff and Sang-Hyun 2015; Konrad et al. 2016). By relying on this approach to technology expectations, we are able to consider the upcoming blockchain digital music infrastructures not just for their expected consequences in the future, but also for the activities they are triggering in our very present, and for articulation of the discourses supporting them as solutions for today's problems and needs of music industry and artists.

As has been said, an emphasis on the infrastructural dimension of music digitization has already been addressed by scholars, who pointed out the role of networks, formats, interfaces, protocols, and data circulation in the changes affecting the music world. A seminal work on this subject is the study by media historian Jonathan Sterne on the development of the MP3 music format (Sterne 2012). As Sterne pointed out in his definition of a *format theory*, the shift from the (already digital) CD to the MP3 implied not just the creation of a new single technical device, but the formation of an infrastructural entity, which should be understood through a multiple-scale analysis that includes 'smaller registers like software, operating standards and codes, as well as larger registers like infrastructures, international corporate consortia and whole technical systems' (2012: 11). A similar approach emerges from the work by Jeremy Wade Morris (2015) on the development of digital music as a commodity, from the 1997 software WinAmp onwards. Morris outlines how the recent history of digital music has been essentially a work through which the value of music as a commodity has been reconfigured in a new form, on the basis of different kinds of tools and infrastructures established for music circulation. Along the path of development of a new digital music infrastructure, the cultural value of music needed to be culturally reconfigured through software interfaces and metadata, but also by discursive and metaphoric efforts displayed by the industry and other related actors. In this new digital landscape, a pivotal role has been assumed by music metadata, not only because they make possible an efficient circulation of music, but also because metadata 'affect how it appears, how it can be used, and how it can be sorted and stored on a user's various devices' as 'it is made up of software code that is largely visible through other interfaces and devices' (Morris 2015).

This brief outline of the notion of infrastructure and the relevance of the discourse and expectations supporting the emergence of new technical innovations also helps to clarify how the recent past of digital music actually developed on an infrastructural scale. And, consequently, to point out that the logic which will drive the future of music could hardly be understood without looking at the shifting intersection between digital infrastructures and the cultural visions that frame the emergence of these new technologies.

What is blockchain and how does it work?

Before exploring the development of blockchain-based music infrastructures more closely, it is useful to outline some of the basic principles about how blockchain technology works. Blockchain is an increasingly popular *cryptographic* and *decentralized* technology that has found a concrete application with the Bitcoin digital currency, which in late 2017 assumed mainstream global visibility as a possible techno-financial bubble. Blockchain is a special kind of *distributed network*, in a similar way to music peer-to-peer networks such as Napster, eMule or Soulseek. Whilst music peer-to-peer networks share songs (or other files) amongst their users, blockchain allows for sharing *certified data* into a public database, which can contain the records of money transactions (in the case of Bitcoin) and also other types of records. A distinctive feature is that these data are recorded in a certified way, as they are stored into a *public ledger* by means of cryptographic techniques, warranting that contents recorded into this ledger cannot be altered or circumvented. The public ledger is organized into ordered 'blocks' of transactions and constitutes a unique, collectively certified database, ordered in a linear and chronological way: with such a distributed model there is no central server where the database resides (for a detailed introduction to blockchain technology, see Swan 2015).

Blockchain technology has been developed in the form of Bitcoins, a cryptographic digital coin enabling a billion-dollar global market of anonymous transactions without any governmental control. Blockchain technology was originally proposed in 2008 in a paper entitled 'Bitcoin: A Peer-To-Peer Electronic Cash System', authored under the pseudonym of Satoshi Nakamoto, whose real existence has not still been definitively cleared. At the beginning of 2009 the first 'block' of the Bitcoin blockchain was created, introducing the idea that, contrary to existing digital forms of exchange (for example conventional bank infrastructures), collective digital transactions can be managed without a third-party authority or mechanism of verification.

A crucial innovation introduced by blockchain pertains to the way the verified transactions are put in chronological order, solving a common and disturbing problem affecting distributed networks, where events can happen contemporarily and conflict each other. A solution was achieved by adopting the idea of ordered blocks of data, linked to each other in a chronological chain and preventing a transaction from being registered twice. To put the blocks in order, a further cryptographic technique was applied called *proof of work*, which avoids invalid and extemporaneous nodes of the network generating fake transactions. This technique requires that any node that certifies recorded blocks should solve a mathematical puzzle by putting a substantive calculating effort into the network. The nodes that make this calculating power available are defined as *miners* and are rewarded with the same Bitcoins that they contribute to regulate.

Another very important piece of how the blockchain technology works are *smart contracts*, which consist in the ability of blockchain to manage the automatic execution of deals between parties: this means that blockchain is able to perform contracts, automatically enforced by computer protocols. Smart contracts were invented in 1994 by computer scientist Nick Szabo, but remained unexploited up to the availability of blockchains, especially until 2013 when young Russian engineer Vitalik Buterin proposed the alternative blockchain infrastructure Ethereum (Greenfield 2017). Ethereum started to operate in 2015, not just to offer an alternative coin (like Bitcoin) but expressly designed to make available a cross-application platform able to run these smart contracts. Since the launch of this alternative blockchain infrastructure in 2015, investments and experiments with blockchain and smart contracts have started in different economic sectors (from banks to tourism reservations, from online gaming to electric car charging management). It is no surprise that the music sector has quickly turned into one of the most important fields of experimentation of this new technology.

Blockchain, the music industry and the rhetoric of fair music

The music sector has historically been particularly ready to adopt new digital technologies for its needs, from the laser writing on the compact disc (1979) to file sharing with Napster (1999) and online selling of digital content with iTunes (2003). Hence, it is no wonder that, in the aftermath of the radical sector reconfiguration generated by MP3 and streaming services, the application of blockchain in the music sector was quickly recognized by both media and industry actors as the next step, as soon as the possibility of running smart contracts over a blockchain infrastructure was circulated in 2015 (O'Dair et al. 2016).

An early input to stir up the hype around blockchain in the music industry was a well-received 2015 report by the Rethink Music initiative (at the Berklee College of Music), titled *Fair Music: Transparency and Payment Flows in the Music Industry* (Rethink Music 2015). This report was one of the first sources to point out the solutions that blockchain could bring to the music sector to solve existing problems affecting the current assets of rights and rewards in the post-digital music industry. As outlined in the report, one of the main current problems in the music industry is the system of distributing revenues from music streaming, which is unanimously considered complex, inefficient and unfair. Indeed, as much as 70 per cent of the revenue from streaming services and other digital distribution platforms goes to intermediaries between artists and fans, such as labels, distributors and other middle-figures (Marshall 2015; Vonderau 2017), whilst musicians and artists receive only a very small fraction of the money spent by consumers. Whilst the process of distributing royalties has always been a rather intricate one, the rise of digital formats and streaming has made it even more complex, multiplying intermediaries and gatekeepers and thus making increasingly opaque the steps that connect the money paid by listeners and the rewards received by artists.

In this landscape, blockchain technology and smart contracts, with their potential to *automatically* attribute and distribute royalties, were immediately recognized as a type of holy grail solution. Tapscott and Tapscott, two of the most visible champions of the benefits of blockchain, state in their book *Blockchain Revolution* that this new technology offers a magic solution for the music sector to solve the power imbalance between artists and platforms. Blockchain will put

> artists at the centre of the model so they can not only 'have their cake' that is, exercise their freedom of expression, but also 'eat it, too', maximizing the value of their moral and material interests in their intellectual property. In other words, to restore their rights. No more big, greedy intermediary, no big government censors.
>
> Tapscott and Tapscott 2016

With this hope in mind, since 2015 excitement has grown around blockchain technology. There are countless journalistic articles in the online and offline press, with titles like 'How blockchain will revolutionize the music industry', from generalist news sites like the *Huffington Post* (Kuznetsov 2017), technology-focused websites like *Techcrunch* (Dickson 2016), or financial sources such as *Forbes* (Chester 2016). However, notwithstanding the newness of blockchain technology, the dominant rhetoric supporting early discourse about the adoption of blockchain technology in the music industry has been a rather old one: the 'rhetoric of revolution', a recurrent and pervasive way of framing the adoption of many digital technologies in recent decades (Balbi and Magaudda 2018: 21–22).

The discourse based on the 'revolutionary technology' is a specific framing, implying that a new technical solution will radically change the way to do things;

this was a key argument explicitly used, for example, in Steve Jobs' theatrical presentations of Apple's new devices such as the iPod and the iPhone. In the case of music blockchain, this revolutionary rhetoric appeared in blogs and magazine articles in a slightly updated version of the 'disruptive technology'. The pivotal idea supporting this discourse is linked to another recurrent cultural framing in music culture: the never-ending 'battle' between artists and the music business. Over the years, the articulation of this battle has taken the shape of the ideological conflict between 'independent' music and 'major labels' (Hesmondhalgh 1999; Magaudda 2011; Hesmondhalgh and Meier 2015). In a digital society, this archetypical struggle assumes renewed negative targets, those represented by global big music digital platforms such as iTunes, Spotify, YouTube and Amazon.

The need to improve the conditions of artists and musicians against big corporations' profits has been, quite unsurprisingly, the major leitmotiv in today's narrative sustaining the future adoption of music blockchain. One of the early blockchain music projects that received attention from the mainstream media has been that associated with the work of the British singer-songwriter Imogen Heap. In October 2015, Heap announced the release of her song 'Tiny Human' over a blockchain system as part of the Mycelia project, an experiment created to develop the possibilities of blockchain technology for artists and independent creators (Bartlett 2015). The aim of this experiment was to show what can be done with a music blockchain for independent artists: each song sold over the blockchain platform can include a smart contract, containing the terms under which the music can be downloaded by listeners or used by third parties, how the royalties earned will be divided, and the automatic routing of payments – via smart contracts – to respective recipients.

On the one hand, Imogen Heap is a British artist who truly represents the need of independent artists against big digital companies, however, on the other hand, there is no doubt that the possibilities outlined by her project describe a selective future, which brings to the forefront only the positive applications of blockchain. Indeed, the projection of future scenarios is never a neutral and transparent activity, as any new innovation in its early stage needs to be supported by specific discourse that envisions the positive implications of a technology and makes them desirable, by affirming specific moral and political orders that can be recognized and embraced by fans and listeners. In other words, positive future scenarios about blockchain should be read as part of the promises and expectations instrumental in supporting the efforts required in the creation and adoption of a new emergent infrastructure.

Five technological promises about music blockchain

As with other emerging technologies, the adoption of blockchain in music requires the concerned people, actors and institutions to converge together on some type of vision or *promise*. The need for new technologies to *perform promises* in their early stages has been pointed out in different ways by STS scholars, who focused on the dynamic patterns by which 'hype' and expectations are mobilized as resources to shape innovation in the present (Selin 2008; Konrad et al. 2016). Expectations and promises are performative in the way they help mobilize the future into the present; the expectations, promises and imagined benefits of a technology are all part of the innovation process into which resources are poured and new actors are 'enrolled' into a supporting network (Latour 2005). These promises and expectations about new technologies became manifest in the form of descriptions of situations of use, potential applications or broader scenarios, and they involve both the technology's technical qualities and political and social implications.

Like other technologies, music blockchain needs to be supported in its early stages by a specific set of expectations and promises, which primarily include the issue of a fairer and better distribution of royalties to artists, but also embrace other issues and questions, as the promises about a new technology need to speak to and mobilize different interests and actors. We can identify at least five types of promise on blockchain infrastructure in these early years in the music industry.

We have already seen the first promise, consisting in the hope for a *perfect royalties distribution* system and the possibility for a system of fast and frictionless royalty payments, running on a dedicated blockchain platform with smart contracts. The new model of music distribution would ideally mean that when a song is streamed this would be instantly registered in the blockchain, a smart contract included in the transaction would record the payment, the profits would be divided automatically between the rights holders (platform, label, artist, songwriter, etc.), and the money could even be deposited into their accounts through a dedicated digital coin. This represents the 'king promise', ensuring the support for blockchain technology by independent artists, fans and those people that believe in the value of creativity and social justice concerning wealth distribution.

A second promise is that of a *perfect music database*, as music blockchain would also contain all the data regarding a song, turning the infrastructure into a certified transparent catalogue of all music production and ownership. Currently in the digital music realm there is no exhaustive database of music, even though an attempt to build such a catalogue was promoted in 2008 by the European Commission. The Global Repertoire Database, as it was named, was an ambitious challenge to build a unique online copyright portal for all musical works. However, in 2014 it collapsed with debts of about $14 million, also leaving a tricky situation in terms of music catalogues, especially in Europe, where there are different copyright management services for each of the 28 EU countries (Milosic 2015). Music blockchain promises to be an institutional solution to this problem, as it would be a public and decentralized registry where any kind of rights and ownership could be stored, splitting the costs of the system in the same way as Bitcoins, i.e., by giving a reward to the machines that offer the calculation power to run it.

This leads us to the third promise performed by blockchain technology: *full transparency over the music value chain,* as the public registry will unequivocally address the rights holders and show clearly the eventual role of any intermediary along the chain, thus reducing the need (and the costs) for these same intermediaries. Indeed, as outlined by Morris (2015), digital streaming and cloud music generated an increasingly thick layer of 'infomediaries' in music circulation, responsible for shaping how audiences encounter music; blockchain promises to eliminate these infomediaries, substituting them with an automated and transparent infrastructure.

Promise four is the possibility to give access to *alternative sources of money* for artists and creators. This is probably the most striking attempt to reconfigure the relationship between music as a commodity and listeners. For example – as I will address in more detail below – blockchain offers the possibility to allocate the fans who purchase a song at the moment it is released a small fraction of the song's royalties, enabling them to invest in and fund their favourite artists.

Finally, there is a fifth promise, which is downplayed in companies' blockchain presentations and journalistic articles, because it looks unattractive for fans: the *elimination of piracy,* connected with increased control over the use of music, assured by an automated and certified infrastructure. In a scenario where all songs are clearly associated with the rights holders, and where playing them is automatically managed by smart contracts, a direct consequence would be that any unauthorized use of music could be traced back and blocked. The dangers of this last promise are linked with worries about technological control over users' practices, but also with the reluctance of the music industry, which still remembers the failure of DRM technology (Gillespie 2007), to restart a fight against piracy already lost in the last decade.

Whilst all these promises look plausible, realistic and easily fulfilled based on the intrinsic features of blockchain, many doubts can be cast on these expectations. Not only should we know that the dynamics of hopes and promises about music blockchain are selective and expressly aimed to build consensus in the present, but a closer look at the actual developments in blockchain competing infrastructures helps to remove the veil of marketing and hype that is driving the early stage of this technology.

Competing infrastructures, the incompatibility of music data and the pressures to music monetization

As already outlined, understanding music circulation increasingly requires focusing on the infrastructural configuration of systems that allow music to move and be commodified, as was done by sociologist and historian Jonathan Sterne (2012) in relation to the MP3 format. It is important to consider not just the technical features of devices and equipment, but the implications and consequences, occurring on different scales, that are promoted and sustained by the new means of music circulation, including infrastructures, formats, databases and the socio-cultural arrangement at the base of all this. Following this approach, we can now reflect on some of the cracks and flaws made apparent by considering how the landscape of blockchain music services is growing up and how competing music blockchain infrastructures articulate alternative visions based on slightly different drives and solutions.

First of all, contrary to one of promises considered before – the possibility to have a unified database with all artistic and copyright-related information – we now have an astonishing multiplication of music platforms and infrastructures based on the blockchain technology. From the start of the blockchain hype in late 2015 until early 2018, the number of services that have announced projects of music distribution based on blockchain has grown constantly: our search in March 2018 of magazine, blog and journal articles dedicated to the music industry adoption of blockchain technology found at least 17 different upcoming platforms and projects, between the US and Europe, expressly devoted to establishing a blockchain system for the circulation of recorded music.[1] Amongst them, we find projects like Imogen Heap's Mycelia, which have been started by artists with the primary aim of supporting fairness in royalties and artistic autonomy. This is also the approach of the platform Choon (www.choon.co), which was started in mid-2017 by the DJ and music producer Gareth Emery, who describes his approach as based on the idea that blockchain could primarily enable artists to run their own career without being exploited by intermediaries, agents and brokers. Also in this category is Bittunes, born in 2013, which stated explicitly that it 'intended to be an *Independent Digital Music Market*, which means that we place special focus on the rights of truly independent bands and songwriters', thus operating 'outside the music industry'.

On the opposite side of the spectrum are other platforms aimed primarily at major industry actors and representing a solution to reorganize the music business from within. The best example is probably the project One-Click License (https://what.ocl.is), which presents itself as a system 'designed to help facilitate almost any type of agreement between disparate parties' by means of centralized management, which is believed to mitigate the flaws of the decentralized philosophy typical of blockchain infrastructures. Whilst many of the platforms focus exclusively on music, others like Patreon (www.patreon. com) and dotBlockchain Media (http://dotblockchainmusic.com) aspire to manage any type of digital content (including movies, books and video games). On the top of this, mainstream platforms such as Spotify and YouTube – the major critical targets of independent artists like Imogen Heap or the community-based platform Bittunes – are moving towards adopting some sort of proprietary blockchain alternative. In April 2017, it was widely reported that Spotify acquired the blockchain start-up Mediachain to implement a new method of royalties distribution across its own platform (Perez 2017). If companies such as Spotify and YouTube choose to shift their distribution platforms to private and proprietary blockchains, the promises of a more democratic and fairer music world triggered by blockchain technology would probably be largely betrayed. Instead, a conservative realignment of powers would perhaps be a much more plausible outcome of the adoption of blockchain in music, following a scenario typical of capitalism in which small players are absorbed by larger and more powerful ones.

As we can see, the actual outcome of blockchain technology in music will also depend on how technical choices are made by different actors in the sector. In this initial stage, there are already many concurrent services, each with distinctive features appealing to different sectors of the music world. Many of the platforms such as Voice, Choon and Ujo Music adopted the

Ethereum infrastructure and the Ether coin as means of exchange; other platforms are instead building their own blockchain infrastructures supported by dedicated digital cryptocurrencies for payments and remuneration. This has been the choice of the Los Angeles-based Vezt platform (www.vezt.co), which is planning to launch its own coin in late 2018, and Muse (https://museblockchain.com), which is developing an autonomous blockchain based on the MUSE Dollar as a primary means for transactions, occurring over a dedicated network called Peertracks. Finally, Bittunes is approaching this by establishing a dedicated peer-to-peer network rather than a centralized platform, adopting the already established Bitcoin digital currency. Bitcoin will be used also by another project, Token.fm (https://token.fm), a platform whose unique selling point is the possibility for fans to 'collect limited editions' and to 'unlock exclusive perks tied to albums', and also receive 'live-stream access, collaborations, pre-sales'. Add to this list other emerging blockchain-related projects that are not focused on the distribution of recorded music, but on other music-related activities such as live music collaborations (Viberate) or merchandising (Project Coral Reef). It is also worth mentioning that artists such as Bjork, 50 Cent and Kraftwerk have started their own particular experiments with blockchain and cryptocurrencies.

The fast multiplication of different and alternative projects, based on diverse blockchains, infrastructures, distribution models, digital coins and services offered, poses the issue of the interoperability of data across these infrastructures. As recognized in information infrastructures studies, data are not self-transparent and taken-for-granted entities (Mongili and Pellegrino 2014), and media historian Lisa Gitleman (2013) points out that expressions like 'raw data' represent a sort of oxymoron, because any kind of data contain some sort of implicit assumption and explicit technical requirements that makes them anything but 'raw'. The issue of the interoperability of data is not just questioning the possibility of having a unique database of music ownership based on blockchain technology, but having frictionless payments and automatic royalty distribution to artists, as any kind of doubt about data could delay or muddle attributions. This problem is already being recognized by another blockchain start-up, Blokùr (www.blokur.com), which explicitly aims to 'reconcile different sources of rights data to a single blockchain state' and solve data conflicts automatically. Hence, paradoxically the early outcome of blockchain is that, rather than reducing intermediaries in the music value chain, it seems to be producing new types of halfway-steps to solve new complications, for example avoiding the problem of 'data friction' (Pelizza 2016) that represents a clear limit for the possibility to distribute automatically revenues on the basis of blockchain smart contracts. If the promise is for a transparent and automatic database with less middlemen, these early outcomes seem to be going in a quite different direction, revealing the emergence of new and highly specialized infomediaries devoted to managing those inconsistencies that are problematic for the correct working of the blockchain infrastructure.

Of course, there are other cracks and faults to be explored in blockchain promises and expectations, for example those platforms based on the idea that fans who buy songs acquire some kind of right over the music, becoming holders of a share in the royalties, in the hope of receiving rewards in a digital currency when these songs are purchased by other people. This model characterizes the aforementioned project Vezt, which has imagined a distribution system based on a so-called *initial song offering* (ISO), mimicking the expression used for the launch of digital currencies (initial coin offering, ICO). With this system, at the moment of the initial release of a song, artists and rights holders can sell a portion of the rights, which are purchased through digital coins issued by Vezt. The song's rights information is encoded on Vezt's blockchain, which will then distribute royalties trough smart contracts when this song is sold to other customers. There is no doubt that, with the ISO model, digital music is taking a further step in the process of subjection to the logic of monetization, a step that primarily turns music into another form of investment – a parallel product of financial capitalism, made possible by automated music micro-markets and having as a direct consequence the reconfiguration of listeners into investors or even financial gamblers.

Conclusion

This early exploration of blockchain's applications in music is unable to forecast the future, but we can say a few things about how current strategies and discourses supporting the development of blockchain infrastructures are performing a selective and partial projection of what the future of digital music could look like. It remains to be seen whether – as imagined by many blockchain-based start-ups – digital music will turn into a new type of transparent and profitable content, circulating automatically by means of a fair, distributed and automated infrastructure. There is a chance that, despite all these efforts, music will escape once more the digital cage imagined for it, as occurred in the past with DRM technology, and listeners will recreate subcultural music values outside the detailed plans coming from industry, investors and other economic actors (as occurred for example with the cassette culture in the 1970s and 1980s and with the recent vinyl revival). We can quite reasonably believe that much energy will be spent by entrepreneurs, firms and musicians in supporting some sort of alternative forms of digital music circulation based on a blockchain distributing infrastructure.

What the past trajectories of technological innovation show us is that the actual consequences of blockchain on the music sector will not depend on the much celebrated positive intrinsic features of this technology, such as decentralization, the bypassing of intermediaries or the transparency of data, but on how digital capitalism processes select, adapt and shape the multiple possibilities offered by this new technology, and by how far listeners and consumers embrace this new step of commodification and monetization of musical contents and data. What emerges from this early phase of music blockchain development is that many attempts will be made to incorporate even more music listeners into the economic process of the exploitation of digital music circulation and distribution and to integrate music content into the automated flow of big data characterizing our current network society. Whilst in the recent past streaming platforms turned music listeners, amongst many things, into actual producers of a new profitable item – their data – with blockchain infrastructures listeners will be increasingly encouraged to play a further functional role within a renewed digital value production chain. The envisioned new musical formats, which imply a share of royalties for fans who buy a song, also promise to transform music listeners into shareholders and investors, bringing us one step further down the path towards the monetization of musical practices and tastes. After all, this type of trajectory can be recognized in many other facets of the upcoming future digital music. Andrew Fry discusses this in Chapter 13 regarding the relationship between streaming platforms and music recommendations, which are already dominated by financial relationships and 'structured not for listener enjoyment, but financial gain for both services and their associates'.

Hence, it is difficult to not interpret the early phase of the music blockchain as the prosecution of what the editors of this book have recognized, in their introduction, as those same digital neoliberal pressures that have influenced how digital music has been produced, circulated and consumed in the past two decades. From many points of view, the critique of contemporary unfairness in the digital music industry, which supports the promise that blockchain will solve musicians' dependence on and exploitation by digital music platforms as Spotify, fits relatively well into the dynamics put forward by French sociologists Boltanski and Chiapello (1999). They described how the 'new spirit of capitalism' works: whilst, this new decentralized and crowd-based technology is supported by a discourse centred on counterbalancing digital capitalism's distortions, actual blockchain applications are likely to lead to a new step along the path of the subjugation of music to economic and financial logics, a step consisting of the incorporation of ownership and 'relations of production' in an automated way into the infrastructure of music circulation, and into the informatics protocols that make file formats work.

Whilst the emerging crowd-based, collaborative, distributed infrastructures based on blockchain technology offer the dream of an alternative to the exploitation of music creativity displaced by dominant digital companies, these infrastructures can however easily become nightmares, in which music becomes an increasingly integrated and automated form of financial transaction and investments.

Note

1   In February 2018, the 17 existing projects recorded and analysed for this study were: Audiocoin, Bittunes, Blokur, Choon, DotBC, Jaak, Mediachain (Spotify), Musicoin, Mycelia, One Click Licence, PeerTracks, Revelator, Token.fm, UJO Music, VEZT, Voise and Zimrii.

References

Balbi, G. and P. Magaudda (2018), *A History of Digital Media: An Intermedia and Global Perspective*. London: Routledge.

Bartlett, J. (2015), 'Imogen Heap: Saviour of the music industry?' *Guardian*, 6 September. Available online: https://www.theguardian.com/music/2015/sep/06/imogen-heap-saviour-of-music-industry (accessed 15 February 2018).

Beer, D. (2013), *Popular Culture and New Media: The Politics of Circulation*. Dordrecht: Springer.

Boltanski, L. and E. Chiapello (1999), *Le nouvel esprit du capitalisme*. Paris: Gallimard. (Eng. trans. *The New Spirit of Capitalism*. London: Verso, 2005.)

Bowker, G. and S.L. Star (2000), *Sorting Things Out: Classification and its Consequences*. Cambridge, MA: MIT Press.

Chester, J. (2016), 'How Blockchain Startups are Disrupting the $15 Billion Music Industry', *Forbes*, 16 September. Available online: https://www.forbes.com/sites/jonathanchester/2016/09/16/how-blockchain-startups-are-disrupting-the-15-billion-music-industry/#5728ac0c407c (accessed 15 February 2018).

Dickson, B. (2016), 'How Blockchain Can Change the Music Industry', *Techcrunch*, 8 October. Available online: https://techcrunch.com/2016/10/08/how-blockchain-can-change-the-music-industry/ (accessed 15 February 2018).

Gibson, J. (1966), *The Senses Considered as Perceptual Systems*. London: Allen and Unwin.

Gillespie, T. (2007), *Wired Shut: DRM and the Shape of Digital Culture*. Cambridge, MA: MIT Press.

Gitelman, L. (ed.) (2013), *Raw Data is an Oxymoron*. Cambridge, MA: MIT Press.

Greenfield, A. (2017). *Radical Technologies: The Design of Everyday Life*. London: Verso Books.

Hesmondhalgh, D. (1999), 'Indie: The institutional politics and aesthetics of a popular music genre', *Cultural Studies*, 13(1): 34–61.

Hesmondhalgh, D. and L. Meier (2015), 'Popular Music, Independence and the Concept of the Alternative in Contemporary Capitalism', in J. Bennett (ed.), *Media Independence: Working with Freedom or Working for Free?*, 94–116. London: Routledge.

Jasanoff, S. and K. Sang-Hyun (eds) (2015), *Dreamscapes of Modernity: Sociotechnical Imaginaries and the Fabrication of Power*. Chicago, IL: University of Chicago Press.

Konrad, K., H. Van Lente, C. Groves and C. Selin (2016), 'Performing and Governing the Future', in L. Smith-Doerr, R. Fouché, U. Felt and C.A. Millerin (eds), *The Handbook of Science and Technology Studies*, 465–93. Cambridge, MA: MIT Press.

Kuznetsov, N. (2017), 'Revolutionizing Digital Music through Blockchain', *Huffington Post*, 14 August. Available online: https://www.huffingtonpost.com/entry/revolutionizing-digital-music-through-blockchain_us_59916850e4b063e2ae058127 (accessed 15 February 2018).

Latour, B. (2005), *Reassembling the Social: An Introduction to Actor–Network Theory*. Oxford: Oxford University Press.

MacKenzie, D. and J. Wajcman (eds), (1985), *The Social Shaping of Technology*. Milton Keynes: Open University Press.

Magaudda, P. (2009), 'Processes of Institutionalisation and 'Symbolic Struggles' in the "Independent Music" Field in Italy', *Modern Italy*, 14(3): 295–310.

Marshall, L. (2015), 'Let's Keep Music Special. F–Spotify: On-demand streaming and the controversy over artist royalties', *Creative Industries Journal*, 8(2): 177–89.

Milosic, K. (2015), 'The Failure of the Global Repertoire Database', *Hypebot*, 31 August. Available online: http://www.hypebot.com/hypebot/2015/08/the-failure-of-the-global-repertoire-database-effort-draft.html (accessed 15 February 2018).

Mongili, A. and G. Pellegrino (eds) (2014), *Information Infrastructure(s): Boundaries, Ecologies, Multiplicity*. Newcastle upon Tyne: Cambridge Scholars Publishing.

Morris, J. (2015), *Selling Digital Music, Formatting Culture*. San Francisco: University of California Press.

O'Dair, M. (ed.) (2016), *Music on the Blockchain*, Report no. 1, July. London: Middlesex University.

Parks, L. and N. Starosielski (eds) (2015), *Signal Traffic: Critical Studies of Media Infrastructures*. Champaign: University of Illinois Press.

Pelizza, A. (2016), 'Disciplining Change, Displacing Frictions. Two structural dimensions of digital circulation across land registry database integration', *Tecnoscienza: Italian Journal of Science and Technology Studies*, 7(2): 35–60.

Perez, S. (2017), 'Spotify Acquires Blockchain Startup Mediachain to Solve Music's Attribution Problem', TechCrunch, 26 April. Available online: https://techcrunch.com/2017/04/26/spotify-acquires-blockchain-startup-mediachain-to-solve-musics-attribution-problem/.

Peters, J.D. (2015), *The Marvelous Clouds: Toward a Philosophy of Elemental Media*. Chicago, IL: University of Chicago Press.

Rethink Music (2015), *Fair Music: Transparency and Payment Flows in the Music Industry*. Boston, MA: Berklee Initiative Institute of Creative Entrepreneurship.

Selin, C. (2007), 'Expectations and the Emergence of Nanotechnology', *Science, Technology and Human Values*, 32(2): 196–220.

Star, S.L and K. Ruhleder (1996), 'Steps Toward an Ecology of Infrastructure: Design and access for large information spaces', *Information Systems Research*, 7(1): 111–34.

Sterne, J. (2012), *MP3: The Meaning of a Format*. Durham, NC: Duke University Press.

Swan, M. (2015), *Blockchain: Blueprint for a New Economy*. Sebastopol: O'Reilly Media, Inc.

Tapscott, D. and A. Tapscott (2016), *Blockchain Revolution: How the Technology Behind Bitcoin is Changing Money, Business, and the World*. London: Penguin.

Van Lente, H. (1993), 'Promising Technology: The Dynamics of Expectations in Technological Developments', PhD diss. Twente University, Enschede, Netherlands.

Vonderau, P. (2017), 'The Spotify Effect: Digital distribution and financial growth', *Television and New Media*, 21 November. Available online: http://journals.sagepub.com/doi/full/10.1177/1527476417741200.

Williams, R. (1974), *Television: Technology and Cultural Form*. London: Fontana.

Wyatt, S. (2008), 'Technological Determinism is Dead; Long live technological determinism', in L. Smith-Doerr, R. Fouché, U. Felt and C.A. Millerin (eds), *The Handbook of Science and Technology Studies*, 165–80. Cambridge, MA: MIT Press.

3

'The Sound of the Future Is Here Today': The Market for Post-rock within the Traditional Small Music Festival Landscape

Kenny Forbes

The post-rock genre is noted for the way in which it circumvents conventional verse-chorus song structures, embraces complexity and pursues forms of music experimentation and otherness almost as a prerequisite, thus creating what can be perceived as unique, futuristic multi-layered soundscapes. Like a 'flashlight pointing into the great unknown' (Chuter 2015: 3), post-rock also eschews the retro inclinations of 'contemporary' music genres (Reynolds 2011) and evades the corporate manifestations of 'alternative' rock (Moore 2005). Furthermore, in its wholehearted espousal of pushing the sonic envelope, it applies a self-imposed neo-tribal distance towards mainstream platforms that engender measures of popular music success (Osborn 2011: 10).

In this respect, terrestrial television viewers are unlikely to encounter post-rock artists such as That Fucking Tank, Alright the Captain and Bearded Youth Quest appearing anytime soon on mainstream BBC music television shows like Jools Holland's *Later*: not so much 'later', more so 'never'.

Yet, the genre achieves increasing measures of new metric popularity in the 2010s, which is a process that has slowly evolved since post-rock was first actualized in 1994 (Reynolds 2007). In short, whilst such otherness eludes notions of the present, post-rock sustains its current high profile within dedicated circles by projecting the sound of the future. Of course, this progression is readily accommodated within the post-Napster Long Tail niche music marketplace, where post-rock's dedicated and growing fan base can digitally cohabitate, thereby expediting interest in its physical manifestation – the live performance.

In this chapter, I argue that the post-rock genre achieves such a distinction by circumventing the vanilla views and cloying corporatization that encapsulate increasingly conventional notions of 'alternative', operating instead within a kind of quasi 'alternative alternative' ecosystem, by embracing notions of non-mainstream inclusiveness and high levels of performance virtuosity.

Methodology

To support these points, ethnographic research was conducted at ArcTanGent (ATG), a niche post-rock festival, with the aim of exploring the contours of the genre and thereafter measuring how it is articulated within a live context. Indeed, considering the vast increase in the UK music festival circuit since the early part of this century, ATG can also be regarded as inhabiting a key space within what amounts to the Long Tail of festivals, thus representing a double enactment of its non-mainstream status. ATG began in 2013 and has, as a result of its nicheness, steadily attracted an increasing number of fans from across the globe, subsequently physicalizing elements of the previously virtual post-rock audience.

By primarily focusing on '*the* music', ArcTanGent serves to enunciate and personify a 'secret club' that assumes cultural space within the larger, more generic, UK festival circuit. With the festival mantra of 'keeping it small' being fully grasped by many of its stakeholders, it is suggested that, framed by a sense of knowingness about the genre's restrictive but empowering values, ATG maintains its mono-genre marketability by virtue of post-rock's alternative-futuristic gaze, shunning notions of the past within this process. Indeed, the prominence of ATG has steadily increased since its inception, leading to the first sold-out festival in 2017, with this trend reflecting the rising 'popularity of the unpopular'. As a result of such developments, one of the key questions that emerge is whether ATG can maintain its perceived level of non-mainstream alternativeness when it now attracts a wider audience.

In order to adequately explore the post-rock perspective as encapsulated by ATG, I attended the festival in 2015 and 2016, immersing myself in this environment by joining the operations team, back stage crew, artists and media at the events. I was thus in a position, by way of participant observation captured through field notes, to view what essentially are 'hidden' operations, set-ups and practices, all from a backstage perspective. Additionally, I conducted several short semi-structured interviews with many of the stakeholders within this environment, including live sound technicians, merchandise sales coordinators, and security staff.

The organizers also provided access to vital information relating to the festival's operational plan, logistics, technical specifications, and audience demographics. Moreover, I viewed several of the performances 'stage front' from the perspective of the audience. Again, participant observation and short interviews were conducted during this process. Such an approach therefore embraced both an 'insider and outsider' outlook (Stadler et al. 2013: 91) and also applied due focus on the social context in which live music was produced and consumed at the festival, aligning with Cohen's (1993: 123) suggestion that ethnographic research on popular music should concentrate 'upon social relationships, emphasising music as social practice and process'.

The remainder of this chapter comprises four main sections. First the post-rock genre is explored in relation to its sonic template and perceived otherness, which precedes a discussion on the notion of the 'alternative alternative' milieu that the genre inhabits. Thereafter, a closer look at the ArcTanGent festival itself further helps to frame the field work analysis that follows in the final section.

Post-rock

ATG's cultural identity is shaped by the specifics of the festival's mono-genreness. As it stands, post-rock's reliance on the manipulation of a myriad of time-displaced technologies is also positioned as a key driver within the genre, which is a process that helps to underpin its compelling otherworldliness within a live setting.

As genre represents an essential tool in which to comprehend a musical culture, post-rock therefore deserves our further consideration. Holt (2007: 2) suggests that, at a basic level, the term 'genre' represents a 'particular type of music with a distinctive cultural web of production, circulation, and signification'. In addition to being situated 'in the music', the genre in question can be seen to circulate within the consciousness of its stakeholders, who share 'certain conventions' in relation to how this music is performed and experienced (ibid.). Such labels and conventions follow Frith's (2002: 88) notion of 'genre worlds', which necessitates a degree of commitment by its investors (artists, audiences, media), who habitually construct an environment where forms of imposed exclusivity help determine the boundaries of the genre.

Likewise, Fabbri (1982) offers five genre stipulations that encompass factors such as formal and technical rules (sound, instrumentation, production), semiotic rules (communication-conveyance of codes), behavioural (performance rituals), social-ideological (social functions), and economic-juridical rules (economic-commercial trajectory). Thus, the comprehensive scope of some advanced music genres can be analysed in sufficient detail.

However, music genre categorization remains problematic, and post-rock is no exception. An anti-genre almost by default, its inherent freedom has led to a plethora of musical styles under the banner of post-rock, inclining Hodgkinson (2004: 223) to posit that it is a 'catch all term' that makes it 'extremely hard to define ... because it attempts to escape mere classification by genre and because it does not represent any subculture'. Certainly, Chuter (2015: 3) is of the opinion that very few bands willingly identity with the term as 'post-rock still struggles to communicate and identify itself with conviction and clarity'.

So, how best to position post-rock? Simon Reynolds ([1994] 2007) first coined the term in 1994 when applying distance between the futuristic soundscapes of a new breed of artists and the distinct limitations within contemporary 'alternative' music, which were said to appear 'like a clapped-out stretch limo in reverse, (whereby) today's "alternative rock" is synonymous with a retreat to one of a number of period genres from rock history' (ibid.: 186). In short, by avoiding such contemporary retro-ness, post-rock's aesthetics can be seen to willingly forgo standardized and celebrated (but ultimately backward looking) trajectories embodied by 'rock' or 'alternative rock' (Reynolds 1994: 42).

Whilst Heller's (2013) claim that post-rock 'has never had mass appeal in mind' may sound rather optimistic, given its enduring self-imposed detachment from notions of the mainstream or perceptions of the alternative, the basis of such a declaration possesses traction within post-rock circles. As a result, the genre's inclination towards an 'alternative alternative' milieu has served to maintain its idealistic norms, with this process being explored further in the next section.

Of course, for all its allusions towards the future, the genesis of post-rock possesses several contrasting 'old world' influences that serve to mirror Fabbri's suggestion that a 'new genre is not born in an empty space but in a musical system already structured' (1982: 62). For Reynolds ([1994] 2007: 188), influential artists of the past include Joy Division, The Jesus and Mary Chain, My Bloody Valentine, Can and Neu!, amongst others. Indeed, whilst the positioning of some selective 'old world' values on the 'modern world' post-rock milieu could be viewed as compromising its futuristic ethos, there is, as Maloney (2017: 32) relates, a 'lucidity in this duplicity', where, by accommodating both worlds, this selective juxtaposition acts to facilitate the necessary detachment from the much larger domain that nostalgia ultimately represents.

Tellingly, writing in 1977, the French philosopher Attali predicted that our confusion about what constituted contemporary retro-nowness would involve embracing new metrics that would lead to a

> new music (which) is on the rise, one that can neither be expressed nor understood using the old tools, a music produced elsewhere and otherwise. It is not that music or the world have become incomprehensible: the concept of comprehension itself has changed; there has been a shift in the locus of the perception of things.
>
> Attali 2003: 133

However, this 'new way of making music' and 'escape from ritual' (ibid.: 134) would involve using some of the 'old tools' dismissed by Attali, such as electric guitars, as a basis for understanding this new soundscape. It also embraced other 'old world' components, such as the inventive Spector-Eno-type soundscapes as a facilitator for the myriad of sonic layers and riffs that the digital recording environment enables by way of samplers and the deconstruction of digital data. As such, it further served to fill space and time with notions of altered acoustic patterns, relying on the re-contextualization of 'rock instrumentation for non-rock purposes, using guitars as facilitators of timbres and textures rather than riffs and power chords' (Reynolds 2007: 186).

As it stands, the distinct 'after-ness' of post-rock supports layers of rich complexities that underline Frith's (1988: 1) pronouncement that rock's reliance on its 'essentially tedious' standard '4.4 beat', could be advanced, as Reynolds, relates, by the way in which post-rock's temporal twists are filtered through the sampler, thereby 'transubstantiating sound into digital data . . . (towards) different eras, different auras, (that) can be combined to form a time-travelling pseudo event . . . (which could be called) "magik" . . . (or) "deconstruction of the metaphysics of presence" ([1994] 2007: 188).

Indeed, within such domains, data delays and displacements further subvert notions of the contemporary and everyday. In this respect, post-rock's capacity to embrace future-ness knows no bounds. The general absence of lyrics within the majority of post-rock texts further serves to evade the conventions and tropes of rock and 'authenticity', towards inclinations of 'absolute' music. In also avoiding forms of lyrical realism that offer a 'direct relationship between a lyric and the social or emotional condition it describes and represents' (Frith 1989: 82), the genre can also place further distance between itself and the mainstream. Instead, according to Jack (2016), instrumental artists like Mogwai can convey emotion perfectly well without the need for lyrics, whereby 'they could say more with a dark, spare, mysterious guitar instrumental than any number of Oasis copyists could in a thousand insipid strums'.

Some similarities between progressive rock and post-rock are also discernible. Outwith their shared circumvention of the mainstream music template, and the emphasis on virtuosity and showmanship in particular (Cateforis 2002), both genres can also be seen to share a predominantly white male artist-audience profile (Sheinbaum 2002: 26). Although a few exceptions exist (Stereolab, You Break, You Buy, Amiina), post-rock artists mainly retain a white male presence, thus reflecting Bradby's claim that rock, despite its post-ness in this case, inclines to exclude women. Whilst technology has served to blur barriers between production and consumption, and between musician and non-musician, it appears that, despite its reliance on technology, it has not widened gender representation, mirroring Bradby's claim that 'traditional representations of women (are) recycled in both live and sampled performance' (Bradby 1993: 156–57).

Alternative alternative

The discussion thus far has attempted to define post-rock, and, whilst no decisive description has emerged, mainly due to the genre's reluctance to avoid specificity, its circumvention of the mainstream has been readily emphasized. Although this could be considered to represent an 'alternative' to the mainstream, such allusions merit further scrutiny and also require to recognize different levels of cultural production.

Not least, the term 'alternative' has become a misnomer, especially given the manner in which any residue of the marginal and the unconventional in popular music (alternative rock, or otherwise) has long since been appropriated by conglomerates and other commercial bodies. Such visible trends have led many of post-rock's stakeholders to eschew any notions of this homogeneous alternative. Instead, their detachment from the mainstream inclines them towards inhabiting a quasi 'alternative alternative' milieu that possesses many of the characteristics and components originally envisaged and embraced within the realm of the independent cultural production of music.

Positive notions of 'independence' as a valid 'other' to the industrial practices of major music companies have permeated popular music history, since rock 'n' roll emerged as potent music genre in the mid-1950s (Peterson and Berger 1975). Indeed, the cultural significance bestowed upon such enterprises by cultural intermediaries has served to extend their aesthetic and social value, also elevating notions of freedom and autonomy that frame the alternative ethos in an affirmative manner (Hesmondhalgh and Meier 2015: 94–95), further acceding to the countercultural flow that has shaped popular music since the mid-1960s.

Of course, once discernible, such feelings can be conveniently co-opted and commercialized by conglomerates, with this configuration between the commercial and the cool remaining a feature of popular music since at least 1944, when teenagers were first defined as a marketing term and their affinity with contemporary music was deemed to represent a sought-after commodity (Savage 2007: xiii).

More contemporary manifestations of 'alternative' or 'independent' music possess a direct impact on post-rock. Whilst notions of the alternative were central to the supposed ethos of both 'independent' and 'indie' music during the 1980s and 1990s, Hemondhalgh and Meier (2015: 96–98) recount how such traits were politically, aesthetically and commercially compromised following the innovative small independent label phase of the immediate post-punk era, further serving to disengage it from the realm of independent production values, the absorption of 'alternative' music within the mainstream music markets being a key component within this conversion to the commercial.

Whilst the digital environment may have facilitated notions of independence and sustainability through low-cost production and direct access to prospective music consumers, as Meier (2017: 55–57) relates, subsequent notions of the digital utopia initiated by Anderson's Long Tail (2006) thesis remain both inaccurate and generalized by virtue of the aggregation of individual creators within the 'tail', and by also failing to take into account the cost of production. In short, the numbers, and the anticipated revenues in particular, do not add up.

For Klein (2010: 114), the commercial wilderness within which many contemporary 'alternative' artists find themselves inclines them towards the lure of the 'alternative' advertising milieu (now embracing a much wider range of platforms within the digital environment), albeit their marginal fan bases may be less than enthusiastic about such practice. However, many bands of this ilk have to make compromises of this nature, balancing the requirement to reach a larger audience, whilst alienating their current smaller audience (ibid.: 131–32).

We therefore find alternative artists being aligned with both alternative and mainstream brands (such blurring between the two is underpinned by artist-brand congruence for the most part), such as Robyn (Volvo), Feist (Apple and Samsung), Cat Power (ATandT, Apple, Garnier, Gap, Lincoln cars, and, somewhat controversially, De Beers diamonds), The Pixies (Samsung, Apple, Galaxy chocolate), Buzzcocks (McDonalds), Iggy Pop (Swift car insurance, Royal Caribbean cruises), Bon Iver (Bushmills whiskey), Skepta (Rolls Royce) and, perhaps most challengingly, John Lydon (Country Life butter). Indeed, the massive global-digital reach of such high-profile consumer brands and internet companies like Apple and Google, and their connective configuration with the three major music companies, makes it extremely difficult for independent labels and artists to avoid the ad-related commercialization of their music (Hesmondhalgh and Meier 2015: 9).

Any allusions about the 'alternative' may therefore rest with the numerous micro-independent record labels that do exist, covering a wide range of music genres and styles (ibid.: 1), which offer hope that independent and alternative forms of artistry can continue to provide some form of balance against the negative market manifestations of neoliberalism and make a cultural and egalitarian impact, embodying the original spirit of alternative forms of cultural production (ibid.: 12) within the realm of the internet's original countercultural ethos (Turner 2008).

As such, varying forms of success do transpire within such environments. Notable post-rock independent record labels that underpin the global dissemination of the genre include Bird's Robe (Sydney, Australia: 65daysofstatic, Sleepmakeswaves), Constellation Records (Montreal, Canada: Godspeed You! Black Emperor, Do Make Say Think), Deep Elm (Hawaii, USA: Goonies Never Say Die, Moonlit Sailor), Rock Action (Glasgow, UK: Errors, Mogwai), Sound In Silence (Athens, Greece: Port-Royal, Good Weather For An Airstrike) and Temporary Residence Ltd. (New York, USA: Explosions In The Sky, Mono).

Indeed, as the US label that issues Mogwai's Rock Action releases, Temporary Residence Ltd (TRL), has established a discernible profile within the post-rock community as an outlet for credible releases that exemplify the genre's underlying ethos. TRL's roster embraces a high-profile post-rock artist, Explosions In The Sky, along with other lesser-known acts, such as Mono, a Japanese instrumental act. As Givony (2007) relates, the credible aura of such artists not only acts as an aesthetic inducement for genre stakeholders, the label can also, through economies of scale (selling anything from 1,000 to 2,500 copies of some releases) avoid forms of large-scale promotion in favour of maintaining a curative-tastemaker presence, adding further value to their presence with the alternative cultural economy that exemplifies post-rock's artistic-creative aesthetic:

> They (TRL) point to a statistically tiny and culturally obscure alternative economy – one that is governed less by the rules of the market and more by symbolism, idealism, and romance that embraces niche genres such as post-rock to which TRL is mainly associated, being regarded as a label that possesses a 'surplus or artistic and professional integrity' striving to apply equal effort in marketing each of their artists.
>
> Givony 2007

Of course, as Sarah Thornton (1995: 116) reminds us, the dissemination of music genres also relies on media platforms that embrace the notion that 'Every music scene has its own distinct set of media relations', whereby 'niche media like the music press construct subcultures as much as document them' (ibid.: 117). Whereas fanzines once served this purpose during post-rock's initial phase, the digital environment offers greater scope whereby such platforms can assume a key presence within the internet's convergence culture, where grassroots intermediaries share space with traditional media, but possess greater autonomy (Jenkins 2008: 222).

With post-rock representing a scene without a location, being disseminated and shaped by discourse over a wide global area (Hodgkinson 2004: 224), new media facilitates a process where consumers can reshape and share media content across a range of electronic platforms. This transmediality process helps shape active and participatory forms of fandom and DIY culture (Jenkins 2008: 126), as well as galvanizing alternative modes of production, which has also led to the 'explicit and implicit critiques of commercial practices' (Jenkins et al. 2013: 53).

Initially disseminated through diary-like entries on MP3 blog sites from the early 2000s (O'Donnell and McClung 2008), the increasingly obsolete MP3 format and advancement towards more professional platforms such as online magazines, where independent sites like *Pitchfork* can advance from a 'glorified blog to institution' through articulation of its zeal for ground-breaking music (Carter and Rogers 2014), also setting the tenor for popular music discourse, by focusing on artists shunned by traditional media (Jokelainen 2014: 30–31).

Occupying a similar position within the post-rock environment is the online magazine *Fecking Bahamas*, which primarily focuses on the post-rock subgenre math rock. It provides regular features and album reviews, and also regularly issues a series of compilations featuring new artists. 'Based' in Melbourne, but with the magazine's main contributors are located globally, its cultural kudos within the genre community is such that a favourable review and a track on one of the magazine's regular compilations can lead to a slot for artists like You Break, You Buy on genre-related festivals like ArcTanGent (ArcTanGent 2017).

Global genre platforms like *Fecking Bahamas* (which features an interactive world map showing the location of some 1,300 math-rock and post-rock artists) further underline that the post-rock scene is both translocal and virtual, whereby isolated pockets of fans in urban areas share affinities across international borders (almost like a long-distance club), but with this environment being subsequently enhanced by the growth of the internet (Peterson and Berger 2004: 8–11). Whilst such virtual genre communities can thrive online through discourse and interaction (Strachan 2017: 144–45), it is, as Peterson and Berger (2004: 11) relate, quite rare for such communities to meet in person. However, as the following section will outline, the ArcTanGent Festival provides such an opportunity for this genre community to gather.

Consequently, such enterprises absorb key elements of the alternative cultural production domain, recouping its original ethos within the realm of an 'alternative alternative' cultural ecosystem.

ArcTanGent

First launched in 2013, the ArcTanGent (ATG) festival, which is named after an earthtone9 album, takes place on the site of Fernhill Farm, an eco-farm near Bristol, catering specifically for a math rock and post-rock audience, with a set capacity of 5,000. With approximately seventy bands being featured across four stages over three days, it has featured high-profile artists such as God Is An Astronaut, Explosions In The Sky and 65daysofstatic.

ATG initially attracted 3,500 festival-goers from across the UK, Europe, North America and Australia. Such trends have continued, with the festival selling out its 5,000 maximum ticket allocation in 2017, and the global dimensions of the ATG audience steadily increasing each year, rising from 6 per cent of the audience total in 2013 to 16 per cent in 2017, including fans from Siberia, Bolivia, South Korea, Fiji and Kenya (O'Callaghan 2018). ATG's post-rock credentials are underpinned by the organizers' collective zeal for the genre, as epitomized by the niche curation process adopted for artist selection. As such, ATG embraces niche-ness by intent, serving to underline its own distinct ethos, and offering a direct dichotomy to larger, more generic, festivals, with this being underpinned by the recognition that post-rock fans wanted something that encompassed different values to the traditional over-large, over-priced festival.

Nonetheless, ATG finds itself in a crowded and somewhat volatile marketplace, with just under 1,000 UK music festivals taking place in 2016 (Jinks 2016), which represents a 34 per cent increase since 2010 (Warman 2010). For some observers, the market has now reached a saturation point (Green 2015; Marks 2016). Amid what is perceived to be the continued success of large-scale festivals such as Glastonbury and Download, which attract 175,000 and 110,000 people, respectively, niche festivals like ATG offer forms of intimacy unattainable at other festivals. As a distinct alternative, ATG find presence within what could be regarded as the Long Tail of UK festivals, again acting as a double enactment of their alternative status, and further reaffirming the 'alternative alternative' realm.

ATG's smallness also presented a rare juncture for the genre community to meet in person, transcending their translocal and virtual origins. Such a community ethos remains an attraction to festival-goers, where it is likely that most of the audience will be familiar with at least one person performing over the weekend, or will have performed at ATG themselves over the previous few years (Schenker 2015).

For the ATG organizers (Goc O'Callaghan, James Scarlett and Simon Maltas), launching the festival represented a commercial gamble, as any new festival enterprise would be (Anderton 2008: 43). The three partners were also aware that its niche-ness was both its USP and its Achilles heel. Indeed, as Dowd (2014: 154) highlights, the smallness of niche festivals does not negate the associated costs, whereby the initial labour of love should not obscure the fact that sufficient tickets have to be sold to cover costs. Whilst all three knew that ATG amounted to a calculated risk, they anticipated that the festival would at least appeal to an audience who were weary of the generic festival, albeit they had no clue how many would turn up. In this respect, no assumptions were made about its global reach, and the 'terrifying' prospect of losing several hundred pounds remained if the festival failed to sell (Dedman 2015a).

Fieldwork

The remaining part of this chapter focuses on the analysis of the fieldwork conducted during the 2015 and 2016 festivals. As well as being named after an earthone9 album, ATG also refers to the mathematical function that applies to the *inverse* of the tangent function, and, in this instance, ATG's engagement with the opposite is worth exploring further.

In attempting to gauge the overall meaning of mono-genre events like ATG, I did not anticipate that its essence would be revealed in an inadvertent way during my first day of research at the 2015 festival, whereby a catering unit was, completely against the genre grain of the festival, loudly playing selections from a pop oldies radio station, much to the amusement of several festival-goers.

In striking such a juxtaposition, the incongruence of the moment was not lost on several of the audience-customers, some of whom jokingly sang along with songs like Wham!'s 'Wake Me Up Before You Go Go' and 'Mamma Mia' by ABBA. With ATG representing the antithesis of ABBA, such skewed bemusement at encountering a mainstream pop song served to expose that the festival participants were keenly aware of this disparity. Indeed, when questioned, one festival-goer remarked, 'Silly choruses are good for a laugh, aren't they?' Another highlighted that Coldplay (a further selection) were 'Obviously catchy, but so mainstream and more or less everything that ArcTanGent isn't'.

Responses of this nature reveal a knowingness about several of the underlying components that underpin and apply meaning to post-rock. Knowingness is defined by Bailey (1994) as representing an assured level of insider knowledge by an audience and artist about the event in hand, and is exposed in their dress, actions and discourse, being both complicit and discriminatory in its articulation. Through such practice both audience and artists can affiliate through coded communication, adding further value to the live music experience. As the analysis will go on to show, this knowingness was transparent in many aspects of ATG's infrastructure, where the festival's genre community ethos was central to its success.

As already indicated, the organizer's passion for post-rock was the initial galvanizer for the launch of ATG. The emphasis placed on 'the music' notwithstanding, be it post-rock or pop, music festivals require vast degrees of planning, know-how and organizational skills. As Clarke (1982: 2–3) reminds us, the logistics required to run even a small festival, be it access, utilities, security, welfare etc., can serve to overwhelm organizers.

Of obvious note, a festival's success or otherwise can depend on all such tasks not only being addressed, but also being coordinated in a timely manner, with the inherent risks involved within the small festival environment being minimized as a result. Ensuring that there are sufficient clean toilets on

Figures 3.1 and 3.2 Audience and artists at the 2015 ArcTanGent festival. Photos courtesy of Kenny Forbes.

site, being stocked with soap, toilet paper and paper towels, with a cleaning schedule also implemented, may seem far removed from the excesses of post-rock, but such factors can help 'make or break' festivals.

For Sundbo and Hagedorn-Rasmussen (2008: 96–99) the sanctity of the 'frontstage' experience (tangible, where the experience of art is produced) relies greatly on the 'backstaging' (intangible, management of experience as commerce), where the logistics, marketing, and other event functions are managed and implemented. For audience and artists to enjoy the positives of the frontstage experience, this process can only materialize through the organizational skillset employed backstage, with the provision that, the more enhanced the frontstage experience, the more the backstage role becomes intangible. Indeed, for the most part, from the perspective of the audience the organizational elements of ATG remain hidden; albeit each of the three organizers were visible throughout the festival, interacting with the audience and taking in a range of the live performances over the weekend.

Of course, like other festivals, much reliance is placed on the network of associates, temporary workers, volunteer helpers and other stakeholders to help deliver ATG. If festivals 'act like "glue", temporarily sticking together various stakeholders, economic transactions and networks' (Gibson and Connell 2012: 9), then, as was certainly the case with ATG, some acknowledgement must be made that many participants are initially drawn towards such festivals by its genre aesthetics (Bennett and Woodward 2014: 12–14).

In the case of ATG, stewards who volunteer through the festival website are required to work two separate four-hour shifts over the course of the weekend in return for festival tickets. Witnessing a volunteer induction briefing session was enlightening in that it served to underline the ATG ethos (which was discernible throughout the festival) of a friendly, outgoing nature.

Whilst it could be claimed that festival organizers profit from such commitment and what is effectively 'free' labour, it is recognized that the volunteer process is necessary for a festival's financial stability, and adds further to the collective-productive experience (Robinson 2015: 167–68). Furthermore, none of the volunteer stewards I spoke to had any reservations about the nature of their employment, and all were more than happy to be part of the ATG experience.

Similar sentiments were also expressed by several of the suppliers, agents and other backstage personnel throughout the course of the two festivals I attended, whereby the professionalism and approachability of the ATG organizers and the proficiency of the aforementioned backstaging were readily acclaimed, as was the focus on 'the music', as typified by this response from a representative from one of the stage utility partners:

> The people that run it see it as less of a money-making scheme and more a way of promoting and supporting the music. You can quite often find the organizers in the crowd, just watching the bands. It is this kind of attitude that makes ArcTanGent one of my favourite festivals.
>
> TPi 2015

Indeed, ATG's emphasis on 'the music' remains its USP and retains its key focus, acting as a magnet for many of its stakeholders. Whilst some commentators (McKay 2000: 150–51; Bowen and Daniels 2005) may suggest that the actual music at festivals 'does not matter', festivals like ArcTanGent would clearly suggest otherwise.

As an extension of this process, and in line with other independently inclined music festivals, ATG is careful not to engage with what Anderton (2008) refers to as 'commercializing the carnivalesque' through consumer–corporate branding, with the V Festival being a key example of such an approach.

Whilst sponsorship is regarded as a vital component for major festival, its potential to taint any forms of alternative status, no matter the size of the event, has clearly influenced ATG's approach. Instead, relationships with carefully selected congruent 'partners' (the term 'sponsors' is specifically avoided) are pursued, thus offering a deviation (albeit in a limited sense) with elements of Anderton's typology of festival sponsorship relationships, such as leveraging, which inclines towards passive and limited forms of sponsorship (2008: 199–212).

In this respect, ATG acts as an alternative-aesthetic magnet for up-and-coming post-rock artists, with groups such as The Fierce and the Dead (Kendall 2015) highlighting what makes ATG unique: 'Festivals like this are like going round someone's house and they play you their records. The people running this festival, they put such faith in it, people respond to it and we want to do the same thing.'

This opportunity to 'see' a record collection in one weekend (Stone 2009: 211) acts to further underscore the significance of ATG's considered selection process for festival acts, whereby curation confers collectivity amongst post-rock artists and audiences.

As a case in point, Hann (2015a) may refer to the indie-folk End of the Road Festival as being unique for the manner in which several artists proclaimed onstage how 'special' the festival was, also thanking the organizers for inviting them to perform, but, almost without exception, every act at ATG 2015 and 2016 declared similar sentiments in a most enthusiastic manner, but without the requisite mainstream media coverage. Indeed, Brighton band Black Peaks underlined this further when they highlighted on stage that, short of an invitation to perform at the previous year's event, they were ready to undertake a flash performance in the festival car park. Likewise, Glasgow band Vasa, who performed at ATG's smallest stage in 2015 amongst like-minded genre stakeholders, found their experience much more prestigious than the mid-sized stage they had played at the previous year's T In The Park, then one of the UK's largest mainstream festivals (Vasa 2015).

Further enhancing the ATG genre community process, it was not unusual to see performers in the audience immediately before or after their festival slot, with this audience-as-performers transformation adding further to ATG's collective mantra, and serving to underline MacKellar's (2014: 2) concept of audience fluidity, whereby performers can become spectators and vice versa.

This sense of oneness was additionally revealed in the good-natured behaviour of the ATG audience. Whilst instances of boisterousness were evident amongst elements of the crowd during some mosh-pit-accommodating performances, it was all in the spirit of the moment, non-threatening and self-contained, bringing to mind Johnson's (2013: 101) suggestion that the physicality of music is central to the music experience. I did not witness any form of violence or threatening behaviour.

People queued; people readily said 'excuse me' where relevant; and I rarely spotted any litter, with audience members walking up to 100 yards to locate a bin. Certainly, the stewards highlighted that it had been common practice since the festival started for mislaid mobile phones and wallets containing cash and credit cards to be frequently handed in to lost property as a matter of course. With regard to the audience, the vast majority were white males (with the gender mix in the region of 85 per cent males), and aged between mid-twenties to mid-thirties for the most part. Dark/black T-shirts and hooded tops proved to be the standard dress code.

In many ways, as in times of such 'cultural pluralization' in the postmodern environment, festivals like ATG provide a facility for the articulation of identity and community (Bennett et al. 2014: 1), as Jeff (26) from Preston related:

> It's hard to explain, but you feel as if you're amongst friends here, even though I don't know anyone outside the group I travelled with. In saying that, I've already bumped into a few people who I met here last year. Yes, there's something about

ArcTanGent that's different from other festivals I've attended, and I've been to quite a few.

For John (23) from Manchester, the reason for the discernible camaraderie amongst the audience was the music:

> It's simple isn't it? We're all here for the music. Not just any music, but for post-rock, or whatever you want to call it. You really can't see all these groups together elsewhere, they're only at ArcTanGent – everyone who's here knows this. That's why it's special.

If we consider ArcTanGent as facilitating a post-subculture environment of some description, then Maffesoli's (1996: 98) concept of neo-tribes assumes relevance, whereby a 'certain ambience' or 'state of mind', based upon 'sentiment, feeling and shared experiences' can serve to provide a common understanding amongst participants. Similar attitudes were expressed by Scott (24) from Glasgow, where he highlighted that ATG retained its uniqueness by

> celebrating this music, which is really *our* music. It's about ignoring all the traditional crap out here and focusing on meaningful music that has nothing to do with the charts. And it's all here in front of you, what more could you ask for?

Indeed, French festival-goer Paul (24) also highlighted that 'the music is everything at ArcTanGent', and German post-rock fan Leo remarked that, 'it's impossible to see all these bands together at another festival, we wouldn't want to be anywhere else'.

Equally, Nikk Hunter (2015), the editor of the aforementioned online magazine *Fecking Bahamas*, suggests that ATG's success is framed by technology, connectivity and social media genre communities, along with the festival's capacity to garner a virtual audience, which then provides a 'real' meeting place for such enthusiasts to gather:

> Things like ArcTanGent wouldn't be able to exist without the internet. It's a local scene created online and shifted into the real world: the niche music equivalent of a sci-fi convention. You create the community then arrange a meeting point.

For the organizers, ATG's community ethos is shaped by its inherent niche-ness, where the non-mainstream can thrive within what amounts to a surreptitious gathering at odds with the homogenous mainstream, whereby for organizer James Scarlett, ATG is

> like being in a secret club isn't it? Let's face it ... music is way-more fun and exciting when you're part of a secret club! The beauty of math rock and post

rock, is it will always be a secret club. There's no chance of post rock suddenly being in the top ten, it's not going to happen. We'll always be niche and that's what I absolutely love about ArcTanGent.

Dedman 2015a

Whilst views of this nature serve to expose several traditional tropes that have framed identities, as well as the aesthetic and cultural divisions within popular music (Riesman 1950; Bourdieu 1984), such traits further underline ATG's mantra.

However, the aforementioned gender mix of the ATG audience (85 per cent male and 15 per cent female) and artist line-up (an average of 93 per cent male, albeit the 2017 festival did feature the most females in the festival line-up to date) is not unique to ATG certainly, but it inclines more towards Download (96 per cent male artists) (Stevens and Sedghi 2015) than to the 56 per cent of male artists at the End of the Road festival (Hann 2015b). Whilst the ATG organizers remain aware of this issue, the general sentiment remains that the post-rock genre remains, for the most part, a male domain. Whilst there is insufficient space to consider such matters in detail, it is useful to note Gibson and Connell's (2012: 3) suggestion:

> Festivals can also include and exclude people by drawing boundaries around 'community', through subcultural affiliation, pre-requisite knowledge to appreciate narrow music styles, specialist knowledge required for entry ... or meaningful participation.

By its very nature, 'the music' remains paramount to ATG's genre niche-ness and cultural identity. Outwith post-rock's focus on instrumental music for the most part (one vocal-inclusive band were suitably castigated by one audience member, whose 'We don't do vocals at this festival' heckle received widespread approval amongst the crowd), the genre's capacity to delay data and alter time signatures (the machine elements) assumes significance within the realm of the hereness and nowness (the human elements) of the live performance.

Conclusion

As the ATG organizers consider its future development, Butler's tourist area cycle of evolution (cited in Stone 2009: 28) offers a useful model to trace the trajectory of the festival, through which conception (devising and gaining support from stakeholders), precedes 'launch' (building awareness and reaching critical mass with audience/media), 'growth' (building on critical mass, retaining old customers and gaining new ones), and 'consolidation' (maintaining original ethos, whilst offering differentials that do not impinge on fundamentals), in the hope that this will not lead to the last two stages of 'decline' (through failure to consolidate) and 'revival'.

With the 2017 festival selling out for the first time, ATG is clearly at the 'consolidation' stage, and questions and possible conflicts about its future development remain uppermost within the consciousness of the various stakeholders. Will it expand? Should it expand? Will it retain its 'secret club' uniqueness and community ethos when the capacity is 7,000 or 10,000?

As such, following the 2017 sell-out of its 5,000 capacity, ATG has now obtained a festival licence to increase this to 10,000 if required, keenly aware that 'success', be it grounded in 'alternative popularity' or otherwise, may compromise the ATG brand. Certainly, for the *Independent* journalist Remfry Dedman (2015b), such an approach serves to enrich the ATG live experience:

> I haven't come across another festival so focused on keeping the vibe and atmosphere so protected. It's simple statistics that the more people you bring into a festival, the more likely you are to sully that great community spirit that is, in my experience, so unique to ArcTanGent. I commend the organizers for taking this approach… I'm sure they could make a lot more money if they increased the capacity to 10–15,000. Personally, I wouldn't want to see it get too much bigger than it is currently.

In summarizing, ATG remains a unique entity within the Long Tail of the UK festival circuit, being shaped and elevated by its niche-ness, affiliation with a non-mainstream music genre and its capacity to facilitate notions of community. It also provides a real-time meeting place for a virtual community. However, it appears that most, if not all, of the festival stakeholders are acutely aware of the delicate balance that must be maintained in order to retain ATG's distinctive vision, whereby the rising popularity of the unpopular can be seen to impinge on its non-mainstream exclusiveness, and thus serve to contemporize (or perhaps 'de-futurize') post-rock.

As it remains, ATG epitomizes the hereness and nowness of the everyday as a live music experience, yet, on the other hand, its articulation via a futuristic sheen enables the virtual and transcendental to juxtapose within an empowering alchemy that functions to underline that, for now at least, the sound of the future is here today.

Acknowledgements

The author is indebted to the ATG organizers (Goc O'Callaghan, James Scarlett and Simon Maltas) for kindly providing facilities and access for this research, with Goc deserving special mention in this respect. Many thanks are also due to the many respondents who agreed to be interviewed during the 2015 and 2016 festivals.

References

Anderson, Chris (2006), *The Long Tail*. London: Random House.
Anderton, Chris (2008), 'Commercializing the Carnivalesque: The V Festival and Image/Risk Management', *Event Management*, 12: 39–51.
ArcTanGent (2017), 'You Break, You Buy'. Available online: http://www.arctangent.co.uk/artist/you-break-you-buy/ (accessed 11 November 2017).
Attali, Jacques (2003), *Noise. The Political Economy of Music*. Minneapolis and London: University of Minnesota Press.
Bailey, Peter (1994), 'Conspiracies of Meaning: Music-Hall and the knowingness of popular culture'. *Past and Present*, 144(1): 138–70.
Bennett, Andy, Jody Taylor and Ian Woodward (2014), 'Introduction', in Andy Bennett, Jody Taylor and Ian Woodward (eds), *The Festivalisation of Culture*, 1–8. Farnham: Ashgate.
Bennett, Andy and Ian Woodward (2014), 'Festival Spaces, Identity, Experience and Belonging', in Andy Bennett, Jody Taylor and Ian Woodward (eds), *The Festivalisation of Culture*, 11–25. Farnham: Ashgate.
Bourdieu, Pierre (1984), *Distinction: A Social Critique of the Judgement of Taste*. Cambridge, MA: Harvard University Press.
Bowen, Heather and Margaret Daniels (2005), 'Does the Music Matter? Motivations for attending a music festival'. *Event Management*, 9: 155–65.
Bradby, Barbara (1993), 'Sampling Sexuality: Gender, technology and the body in dance music', *Popular Music*, 12(2): 155–76.
Carter, David and Ian Rogers (2014), 'Fifteen Years of "Utopia": Napster and Pitchfork as technologies of democratization', *First Monday*, 19(10): 6 October. Available at: https://journals.uic.edu/ojs/index.php/fm/article/view/5543/4122 (accessed 16 November).

Cateforis, Theo (2002), 'How Alternative Turned Progressive. The strange case of math rock', in K. Holm-Hudson (ed), *Progressive Rock Reconsidered*, 243–60. New York and London: Routledge.

Chuter, Jack (2015), *Storm Static Sleep. A Pathway through Post-Rock*. London: Function Books.

Clarke, Michael (1982), *The Politics of Pop Festivals*. London: Function Books.

Cohen, Sara (1993), 'Ethnography and Popular Music Studies'. *Popular Music*, 3(10): 123–38.

Dedman, Remfry (2015a), 'ArcTanGent Interview: "It's Like Being Part of a Secret Club"', *Independent*, 13 August. Available online: http://blogs.independent.co.uk/2015/08/13/arctangent-interview-'it's-like-being-part-of-a-secret-club'/ (accessed 23 August 2015).

Dedman, Remfry (2015b), 'Re Independent/ArcTanGent'. Email correspondence with the author, 9 December.

Dowd, Timothy (2014), 'Music Festivals as Trans-national Scenes: The case of progressive rock in the late twentieth and early twenty-first centuries', in Andy Bennett, Jody Taylor and Ian Woodward (eds), *The Festivalisation of Culture*, 147–68. Farnham: Ashgate.

Fabbri, Franco (1982), 'A Theory of Popular Music Genres: Two applications', in David Horn and Philip Tagg (eds), *Popular Music Perspectives*, 52–81. Göteborg and Exeter: A. Wheaton.

Frith, Simon (1988), *Music for Pleasure*. London and New York: Routledge.

Frith, Simon (1989), 'Why Do Songs Have Words?' *Contemporary Music Review*, 5(1): 77–96.

Frith, Simon (2002), *Performing Rites*. Oxford: Oxford University Press.

Gibson, Chris and John Connell (2012), *Music Festivals and Regional Developments in Australia*. Farnham: Ashgate.

Givony, Ronen (2007), 'Temporary Residence Records', *Perfect Sound Forever*, May. Available online: http://www.furious.com/perfect/temporaryresidence.html (accessed 6 November 2017).

Green, Thomas (2015), 'Have We Finally Hit Peak Festival?' *Telegraph*, 25 April. Available online: http://www.telegraph.co.uk/culture/music/music-festivals/11560934/Have-we-finally-hit-peak-festival.html (accessed 23 June 2016).

Hann, Michael (2015a), 'End of the Road Festival Review – The bands love it as much as the crowd', *Guardian*, 7 September. Available online: http://www.theguardian.com/music/2015/sep/07/end-road-festival-review-sufjan-stevens (accessed 17 November 2015).

Hann, Michael (2015b), 'End of the Road Proves You Can Still Fill Bills with Women and Still have a Sellout Music Festival', *Guardian*, 8 September. Available online: http://www.theguardian.com/music/2015/sep/08/end-of-the-road-festival-women-acts (accessed 17 November 2015).

Heller, Jason (2013), 'Picking a Path through the Nebulous Terrain of Post-rock', *AV Club* 20 June. Available online: https://music.avclub.com/picking-a-path-through-the-nebulous-terrain-of-post-roc-1798238882 (accessed 22 October 2017).

Hesmondhalgh, David and Leslie Meier (2015), 'Popular Music, Independence, and the Concept of the Alternative in Contemporary Capitalism', in James Bennett and Nikki Strange (eds), *Media Independence*, 94–116. London and New York: Routledge.

Hodgkinson, James (2004), 'The Fanzine Discourse over Post-rock', in Andy Bennett and Richard Peterson (eds), *Music Scenes*, 221–37, Nashville, TN: Vanderbilt University Press.

Holt, Fabian (2007), *Genre in Popular Music*. Chicago, IL, and London: University of Chicago Press.

Hunter, Nikk (2015), 'Re ArcTanGent Questions'. Email correspondence with the author, 3 December.

Jack, Malcolm (2016), 'Mogwai – 10 of the Best', *Guardian*, 14 December. Available online: https://www.theguardian.com/music/musicblog/2016/dec/14/mogwai-10-of-the-best (accessed 7 October 2017).

Jenkins, Henry (2008), *Convergence Culture: Where Old and New Media Collide*. New York: New York University Press.

Jenkins, Henry, Sam Ford and Joshua Green (2013), *Spreadable Media: Creating Value and Meaning in a Networked Culture*. New York: New York University Press.

Jinks, David (2016), 'Facing the Music. The hidden costs of festivals', *Parcelhero*, Industry Report. Available online: https://www.parcelhero.com/content/downloads/pdfs/festivals/festivalreport.pdf (accessed 20 June 2016).

Johnson, Bruce (2013), 'I Hear Music: Popular music and its mediations', *Journal of the International Association for the Study of Popular Music*, 3(2): 96–110.

Jokelainen, Jarkko (2014), 'Anyone Can Be a Critic. Is there still a need for cultural journalism in the digital age?' Reuters Institute Fellowship Paper, University of Oxford.

Kendall, Jo (2015), 'The Fierce and the Dead: Four go wild in the country', *Team Rock*, 13 November. Available online: http://www.teamrock.com/features/2015-11-13/the-fierce-and-the-dead-four-go-wild-in-the-country (accessed 17 December 2015).

Klein, Bethany (2010), *As Heard on TV: Popular Music in Advertising*. London and New York: Routledge.

McKay, George (2000), *Glastonbury: A Very English Fair*. London: Victor Gollancz.

Mackellar, Jo (2014), *Event Audiences and Expectations*. London and New York: Routledge.

Maffesoli, Michel (1996), *The Time of the Tribes. The Decline of the Individual in Mass Society*. London: Sage.

Maloney, Sean (2017), *The Modern Lovers*. New York: Bloomsbury.

Marks, Olivia (2016), 'How Crowdfunded Music Festivals are Offering an Alternative to Increasingly Corporate Ones', *Independent* ,12 January. Available online: http://www.

independent.co.uk/arts-entertainment/music/festivals/how-crowdfunded-music-festivals-are-offering-an-alternative-to-increasingly-corporate-ones-a6808261.html (accessed 23 June 2016).

Meier, Leslie (2017), *Popular Music as Promotion: Music and Branding in the Digital Age*. Cambridge: Polity Press.

Moore, Ryan (2005), 'Alternative to What? Subcultural capital and the commercialization of a music scene', *Deviant Behavior*, 26(3): 229–52.

O'Callaghan, Goc (2018), 'Event Attendees by Location 2017'. Email correspondence with the author, 13 February.

O'Donnell, Patrick and Stephen McClung (2008), 'MP3 Music Blogs: Their efficacy in selling music and marketing brands', *Atlantic Journal of Communication*, 16: 71–87.

Osborn, Brad (2011), 'Understanding Through-Composition in Post-Rock, Math-Metal, and Other Post-Millennial Rock Genres', *Music Theory Online*, 17(3): 1–17.

Peterson, Richard and David Berger (1975), 'Cycles in Symbol Production: The case of popular music', *American Sociological Review*, 40(2): 158–73.

Peterson, Richard and Andy Bennett (2004), 'Introducing Music Scenes', in Andy Bennett and Richard Peterson (eds), *Music Scenes*, 1–16. Nashville, TN: Vanderbilt University Press.

Reynolds, Simon. [1994] 2007 'Post-Rock', in S. Reynolds, (ed.), *Bring the Noise*, 186–193. London: Faber and Faber.

Reynolds, Simon (1994) 'RU Ready to Post-rock?' *Melody Maker*, 12 July: 42–43.

Reynolds, Simon (2011), *Retromania. Pop Culture's Addiction of its Own Past*. London: Faber and Faber.

Riesman, David (1950), 'Listening to Popular Music', *American Quarterly*, 2(4): 359–71.

Rik (2013) 'ArcTanGent – Goc Interviewed', *Bleeder*, 2 July. Available online: http://www.bleedermagazine.com/arctangent-interview-with-goc/ (accessed 7 December 2015).

Robinson, Roxy (2015), 'No Spectators! The art of participation, from Burning Man to boutique festivals in Britain', in G. McKay (ed.), *The Pop Festival. History, Music, Media, Culture*, 165–82. New York: Bloomsbury Academic.

Savage, Jon (2007), *Teenage: The Creation of Youth 1875–1945*. London: Pimlico.

Schenker, David (2015), 'ArcTanGent Festival: Fern Hill Farm, Somerset – live review', *Louder Than War*, 5 September. Available online: http://louderthanwar.com/arctangent-festival-fern-hill-farm-somerset-live-review/ (accessed 7 December 2015).

Sheinbaum, John (2002), 'Progressive Rock and the Inversion of Musical Values', in Kevin Holm-Hudson (ed.), *Progressive Rock Reconsidered*, 21–42. New York and London: Routledge.

Stadler, Raphaela, Sacha Reid and Simone Fullagar (2013), 'An Ethnographic Exploration of Knowledge Practices within the Queensland Music Festival', *International Journal of Event and Festival Management*, 4(2): 90–106.

Stevens, Jenny and Ami Sedghi (2015), 'Glastonbury, Reading or Creamfields: Which 2015 festival has the fewest female artists?' *Guardian*, 23 June. Available online: http://www.theguardian.com/music/2015/jun/23/glastonbury-reading-creamfields-2015-festival-female-artists-charts-lineups-male (accessed 17 November 2015).

Stone, Chris (2009), 'The British Pop Music Festival Phenomenon', in J. Ali-Knight, M. Robertson, A. Fyall and A. Ladkin (eds), *International Perspectives of Festivals and Events*; *Paradigms of Analysis*, 205–24. Los Angeles, CA: Elsevier.

Strachan, Robert (2017), *Sonic Technologies. Popular Music, Digital Culture and the Creative Process*. New York: Bloomsbury.

Sundbo, Jon and Per Hagedorn-Rasmussen (2008), 'The Backstaging of Experience Production', in Jon Sundbo and Per Darmer (eds), *Creating Experiences in the Experience Economy*, 83–110. Cheltenham: Edward Elgar.

Thornton, Sarah (1995), *Club Cultures*. Cambridge: Polity.

TPi (2015), 'ArcTanGent', *Festival Insights*, 4 September. Available online: http://www.festivalinsights.com/2015/09/arctangent/ (accessed 17 November 2015).

Turner, Fred (2008), *From Counterculture to Cyberculture: Stewart Brand, The Whole Earth Network, and the Rise of Digital Utopianism*. Chicago, IL: Chicago University Press.

Vasa (2015). Interview with the author, Glasgow, 27 October.

Warman, Janice (2010), 'How Music Festivals are Singing the Changes', *Guardian*, 27 August. Available online: https://www.theguardian.com/business/2010/aug/27/music-festivals-record-industry (accessed 23 June 2016).

4

'They Sold the Festival Out!' Axionormativity as the Future of Festivals

Waldemar Kuligowski

'This festival is over!' shouted a group of young women and men, their clenched fists up in the air. 'They sold the festival out!' A 30-year-old punk wearing a studded jacket was the loudest. The words chanted by a dozen or so people for a short moment drew the attention of other rock fans hurrying to the next performance of the Jarocin festival in Western Poland. 'This is a festival with a message', a Dutch DJ repeated over and over again, in a car on a narrow, bumpy road in Southern Hungary. 'The most important thing is the message', he kept repeating, 'and that is why *they* don't like us here so much', pointing to another police car controlling the access to the O.Z.O.R.A. Festival grounds. 'Serbia, Serbia!' shouted a boy in a 'Kosovo is Serbia' t-shirt, with joy and pride and with three fingers of his hand raised in the air. The words 'This is Serbia!' blended together with the loud music of trumpets, which since early morning had dominated Guča, a small town in central Serbia, home to the largest European brass bands festival.

What connects these three events? Is there any common denominator for punk fans from Poland, a psytrance fan from Hungary and a Serbian lover of trumpet sounds? In their anger, pride and joy they expressed their attitude towards values they associated with a specific festival. In each of the above cases, genre is merely a medium for emotions that are triggered by certain values. The fans from the Polish Jarocin festival opposed the change in the event's formula, which had been previously associated with the 'mecca of subcultures' and massive pogo dancing during punk concerts. The Dutch DJ spoke about the 'message', which was treated as the main course in the festival's menu by the post-hippie organizers of the O.Z.O.R.A. The young Serb expressed his nationalistic dreams in a place that transformed them into a festival attraction.

My ethnographic research of music festivals confirms that the axio-normative sphere is becoming increasingly important and may, to a significant degree, influence the future form of festivals. Therefore, in this chapter, I would like to analyse selected contemporary music festivals from this perspective.

The axio-normative orders of festivals

The notion of 'the festival' occupies an important place in many disciplines, such as cultural anthropology, social psychology, folklore, comparative religion, sociology, history, management and economics. The 'festival' also features prominently on various levels of colloquial, political and economic discourse. In the field of cultural research, there are several well-known approaches to festivals: the sacred/profane opposition (Durkheim 1986; Mauss 2004); studies focused on the paroxysm of the festival (Caillois 2001a,b); categorizing festivals with the concept of secular and holy time (Eliade 1959); analysis of subversive practices (Bakhtin 1968, 1984); the performative perspective (Schechner 1988); associating them with liminality and *communitas* (Turner 1969), as well as the most recent contribution of event studies (Getz 2005, 2010). This spectrum is complemented by studies in the field of management, as part of the humanities, and by studies on cultural policy and the organizational dimensions of cultural practices and creativity (Maughan and Bianchini 2004; Klaic 2009; Negrier et al. 2013).

The majority of researchers agree that the culture of festival is one of the most intriguing elements of European culture, a manifestation of its tradition. Whilst in the Middle Ages most festivals took place under the patronage of local church organizations as part of the sacred calendar, Ronström states that at the end of the twentieth century 'festival began to be used as a generic term for a large array of celebrations that carry few or no religious connotations ... The world has been festivalized' (Ronström 2011). There are many aspects to this process. On the one hand, there are still functioning festival events that are homogeneous – organized by people with similar cultural competences and comparable strategies for their reception or consumption. On the other hand, fairs, meetings, 'days', feasts or celebrations are organized 'for everyone', during which the main activities of the participants are walking, eating, drinking, smoking and engaging in brief conversations (Hunyadi et al. 2006; Delanty et al. 2011; Anderton 2015).

Even a cursory review of national, regional and local calendars confirms that festivals have come to dominate cultural life. Festivals are organized by public institutions, local governments, non-governmental organizations and private entities. Investment plans are adapted around them, as are the schedules of classes at schools and universities; they also have an impact on traffic regulations, trade, alcohol sale and consumption, etc. The festival has ultimately become an autonomous entity, in institutional, financial and organizational and cultural terms.

All these processes combine in the efforts undertaken by cities applying to be European Capitals of Culture, and the competitive activity associated with this phenomenon. Many authors note that the popularization of festivals as quantitatively dominant forms of cultural activity has triggered positive processes that had previously been absent in the local cultural 'ecosystems' (Holden 2015). The scholarly literature in this field (Autissier 2008; Klaic 2009), as well as research conducted in Poland (Poprawski 2015), indicates that festivals have become a unique space for cooperation between entities from the public, civic and private sectors, on a scale absent in any other form of activity. The festival is often a source of mutual inspiration or for the stealing of ideas; an intersectoral synergy laboratory. Furthermore, well-designed festivals are irreplaceable zones of intercultural dialogue (Dragicevic-Sesic and Dragojevic 2004).

Given the number and scope of festival events, we can now formulate a thesis on the festivalization of culture (Bennett et al. 2014; Kuligowski 2017a). At the most general level, this phenomenon consists in treating festival events as follows: (1) a means of ensuring access to culture/education/entertainment; (2) a tool for promoting a local area or region; (3) an element in the creation of cultural/historical policy; (4) a space for social gatherings, a setting for maintaining relationships in the community, and as a backdrop for shaping personal image, for example through social media; and (5) a medium for promoting certain moral and ideological values. The aim of the research is to focus on the fifth aspect, which is, so far, the least-studied.

Despite the fact that the notion of festivalization has been widely disseminated and popularized, along with related studies, this has not been accompanied by any reflection connecting this process directly with the sphere of values. Whilst conducting research on music festivals in Serbia, Hungary and Poland (Kuligowski 2014, 2015, 2016, 2017a, 2017b), I noticed the great importance of what, following Florian Znaniecki (1971: 511), can be described as the 'axio-normative order'. The Polish sociologist distinguished four classes of social systems: social relations/interpersonal relations, social roles, social groups, and societies as systems of diversified and functionally integrated social groups. All these social systems have a specific cultural base and can function cooperatively only through communicated and at least partially shared knowledge, norms, and values. The cultural base includes 'axiological standards' that persons and groups are supposed to apply in evaluating each other and the system as a whole: 'Insofar as they accept and conform with these standards and norms, the social system manifests a dynamic inner order which can be termed axio-normative' (Znaniecka-Lopata 1976: 205).

As Znaniecki emphasized:

> Actions that really aim to comply with a given ideological model are similar to each other, and can be objectively categorized in the same class to the extent that they all reveal a common order of composition and organization. The most important of the values contained in them were selected and defined on the basis of the same patterns, and the intentions were shaped in accordance with the same standards.
>
> Znaniecki 1971: 511

What does this mean for contemporary festivals and their cultural bases? Participants at music festivals strongly identify with the festival as a specific brand: with the idea, message and visual symbolism, and sometimes also with activities associated with the festival that are social or political in nature. To use Znaniecki's terminology, festival 'axio-normative orders' – interrelated values, patterns and standards – are important factors that both attract participants and encourage their identification. This has led to the growing number of festivals that build their 'identity' on the basis of a clearly defined package of values/norms or 'axiological standards'. The rhetoric of festival organizers increasingly contains assertions that certain festivals are organized 'in contrast' to others. Of course, the study of festival axio-normative orders should take the difference between the idealistic and the actual into account (Parsons 1937: 91; Znaniecki 1971: 297).

Acknowledging the expansive nature of the festivalization process, this study assumes that grounding festivals in specific values and norms is becoming an increasingly important element of contemporary festival policy. Festival organizers consciously present various axio-normative orders, and their participants identify with these in a variety of ways. Thus, a new, festivalized map of values emerges, which then shapes – at local, regional and national levels – cultural and historical policies, promotional strategies, and social and political discourses. From this perspective, it is worth noting that whilst some of the value-oriented festivals are primarily spaces for integrating people who hold a given set of beliefs (energized by shared content reinforcing their views), other festivals – a minority, it would seem – take the form of an exploratory space, unpredictable meetings, dialogue, and a meeting of values (Dragicevic-Sesic and Dragojevic 2004).

The focus on festival axio-normativity at music festivals has another justification. Music is a medium that evokes strong emotions; some researchers even go so far as to assert that music is simply 'about emotions', that it creates a special representation of 'emotions, moods, mental tension, and resolutions' (Langer 1957: 100). Other researchers emphasize that music can integrate and disintegrate; inclined to activity but also to reflection, can create 'specific' places and spaces, and establish social differences, political orders and moral hierarchies (Lomax 1968; Feld 1990; Chapman 1997; Hudson 2015). The anthropologist John Blacking (1977) wrote about music in the context of emotions like falling in love, ecstasy, and joy of dancing. Daniel Cavicchi (1998), in work on music and meaning amongst Bruce Springsteen fans, uncovers the complex practices fans experience of music: 'The feeling that one has just been to a religious revival', says one of them, 'Faith and Hope and Joy!' (Cavicchi 1998: 93).

On a general level Theo Van Leeuwen, renowned social semiotician, suggests that 'listening is connection, communion' (Van Leeuwen 1999: 197) and music performances have been seen as occasions to (re)create a sense of *communitas*, or of transformation from one state to another. In a similar way Tia DeNora presents 'music as a material that actors use to elaborate, to fill out and fill in, to themselves and to others, modes of aesthetic agency and, with it, subjective stances and identities, a resource for producing and recalling emotional states' (DeNora 2000: 107). At this point, I can conclude that music is an element of culture that operates on many levels, is polysemantic, is based on emotions, and generates social practices. I therefore assume that it also has a particular significance for generating norms and values in the context of music festivals.

Values in action

The axionormativity of festivals has many faces and levels. For many years 'villages' promoting religious ideas have been present at most music festivals.

Both Krishna's Village of Peace (Pokojowa Wioska Kryszny) and the Jesus Station (Przystanek Jezus) operate at the huge, free open-air Woodstock Festival, organized in Poland to crown a charity fund-raiser. Such proximity is not conflict-free. At other festivals volunteers distribute pocket editions of the 'Festival Bible'. First published in 2001, it was created as part of the international organization of 'Bible for the Nations'. It includes the New Testament and many prayers, accompanied by colourful pages presenting the statements of famous 'converted' musicians (members of such bands as Iron Maiden, Megadeth and Accept), as well as testimonies of women and men who describe their experience of God. The extra-musical, additional activities usually include presentations, exhibitions or discussions aimed at promoting various ideas: environmental, charity work, meditation, yoga, healthy lifestyle, patriotism, Catholicism, Krishnaism, vegetarianism, etc. It may be concluded that the 'soft' (or even 'trivial') axionormativity is a fixed element of all festival types.

Moreover, a growing trend may be observed in Poland, wherein the increasing number of music festivals define themselves by direct association with specific sets of norms and values, with axionormativity being their typical mark and attraction at the same time. Examples of such attitudes include the selected contemporary music festivals. A number of distinct axio-normative orders may be distinguished amongst them:

- Axionormativity promoting nationalist and conservative values: the Eagle's Nest Festival (Orle Gniazdo), the Indomitable and Independent Song Festival (Festiwal Piosenki Niezłomnej i Niepodległej) and Cieszanów Rock Festival
- Axionormativity promoting the idea of multiculturalism: the Cross Culture Festival (Festiwal Skrzyżowanie Kultur), the Jewish Culture Festival (Szalom na Szerokiej) and Ethno Port Festival
- Axionormativity promoting subcultural values: Goth (Bolków Party), punk (Rock na Bagnie) and the Ostróda Reggae Festival (reggae)
- Axionormativity promoting Catholic values: 'If Not God Then Who' Festival (Któż jak Bóg) and the Salvatorian Festival of Religious Songs (Salwatoriański Festiwal Piosenki Religijnej)
- Axionormativity promoting tradition and heritage: the Song of Our Roots Festival (Festiwal Pieśń Naszych Korzeni), the Festival of Highland Folklore (Festiwal Folkloru Ziem Górskich) and the International Chopin Piano Festival (Międzynarodowy Festiwal Chopinowski)

The above division as well as assigning specific festivals to separate axio-normative orders works in principle only, as they are based solely on the analysis of promotional materials and press releases. This division, however, clearly indicates that the axio-normative sphere is both important and diverse. The second part of the paper is an attempt to analyse the axionormativity of festivals using three festivals as examples: in Serbia, Poland and Hungary. At each of these events, I conducted ethnographic fieldwork using various tools from standard questionnaire-based interviews through participant observation to field recording.

'Serbian essence', 'Polish mecca' and 'Hungarian Woodstock'

The Dragačevski Sabor Trubača/Guča Trumpet Festival was originally a small regional event that took place in a tiny Serbian town. The first event in 1961 was modest, but year-by-year the festival's popularity was growing. The local event eventually became the largest regular European festival for brass bands, and by 2010 the number of attendees reached 800,000. *Politika*, a high-circulation Belgrade newspaper, described the 2010 festival as 'the largest gathering of people in Serbia's history' (Ostašević 2013).

A new chapter in the history of the Sabor began in 1993, when Yugoslavia broke up into a number of states and the festival in Guča became an element of ethnic conflict. It began to be considered as the most prominent expression of the 'essence' of Serbian national culture. First, a large amount of money was provided to finance the subsequent editions of the festival. Second, senior government officials personally appeared at the Guča festival. Consequently, the Prime Minister of the Republic of Serbia, Milorad Dodik, declared, 'If you love Serbia, you must also love Guča – the most important town of the whole country during the festival' (Mikeska 2007: 28).

The Jarocin Rock Festival is one of the oldest music events in Poland. It was started in 1980 in a small town in the western part of the country. As the biggest rock festival not only in Poland, but also in the whole Eastern Bloc, it was a great cultural sensation. Every year, it attracted several thousand people who could display subcultural values, dress and behaviour. The festival took place with the consent of the socialist government, which did not fully understand its subversive potential. The name of the festival quickly became a symbol of freedom and attitudes alternative to the dominant ideology. The transformation that started

Figure 4.1 The Jarocin Rock Festival. Photo courtesy of Waldemar Kuligowski.

in 1989 redefined the meaning of the festival. The organizers first tried to change its format in the vein of other commercial festivals, but in the face of street riots and permanent conflicts between the audience and the police, the festival was held for the last time in 1994. It was reactivated in 2005 and currently seeks to connect with its former importance and status of being a 'mecca of subcultures' (Kuligowski 2015).

The O.Z.O.R.A. Festival has been held since 2004 in the buildings of what used to be a farm in the central part of Hungary, in a village of the same name (Ozora). However, its origins date back to 1999, and involve a total eclipse of the sun accompanied by psytrance music and its many genres, with an audience of 20,000 people (St John 2010: 1–17). Today, the festival attracts fans of psytrance music, offering them all-day performances, yoga and meditation practice, sessions of Capoeira, Pilates, Aikido, Tai Chi, many lectures on naturopathy, culinary traditions from various regions of the world, and so-called 'spiritual wisdom'. It should be noted that organizationally and financially, O.Z.O.R.A. relies on the activities of people from outside Hungary: the post-hippie communities from Goa (India) and the USA. Stereotypically, in Hungary and abroad the festival is associated with the availability of drugs, naked people and has been dubbed the 'Hungarian Woodstock'.

The three festivals described above are very different from each other in many respects: country, genre, origin. From the perspective of my analysis, another material difference is the audience. It is hard to assume that a brass band fan will

Figure 4.2 The O.Z.O.R.A. Festival. Photo courtesy of Waldemar Kuligowski.

also enjoy morning yoga classes at the O.Z.O.R.A or pogo dancing in Jarocin. Putting all these fundamental differences aside, the audiences of these three festivals have something important in common: orientation of values. Each year, thousands of people flock to Guča, Ozora and Jarocin, drawn by the axio-normative dimension of the festivals. Each of these events has built its individual set of values with which it is associated. In consequence, there is also a set of counter-values each festival is opposed to, either as declared by organizers or participants, or both.

Visuality, fans, organizers

First, let us analyse the visual aspects of these festivals. As Gillian Rose (2007) suggests, visuality has many meanings, but the most important is to stress cultural difference. The images, symbols and signs may make the difference invisible or, quite on the contrary, they may stress it. My fieldwork shows that the visual aspect of festivals is highly axio-normative, and therefore differentiating in nature.

In Guča, the most dominant objects are those that directly refer to Serbia and Serbianness. They include flags, coats of arms, emblems, images of national heroes as well as the map of the 'great' Serbia from before the Yugoslav Federation. Such symbols can be seen on t-shirts, mugs, plastic trumpets, caps and countless other objects. They can be purchased at festival shops or seen in the crowd of fans. The Serbian flag flutters in the main town square, and accompanies groups of people on the camping site, in nearby orchards or simply in the small river, who sing, dance and drink alcohol whilst listening to music. Such a situation brings to mind the observations of Michael Billig (1995: 93) who regarded 'flagging' as an everyday manifestation of nationalism. Eager and constant 'flagging' guarantees refreshing the memory of the fatherland, reproduces the nation state and updates the national identity.

As regards the Jarocin festival, the visual aspect is very different. A monument of an army boot (*glan*) adorns a square next to the crossing of the town's major roads. Unveiled in 2011, it is an image of a heavy leather boot and has become the icon of the punk subculture. Mohawk hairstyle, leather jacket, colourful trousers and army boots – to this day they are the iconic punk fashion style. Although the subculture costume may be regarded in the categories of a postmodern style, fashion identity, or an expression of class affiliation (Muggleton 2002), in Jarocin the punk style was adopted to promote the festival and even the town itself. It is one of the few cases where the name of the town has become recognisable nationwide, what is more, the fans attended not 'the festival' but 'Jarocin' and such an expression was perfectly understood by everybody. The festival magazine and souvenirs are based on punk style. Even at the entrance to the Regional Museum there are two large wicker army boots made by a local artist.

However, neither the flags in the Serbian Guča, nor the punk style in Polish Jarocin, are as visible and omnipresent as the axio-normative visuality in Hungarian Ozora. The fans are greeted at a huge gate with a notice reading 'Welcome to Paradise'. This leads the way to a vast area full of fluorescent images, totems, buildings called Dragon Nest or Chambook House or places called Cooking Grove, The Wheel of Wisdom or Labyrinth. This post-hippie space combines the elements of nature (wood, thatched roofs) and technology (laser beams, music 24 hours a day), localness (the Hungarian folklore in the festival-opening parade) and globality (costumes, tattoos, symbols). Crossing the threshold means entering a different reality. Moreover, when put in this space, festival fans experience 'topophilia' (Tuan 1990), a source of joy, inspiration and identity. Many participants told me about the 'psychedelic space' of festival: 'This

is amazing part of nature. Here music is always. And everything is lit up'
(23-year-old female). The next section will focus on what the fans say about
these three festivals and the values they promote.

Let us take Guča first (Kuligowski 2014):

'We have it all here: the trumpet is our national instrument and rakija is our
national drink.'

24-year-old female

'The festival promotes Serbian identity, particularly through music and fun, so
characteristic of our tradition and stemming from it ... The festival increases
our prestige throughout Europe.'

42-year-old male

'Guča is Serbia ... This is the most important festival promoting Serbia, the
symbol of fun and happiness ... the festival brings people together and that is
why there are visitors from all over the world.'

24-year-old male

'I come here to see the folklore and folk customs.'

52-year-old male

'This festival promotes Serbian culture because the brass bands play our national
music ... We can be proud of this festival, as it is the most famous festival in the
whole Europe.'

26-year-old male

The significance of the Jarocin Rock Festival is stressed using very different
categories and values:

'I come to the festival on Thursday, I leave on Monday, leaving behind my job,
Warsaw, the city, traffic jams, newspapers, television, the internet, and I don't care
about anything. I am alienated from life, all I do is have fun, I'm in a great mood.
It is the most important thing, it's the essence of the festival.'

42-year-old male

'It was, let's say, the barricade of that generation. And maybe it was the core of
Jarocin, as I judge today. Punk and another strong beats, this is probably the face
of Jarocin, which everyone wants to watch. The iconography of this place shows
it best.'

67-year-old male

'For me it's rest. Although it's common knowledge that you drink from morning
to morning. Yesterday we finished about half past seven in the morning. But

we're alive, we're breathing. There's a group of friends, it's fun, and that's what it's about. We have recharged in a safe company, without aggression, completely relaxed. We came here to rest.'

48-year-old male

'Now there is a healthy climate here. We can talk, sit out all night. Old and young people sit down after all concerts, almost to the morning and talk about things important to us. There is such a climate. We just become happy people.'

50-year-old female

The O.Z.O.R.A. Festival fans believe in yet another set of values:

'I feel pure freedom here. I can feel the positive energy of the people, music and place. I can get away from everything negative. It's great!'

32-year-old female

'The message is the most important. And the message of this festival is freedom. An internal freedom, first of all. It's the source of other positive things.'

25-year-old male

'Here you can be who you want. Your body, your freedom. You can be afro or trans. Or you can shine all night. It does not bother anyone.'

25-year-old male

I would like to conclude this part of the chapter with the views of the festival organizers. As was mentioned before, the 'missions' of festivals and official declarations of their organizers are important expressions of their axionormativity.

The official brochure *Guča: A Tin Soul of Serbia* (Bogabac 2007) contains such terms as 'the Serbian carnival', 'Guča is our freedom', or 'the heart of Serbia beats in Guča'. The whole narrative ties strongly together the festival and brass band music with the history and culture of Serbs. The festival itself is supposed to be the manifestation of this culture and its symbolic centre. As a result, the sound of trumpets creates a national audio-sphere. In line with John R. Short's (1991) 'national landscape ideology', when referring to this festival one can speak about the national sound landscape that evokes the past and is identical to the rural landscape (Nash 1993).

As has been mentioned above, in the case of Jarocin, the brand of the festival has become a recognisable symbol of the town, regarded as the capital of Polish music of rebellion. In 2014, the Museum of Polish Rock (Spichlerz – Muzeum Polskiego Rocka) was opened, which documents the history of the genre in Poland, as well as the successive editions of the festival. The official statements by the organizers discuss the legendary history of the festival as the place of rebellion against socialist authorities. A multi-volume publication representing the oral history trend, which contains recollections of the festival, is called *Grunt to bunt* (*Rebellion is the main thing*; Witkowski 2011–2013). A feature length documentary telling the story of the festival was given a similar title: *Jarocin, Rock for Freedom* (Leszek Gnoiński and Marek Gajczak, 2016).

The O.Z.O.R.A. festival is the event with the most complete character. Organizers refer directly to the tradition of New Age and hippie ideology. Titles of articles from the festival newspaper, *The Ozorian Prophet*, include 'Sound of the universe', 'Goa state of mind', and 'Redefining the ancient tribal ritual for the 21st century', and the authors make references to Victor Turner and his way of thinking about ritual and *communitas*. Thus they stress the community dimension of what is going on at the festival grounds, and, concurrently, they distinguish themselves from *orbis exterior*, which is tedious, commercialized and lacking spiritual values.

Conclusions

'They sold the festival out!', 'This festival is over!' Such alarming opinions could be heard during the 2017 Jarocin Rock Festival. What triggered such a loud protest by some fans was the change of the festival's formula, which covered most of its key elements: location, preferred genre and the idea of the festival as such. The last year was indeed different from the previous ones: the festival was divided between a number of stages dispersed throughout the town, instead of a single, main festival ground on the outskirts; punk musicians were almost absent from the new line-up, replaced by bands playing different genres; also the festival's mission was thoroughly redefined as its organizers stopped referring to rebellion and the 'mecca of subcultures' and focused on musical experiments and 'idioms' dedicated to late Polish musicians (Czesław Niemen). Such a transition from the previous category of protest to the currently promoted artistic experiment and recreation was unacceptable to many fans.

The change in the axionormative sphere of the Jarocin Rock Festival led to a crisis, demonstrated by a dramatic reduction in the number of people attending, negative comments by former fans on social media, as well as many voices of protest made during the festival itself. At this point I do not wish to discuss the reason for changing the festival's formula, as this is an independent decision made by the organizers, who wanted to be free from the burden of history and to create a new and different festival. The process I observed in the Polish town, however, spoke volumes about the future of music festivals in general.

My basic hypothesis is that one of the key attractions of festivals in future will be their axionormative sphere. This refers to a set of values that the organizers and fans regard as attractive, distinguishing from others and building their identity and community. The festival's system of values and norms may be built using a number of tools: genre, visual identity and the visual aspect of the festival itself, the mission and declarations of the organizers and as a consequence, thanks to the internalization of the system, by the fans.

The festivals I researched confirm this hypothesis. Each functions as an opposition to another festival and another axionormative system. Dragačevski Sabor Trubača is defined as an opposition to the Exit Festival in Novi Sad, which was created in 2000 on the initiative of the local university students who wanted to open up to Europe, a step outside the values dominating the state ruled by Slobodan Milošević. In many statements and publications, and also in the modern Serbian prose (Jergović 2008), the opposition between the Guča and Novi Sad festivals is indicated as a deep and permanent difference. The O.Z.O.R.A. festival was created as an extraterritorial space within contemporary Hungary. The festival grounds are private and called 'Field of Dreams' (St John 2009), with unique rules formulated by the organizers and the availability of drugs and derivative substances as the most explicit example (this is the reason for searches by the police surrounding festival grounds). The fans of the festival stress its alternative nature and criticism of Hungary and the conservative policy of Victor Orbán's government.

In both these cases axionormativity is clear, although its sources are dramatically different. With Guča, the foundation is the local nationalism and brass band genre monopolized by the Serbian discourse; with O.Z.O.R.A., it is the global post-hippie idea and transnational genre of psytrance. In both cases, the political component is strong, bolstered by the relationship with other values and norms.

The Jarocin Rock Festival shows the effects of deviating from the defined and fixed axionormative sphere.

In future, the locations of festivals, their programmes, line-up and other attractions such as the original food, entertainment and education sessions will still be important. However, I think that axionormativity will be one of the fundamental elements of building, sustaining and succeeding with music festivals. The fans seek strong identification and affiliation with empathic communities (Preece 1997; Rifkin 2009), based on shared values. Thanks to the music, which evokes strong emotions, music festivals may successfully integrate such communities. An important cultural context may be that mainstream music is rather devoid of ideas and distant from 'axiological standards'. Digitalization of music and the dissemination of individual/solitary listening practices further strengthens the importance of places where music is performed live and listened to with others. One can risk a statement that the axio-normative 'turn' of the festival is a backlash against the conditions imposed by new technologies.

In this light, important questions pertain to whether future festivals will be 'contact zones' or rather 'exclusion zones' (Chang 2005). Axionormativity integrates and establishes communities, but at the same time excludes and creates strangers/opponents. This ambivalence will be one of the most important challenges that future festival organizers will face, for as Znaniecki argued, the human world is a world of values.

References

Anderton, Chris (2015), 'Branding, Sponsorship, and the Music Festival', in George McKay (ed.), *The Pop Festival: History, Music, Media, Culture*, 199–212. New York: Bloomsbury Academic.

Autissier, Anne-Marie (2008), *Festivals in Europe, Crossing Approaches from Edinburgh to Zagreb*. Paris-Toulouse: Les Editions de l'Attribut.

Bakhtin, Mikhail (1968), *Rabelais and His World*. Bloomington: Indiana University Press.

Bakhtin, Mikhail (1984), *Problems of Dostoevsky's Poetics*. Manchester: Manchester University Press.

Bennett, Andy, Jodie Taylor and Ian Woodward (eds) (2014), *The Festivalization of Culture*. London and New York: Routledge.

Billig, Michael (1995), *Banal Nationalism*. London: Sage Publications.

Blacking, John (ed.) (1977), *The Anthropology of Body*. New York: Academic Press.

Bogabac, Zoran (2007), *Guča. Limena dusza Serbije*. Beograd: Politika.

Caillois, Roger (2001a), *Man, Play and Games*, Urbana and Chicago, IL: University of Illinois Press.

Caillios, Roger (2001b), *Man and the Sacred*, Urbana and Chicago, IL: University of Illinois Press.

Cavicchi, Daniel (1998), *Tramps Like Us: Music and Meaning among Springsteen Fans*. New York: Oxford University Press.

Chang, T.C. (2005), 'Place, Memory and Identity: Imagining "New Asia"', *Asia Pacific Viewpoint*, 46(3): 247–53.

Chapman, Malcolm (1997), 'Thoughts on Celtic Music', in Martin Stokes (ed.), *Ethnicity, Identity, and Music. The Musical Construction of Place*, 29–44. Oxford: Berg.

Delanti, Gerard, Liana Giorgio and Monica Sassatelli (eds) (2011), *Festivals and the Cultural Public Sphere*. Abingdon: Routledge.

DeNora, Tia (2000), *Music in Everyday Life*. Cambridge: Cambridge University Press.

Dragicevic-Sesic, Milena and Sanjin Dragojevic (2004), *Intercultural Mediation in the Balkans*. Sarajevo: OKO.

Durkheim, Emile (1986), *The Elementary Forms of the Religious Life*. Beverly Hills, CA: Sage Publications, Inc.

Eliade, Mircea (1959), *The Sacred and the Profane. The Nature of Religion*. New York: Harcourt, Brace.

Feld, Steven (1990), *Sound and Sentiment. Birds, Weeping, Poetics and Song in Kaluli Experience*. Philadelphia: University of Philadelphia Press.

Getz, David (2005), *Event Management and Event Tourism*. New York: Wiley.

Getz, David (2010), 'The Nature and the Scope of Festival Studies', *International Journal of Event Management Research*, 5(1): 1–47.

Holden, John (2015), *The Ecology of Culture*. London: AHRC.

Hunyadi, Zsuzsa, Péter Inkei and János Zoltán Szabo (2006), *Festival-world Summary Report. National Survey on Festivals in Hungary. Deliberations on Public Funding, Evaluation and Monitoring*. Budapest: KulturPont Iroda, The Budapest Observatory. Available online: http://www.budobs.org/pdf/Festival_en.pdf (accessed 2 December 2017).

Jergović, Miljenko (2008), *Freelande*. Zagreb: Naklada Ljevak.

Klaic, Dragan (2009), 'The Economy of Arts Festivals: An elusive, untransparent dimension', *Economia della Cultura*, 19(3): 317–24.

Kuligowski, Waldemar (2014), 'Nationalism and Ethnicization of History in a Serbian Festival', *Anthropos. International Review of Anthropology and Linguistics*, 109(1): 249–59.

Kuligowski, Waldemar (2015), 'Sentymentalizacja, topofilia i pokoleniowość. Jarocin re-study', *Czas Kultury*, 187(4): 32–42.

Kuligowski, Waldemar (2016), 'Festivalizing Tradition. A fieldworker's notes from the Guča Trumpet Festival (Serbia) and the Carnival of Santa Cruz de Tenerife (Spain)', *Lithuanian Ethnology: Studies in Social Anthropology and Ethnology*, 16(25): 35–54.

Kuligowski, Waldemar (2017a), 'Festiwalizacja kultury. Jak megaiwenty tworzą megatrendy', *Czas Kultury*, 192(1): 83–98.

Kuligowski, Waldemar (2017b), 'Collective Vertigo. Roger Caillois' "théorie de la fête" toward contemporary music festivals in Poland and Hungary', *Acta Ethnographica Hungarica. An International Journal of Ethnography*, 63(2): 389–406.

Langer, Susan (1957), *Philosophy in a New Key. A Study in a Symbolism of Reason, Rite, and Art*. Cambridge, MA: Harvard University Press.

Lomax, Alan (1960), *Folk Song Styles and Culture*. Washington, DC: American Association for Advancement of Sciences.

Maughan, Christopher and Franco Bianchini (2004), *The Economic and Social Impact of Cultural Festivals in the East Midlands of England. Final Report. Part 1*. Leicester: De Montfort University. Available online: http://www.artscouncil.org.uk/documents/publications/phpvY0hNv.pdf (accessed 2 December 2017).

Mauss, Marcel (2004), *Seasonal Variations of the Eskimo: A Study in Social Morphology*. London: Routledge.

Mikeska, Marek (2007), 'Krátce a aktuálně ze Srbska', *Navýchod*, 7: 28–29.

Muggleton, David (2002), *Inside Subcultures. The Postmodern Meaning of Style*. Oxford: Berg.

Nash, Catherine (1993), 'Embodying the Nation: the West of Ireland landscape and national identity', in Michael Cronin and Barbara O'Connor (eds), *Tourism and Ireland: A Critical Analysis*, 86–112. Cork: Cork University Press.

Negrier, Emmanuel, Lluis Bonet and Michel Guerin (2013), *Music Festivals: A Changing World*. Paris: Editions Michel de Maule.

Ostašević, Gvozden (2010), 'U Guči potrošeno 40 miliona evra', *Politika*, 23/24. Available online: www.politika.rs/rubrike/Srbija/Trubazaradila-40-miliona-evra.lt.html (accessed 26 June 2016).

Parsons, Talcott (1937), *The Structure of Social Action*. New York: Free Press.

Poprawski, Marcin et al. (eds) (2015), *Oddziaływanie festiwali na polskie miasta. Studium kompetencji kadr sektora kultury oraz synergii międzysektorowej*. Available online: http://www.zmp.poznan.pl/zwiazekmp/portal/web/uploads/pub/news/news_1709/text/Oddziaływanie per cent20Festiwali per cent20na per cent20Polskie per cent20Miasta per cent20- per cent20Raport per cent20z per cent20badan? per cent202014-15 per cent20ZMP per cent20ROK per cent20v2.2.pdf (accessed 12 December 2016).

Preece, Jenny (1999), 'Emphatic Community: Balancing emotional and factual communication', *Interacting with Computers*, 12: 63–77.

Rifkin, Jeremy (2009), *The Empathic Civilization: The Race to Global Consciousness in a World in Crisis*. London: Jeremy P. Tarcher.

Ronström, Ove (2011), *Festivalisation: What a Festival Says – and Does. Reflections over Festivals and Festivalisation*. Sweden: Gotland University. Available online: https://uu.diva-portal.org/smash/get/diva2:461099/FULLTEXT01.pdf (accessed 15 December 2017).

Rose, Gillian (2007), *Visual Methodologies. An Introduction to the Interpretation of Visual Materials*. London: SAGE.

Schechner, Richard (1988), *Performance Theory*. London: Routledge.

Short, John. R. (1991), *Imagined Country*. London: Routledge.

St John, Graham (2009), *Ozora: Field of Dreams*. Available online: http://www.undergrowth.org/ozora_field_of_dreams_by_graham_st_john (accessed 5 January 2018).

St John, Graham (2010), *The Local Scenes and Global Culture of Psytrance*. New York: Routledge.

Steiner, George (1996), 'A Festival Overture'. Lecture. Edinburgh: University of Edinburgh.

Tuan Yi-Fu (1990), *Topophilia: A Study of Environmental Perception, Attitudes, and Values*. New York: Columbia University Press.

Turner, Victor (1969), *The Ritual Process: Structure and Anti-structure*. Chicago, IL: Aldine Publishing Co.

Van Leeuwen, Theo (1999), *Speech, Music, Sound*. Basingstoke: Macmillan.

Witkowski, Grzegorz (2011–2013), *Grunt to Bunt*. Vol. 1–3. Poznań, in Rock.

Zatezić, Novica and Velimir Illić (2007), 'Pucaj trubo', *Večernje novosti*, 16: 12 August.

Znaniecka-Lopata, Helena (1976), 'Florian Znaniecki: Creative evolution of a sociologist', *Journal of the History of the Behavioral Sciences*, 12: 203–15.

Znaniecki, Florian (1971), *Nauki o kulturze. Narodziny i rozwój*. Warszawa: PWN.

5

The Hidden Worker Bees: Advanced Neoliberalism and Manchester's Underground Club Scene

Kamila Rymajdo

This chapter identifies the contributing factors to the last decade's changes in British clubbing trends, culminating in widespread nightclub closures widely reported by the national media in 2015. It discusses the ensuing optimistic tone of the media coverage of the north's music scenes, speculating on their motives and the effect of the coverage. Drawing on theories of work within the creative industries under advanced neoliberalism, it presents findings from venue and promoter interviews conducted in 2016 and 2017, to draw conclusions from the operational practices within Manchester nightclubs opened during and since 2015. In doing so, it investigates how nightclubs are adapting to reflect shifts in leisure-time trends. Finally, in line with Jacques Attali's claim (Attali 1977: 10) that music foretells wider societal changes, it speculates on what role nightclubs play in today's society.

Club culture within British society

In the past, certain genres of music were associated with particular cities: Detroit and techno, Manchester and acid house, London and grime. But because music is made increasingly diasporically, these long-established ties are getting looser and their legacies have been replaced by the bricks and mortar of nightclubs. Former Haçienda DJ and club culture critic Dave Haslam asserts that 'Clubs and venues like Bolton Palais, Nottingham's Rock City and the Barrowland Ballroom in Glasgow have played a central role in towns and cities for years and become embedded in the cultural and social life of a community in the same way that, traditionally, a university, cathedral or a factory might have done' (Haslam 2015a:

ix). Sarah Thornton pinpoints the seed of the modern nightclub as being planted in the 1950s, when 'records supplanted musicians as the source of sounds for most social dancing' (Thornton 1995: 51). But it was not until the 1960s that the aesthetic of the modern nightclub was born, with 'discotheques' differentiating themselves from the dancehalls and youth clubs of the previous decade by being 'self-consciously unconventional. They were *lounges, rooms* or simply *spots*; they were *places* with presence rather than palaces' (Thornton 1995: 54). By the 1990s it was all about raves that 'catered for up to tens of thousands of dancers, often in premises unlicensed for dancing, including warehouses, disused airfields and agricultural land' (Longlois 1992: 230).

For scholars, clubbing presents a variety of angles for exploration. For example, in his 1999 book *Clubbing*, Ben Maldon asserts that it 'offers a myriad of insights into our conceptualizations of a whole range of social interactions, notions of communality and play, and of being young' (Malbon 1999: 4). Sarah Thornton notes its cross-race and demographic-wide appeal: 'For a broad range of British youth . . . going out is an integral part of growing up' (Thornton 1995: 16). So ingrained is clubbing to every generation's maturation that in *Generation Ecstasy* Simon Reynolds goes further, arguing that even 'organized religion has noticed the way rave culture provides "the youth of today" with an experience of collective communion and transcendence' (Reynolds 1999: 242). Today, clubbing remains a pertinent subject for scholars because of its continued evolvement and adaptation to societal changes. For example, the 'silent disco', which appeals to clubbers because of its 'voyeuristic passerby factor' (Taylor 2015: 75), reflects the pervasive surveillance characterizing social media. Brands such as Morning Gloryville, self-described as 'the pioneers of sober morning raving' represent a time-strapped society more focused on healthy lifestyles, and immersive clubbing experiences such as Elrow Bollywood are symptomatic of an era pushing towards total virtual reality. Clubs are also of interest to scholars because of what they reveal about tourism (Sellars 1998) or for their expression of glocalization, that is, 'the interpenetration of the global and the local, resulting in unique outcomes in different geographic areas' (Ritzer 2007: 13).

Nightclubs, as part of musical subcultures, play a significant role in cities' economies too, enabling an upward domino effect by attracting other sectors of the music business. Investigating how Berlin became such a major focus of the international music industry, Ingo Bader and Albert Scharenberg go as far as to assert that clubs and their associated musical subcultures are 'the *main* [emphasis added] reason that global players and major music industry associations have moved their headquarters to Berlin' (Bader and Scharenberg 2010: 76). The German government proved to be in agreement, as in 2016 courts ruled that Berlin's techno mecca Berghain should be in the same tax category as concert venues and museums, given that it produces work of cultural significance (Oltermann 2016). A similar narrative of cultural impact can be traced in Britain. 'We've seen how often a venue getting critical acclaim or helping achieve critical mass can go on to have a much wider impact,' Haslam has argued (Haslam 2015a: 345–46). Indeed, the establishment's recognition of the importance of the nightlife economy began in the 1980s. The deindustrialization of former smokestack cities such as Sheffield and Manchester saw economic, aesthetic and cultural reinvention take place, with councils recognizing the potential of music industries as a catalyst for change. However, the collaborative efforts of councils and the music-based creative industries did not necessarily yield successful outcomes. 'Anthony Wilson, constantly point(ed) to the "success" and vibrancy of the music scene in Manchester, contrasting it to that of Sheffield as a salutary lesson in irrelevant municipal meddling in a sector it cannot understand' (Brown et al. 2000: 443). Still, even when they were not getting involved directly, councils exploited their cities' vibrant music scenes as a source of good PR' (Brown et al. 2000: 439).

Concurrently, big shifts were underway within club culture itself and potential for profit increased. 'Among the changes in nightclubbing through the 1990s would be the increased status of DJs,' asserts Haslam (Haslam 2015a: 345). Not just DJs, but venues too were cashing in. 'By the mid–90s, nightclubs like Cream weren't just venues with flashing lights and dancing – they became "brands" with major commercial clout' (Haslam 2015a: 345). So apparent were the cultural gains that the creative industries were at the forefront of the New Labour government's view of Britain's future, with the former Prime Minister Tony Blair writing in 1997, 'I believe we are now in the middle of a second revolution, defined in part by new information technology, but also by creativity' (Blair, quoted in Brown et al. 2000: 437). But Blair's enthusiasm for creatives was not universal. That same year, he backed the ban on 'hoodies' in shopping centres, the clothing associated with urban music genres such as grime. The message reverberated within policy with the introduction of Form 696. Effective from 2005, it was the paperwork used by London's Metropolitan Police to measure the risk of violence at music events by gathering the personal details of artists and promoters, targeting genres such as grime, garage, R&B and house. So pervasive was its use that the whole London grime scene was nearly derailed, with a similar approach adopted by police across the rest of the country (Rymajdo 2017b, 2018).

Whilst the 1990s and early 2000s saw rave shutdowns and club closures resulting from drugs and (real and perceived) violence, as was the fate of the Haçienda, by the mid-2000s other factors came into play, contributing to club culture's decline. Writing in 2005, Heather Skinner, Gloria Moss and Scott Parfitt asserted that 'The town and city centre late-night economy is a highly competitive saturated market, where boundaries are blurring between nightclubs and other types of mainstream late night venues' (Skinner et al. 2005: 121) and this continued into the 2010s, with clubs' losing streak accelerated by the fashion for city centre living and the resulting noise complaints. The economic crash of 2008, increased university fees and the growth of the festival market both in the UK and abroad, as well as the popularity of party island holidays to destinations such as Ibiza and Ayia Napa, also had a major impact on club culture in Britain. Vice's 2016 UK census, which asked 2,500 participants aged 18–34 about their views on a variety of topics, reflected these wider factors, reporting the resultant shift in leisure-time trends amongst young people: 'Once upon a time, going out was all about the great British pub. In a different, pill-ier age, the hottest spots were fields in the middle of nowhere. For this generation, it turns out the ultimate night out is actually a night in' (Ewens 2016). The survey found that 63 per cent of people preferred spending their downtime attending a house party, compared to 34 per cent who chose clubbing. The results corroborate club closures across the country, which hit both clubs in small towns and in big cities, even taking the most iconic, from London's Plastic People to Manchester's Roadhouse.

Although 2015 was the year that the press reported widely on the downturn, quoting figures released by the Association of Licensed Multiple Retails that showed the number of clubs in the UK dropped from 3,144 in 2005 to 1,733 in 2015 (Connolly 2015), it was the revoking of Fabric's licence in 2016 following the drug-related deaths of two teenagers that galvanized the music industry to take action and save at least that particular club. Indeed, a national and sustained campaign that lasted five months followed the London club's closure, with Fabric reopening under a stricter licence in January 2017. Shortly after Fabric's resurrection, recently elected London Mayor Sadiq Khan created the role of a Night Czar, appointing Amy Lamé to ensure London remained a '24-hour city' (Sherwood 2016).

The media too began to paint a more positive picture. Dave Haslam argued in the *Guardian* that the reported club closures were not representative of the reality, asserting that 'There's no evidence that interest in music and going out itself has dropped since the 1970s, let alone in the period surveyed by the ALMR', proposing that rather people's interests had shifted to live music, with associated venues not included in the audit (Haslam 2015b). Still, it was impossible for the press to ignore the pervasive gentrification in London or indeed propose a solution and thus a third, simpler option presented itself in how to continue to write about club culture with optimism: turning to the North of England. Some drew attention to the possibilities afforded by the North's cheap rents, with music culture website *The Quietus* suggesting that 'taking money out of the equation – the sort of money attached to a high-cost, industry-centred city – creates a sense of freedom and enhances community' (Wray 2017), whilst others celebrated the North's ability to stay underground (Turner et al. 2017). Perhaps most common amongst articles celebrating the creativity of the North, however, was the foregrounding of the DIY approach, its success succinctly surmised by Mark O'Donnell in a 2017 *Mixmag* article: 'Putting the work in comes easy to Manchester; it's a city full of grafters' (O'Donnell 2017). Such an overview is predictable given that, 'independence is rarely perceived in a "bad sense", stemming from Western notions of individual and political freedoms' (Bennett 2014: 1), and I have also written positively about Manchester's self-sufficiency. But it must also be conceded that the resulting subtext of these articles is that cities like Manchester do not need the kind of arts funding that is afforded the South – that they do just fine, if not better, without it – thus helping to uphold the old systems of inequality and contributing to continuation of a culture where Mancunians and northerners must work that much harder than their southern counterparts. Indeed, in 2017 'the Institute for Public Policy Research North revealed the scale of the funding gap between northern cities and London. It found that for the North to get the same Arts Council England funding per head as the capital it would need £691m more in the 2018–22 funding round' (Marsh 2017).

Manchester clubbing history

It comes as no surprise then, that Manchester's long and unique clubbing history is characterized by resilience, adaptability and reinvention. In the 1960s, when the city's music scenes centred around genres such as beat, jazz, blues, folk, pop and psychedelic, DJs were often found spinning records in the city's coffee shops which 'did not need a licence to operate and could open until the early hours' (Gatenby and Gill 2011: 16), but by the 1980s and 1990s, with the ascent of the Madchester movement, it was all about clubs and raves. The Haçienda, aligned with Tony Wilson's Factory Records, was at the centre of the rise of acid house and '"Madchester" attracted the attention of the international media and music industry' (Brown et al. 2000: 441). 'With its combination of bohemia (a large population of college and art students and the biggest gay community outside London) and demographic reach (around fifteen million people live within a couple hours' drive from the city centre), Manchester was well placed to become the focus of a pop cultural explosion' (Reynolds 1999: 94). Since the Haçienda, the city has birthed other globally recognized brands within club culture – Sankeys and The Warehouse Project – whilst its large student body has been the emollient of the city's indie and urban music scenes, exemplified by iconic venues and club nights such as the Star and Garter and its indie night Smile or South's bass, grime and trap focused Murkage.

According to Bader and Scharenberg (2010: 80), the cities that birth subcultures and their venues are usually undergoing change, for example, because of the collapse of their economic base, and Manchester proves its credentials every decade, if not economically, then aesthetically, but usually both. Describing a video by Factory Records band Northside, Gatenby and Gill write, 'you can see how the city centre looked in 1990 and realize how much development has taken place since the Madchester days' (2011: 25). A major effect of this redevelopment was the concentration of the city's music in and around Oldham Street, an area that is now known as the Northern Quarter. Its evolvement into Manchester's creative hub came following the erection of the locally derided shopping mall, the Arndale Centre, which was built in the 1970s. With businesses clamouring to secure space within it and on nearby Market Street, Oldham Street was virtually abandoned and rent plummeted. Dive bars and sex shops moved in, but so did record shops, nightclubs and creatives, for whom the area offered affordable studio space.

As Gatenby and Gill point out, there were 'similarities between the coffee bar scene of the early 1960s and the rave culture of the late 1980s and early 1990s' with both falling victim to police clampdowns due to drug use. Whilst the latter was tackled with the Manchester Corporation Act of 1965, the Haçienda and its contemporaries such as Konspiracy found themselves at the mercy of controversial Chief Constable James Anderton after the 'doors wars' of competing gangs trying to control security at the venues, and thereafter the selling of drugs within the clubs (Gatenby and Gill 2011: 16). Nowadays club culture in Manchester has new enemies. Whilst noise complaints have led councils to review licences of well-known venues such as Night and Day (Thompson 2014) and Islington Mill (Rymajdo 2017a), others, such as the iconic Dry Bar, have been sold off to developers (Heward 2017), with ever more venues, even those out of the city centre such as the warehouse space Mantra, also under threat. But perhaps the biggest changes within nightlife trends in the mid- to late-2010s have been brought on by the gentrification of the city's creative hub. Accelerated by another regeneration, driven by the partial relocation to Salford's Media City of several national media companies including the BBC, ITV and Channel 4, as well as the success of locally grown online media megaplayers LADBible and UNILAD, the Northern Quarter became an area populated by hipster bars and cafes playing homogenized playlists synonymous with commercial town centre venues across the country (Rymajdo 2018). Their free or low entry fees have pushed out independent promoters, resulting in an underground on the move yet again.

But such a homogenization is inevitable if one accepts that 'clubbing is usually subdivided by clubbers and the clubbing media according to sexuality, age and location into types or strands, such as mainstream, gay, student, S&M, indie, "local", as well as being differentiated into musical genres, such as house, techno, drum 'n' bass and big beat to name only a handful of genres that might themselves be further sub-classified' (Malbon 1999: 32). Or as Thornton puts it, 'Club cultures are *taste cultures*. Club crowds generally congregate on the basis of their shared taste in music, their consumption of common media and, most importantly, their preference for people with similar tastes to themselves' (Thornton 1995: 3). Rather than becoming an area of identikit establishments playing the same music, the Northern Quarter was perhaps always to some degree uniform, maturing from a subcultural hub in its 'youth' into a more profit-driven mainstream-focused space in its 'adulthood'. Within club culture, it seems, the underground and mainstream cannot co-exist in close proximity. Thornton writes, 'clubber and raver ideologies offer "alternatives" in the strict sense of the word' (Thornton 1995: 115) because 'the mainstream is a powerful way to put themselves in the big picture, imagine their social world, assert their cultural worth, claim their subcultural capital' (Thornton 1995: 115). For clubbing to offer the kind of sanctuary that people with these shared values need, it must figuratively and to an extent physically, be under the ground.

The new independents – Hidden and The White Hotel

With a name and location that signalled an understanding of this, Hidden's arrival was announced in February 2015 by an article in the *Manchester Evening News*, describing how two entrepreneurs applied for a licence to open a nightclub and arts space within the disused Downtex Mill, on the edge of Manchester city centre. Their licence, granted by Salford Council five months prior to publication of the piece, would allow them to run a similar operation to Islington Mill, a multi-use space close by popular with Manchester underground promoters and artists, but on a bigger scale, with a 650-capacity club space across several rooms. In an interview with the newspaper, director Jobie Donnachie 'admits the venture is unlikely to be a money-spinner' but expresses the desire 'to create a thriving atmosphere of like-minded people in which they can express themselves on a platform from which their talents can grow' (Williams 2015). The owners enlisted the help of two bookers with experience from rival establishments of international renown – Sankeys' Jay Smith and The Warehouse Project's Anton Stevens – who began to organize in-house events, ranging from big-name DJ line-ups to themed parties focused on a specific genre, where local DJs were enlisted to play.

Concurrently, The White Hotel was also emerging as a new subcultural hub. The close proximity of the 300-capacity venue to HM Prison Manchester, locally known as Strangeways, imbued its immediate surroundings with an ominous atmosphere, further intensified by its precise location on a darkly lit one-way street popular with sex workers. However, in opposition to Hidden, which opened with a degree of fanfare, according to hearsay the former car mechanic's shop turned music venue began operating with no licence and no bouncers. It certainly operated with zero social media presence for a time and, like Hidden, was near impossible for taxi drivers to find. Now a fully legal enterprise, its popularity is partly owing to a continuation of flexible opening hours permitted by Salford Council's less-restrictive licensing laws (when compared to those of neighbouring Manchester City Council).

One of The White Hotel's earliest club nights was techno imprint Lost Control. Its organizer Matthew Earnshaw explained that his move from the Northern Quarter was prompted by the area's 'venue owners [who] don't really care about the events that are on'. He criticized them for 'strict last entry times, bouncers on power trips and having no free spirit'. The White Hotel, he argued, was different because the owners are really into using it as an art space, as a music space. Ben [Ward, licence holder] is one of the most genuine people I know, he's really sound, you can tell he really enjoys owning the place. He'll go round and talk to people, he'll talk to people in the club, he'll talk to the promoters. I've never seen that anywhere else.

Indeed, both clubs sought the patronage of established local promoters with strong followings across a broad range of genres and demographics, with promoters who have used both venues including the LGBTQ-marketed Homoelectric, techno imprint Meat Free and house and techno focused Love Dose. However, the crossovers in their booking policies have resulted in similar audiences across the two venues.

Writing about the club culture of the 1990s, Tony Langlois describes the climate surrounding the rise of house as resulting from 'the failure of technological and political utopias to materialize', breeding 'a generation appreciative of a quasi-mystical and somewhat hedonistic aesthetic' (Langlois 1992: 237). What Hidden and The White Hotel illustrate is a shift from the search for utopia within the club to the world of work, observed within the wider creative industries by scholars such as Angela McRobbie:

> In fields like film-making or fashion design there is a euphoric sense amongst practitioners of bypassing tradition, pre-empting conscription into the dullness of 9–5 and evading the constraints of institutional processes. There is a utopian thread embedded in this wholehearted attempt to make-over the world of work into something closer to a life of enthusiasm and enjoyment.
>
> McRobbie, quoted in Bennett 2014: 17

Indeed, according to Ruth Levitas, the utopian scholar, utopias are 'not just a dream to be enjoyed, but a vision to be pursued' (Levitas 2010: 3). In such visions, utopias become an 'expression of the desire for a better way of being' (Levitas 2010: 9). Hidden's Smith revealed that the club wanted to create its own utopian spirit by 'keeping an illegal feel to it but being legally run' whilst The White Hotel's creative director Austin Collings said, 'I think a part of it is trying to destroy it, a certain part of me tries to break it down constantly'.

Despite these utopian ideals, work within the creative industries under advanced neoliberalism is characterized by precariousness. Workers, even when employed by an organization, are expected to be self-reliant and adaptable, their unstable position justified by the neoliberal values of autonomy and individuality. Writing about the music business, Timothy Taylor traces this back to France's

1968 civil unrest, quoting Pierre Bourdieu and Luc Boltanski to argue that the resultant tropes of liberation, freedom of expression and sexual relationships were 'in the process of supplying the economy with the perfect consumer' (Taylor 2015: 46). Referencing Thomas Frank, Matt Stahl makes a similar point in *Unfree Masters*, his 2013 book about recording artists and the politics of work:

> the twin development of business and countercultural revolutions – in which sensation-seeking middle class youth and intrepid ad agency creatives rejected conformity and endorsed individuation and self-actualization more or less simultaneously and on a large-scale – resulted in the institutionalization of 'a hip consumerism driven by disgust with mass society itself.
>
> Stahl 2013: 69

The characteristics of the consumer identified by Bourdieu eventually became the traits of the creative industries worker: McRobbie asserts that the creative sector 'relies on disembedded and highly individualized personnel' (McRobbie, quoted in McGuigan 2009: 187). Meanwhile, their autonomy is a prerequisite of good work. Quoting David Hesmondhalgh, Stahl writes, '"creative autonomy" is essential to work in the creative industries because "autonomy itself is bound up with the interests of cultural-industry businesses"; without freedom from constant monitoring and control, creative workers would not (the industry fears) be able to come up with potentially valuable new cultural properties' (Stahl 2013: 7). Indeed, Hidden's Smith revealed that autonomy was the central characteristic of his role: 'We could have gone for certain DJs who we knew would have filled the venue but me and Anton stuck to our guns, we said, we want certain DJs that are not ticket sellers, but we know are gonna bring a good crowd to Hidden'. Meanwhile, The White Hotel's Collings said, 'A lot of my ideas come out of the opposition to things, out of being a natural contrarian. The music, books and films I've always liked are the ones that try and do something majorly different so by nature you bring that to this environment'.

With Ward previously at the helm of indie imprint Sways Records, and Collings simultaneously a novelist and film-maker who previously worked as a journalist, The White Hotel directors are emblematic of a generation of creative industries workers described by Mark Deuze as, 'unlearning old skills whilst reflexively adapting to new demands' (Deuze 2007: 10). Conversely, 'individualized work in the creative industries demands "creative compromise" that is appropriate to a relentlessly "upbeat business", and furious networking by ambitious young people' (McGuigan 2009: 188). Smith confirmed this was the case: 'You've got to be six months ahead of everyone else, so it's constantly emails, it's keeping up a reputation with agents'. As Leadbeater and Oakley assert, 'Life as an Independent is not nirvana, nor even necessarily a recipe for making money. It can provide choice, autonomy and satisfaction, but it also involves constant uncertainty, insecurity and change' (Leadbeater and Oakley 1999: 15). Indeed, whilst Collings said, 'If I had my way I wouldn't deal with any promoters but we have to rely on them to substantiate our own ideas', Smith revealed that working for Hidden came with personal financial hardship: 'We gave up everything to get the club up and running so on our personal lives, it did take a lot out of us.'

On a marketing level, whilst forging strong links with the city's existing music scene, Hidden tried very hard to individualize itself by replicating the scarcity approach adopted by independents whose limited economic resources force them to find novel ways to stand out (Hracs et al. 2012: 1154). This was successful for a variety of industries including music, fashion and hospitality, and it worked for Hidden too, as manager Martin Moffat confirmed: 'It gets people coming for the right reasons, for the party. We don't get the passing trade, which obviously isn't always the best from a business point of view but it means that we get to kind of get a better crowd, it adds to the excitement.'

The approach illustrates that for the club's owners and bookers, the social capital accrued by attracting customers who reflect their values and their cultural capital, is more important than economic capital.

The White Hotel's operation paints a similar picture, utilizing a highly stylized approach and aesthetic, its website offering no information, but instead a short clip of a wine bottle smashing upon impact with a brick wall. In email communications, Ward also resists a traditional role title and instead signs off as 'Caretaker' whilst Collings is 'Madness'. Within the venue itself, the bar is situated below ground level, requiring the customer to kneel down to speak to the bartender, whilst on the other side of the room, another bar, offering cocktails and vintage wine from menus custom-designed to complement specific events, serves its drinks with altar bread wafers associated with the sacrament of holy communion. The resultant atmosphere is church-meets-warehouse-rave-meets-Prohibition-era-speakeasy, and Collings confirmed that the aim was blurring the lines: 'It's like a sensory overload so you don't know whether you're coming into a cinema, a club, a boozer, a brothel or anything.'

On the one hand, the venue's originality can be celebrated for its reflection of Manchester's rich subcultural scene, but on the other, it can be argued they reflect neoliberalism's penchant for high-risk strategies: 'Advanced industrialism, especially impelled by the dynamic of capital accumulation, takes risks that are incalculable. For instance, products are released on to the market with precious little knowledge as to whether they are safe or not' (McGuigan 2009: 117).

Ward explained that a high-risk strategy was intrinsic to creating the venue's unique character, which differentiated it from competitors:

> We commission nights with people we really like and rather than just say we'll put them on among a night, we say, we'll commission you, you pick the line-up, we'll take the risk and we've given them a budget. It's our own money, it's a lot of money and we put it on the line.

Meanwhile, Hidden's initial high-risk strategy was in part resulting from The Warehouse Project's dominance and their ability to afford DJ exclusivity contracts, which had put previous competitors out of business (Rymajdo 2016a). According to Stevens, Hidden's counter strategy involved 'going against the grain of what's happening in the city and what's working in the city', with Smith adding that, 'in the first six months we did sort of question if we were doing the right thing'. Owner Nikos Arnaoutis revealed the financial hardship was almost unbearable, saying 'When it was November [2015] I remember not wanting to get out of bed'.

Both Hidden and The White Hotel's approaches proved to be successful, however. Hidden won the *Manchester Evenings News* annual CityLife Awards Best Club prize with an overwhelming majority, garnering 45 per cent of the votes (Walters 2016) and national recognition followed. A year after opening, the venue won in the 'Best Small Club in the UK' category at the Best of British 2016 DJ Mag Awards, beating much longer-established venues from London, Southampton, Sheffield and Glasgow, whilst The White Hotel has been the subject of articles in both the local (Cooper 2017) and national press (Rymajdo 2017d). At the time of writing (March 2018), it is rated as the second best Manchester music venue by Skiddle users, out of a listed 303. But in the end, the biggest winner is perhaps their competitor. Stevens said:

> The Warehouse Project are really happy that we're taking the risk, because not only are we not going for what they're going for, but we're adding value to artists who haven't played in Manchester before. That's meant that we've had a lot of people who've played here, who've had their debuts here and those people are now being booked by The Warehouse Project whereas they wouldn't have been before.

Whilst no doubt such developments are positive for the bookers themselves, proving their tastemaker credentials and thus increasing their cultural capital, in some way the situation is a sad echo of the argument put forward by Horkheimer and Adorno, that the constant pursuit of novel commodities only creates homogenization.

The club culture hybrids: Eastern Bloc, Partisan Collective and sponsored house parties

Although Hidden and The White Hotel have become the beacons of Manchester's underground music scene (Rymajdo 2017c), the pioneering practices of other venues and promoters – what I will call the 'club culture hybrids' – are also pertinent to this chapter. Intuitive to the changing demands of clubbers and the hardships facing promoters, they have challenged the concept of what is understood as a nightclub and a club night, taking them outside the traditional venues and operational structures. In doing so, they have for the most part been successful and from the perspective of the clubber and in some instances, the council, positively impacted on the scene, turning around failing business models, disused buildings and monetizing the 'staying in' strain of 'going out', thus helping struggling local DJs. But whilst being pioneering in one way, they, much like Hidden and The White Hotel, mimic the exploitative practices characteristic of advanced neoliberalism, from the gift economy and free labour found on the internet and utilized by corporations (Terranova 2014), the curatorial structure of online streaming companies where the middleman profits whilst the artist loses (Hall 2017), to the attention-demanding features of social media deployed by conglomerates such as Facebook (Lewis 2017).

The record-store-cum-vinyl-cafe/bar Eastern Bloc has always operated with the spirit of taste-making, but in recent years has multiplied the ways in which it demonstrates its credentials. Opened in 1985, it started as a record store in the independent shopping complex Afflecks Palace, before moving to Afflecks Arcade in 1987 and then Stevenson Square in 2011. It was then that the once-law-flaunting shop, which sold tickets to illegal raves during Madchester's heyday, began trading as a fully licensed bar, thus saving itself from closure following dwindling vinyl sales. However, it is in its concurrent reinvention as a curator that it showcases how much venues in Manchester have adapted to the wider trends within the music industry, with Eastern Bloc fashioning itself after Spotify and other such platforms that pride themselves on expertise. Eastern Bloc's staff, such as Kerrie Anderson, Black Eyes (the aforementioned Matthew

Earnshaw) and Meanand3rd are more than baristas, chefs and sales clerks. They are active members of the city's music scene.

Detailing her highly-skilled and varied role, Kerrie Anderson describes how alongside local promoters she curates club night pre-parties, 'serving as warm up to the main events, where the main act comes down and plays records sometimes in a different style to what they usually would'. She works with organizations such as Manchester University DJ Society, supporting with recruitment and DJ lessons and co-ordinates the live streaming of Eastern Bloc events. With Eastern Bloc situated in the heart of the Northern Quarter, competing with bars at every corner of its Stevenson Square address, the events Anderson curates are free and indeed bring in a crowd, especially when acts as iconic as Marshall Jefferson or Daniel Avery are on the bill. But with some DJs playing two-hour sets before their official gig begins, such an add-on to club nights does beg the question of who profits and who has to work twice as hard.

While local promoters Meat Free were the first in the city to adopt 'a pay what you like policy' at their then home Joshua Brooks, thus forgoing any guaranteed income, it was Partisan Collective, a democratically owned venue valorized by the *Guardian* (Hardy and Gollespie 2017) that introduced tactics to mimic the exploitative methods of neoliberal companies, its volunteer-driven operation similar to corporations' reliance on the internet's free labour and gift economy. Opened in July 2017, it launched with a two-day festival, eighteen months after a group of dissatisfied local music and arts enthusiasts discussed it into existence at a meeting in a Northern Quarter pub. In opposition to every other music venue in Manchester, its hire policy is sensitive to promoters' capacity to turn a profit and social impact, with its website stating 'We have a sliding scale fee structure for different kinds of organizations, which varies dependent on length and time of booking'. This provides a no doubt much welcome second option to cash-strapped promoters. But this model thrives on not only being accessed, but built by users (Terranova 2004: 91) and is an approach now as exploited by musicians as it is by companies, with Kanye West's 2016 album *The Life of Pablo* a pioneering example of participatory culture (Carmanica 2016). Partisan's visibility and indeed success is dependent on a sustained attack on its users' time and attention, with the cooperative simultaneously praising its members, writing how they 'transformed two junk-filled floors into a community arts and social space, housing a basement venue, two bars and offices'. However – always demanding more – they encourage monetary and physical donations as well as existing volunteers driving further volunteer recruitment. As Terranova asserts,

'After all, the goal of the access people and telecoms is to have people spend as much time on the net as possible, regardless of what they are doing. The objective is to have you consume bandwidth' (Terranova 2004: 93). Partisan too, not only wish for you to attend their events, but help run them and be party to their every decision.

Finally, hedonism combined with the entrepreneurial spirit of neoliberalism within the DIY framework is what characterizes a new generation of house parties in Manchester, the UK city with the biggest student population. In a 2016 Thump article entitled 'Manchester and the Evolution of the Student House Party', Duncan Harrison describes how professionally organized such events are, with hired sound systems, paid DJs, bouncers and guest lists. Their attractiveness to organizers and attendees alike stems from cost – an average of five or six students sharing a house will still find putting such an event on cheaper than a traditional night out, not to mention the kudos organizing such a night brings (Harrison 2016). But as Harrison points out, it is not only the students' own entrepreneurial spirit that makes these parties exemplary of advanced neoliberalism's pervasiveness:

> The scale of these events doesn't just end at selectors and sound systems. Brands like Spotify, Red Bull and Propercorn have all offered students the sound systems, refreshments, decor and DJs to elevate their parties to new heights, basically in the hope that some spangled sociology student will unintentionally advertise for them in her new profile picture.
>
> Harrison 2016

Conclusion

In a way, Jacques Attali's claim in his 1977 book, *Noise: The Political Economy of Music*, still stands as music continues to predict and reflect societal changes. Much like technologies that wreak havoc with users' attention spans, so does club culture offer ever more options. Successful nightclubs are no longer just clubs, they are multi-purpose venues that, like the multi-skilled and highly indvidualized people who run them, are constantly evolving their skillset. Like follower-number-obsessed social media celebrities and influencers, club owners and bookers are also less driven by profit (because there is less money to be made) and instead focus on increasing their cultural capital. What these characteristics reveal is that rather than trying to resist the status quo, subcultural spaces are finding ways to adapt to the conditions of advanced neoliberalism, to operate within it as smoothly as possible.

In many of their operations, underground nightclubs reflect recent changes in the wider music industry. Similarly to the streaming services that have become ubiquitous to our music consumption, they have taken on the role of curators, whilst their investments in less-well-known musicians mimic the patronage model adopted by brands such as Red Bull or Converse. They also emulate the changing approach of record labels, which have adapted to shrinking record sales by locking artists into 360 deals, where revenue from other sources of income such as merchandizing and publishing is included in their contracts (Marshall 2012). The venues' version of this is drawing on the opportunities afforded by the specifics of the buildings where they are located, converting extra space into studios that can be rented out or creating unique experiences, such as intimate pre-club performances. Whilst these strategies keep the nightlife economy afloat, oversaturation leads to an overall decrease in profit, which is ultimately paid for by the workers, who toil harder, longer or even for free, reflecting the increasing value gap present in other systems within advanced neoliberalism. The beneficiaries of this extra free labour are those at the top of the food chain, namely the bigger venues, who draw on the cultural capital accrued by smaller venues' bookers.

As with recorded music, where the democratization of its production has increased its disposability, clubbing too has lost in cultural (and subcultural) importance. Identities are forged elsewhere, in new meeting places online and on the ground. Moreover, the acceleration of production means that 'competition and the search for scarcity lock producers and consumers into a never-ending cycle of discovering and discarding sources of uniqueness and value' (Hracs et al. 2012: 1158). The situation seems even more bleak when we consider not much has changed from nearly a decade ago, when McGuigan argued that 'The conditions of work and, therefore, of life have become more precarious everywhere, giving rise to "a political economy of insecurity" that does not, strangely enough, seem to call capitalism into question' (McGuigan 2009: 176). Indeed, even Manchester's most socialist leaning venues do not seem so socialist under closer inspection.

However, whilst the practices of free labour and drawing on the gift economy are ever more commonplace and perhaps inevitable for a start-up operating under advanced neoliberalism, what the ambition of a venue such as Partisan illustrates is the potential for a more transparent system, where labour required for the successful running of a venue is calculated and because of the cooperative nature of operation, has a better chance of being fairly rewarded. The philosophy behind Partisan brings to mind the 'smart contract' blockchain technology being adopted by some musicians, where royalties are instantly split 'with no need for traditional middlemen like labels, publishers, or collecting societies' (Dredge 2018), thus recompensing those who are putting in the work. Unlike the original P2P system that came into play two decades ago, 'this time, the revolution promises to be different. Whereas digital and illegal downloading once wreaked havoc on the industry at large (from music creators to record labels, none were spared), a blockchain-based model for music pledges to boost the fortunes of artists' (Elder 2017). With Partisan aiming to bring audiences and culture-makers closer together, it too has the desire to cut out middlemen such as venue owners. Much in the same way that blockchain technology might reward artists played by DJs (Hall 2017), further down the line, it perhaps also has the potential to safeguard the cultural capital accrued by bookers, which at present, is often stolen by others.

Whether in the future nightclubs become fairer and more rewarding for their employees, they will always play an important role within wider society, because as Levitas explains, 'Whatever we think of particular utopias, we learn a lot about the experience of living under any set of conditions by reflecting upon the desire which those conditions generate and yet leave unfulfilled' (Levitas 2010: 9). Whilst Manchester's new independent venues are currently by no means perfect examples of the type of resistance we might hope to foster to overcome advanced neoliberalism, they do perfectly illustrate the continued complexities and increasing struggles of life and work under this system, and because of that it is important we both study and support them. And as Marxist philosopher Ernest Bloch once argued, 'hope was a practical as well as a theoretical matter' (Levitas 2010: 98) and therefore, for both their workers and users, these spaces are vital for the respite needed to ponder on more fulfilling ways of living, working and partying in the future.

References

Araujo, Rosane (2013), *The City is Me*. Bristol and Chicago, IL: Intellect.

Attali, Jacques (2014) [1977]. *Noise: The Political Economy of Music*, trans. Brian Massumi Minneapolis: University of Minnesota Press.

Bader, Ingo and Albert Scharenberg (2010), 'The Sound of Berlin: Subculture and the global music industry', *International Journal of Urban and Regional Research*, 34(1): 76–91.

Bennett, James (2014), *Media Independence: Working with Freedom or Working for Free?*, ed. James Bennett and Niki Strange. Abingdon-on-Thames: Taylor and Francis.

Brown, Adam, Justin O'Connor and Sara Cohen (2000), 'Local Music Policies within a Global Music Industry: Cultural quarters in Manchester and Sheffield', *Geoforum*, 31: 437–51.

Caramanica, Jon (2016), 'Kanye West Is Fixing His Album in Public. You'll want to read the edits', *The New York Times*, 19 February. Available online: https://www.nytimes.com/2016/02/21/arts/music/kanye-west-life-of-pablo-tlop.html (accessed 1 March 2018).

Connolly, Jim (2015), 'UK Nightclubs Closing at "Alarming Rate", Industry Figures Suggest', *Newsbeat*, 10 August. Available online: http://www.bbc.co.uk/newsbeat/article/33713015/uk-nightclubs-closing-at-alarming-rate-industry-figures-suggest (accessed 31 January 2018).

Cooper, Matthew (2017), 'Where is the The White Hotel and What's on this Weekend? Everything you need to know', *Manchester Evening News*, 23 February. Available online: https://www.manchestereveningnews.co.uk/whats-on/music-nightlife-news/where-the-white-hotel-salford-11928207 (accessed 21 February 2018).

Deacon, Liam (2014), 'Challenging Generation K: The dangerous rise of ketamine in UK club culture', *Talking Drugs*, 2 July. Available online: https://www.talkingdrugs.org/generation-k-the-rise-of-ketamine-in-uk-club-culture (accessed 1 February 2018).

Deuze, Mark (2007), *Media Work*. Cambridge: Polity Press.

Deuze, Mark (2012), *Media Life*. Cambridge and Malden: Polity Press.

Dredge, Stuart (2018), 'What Could Blockchain Do for Music?', *Medium*, 24 January. Available online: https://medium.com/s/welcome-to-blockchain/what-could-blockchain-do-for-music-4f60220e9709 (accessed 3 March 2018).

Ekanayake, Manu (2018), 'Daniel Avery: The techno auteur doing things with a distinct touch', *Mixmag*, 29 January. Available online: http://mixmag.net/feature/techno-auteur-daniel-avery (accessed 9 February 2018).

Elder, Robert (2017), 'Blockchain Tokens Could Transform the Music Industry', *Business Insider*, 8 November. Available online: http://uk.businessinsider.com/blockchain-could-transform-the-music-industry-2017-11 (accessed 3 March 2018).

Ewans, Hannah Rose (2016), 'How Young People Feel About Going Out, Housing and Mental Health', *VICE*, 23 September. Available online: https://www.vice.com/en_uk/article/mvnk94/how-young-people-feel-about-going-out-housing-and-mental-health (accessed 29 January 2018).

Gatenby, Phill and Gill Craig (2011), *The Manchester Musical History Tour*. Manchester: Empire Publications.

Hall, Josh (2017), 'How the Technology behind Bitcoin Could Change the Music Industry – and Help Everyone Get Paid', *FACT*, 21 February. Available online: http://www.factmag.com/2017/02/21/blockchain-bitcoin-music-industry/ (accessed 3 March).

Hardy, Kate and Tom Gillespie (2017), 'London's Exodus Offers a Stark Warning to Other UK Cities: Your culture is at risk', *Guardian*, 4 August. Available online: https://www.theguardian.com/commentisfree/2017/aug/04/london-exodus-warning-uk-cities-culture (accessed 8 February 2018).

Harrison, Duncan (2016), 'Manchester and the Evolution of the Student House Party', *Thump*, 18 January. Available online: https://thump.vice.com/en_uk/article/8q7xe5/manchester-and-the-evolution-of-the-student-house-party (accessed 9 February 2018).

Haslam, Dave (2015a), *Life After Dark*. London and New York: Simon and Schuster.

Haslam, Dave (2015b), 'UK Clubs are Closing – This is how a nightclub revolution begins', *Guardian*, 11 August. Available online: https://www.theguardian.com/commentisfree/2015/aug/11/clubs-closing-nightlife-uk (accessed 9 February 2018).

Howard, Emily (2017), 'Manchester Institution Dry Bar is Sold – With planning permission for a boutique hotel', *Manchester Evening News*, 14 March. Available online: https://www.manchestereveningnews.co.uk/whats-on/whats-on-news/dry-bar-manchester-sold-hotel-12741252 (accessed 1 March 2018).

Hracs, Brian J., Doreen Jakob and Atle Hauge (2012), 'Standing Out in the Crowd: The rise of exclusivity-based strategies to compete in the contemporary marketplace for music and fashion', *Environment and Planning A*, 45: 1144–61.

Khawaja, Jemayel (2015), 'Seth Troxler Rallies against Ketamine, Inauthenticity, and Aoki (Again)', *Thump*, 24 March. Available online: https://thump.vice.com/en_uk/article/9avw4e/seth-troxler-rallies-against-ketamine-inauthenticity-and-aoki-again (accessed 31 January 2018).

Langlois, Tony (1992), 'Can You Feel It? DJs and House Music culture in the UK', *Popular Music*, 11(2): 229–37.

Leadbeater, Charles and Kate Oakley (1999), *The Independents: Britain's New Cultural Entrepreneur*. London: Demos.

Levitas, Ruth (2010), *The Concept of Utopia*. Oxford and Bern: Peter Lang.

Lewis, Paul (2017), '"Our Minds Can be Hijacked": The tech insiders who fear a smartphone dystopia', *Guardian*, 6 October. Available online https://www.theguardian.com/technology/2017/oct/05/smartphone-addiction-silicon-valley-dystopia (accessed 1 March).

Malbon, Ben (1999), *Clubbing*. London and New York: Routledge.

Marsh, Sarah (2017), 'Arts Funding: £700m needed to bridge north–south divide, study finds', *Guardian*, 4 August. Available online: https://www.theguardian.com/culture/2017/aug/04/arts-funding-700m-needed-bridge-north-south-divide-study-finds (accessed 1 March 2018).

Marshall, Lee (2012), 'The 360 Deal and the "New" Music Industry', *European Journal of Cultural Studies*, 16(1): 77–99.

McGuigan, Jim (2009), *Cool Capitalism*. London: Pluto Press.

McRobbie, Angela (1998), *British Fashion Design*. London and New York: Routledge.

Ministry of Sound Staff (2016), 'Are Immersive Club Nights the Way to Forget Yourself?', *Ministry of Sound*, 23 February. Available online: http://www.ministryofsound.com/posts/articles/2016/february/are-immersive-club-nights-the-way-to-forget-yourself/ (accessed 8 February 2018).

Morning Gloryville. Available online: http://morninggloryville.com/ (accessed 9 February 2018).

Nur, Yousif (2016), 'Dance Yourself Happy: The rise of the sober rave', *Guardian*, 17 March. Available online: https://www.theguardian.com/music/2016/mar/17/sober-raving-clubbing-morning-gloryville (accessed 8 February 2018).

O'Donnell, Mark (2017), 'Manchester is the Beating Heart of New Music in the UK', *Mixmag*, 5 December. Available online: http://mixmag.net/feature/mcr-scene-piece (accessed 9 February 2018).

Olttermann, Philip (2016), 'High Culture Club: Berghain secures same tax status as Berlin concert venues', *Guardian*, 12 September. Available online: https://www.theguardian.com/music/2016/sep/12/berlins-berghain-nightclub-classed-as-culturally-significant-venue (accessed 31 January 2018).

Partisan Collective. Available online: http://partisancollective.net/ (accessed 9 February 2018).

Reynolds, Simon (1999), *Generation Ecstasy*. New York: Routledge.

Ritzer, George (2007), *The Globalization of Nothing 2*. Thousand Oaks, A, London and New Delhi: Fine Forge Press.

Rymajdo, Kamila (2016a), 'How a Student Night Started on a Whim Became One of the North's Best Loved Parties', *Thump*, 19 July. Available online: https://thump.vice.com/en_uk/article/nzyzam/micron-manchester (accessed 8 February 2018).

Rymajdo, Kamila (2016b), 'Here's Why British Nightlife Needs to Explore New Places and Different Spaces to Survive', *Thump*, 13 October. Available online: https://thump.vice.com/en_uk/article/53awyk/club-culture-spaces-and-places (accessed 31 January 2018).

Rymajdo, Kamila (2017a), 'Long Live Islington Mill, Manchester's Most Beloved Independent Venue', *Noisey*, 3 February. Available online: https://noisey.vice.com/en_uk/article/3dppyn/long-live-islington-mill-manchesters-most-beloved-independent-venue (accessed 31 January 2018).

Rymajdo, Kamila (2017b), 'We Asked Promoters About Exactly How an Outdated Form Polices Grime Gigs', *Noisey*, 31 March. Available online: https://noisey.vice.com/en_uk/article/yp9k3y/we-asked-promoters-about-exactly-how-an-outdated-form-polices-grime-gigs (accessed 29 January 2018).

Rymajdo, Kamila (2017c), 'Salford is the Most Exciting Place to Party in the UK Right Now', *Thump*, 5 July. Available online: https://thump.vice.com/en_uk/article/vbmdnm/salford-best-clubbing-in-uk (accessed 8 February 2018).

Rymajdo, Kamila (2017d), 'Manchester's White Hotel is the City's Experimental Centre', *Mixmag*, 13 December. Available online: http://mixmag.net/feature/manchesters-white-hotel-is-the-citys-experimental-centre (accessed 8 February 2018).

Rymajdo, Kamila (2018), 'Meeting Manchester's New Wave of Neo-noir Trap Artists', *Dazed*, 8 January. Available online: http://www.dazeddigital.com/music/article/38560/1/iamddb-bipolar-sunshine-just-banco-manchester-new-sound (accessed 8 February 2018).

Sellars, Alethea (1998), 'The influence of dance music on the UK youth tourism market', *Tourism Management*, 19(6): 611–15.

Sherwood, Harriet (2016), 'Sadiq Khan to Appoint London "Night Tsar" in Light of Club Closures', *Guardian*, 22 October. Available online: https://www.theguardian.com/uk-news/2016/oct/22/london-sadiq-khan-night-tsar-club-closures-24-hour-city-fabric (accessed 30 January 2018).

Skiddle Staff (2017), 'Petition Launched to Save Mantra Warehouse', *Skiddle*, 9 August. Available online: https://www.skiddle.com/news/all/Petition-launched-to-save-Mantra-Warehouse/31997/ (accessed 1 March 2018).

Skinner, Heather, Gloria Moss and Scott Parfitt (2005), 'Nightclubs and Bars: What do customers really want?', *International Journal of Contemporary Hospitality Management*, 17(2): 114–24.

Stahl, Matt (2013), *Unfree Masters: Recording Artists and the Politics of Work*. Durham, NC and London: Duke University Press.

Taylor, Timothy D. (2015), *Music and Capitalism: A History of the Present*. Chicago, IL: University of Chicago Press.

Thornton, Sarah (1995), *Club Cultures*. Cambridge: Polity Press.

Terranova, Tiziana (2004), *Network Culture: Politics for the Information Age*. London: Pluto Press.

Thompson, Dan (2014), 'Gig Venue Night and Day Cafe Threatened with Closure after Neighbour Complains about Noise', *Manchester Evening News*, 16 January. Available online: https://www.manchestereveningnews.co.uk/whats-on/whats-on-news/night-day-cafe-under-threat-6512779 (accessed 1 March 2018).

Turner, Luke, Dave Simpson, Daniel Dylan Wray and Joe Muggs (2017), 'How the North Stayed Underground', *Guardian*, 30 October. Available online: https://www.theguardian.com/music/ng-interactive/2017/oct/30/how-the-north-stayed-underground-grime-makina-psychedelia (accessed 20 February 2018).

Walters, Sarah (2016), 'Hidden Takes the Best Club Title in the CityLife Awards 2015', *Manchester Evening News*, 7 January. Available online: https://www.manchestereveningnews.co.uk/whats-on/whats-on-news/hidden-best-club-citylife-awards-10699991 (accessed 31 January 2018).

Williams, Jennifer (2015), 'Plans for New Nightclub and Arts Venue at "Neglected" Textile Mill Get the Go-ahead', *Manchester Evening News*, 19 February. Available online: https://www.manchestereveningnews.co.uk/news/greater-manchester-news/plans-new-nightclub-arts-venue-8680795 (accessed 31 January 2018).

Wray, Daniel Dylan (2017), 'Sound Cities: London vs The Music Industry', *The Quietus*, 5 December. Available online: http://thequietus.com/articles/23716-sound-cities-hull-city-of-culture-hebden-bridge-glasgow (accessed 8 February 2018).

Part Two

The Musicians and their Music

The Adaptive Musician: The Case of Peter Hook and Graham Massey

Ewa Mazierska and Tony Rigg

This chapter examines the artistic trajectories of two musicians originating from the North-West of England, Peter Hook and Graham Massey. Their music careers began in the 1970s, spanning five decades at the time of writing. Each attained major chart success in the UK and many other countries around the world, they both had record deals with culturally significant record labels, they used various vehicles and permutations for their creative output, and they both continue to make their living from music-related activities. The question we pose in this chapter is how these two musicians managed to sustain their careers for such a long period of time, given the changing fashions and climate in music. This is particularly relevant given the crisis in the recording industry that began in the late 1990s, the impact of which continues to resonate, particularly for artists whose practice began before the digital music revolution. To answer this, we consider factors pertaining to their personal circumstances, most importantly their talent and desire to live for and from music, and the wider context in which they operated, especially the time and place they started their work as professional musicians. We also consider whether there are any lessons that younger generations of musician can draw from their successes and failures. In order to do so, one of the authors, Tony Rigg, conducted in-depth interviews with these musicians in early 2018. Our research takes into account the circumstance of the genesis of Hook's and Massey's artistry, their subsequent rise to prominence and the history of music in the North-West of England in the 1970s up to the 1990s. To this history we devote the first part of the chapter.

The late 1970s and 1980s in the North-West: swimming against the tide

The 1980s are regarded as the period when neoliberalism began in the UK and the USA, following the election victories of Margaret Thatcher (1979) and Ronald Reagan (1981), whose politics were informed by the ideology of the 'New Right'. In cultural industries, as Timothy Taylor argues, the early neoliberalization was marked by increased corporatization:

> held much more to the bottom line than [it was the case] in the past, in part also because of the increasing ownership role played by managers, who through the mechanism of stock options began to think of themselves more as owners with a responsibility to stockholders.
>
> Taylor 2016: 48

However, whilst Taylor is correct about the 'general direction of travel' of the culture industries marked by centralization and ruthless monetization, including the popular music industries, there were exceptions to this rule. One of these exceptions was the North-West of England and Manchester especially. Following the period of deindustrialization, at the beginning of the late 1970s Manchester was a city in decline, known for dilapidated housing estates, empty shells of factories and a high level of crime. It was a city in ruins, feeding on its past. Although there were popular bands originating from the city and its surrounding areas, such as 10cc, the Hollies, Sweet Sensation, even the Bee Gees, the individual successes did not constitute a sense of a thriving music industry or scene. There was a lack of animators of culture willing to invest in the local talent. This situation also mirrored what was happening in other parts of the North of England. Those who were seeking success in popular music typically headed to the South of England or overseas. This was the case with the Beatles, who tried their luck in London, a journey depicted in Richard Lester's *A Hard Day's Night* (1964) in which the band leaves Liverpool by train to appear on television. The ascent of punk in the UK between 1976 and 1977 however, represented the dawn of a new era.

Punk is widely seen as not only a specific subgenre of rock, but also a distinct subculture and attitude to creating music and conducting music business. It is seen as a response to and marked by a rejection of musical virtuosity and the excesses often associated with preceding incarnations of rock typified by bands such as Led Zeppelin, Queen and Emerson, Lake and Palmer and, by the same token, breaking down the division between performers and consumers of music. Punk musicians were also hostile towards the dominant players in music and the media, including the large record companies. This was because these players represented the conformist political world against which punk rebelled, but also because these dominant institutions initially rejected them. Instead, punk musicians favoured small independent companies, which they often set up themselves. As Al Spicer remarks, the essence of punk was 'a "fuck you" attitude and a DIY aesthetic that meant any snotty-nosed teenager could join in' (Spicer 2006: 5). This attitude presented a cohesive ideology for a lifestyle movement beyond that of simply consuming music.

Punk musicians, despite their rebellious posture, proved to be very adaptable to the changing fashions and conditions of making music, thanks to their ability to rely on their own entrepreneurial spirit, rather than the support of large companies. Punk ideology emboldened outsiders, aspiring musicians operating outside the centres and in the case of Britain, outside London in the North-West, which is of specific interest here. However, the ascent of punk would not change the fortunes of the musicians discussed in this chapter, if not for the fact that it was coupled with the emergence of cultural entrepreneurs willing to invest in the new phenomenon and keep it local, rather than being relocated to London. Tony Wilson was the most important of such local entrepreneurs and subsequently became an object of most sustained research and mythologization, through several books and films devoted to him (Mazierska and Rymajdo 2017; Witts 2018).

Wilson came from Salford and studied at Cambridge University. On completing his study there in the early 1970s he returned to the North and started working as a reporter for Granada Television. Attending a Sex Pistols concert at Manchester Lesser Free Trade Hall in 1976 inspired him to start building up a music scene in Manchester (Nice 2011: 7–8). Before that, as Dave Haslam asserts, 'the notion of Manchester as a taste-making rock and roll town was unthinkable' (Haslam 1999: 110).

Wilson achieved this by creating an infrastructure that consisted of a record label, a club initially manifested in 1978 as the Factory Club Night and later the Haçienda (although Dry Bar should not go unmentioned), and a collective of like-minded individuals, keen to develop and harness the potential of Manchester's creative communities. Wilson's ambitions went beyond creating a music scene: he tried to reinvent the city by associating it with music culture, creativity and a particular brand of socialism: a Wilsonian version of Situationism.

As James Nice puts it, he had 'faith in the romantic magic of Manchester' (Nice 2011: 12).

Wilson's ambitions about Manchester are conveyed in his book, *24-Hour Party People: What the Sleeve Notes Never Tell You* (2002). This is a hybrid of the script of the biopic devoted to him (*24-Hour Party People* (2002), directed by Michael Winterbottom) and Wilson's thoughts about his own life in the context of a wider history of the North of England. At the beginning of Chapter 2, entitled 'Granadaland', Wilson writes:

> England's North-West, the background to our little tale, is a bit like that bit of semi-desert between the Tigris and the Euphrates in Iraq; a piece of land and a bunch of people that changed the world forever and then sank back into obscurity. In their aridity and poverty they seem to pay the price for ever daring to kick evolution's arse. . . .. This was the land that gave us the modern world. This was the home of the Industrial Revolution, changing the habits of homo sapiens the way the agrarian revolution had done ten thousand years earlier. And what did the heritage mean? It meant slums. It meant shite. Burnt out by all that 'production'. Capital strides the globe and it walked out on this lot around the time Queen Victoria popped it. The remnants, derelict working-class housing zones, empty redbrick mills and warehouses and a sense of self that it included loss and pride in equal if confused measures.
>
> Wilson 2002: 14

Wilson's mission seems to be the restoration of pride in being from the North West and especially being a musician from this region. Factory Records and the Haçienda became the pillars of the musical phenomenon known as Madchester. By investing in this enterprise Wilson not only acted against the neoliberal trend of increased corporatization, as mentioned by Taylor, but also against the idea of putting profit above art. Factory was known for its nonchalant approach to spending money, almost making a virtue of creating a deficit rather than surplus. The best-known example of this is reflected in the production of Factory Records' most commercially successful single, New Order's 'Blue Monday'. The single's original sleeve, created by Factory designers Peter Saville and Brett Wickens, showed disrespect for the way records are normally produced, by not including basic information about the product, as if to deter 'ordinary' consumers from buying it and appealing only to 'Factory insiders'. Moreover, due to the use of die-cutting and specific colours (all features used to make the record unique, even if mass-produced), the production cost of the sleeve was so high that the single sold at a loss (Nice 2011: 207–8).

The two musicians discussed in this chapter had different relationships with Wilson and Factory. Peter Hook, who was a member of Joy Division and New Order, was central to the operations of Wilson's musical 'empire'. Wilson saw Factory as 'a laboratory experiment in popular art' and its survival was propped up by the success of its major acts, Joy Division, New Order and the Happy Mondays (Robertson 2006). The commercial success of Hook's bands provided a significant contribution to Factory's creative and cultural legacy as well as resourcing the label's operations and the maintenance of the famously loss-making Haçienda, which became the subject of Peter Hook's first biographical book (Hook 2008).

Despite having music released on Factory Records, Massey's involvement with Factory was more peripheral, due to the bulk of his business dealings being with other organizations. However, our argument is that, as much as the 'punk revolution' provided the foundations for the rise of Joy Division, New Order, and 808 State, Manchester and the North West served to further these bands' artistic agenda by 'swimming against the tide' of neoliberalism in popular music. They felt compelled to try their hand in music, despite coming from modest social backgrounds and to develop their talent locally.

Peter Hook: punk to payment

Peter Hook came from a working-class family in Salford. His father was a driver for Frederick Hampson Glassworks in Salford. His father was abusive to his mother and his parents split when Peter was a child. Subsequently he and his younger brother lived with his mother and then with his stepfather, Ernest William Hook, whose name he adopted. In his second biographical publication, Hook paints a vivid picture of his North-West childhood:

> We were for a while a pretty normal single-parent working-class family: two-up, two-down, outside toilet, coal hole, living in Jane Street, Langworthy, in wonderful, dirty old Salford. When I saw Control, all those years later, I didn't even notice it was in black and white because it was exactly what my childhood had looked and felt like: dark and smoggy and brown, the colour of a wet cardboard box, which was how all of Manchester looked in those days.
>
> Hook 2012: 3

Hook's music career began in 1976 at the age of twenty. The aforementioned Sex Pistols concert on 4 June at the Lesser Free Trade Hall, attended by Tony Wilson and a number of other soon to be important figures, inspired Hook and his then friend Bernard Sumner to promptly acquire instruments and form a band. Hook went on to cofound two of the most influential British music groups of his generation and to enjoy success independently with many other music projects. The substantial revenues generated by his creative endeavours, as well as the cultural significance of his work, make him a perfect example of the 'adaptive musician'.

When we asked Hook about his motivations at the time of forming Joy Division, he replied that then he did not think in such terms:

> I had no idea what I wanted to do. I just wanted to emulate the Sex Pistols. It was as simple as that. There was no thought other than wanting to get on stage and tell everyone to fuck off. It was about being a punk and it was about channeling the aggression and the frustration you felt as a human being and as a teenager, not knowing what you wanted to do, what you wanted to achieve. When your hormones are boiling, that's how you feel: angry, nihilistic and aggressive. Music is a perfect antidote to this aggression.

What Hook is describing here are the characteristics of a romantic artist, who embarks on a career in music out of desire for self-expression rather than to achieve a stable income or even to become a star. He also testifies to his allegiance to punk culture, by emphasising strong emotions, as opposed to rational considerations. What connected the young Hook to punk culture was also a belief that to be a punk musician one does not have to be a virtuoso of an instrument, because the attitude is more important than knowledge or skill. According to Hook's testimony, at the point of deciding he was going to form a band in 1976 he did not have any musical training whatsoever. He taught himself to play bass guitar and he suggests that his auto-didacticism might be an important factor in the development of his unique style as an instrumentalist and composer (Hook 2012: 39).[1]

Whilst the nucleus of Joy Division – Peter Hook, Bernard Sumner and Ian Curtis – came together in 1976 with the intent of forming a band, it was not until 1977 that the line-up was completed with the addition of Stephen Morris. With the pre-Joy Division name of Warsaw, they began developing a cohesive musical entity. Hook considers that their musical naivety at that time was beneficial, as it liberated them from the rules and conventions that restricted other musicians. There were numerous other factors contributing to the appeal of Joy Division, including the distinctive performance style of its front man and the lyrical content that connected them thematically with the youth of the era. Another important factor in the band's transition from amateur to professional status was the introduction of manager Rob Gretton. Only twenty-three when he took over the helm, Gretton kept the band together and freed its members from many organizational tasks, allowing them to focus on their creative outputs. By Hook's admission, the members of Joy Division were making limited progress as a self-managed band, so Gretton's arrival was seen as a very positive development. He coordinated recording activities, television and radio appearances, logistics and touring schedules, initially in the North, then further afield, advancing into Europe, consequently growing the band's fan base. As the band were about to embark upon a tour of North America, Ian Curtis died by suicide on 18 May 1980. Whilst the band had gained significant traction prior to the untimely death of Curtis, paradoxically, interest in Joy Division, increased substantially in its wake. The premature demise of the band on the brink of wider success, and the relative shortage of material, served to further reinforce its cult status.[2] The music from Joy Division is still very popular today, in part thanks to the sense of its authenticity, to which Hook alludes in the interview.

The death of Ian Curtis changed the situation of the members of the band, renamed New Order, in a dramatic way. For a start, they lost the focal point of the band and the principal lyricist. In the light of the difficulty of replacing

Figure 6.1 Peter Hook performing live with 'The Light' at the inaugural Unknown Pleasures concert, 18 May 2010, at his club Factory251, Manchester. Photo courtesy of Mark McNulty.

Curtis, the vocalist role was taken by Bernard Sumner, who was previously the guitarist and keyboard player in Joy Division, whilst Gillian Gilbert was introduced to take the pressure off Bernard instrumentally. Perhaps more importantly, the band changed its formula – from a punk-oriented, guitar-based format to a hybrid band, drawing heavily on electronic instruments and new technology. It should be noted that Joy Division were keen to explore technology and their music did incorporate the use of synthesizers, however emerging technologies became a key feature of New Order. Hook's bass guitar work continued to be a prominent feature in the new sound. The new approaches helped locate them at the cutting edge of British popular music. This transition was strongly encouraged by Gretton, who recognized the potential of combining electronic and conventional rock instruments before New Order's competitors did and provided the band with equipment that at the time was expensive and difficult to access, including prototypes.[3] Hook suggested that the band's reputation for embracing new technology led to them becoming a testing ground for new equipment produced by the manufacturing companies. New Order achieved even greater commercial success than Joy Division, whilst still maintaining its status of authenticity.

Although Joy Division and New Order found substantial audiences and had chart successes, this did not translate into its members earning a high income from making music. As Hook admits, their material needs were taken care of by Gretton, but they weren't rewarded financially in the manner commensurate with their chart success. Although it is impossible to say with precision why was there this gap, the most likely factors were Gretton's prioritizing 'investment' in the band over instantaneous gratification, as well as the fact that they were the most profitable of 'Wilson's projects'. The revenue the band created was thus in part used to subsidise other Wilson operations, in a way typical for the period. It is also plausible to suggest that Gretton represented the new type of 'neoliberal' manager, as described by Timothy Taylor (Taylor 2016: 48): somebody who not only managed but also largely 'owned the band'.

The arrangements with Gretton presented both advantages and disadvantages for the band. The advantage, as Hook admits, was freeing the musicians from financial considerations, which allowed them to focus on their music. At the same time, he alludes to the relationship with Gretton as having hegemonic overtones. 'A Manager always keeps the band poor and when they complain, he throws them a bone', he told us. Such an approach helped Gretton to keep the members of New Order focused and motivated them to work with a high level of productivity. The downside was the lack of money to plan long term and the discouragement of engaging in activities outside the band. The firm grip of Gretton may also explain why the members of New Order were known for not giving interviews. For Hook, who is an extravert, it must have been difficult not to be able to express himself this way.

As Hook attests, ten years after he began his career in music he still hadn't accumulated any wealth for himself, despite his role in the creation of numerous hit records. This made it increasingly difficult for Gretton to not acknowledge by financial reward. Moreover, as the members became older and more experienced, their material needs increased and this was again, causing them to question what had happened to the wealth generated by their activities.

As was the case with New Order, it is not uncommon for band members to seek alternative vehicles to express their creativity. Hook invested in the Suite Sixteen recording studio in Rochdale in 1984, providing him with an environment to independently explore the role of producer and subsequently produce music for other musicians, such as *Elephant Stone* for the Stone Roses in 1990 and *Paranoid* by Inspiral Carpets in 1994. From the early 1990s, Hook was able to benefit by compounding the revenues from the legacy of the Joy Division and New Order catalogues and adding personal projects, such as the two band projects Revenge (formed in 1989) and Monaco (formed in 1996). The combination of legacy and new projects resulted in Hook finally 'seeing money', as he put it. However, as was the case with all break out projects from the members of New Order, none attained the level of success the band achieved together.

Hook remained a member of New Order until 2007, although the band was on hiatus between 1993 and 1998. Rob Gretton died in 1999, but his estate still benefits from the earnings of Joy Division and New Order, an arrangement that was not uncommon at the time he started to work as a manager for these bands. After his death, Gretton's assistant Rebecca Boulton became the new manager. Although the band still worked in the shadow of Gretton, New Order's relationship with their management has changed. If Gretton were still around, would his strong personality and influence have been able to help to prevent the development of irreconcilable differences between the members of the band, which finally led to the widely publicized dispute between Hook and the remaining members of New Order? This dispute not only affected negatively the myth and reputation of the band's members, but also cost them a significant proportion of their earnings which may have been factor in their increased activities as producers and performers of music. Hook's current managers are hand-picked and whilst his team is comprised of accomplished and successful professionals, they are seen by him more as facilitators of his agenda than its architects. As he puts it, now he 'directs his career'.

Hook has continued through the 2000s and subsequent years to instigate and participate in new music projects, including Man Ray (2010) and Freebass (2010), a collaboration with two other bass players from important Manchester bands, Gary (Mani) Mounfield from the Stone Roses and Andy Rourke from the Smiths. Hook's own record label Haçienda Records served as a vehicle to release these recordings, further illustrating his tendency towards directing his own activities.

Hook has diversified his portfolio even more and has become a brand in his own right. He is a sought-after media personality and raconteur, appearing regularly on radio, television and at other public events. Most frequently he talks about his active projects and his time in Joy Division and New Order, but he also engages in other topics, such as the state of music, music technology and culture at large. He has also written three bestselling books, one that revisits Joy Division, which we quoted in this chapter, and another that revisits New Order. His first book that catalogued the rise and fall of the Haçienda, titled *The Hacienda: How Not to Run a Club* (2008), was ironically followed by a collaboration with music venue magnate Aaron Mellor and Ben Kelly, the architect who originally designed the Haçienda club. They created another club called Factory251, located in the site of the former Factory Records offices in Manchester and launched in 2010. Despite the difficult climate for clubs, this venture has continued to thrive as one of Manchester's most popular night spots.

A key activity for Hook is his work with his band, Peter Hook and the Light, which began in 2010. The band also features his son Jack who plays bass, like his father, enabling Hook to concentrate on vocals and key bass motifs. This vehicle was initially intended by Hook to recreate and provide fans with an experience, as close to seeing Joy Division live as possible, subsequently moving on to touring the New Order catalogue. Hook's work in this period also reflects the changing relationship between recorded and live music as dominant revenue streams. Whilst in the 1980s and the 1990s New Order's success was based predominantly on sales of recorded music, in recent times a substantial proportion of Hook's earnings comes from touring. To illustrate, in the second half of 2017 Peter Hook and the Light played forty gigs in the UK, Europe, Australia and New Zealand. In 2018, the band played thirty concerts in the United States in two months, equating to one in every two days.

Hook is also known for his DJing. As a consequence of the credibility of his artistry Hook is seen as a purveyor of taste. This activity allows him to travel flexibly with little equipment and present his music choices to audiences all over the world.

Another notable project Hook has played a key role in is 'Haçienda Classical'. This has been designed as a live experience combining a large symphonic orchestra with electronic instruments as a reimagining of the music and the Haçienda club experience. Starting off in Manchester's classical music venue the Bridgewater Hall, the show has been seen in major venues including the Royal Albert Hall in London and had outdoor festivals built around it. Other legacy brands such as Gatecrasher and Cream have also replicated this formula. Hook is the owner of the Haçienda brand and also the protagonist of Haçienda Club nights, which are typically concert-level and often 'pop up' events on key calendar dates, attended by thousands of people. It is worth noting here that from its launch in 1982 until its demise in 1997, the Haçienda was a significant drain on the revenues generated by New Order. Whilst its commercial performance was arguably disastrous during its lifespan, its cultural legacy continues to endure, presenting opportunities for Hook to recoup some of his losses from the venture, in the present day. In this sense, Hook can be seen as a successor to Wilson, who managed to learn from the mistakes of his predecessor, whilst also recognizing his achievements. Clearly having found a satisfactory way to balance his creative and business agendas Hook is able to acknowledge 'There is nothing nicer than being in control of your own destiny'.

Graham Massey: payment from punk

Graham Massey was born in 1960 and like Hook, is also from a modest working-class background, being the third of four brothers raised in Levenshulme, Manchester. At the time of his childhood and teenage years, progressing to higher education was not common in his social milieu however, his academically gifted older brother attended grammar school and later studied at Oxford University. This success provided a context of expectation for Massey, even though, by his own admission, he was not particularly academic. Massey considers that the success of his brother contributed to him gravitating towards an 'arty persona' however, opportunities to become such were not facilitated by the education system. Despite his fascination with musical instruments, he was denied music education at school due to not passing a simple test to get into the choir: 'I felt aggrieved that music had been shut out of my life at school', he confessed to us.

Another factor contributing to his draw towards music was the contradiction of Thatcher's Britain. There was an expectation that everybody had to get a job, but actually finding a job was not a 'serious option' in the 1980s, especially in the North of England where the Fordist order was crumbling and unemployment rates were very high, fuelling frustrations, especially with the younger generation. Under such circumstances, in some ways very similar to the situation in contemporary Britain, where opportunities for young people are very limited, taking up music seemed like a natural thing to do, as it offered a chance of channeling one's energy and making a career.

Consequently, despite not having formal musical training, Massey taught himself how to play a range of musical instruments. In this sense, not unlike Peter Hook, he was a product of punk, with its rejection of virtuosity and putting attitude higher than technical skill. Another source of inspiration for Massey were 'noise artists' such as Brian Eno, who likewise were not pursuing conventional virtuoso practices. That said, he was also influenced by styles such as progressive rock and space rock, where musical virtuosity was treated with a higher esteem.

Between 1978 and 1988, Massey was involved in various music projects in the Manchester area, representing different genres and influences, including punk, jazz and hip-hop. This period he describes as a time of preparing himself for the music industry. Massey's first record release in 1980 was the *Weird Noise* EP under the mantle of 'Danny and the Dressmakers'. This was a nine-track seven-inch record featuring four additional bands. Massey describes this as an LP condensed onto a seven-inch vinyl. The allegiance to punk aesthetics and ideology of this production was not just reflected by the low-fi recordings and the degradation through format choice but also the name of the record label, Fuck Off Records, which was based in a squat in London and was affiliated with Better Badges and Rough Trade. Massey himself admits that at the time, despite the dominance of punk ideology, getting a record out was 'a rare thing'. To this young musician, just to have a record put out was a major achievement. As Massey attests', to have been able to contribute to the history of music in any way was such a badge of honour', and even more so if it was played by John Peel.

One of the key developments in the late 1970s and early 1980s in Manchester music was the Haçienda's predecessor, the Factory Club, a regular occurrence held at the Russell Club in Hulme, set up by Tony Wilson and associates. It became a vital conduit and testing ground for the Manchester creative community, offering a space for alternative music and multimedia art. The

Factory Club provided the reason for the formation of another Massey project called Biting Tongues, which was instigated by Howard Walmsley with the intention of producing a sound track for his silent film of the same name. Massey and fellow band member Colin Seddon disbanded the Post Natals to join Walmsley and others, including Eddie Sherwood who later joined Simply Red. In the interview, Massey referred to the notion of 'musical socializing' as part of his preparation for the music business. It is likely that Massey's presence in the creative communities and consequential networking would later help him to become a central figure in the Manchester music scene. Biting Tongues released on a number of record labels, initially on Situation 2, a subsidiary of Beggars Banquet. Massey points to the fact that whilst many Manchester musicians in this period tried to remain true to their northern roots, it was not always possible and they had to integrate their careers with conducting some business operations in London. Despite interfacing with London institutions, Massey felt that it was important not to relocate there and hence has always maintained his base of operations in Manchester.

Massey recalls that DIY record labels in the 1980s were often poorly resourced and could go bankrupt in between commissioning a recording and it being completed. This was the case with New Hormones, a pioneering Manchester-based

Figure 6.2 Graham Massey performing at his fiftieth birthday celebration event at Blueprint Studios. Photo courtesy of Joel Fildes.

DIY-label, which was founded by the Buzzcocks and their manager Richard Boon and was responsible for releasing the Buzzcocks' 'Spiral Scratch' EP (1977). Massey considers New Hormones to be a precursor to Factory in its somewhat idealistic, yet haphazard approach to making and selling music. In particular, unlike the successful independent record labels with one or more successful bands on their roster that allowed the funding of more obscure projects, New Hormones did not sufficiently care to balance more commercial projects with the experimental ones and thus was constantly in danger of going bust. In 1981, Biting Tongues released *Live It,* their second New Hormones album, on cassette but for the following planned release the label literally ran out of money half way through the recording. Consequently, the material was released by Paragon in 1983. After this, Biting Tongues went on to release three records on Factory Records, the first being in 1984.

As we mentioned earlier, Wilson was notorious for informal business practices. It is thus perhaps not surprising that there was no long-term commitment between the band and the label. In its place, there was a release-by-release arrangement where Factory financed recording and production, with profits being evenly shared between band and label. This type of deal was very different to those issued by the major labels at the time, again marking a different ideology to that pertaining to neoliberalism, as discussed by Taylor. From Massey's perspective, the advantage of such an approach was giving the chance of making a record to a large number of artists who otherwise might never make their debut, without much economic pressure. The disadvantage consisted of the lack of long-term planning and sustainability, hence a difficulty for these artists to move from amateur and semi-professional status to becoming professionals. It could be argued that being under Wilson's wing forced the artist to 'adapt', which was the case with the protagonists of this chapter.

In the case of Massey, part of this strategy was learning new skills, in particular moving from performing to producing music. In the years 1985 to 1987, Massey sought formal education in the technical aspects of music production by studying at the School of Sound Recording (SSR) in Manchester. Learning production skills provided the foundation for Massey taking a prominent role within 808 State studio activities, to which we will soon turn. In the second half of the 1980s, Massey added a further dimension to his repertoire by becoming what Brian Eno describes as a 'studio musician', for whom the studio, rather than a guitar or piano, is a principal instrument (Eno 2004). This made him more akin to scientists or engineers who labour in their labs in solitude, rather than to ordinary musicians who jam. Massey, probably intuitively rather than by design, tried to reconcile his affinity to studio work with his punk heritage.

In 1987, Massey formed a hip-hop collective called 'Hit Squad MCR' with fellow Mancunians A Guy Called Gerald (true name Gerald Simpson) and Martin Price. This morphed into 808 State in 1988, and the name was derived from Roland's 808 electronic drum machine, in this way announcing the band's affinity to electronic music. Price already had a footing in the music business, gained with his record shop Eastern Bloc in Manchester's Northern Quarter. This was beneficial in many ways, such as providing a window to the musical output of the time, including niche music from the UK and overseas. It also provided a component to inform the overall 808 State approach to business. In 1988, Price's record label, Creed, self-financed the release of 808 State's debut album *Newbuild*, by way of a manufacturing and distribution deal with Southern Records. Whilst receiving critical acclaim and being cited as seminal by artists such as Aphex Twin, the record initially was not a commercial success.[4]

At the time, rave culture was coming to prominence in Britain in places like the Haçienda and Warehouse Parties, which made Massey, Simpson and Price aware of the great impact of this music on social behaviour and the formation of subcultures, an agenda that was synchronized with the music they were then making. He describes how they were able to combine avant-garde, leftfield practice and punk attitude and re-platform it into dance music. To Massey, what had previously been fringe music was now a social music that had come to the centre. Consequently, when talking to record companies, they were the experts and ahead of the curve, a fact no doubt contributing to the creative freedom they were afforded. At the same time, the relationship with Factory and Tony Wilson continued to develop, with Wilson providing exposure for 808 State to TV audiences, when the band was in relative infancy and could not afford to pay for publicity. 808 State continued to develop their operations in the manner of DIY, controlling their own creative agenda and organizing their activities.

The next step was the signing of a record deal with ZTT records, a London-based independent label with the backing of a major record label (Warner), affording the band 'the power of a major but the front end of an indie'. ZTT was known for its cutting-edge approach to making music and avant-garde taste, as signified by its name, which was taken from FT Marinetti's sound poem, *Zang Tuum Tumb*. Yet, at the same time, it was successful in reaching a wider audience (Gillon and Mazierska 2018).

808 State was drawn to the attention of ZTT's Paul Morley by a Friday evening alternative culture TV programme on BBC2 called *Snub TV*, which ran a feature about the band, in itself testimony to the progress they had made independently, without external music business intervention. The notion of a 'ready made' artist who has established their potential to be a bankable investment for a record label was a relatively new concept at the time, but 808 State was seen this way by ZTT. While working with this label, Massey enjoyed the benefit of strategic advice and the major marketing engine of Warner music, as is evident from promotional videos such as 'Cubik' and 'In Yer Face', as well as what may or may not have been contrived publicity such as Massey being cited as the 'Most Eligible Bachelor of 1991' in lifestyle magazine *Company*. Massey recognizes that they were being commodified through such means. However, the foundations they had established and continued to pursue were based on authentic music, hence they were able to maintain the perception of being credible.

The testimony of 808 State's success in the late 1980s and the 1990s was measured not only by the popularity of their own output, but the demand for collaboration and remixes. In this period, Massey collaborated with artists such as Bjork, David Bowie and many others. Such brand association was often based on strategic alliances. He became a model example of a musician whose work is organized around discrete units, 'projects', which have a specific time span. This involves employing workers on short contracts and paying them on the basis of accomplishing specific tasks, unlike a band, which is a long-term project to which members dedicate all their energy and typically share costs and profit evenly. As one of the authors of this chapter argued elsewhere, production of music this way is typical for electronic musicians and fits well the approach to work pertaining to neoliberalism (Mazierska 2018; see also Webb 2004).

Inevitably, being in demand meant that Massey could support himself through music and amassed a significant reputation and wider cultural capital, which proved important for the sustainability of his career. This means, for example, being able to invest in resources such as equipment and being able to produce music independently of external circumstances. Massey also adds that an important factor in his and 808 State's sustainability was the way the band managed their finances, creating a limited company that they controlled as their commercial vehicle, paying themselves modest salaries and supplementing this with the periodic royalty payments.

By the late 1990s, Massey had become a musician with a large portfolio of genres and projects. This included film and television music such as the 808 State produced theme tune for the popular Channel 4 youth culture programme *The Word*. This aspect grew in significance from the 2000s, namely during the crisis years of the recording industry. His current portfolio includes a range of performance and production vehicles, including Sisters of Transistors and Massonix, the latter of which he was encouraged to embark upon by Autechre. This incarnation is an experimental solo project, as well as a vehicle of collaboration with other electronic artists, particularly in live contexts. Another of his projects is the jazz-influenced Toolshed, an ensemble of musicians whose line-up and size depends on the circumstances. These projects function flexibly – they can be used in the studio and easily assembled in performance contexts.

As we mentioned, Massey fits well the idea of a studio musician and the studio also is the means of his income. That said, Massey is aware of the importance of live events under current circumstances and he plays live regularly in a plethora of scenarios, from solo performance as a DJ to large ensembles playing traditional instruments, such as the 'Part Time Heliocentric Cosmo Drama After School Club', which was formed in 2013 as a tribute to Sun Ra.

In common with Peter Hook, Massey can be seen as a musician who continues to build his portfolio. The proof of that is his continued maintenance of 808 State, through building his digital legacy and presence on social media. A sign of his awareness of the value of the brand was to appoint Key Music Management and the recent decision to produce new material under this name and tour with his band. 808 State's live shows are not only in demand for heritage and nostalgia events, but also as a key feature of contemporary youth music events, such as Galaxiid (by Russian DJ and producer Nina Kraviz) in 2017.

Conclusions

This chapter compares two musicians from the North of England, with the aim of identifying the main factors in the longevity of their careers. The largest part of their success is due to their talent, commitment and, to use the old-fashioned word, 'authenticity'. Hook and Massey did not approach their music making with the intention of getting rich. Rather their orientation was towards self-expression.

However, we also argued that both Hook and Massey benefited from embracing counter culture, particularly the punk ideology, deciding to pursue a career in music, despite the lack of formal training, family tradition and, initially, the scarcity of financial means to support themselves. They also took advantage of the fact that in the 1980s Manchester became a major centre for the production and consumption of music, able to compete with London, which increased the options in terms of signing record deals at a time when having such a deal was a crucial factor in having a music career. What connects them is also their embrace of new technology, especially electronic. This allowed Hook and Massey to move from rock to electronic music and to also develop new approaches to making music, placing them ahead of the curve and translating to dominant position in the youth-oriented popular music. Their relationships with the music industry may have also been a key factor in their success. In the case of Hook there was Rob Gretton and Factory; in the case of Massey his consortium, ZTT and Warner. These agents facilitated the proliferation of their musical output. According to Hook, Rob Gretton was of the view that you should 'never let your band peak'. It could be suggested that this in part explains why New Order were able to produce hit records over such a long period of time.

They are both artists with a large portfolio of activities, which increases their income and cushions them against the volatility of the music industry. Both artists also devote a substantial part of their energy to maintaining their legacy. What connects, yet also differentiates them, is also an ability to direct and manage their own financial affairs. However, whilst Massey learned it from the beginning, in part because his operations were not as profitable as Joy Division and New Order, Hook learned it with the passage of years and is currently in the position of 'managing his managers', namely using them to organize his artistic life whilst being in charge of his overall strategy.

What can the aspiring musicians of today learn from the trajectories of Hook and Massey? In our opinion, further to the lessons learned by Hook and Massey, success in music, probably more than in most professions, is an outcome of many factors that are outside of the musician's influence, such as the existence of conducive environments accessible to the artist for the production, commoditization and consumption of music. From this perspective, English musicians were always privileged over their counterparts in continental Europe and those from the North found themselves in this position in the 1980s. Another lesson is that it can be difficult to make a proper living in a music scene while it is still booming, although with the passing of time it can open itself to 'heritage-ization' and commodification. Finally, most successful musicians need to endure a long period of 'apprenticeship', accepting not 'seeing money' at age thirty or working for ten years as an amateur before becoming a professional. In short, to be successful in music, one has to be as ready for success as for failure.

Notes

1   Hook cites a number of factors that contribute to his distinctive sound and playing
    style, including his posture and the influence of Stranglers Bass guitarist Jean-Jaques
    Burnel. However, the technique of playing the higher notes on instrument was a
    response to him being dissatisfied with how his early equipment, pertinently his bass
    speaker, sounded when playing the lower frequencies. Consequentially Hook's bass
    changed from being a supportive instrument to a prominent feature carrying many
    key motifs. This gave his playing an authentic dimension, serving to differentiate
    both Joy Division and New Order from other bands of the time.

2   Several successful films devoted to Joy Division, most importantly *Control,* act as
    confirmation of this longevity, as well as being a means to prolong it. Joy Division
    has also been cited as influential by many musicians, with prominent bands
    including Radiohead and Smashing Pumpkins recording and performing Joy
    Division songs.

3   One of the distinctive elements of *Blue Monday* was the kick drum used on the
    introduction and throughout the song which, as Hook recalls, was created using an
    early version of the Oberheim DMX drum machine. According to Paul White, who
    was the person at Oberheim Electronics responsible for the DMX, there were only a
    handful of the first version of these drum machines made, and there were significant
    differences between that and the commercially available unit.

4   Only when 808 State became more prominent did the limited production run of
    this record make it sought after, which was reflected in the inflated second-hand
    price.

References

Eno, Brian (2004), 'The Studio as Compositional Tool', in Christoph Cox and Daniel
    Warner (eds), *Audio Culture: Readings in Modern Music*, 127–30. London:
    Continuum.

Gillon, Les and Ewa Mazierska (2018), 'The Missing Star of MC Tunes', in Ewa
    Mazierska (ed.), *Sounds Northern: Popular Music, Culture and Place in England's
    North*, 174–89. Sheffield: Equinox.

Haslam, Dave (1999), *Manchester England: The Story of the Pop Cult City*. London:
    Fourth Estate.

Hook, Peter (2008), *The Hacienda: How Not to Run a Club*. London: Simon and
    Schuster.

Hook, Peter (2012), *Unknown Pleasures: Inside Joy Division*. London: Simon and
    Schuster.

Mazierska, Ewa (2018), *Popular Viennese Electronic Music 1990–2015: A Cultural History*. London: Routledge.

Mazierska, Ewa and Kamila Rymajdo (2017), 'The North and Europe in *24-Hour Party People* and *Control*', in Ewa Mazierska (ed.), *Heading North: The North of England in Film and Television*, 235–55. London: Palgrave.

Nice, James (2011), *Shadowplayers: The Rise and Fall of Factory Records*. London: Aurum.

Robertson, Matthew (2006), *Factory Records: The Complete Graphic Album*. London: Thames and Hudson.

Spicer, Al (2006), *The Rough Guide to Punk*. London: Rough Guides.

Taylor, Timothy D. (2016), *Music and Capitalism: A History of the Present*. Chicago, IL: The University of Chicago Press.

Webb, Peter (2004) 'Interrogating the Production of Sound and Place: The Bristol phenomenon, from Lunatic Fringe to worldwide Massive', in Sheila Whiteley, Andy Bennett and Stan Hawkins (eds), *Space and Place: Popular Music and Cultural Identity*, 66–85. Farnham: Ashgate.

Wilson, Tony (2002), *24-Hour Party People: What the Sleeve Notes Never Tell You*. London: Channel 4 Books.

Witts, Richard (2018), 'Manpool, the Musical: Harmony and counterpoint on the Lancashire plain', in Ewa Mazierska (ed.), *Sounds Northern: Popular Music, Culture and Place in England's North*, 17–36. Sheffield: Equinox.

7

Where Do We Go From Here? The Future of Composers in the Post-digital Era

Lars Bröndum

The aim of this chapter is to discuss some of the effects that digitalization has on the daily life of composers. Digitalization has changed the music world in ways we never could have imagined. The CD first came to the market in 1982 and other formats such as CD-ROM, CD-R and the CD-RW followed shortly after (Peek 2010:16). The digital CD was very successful commercially and quickly replaced vinyl LPs. Techniques to crack the copy protection and rip the CDs soon followed and perfect copies could be made without any signal degradation (Dahlstrom et al. 2006: 7). The development of compression algorithms, such as the MP3 format, allowed the file size to be reduced, thus making it easier to share the music. In the beginning of the 2000s, the growth of the internet was substantial and digital services such as Napster and Pirate Bay paved the way for illegal file sharing (Sundberg and Rydell 2009). In the last decade, legal streaming services and music download services such as Spotify and iTunes have replaced much of the illegal file sharing. It is now easy, cheap and convenient to listen to streamed music. Digitalization also has changed the way we create music. Music software has become very sophisticated and affordable. The internet has opened up new possibilities for marketing music and selling it all over the world.

We are now almost two decades into the twenty-first century and it is interesting to reflect and ask how digitalization has changed the reality for composers. The first part of this chapter is a short background examining some opposing views on what music is, what a composition is, and how to define a musician and composer in a pre-and/post-digitalization context. The second part presents interviews with four contemporary Swedish composers, which focus on questions relating to marketing, distribution, economy, community and the possible future of the music industry in the post-digital era. The composers represent a wide span of music genres: pop music, free improvizational music, live electroacoustic music and computer game music.

The new tools

In the 1970s, the music industry focused on a few fortunate bands that had the privilege to record albums in studios, followed by tours and promotion to sell the albums. Studio time was very expensive. Buying music (primarily LPs) was generally how I spent my weekly allowances. Roughly fifty years later the digital technology has developed fast. With the development of personal computers, easy-to-use software and the internet, music creation has changed. Digitalization has affected how we create music, how we listen to music and how we communicate about music. Instruments are today inexpensive and many people order them online. Actually, today you do not even have to invest in instruments: in low-cost or free computer programs such as Garageband (Apple Inc. 2002), many virtual instruments are included for free. Furthermore, you no longer have to get blisters from hours of practising the guitar. You can simply drag pre-recorded loops to tracks in your favourite digital workstation and your music can be made available to almost anyone in the whole world through the internet – just a few mouse clicks away. So what is the problem? Everything is affordable, easy and everyone has a fair shot at becoming a music creator. This was the stuff one could only dream of back in the 1970s. But there is a dark flip-side to this development. One serious problem is that the economy has drastically changed and streaming services such as Spotify and Youtube pay almost nothing to the indie composers. Another problem is that since the digital music tools are very affordable and easy to use, the competition has increased. The consequence is that many professional composers have to survive with almost no revenue from their music.

> The industry was said to contribute towards high levels of anxiety and depression given the precarious nature of the work, an inability to plan one's time/future, the nature of self-employment, anti-social hours, exhaustion, and, crucially, low or often zero pay.
>
> Gross and Musgrave 2016: 13

The exponentially growing options of digital tools should bring new creative possibilities, but may do the opposite. It may bring a feeling of becoming creatively stressed, constantly looking for and learning new tools. Psychologist Barry Schwarts draws attention to the 'paradox of choice':

There's no question that some choice is better than none, but it doesn't follow from that that more choice is better than some choice. There's some magical amount. I don't know what it is. I'm pretty confident that we have long since passed the point where options improve our welfare.

Schwarts 2005

If one looks at iOS, Apple's highly successful operating system for iPhones and iPads, the amount of available software has exploded, from a few apps to now millions (Statista 2017). The longevity of many of these software applications is also sometimes limited, meaning the composers have to regularly learn new software.

Changing definitions

What is music, who is the musician and what is composition? As stated earlier, it is not the aim of this chapter to try to define or answer those questions in depth. It is, however, of interest to look briefly at some definitions that other writers/ researchers have stipulated and how it has changed in a pre-digital and post-digital context. A pre-digital definition from an ethnomusicologist view is presented by Alan Merriam: 'There is no question that music is symbolic, but the difficulty lies in the precise nature of what is meant by symbolism' (Merriam 1964: 230). The society we live in interprets this symbolism and gives the symbols meaning. Merriam continues to describe music and musicians:

> The formation of a sub-culture based on music, as well as the identification of a sub-culture partially through music, seem to be fairly widespread both in nonliterate and Western societies, and particular kinds of roles and behavior for the musician are equally widely distributed. Such problems are of high importance if we are to understand the behavior of the musician as a human phenomenon. To what extent and in what areas of the world is the musician a specialist? What constitutes professionalism in given societies? Is the role of the musician ascribed or achieved, and what are the requirements for being a musician?
>
> Merriam 1964: 144

It is interesting to note here that Merriam states that a subculture often can be defined by its music. An opposing post-digital view may be found in Rasmus Fleicher's *Post Digital Manifest* (2009), as Fleicher suggests that music does not assign us to a group but to a global community instead. Fleicher is a proponent of free file sharing and was active in 'Piratbyrån'[1] (Sundberg and Rydell 2009: 84). He asks:

> 'What kind of music do you like?' There was a time when this question was a given when new friendships where made. These days it is on the impolite side, or at best comical in its unstated reference to the record shelf in the living room. Today, we discover new music infinitely much faster than before the Internet. We are familiar with much more of it, filling our pockets with amounts that not long ago were unfathomable. But how can we possibly choose? What about our ability to be touched by music, or more materialistically: our bodies' ability to be set in motion by music? Has it been heightened or reduced?
>
> Fleischer 2009

In this context it may be argued that subcultures are less important in the post-digital world. Music is perhaps no longer such a strong force in uniting small groups of people. We have a larger international reach today and music expands beyond our own countries and cultures. The skate punk lover may join a community on the internet that has members from all over the globe and of differing age, race and sex (no longer just a tight net of friends in the neighbourhood or tribe), and perhaps the 'sub' in a subculture is not applicable anymore. Merriam writes, 'who the musician is, how he behaves, what society thinks of him, and why these patterns emerge are questions of vital importance to a thorough understanding of music as a human behavior' (Merriam 1964: 144). It is, in other words, an integral part of humanity to express ourselves through music. Fleicher (2009: 69), on the other hand, has quite a different idea of what music is: 'Music gathers crowds. Music takes time. Music takes place.' Thus, it is interesting to look at Merriam's definition of what composition is in a pre-digital context:

> Composition seems clearly to be the product of the individual or a group of individuals and not to differ radically between literate and nonliterate peoples save in the question of writing. All composition is conscious in the broadest sense of the word when viewed from an analytic standpoint. Composers may be casual individuals, specialists, or groups of people, and their compositions must be acceptable to society at large. Techniques of composition include at least the following: the reworking of old materials, the incorporation of borrowed or old material, improvization, communal re-creation, creation arising out of particularly intense emotional experience, transposition, and composition from individual idiosyncrasy.
>
> Merriam 1964: 184

What has changed from this definition? A few things come to mind. For example, the statement that Merriam makes that 'creating arising out of particular intense emotional experience' may in a computer-generated piece not be applicable here. In electroacoustic music, computer-generated pieces have been around for a while, where stochastic principles might be the determining factor in programs such as Music V (Koenig 1970: 3). Developments with algorithmic composition have progressed far, and an example of this in pop music today is Hatsune Miku, a completely digital product who does not exist in reality. As described on Wikipedia:

> Hatsune Miku (初音ミク?), sometimes referred to as Miku Hatsune, is a humanoid persona voiced by a singing synthesizer application developed by Crypton Future Media, headquartered in Sapporo city. She uses Yamaha Corporation's Vocaloid 2 and Vocaloid 3 singing synthesizing technologies. She also uses Crypton Future Media's Piapro Studio, a singing synthesizer VSTi Plugin.
>
> Wikipedia 2014

Her voice is constructed from samples of voice actress Saki Fujita and the vocals are programmed with Yamaha Corporation's programs Vocaloid2 and Vocaloid3. Hatsune Miku also performs live using video projections. The digital girl is portrayed to be a 16-year-old girl with long turquoise pigtails.

Hyperinflation of music

According to *Dagens Nyheter* (a leading Swedish newspaper), Daniel Ek, CEO of Spotify, was in 2017 one of the ten highest earning CEOs in Sweden (Flores 2017). According to Daniel Seabrook's article in *The New Yorker*:

> Ek was one of the pirate band. Before starting the Spotify company, he had briefly been the CEO of uTorrent, which made money in part by monetizing pirated music and movies on BitTorrent, a major file-sharing protocol ... Later, the Napster co-founder Sean Parker, for years Public Enemy No. 1 to record-company executives, joined forces with Ek.
>
> Seabrook 2014

So how has the post-digital attitude of music changed our view of music? Some vivid examples can be noted in the trial against Pirate Bay. In her closing statement, prosecuting attorney Monique Wadstedt described the people behind Pirate Bay:

It's like lying on your back and letting the fried sparrows fly into your mouth, whether you are hungry or not. Sparrows also lie around you so you can consume them whenever you want to, without it requiring any sacrifice from you. Of course you get a certain feeling of fullness.

Wadstedt quoted in Fleicher 2009: 6[2]

Fleisher describes the digital multitude as follows:

The abundance is an abyss. We all know what it is like to sit paralysed, staring down into an all too large playlist. 16381 objects. 63 days, 10 hours, 38 minutes, 19 seconds total time. 131.92 GB. The same feeling also arises when we use a service where the music is streamed directly from a central server, where one only has to search and push the play button. In both cases we are given options verging on the infinite. All of the alternatives are equally close at hand.

Fleicher 2009: 14

Or as one reviewer, Rasmus Landström, interprets Fleicher:

Suddenly I've got a word for what has happened to my own music listening. From [my record collection] being a capital product with recorded music [it] has become a consumer product. And from being identity-building my collection has become almost irrelevant. I can still get what I want when I want it. Suddenly I get an expression of that feeling that makes me sometimes think that my music listening has become less important. The feeling of 'shuffle nihilism' and that the music is just a background noise suddenly has hit me.

Landström 2010

In a lecture at Moderna Museet (The Modern Art Museum) in Stockholm, Brian Eno called digital streaming 'the endless tap of music' (Eno 2014). He expressed tedium over the thought that music can surround us 24 hours a day.

When the internet was in its infancy, slow modems were used to transfer files and documents. But gradually the transfer got faster and, as previously mentioned, the compression algorithm MP3 was developed. MP3 enabled compressing the music to make it small enough to distribute it on the internet; this happened around the turn of the millennium. It was pretty innocent and geeky at the beginning, but when revenue was beginning to shrink for record companies, composers and musicians, and record stores were closing down, the music industry reacted by suing people for sharing music. The downloaders started to counter-react and radically proclaimed that music should not be owned (Fleicher 2009). For example, Fleicher in his *Post Digital Manifest* postulates ways on how music shall be enjoyed. Gone was the old capitalist idea of 'owning' music.

This was great for everyone, except for those for whom music was their main source of income. From Napster and Pirate Bay and onwards to legal ways to enjoy music, such as Youtube and Spotify, things haven't changed so much for the artists. Spotify lets the user have the entire music catalogue where the revenue is partly collected by using commercials and subscriptions. And, slowly, we see meagre payments now dripping into the music creators' bank accounts, but it is nothing like the revenue generated by sales of LPs and CDs in the 1970s and 1980s. According to IFPI statistics:

> In 2016, the global recorded music market grew by 5.9 per cent, the fastest rate of growth since IFPI began tracking the market in 1997. This was a second consecutive year of global growth for the industry with revenue increasing in the vast majority of markets, including nine of the top ten. This growth, however, should be viewed in the context of the industry losing nearly 40 per cent of its revenues in the preceding 15 years ... The revenue stream accounts for 14 per cent of the market but remains significantly undervalued.
>
> IFPI 2016

However, the report does not show who benefits from this increasing growth in the revenue. Is it shareholders in Spotify and Youtube (which is owned by Google) or the most commercial artists that benefit? The indie composers and musicians are still waiting for a fair share of the revenue. Spotify's algorithm favours most famous artists at the expense of those who are less well known. Seabrook explains it as follows:

> But exactly what is the royalty rate for a single stream? It depends on many factors. The more popular you are, the higher your metric. Some countries' streams are worth more than others. Free, ad-supported streams are worth less than subscriber streams, because the company makes less on ads than on subscriptions ... According to the company's web site, the average stream on Spotify is worth between six-tenths and eight-tenths of a cent. If you do the math, that means that around a hundred and fifty streams equal one ninety-nine-cent download. But that metric is hard for many musicians and record executives to accept.
>
> Seabrook 2014

The big acts are also at an advantage in finding new ways to spread their music. For example, 2.8 million copies of Prince's album *Planet Earth* were distributed in cooperation with the *Daily Mail* (Rydell and Sundberg 2009: 235). U2 and Apple tried a joint venture by uploading the album *Songs of Innocence* to unknowing iPhone users via iTunes. Bono eventually had to apologize for this as it angered many listeners (Grow 2014).

In conclusion, a few observations can be made. It seems clear there has been a change in the post-digital society in regard to attitudes to most aspects of music. There is a sense of devaluation of music because of the abundance of free or almost free music. There also seems to be a difficulty with which music creators are racing to catch up with the increasing speed of technological advancements and trying out new ways to make a living from music. And, importantly, the revenue from digital streaming and downloading is still lagging behind, especially for smaller labels and artists.

A Swedish context

In Sweden, music export has grown since the 1970s and has become very successful. In the article 'Beyond ABBA: The Globalization of Swedish Popular Music', Ola Johansson lists reasons for this success, such as governmental and institutional support, high levels of technology and early musical training in subsidized 'after school' programmes (Johansson 2010: 134–41). Johansson points out that because of a shift towards a neoliberal economy and negative changes to the welfare system, there is now less money in Sweden for supporting music and asks, if the support continues to decline, can talent continue to develop? (Johansson 2010: 140). In an investigation for a Konstnärsnämnden (Swedish Art Council) report from 2009, Fredrik Östling states:

> I have observed that most composers combine composing with other forms of work. Security is from that point low. Whatever the genre the composer/ songwriter belongs to, it is a form of 'star-economy', where only a few can live solely on the income from his or her compositions.
>
> Östling 2009: 75

I have already mentioned examples of the star-economy, such as hefty endorsements from major companies for U2 and Prince. Another such example is Metallica playing the online game *World of Warcraft* (Andy 2014) as promotion.

There is still a lot of money in music, but it is more concentrated and for a smaller list of celebrity musicians. How does the small-scale, independent artist survive without these sponsorships? Artists can supplement their income, as mentioned earlier, through applying for grants and running small companies as entrepreneurs. However, depending on grants is difficult and unpredictable as there is no guarantee of receiving them. It also very time-consuming to apply for grants, as there is no standardized system between the different grants providers. In Sweden, the government has encouraged artists to form their own companies called 'egenföretagare' (small-scale entrepreneurs, or one-man businesses). This is for many music creators a burden that involves complicated book keeping and tax declarations, and they may have to hire consultants to manage their businesses, which of course is an additional expense for an already strained budget. Östling's investigation concludes that, 'the cultural entrepreneurs are according to their self-image not regular entrepreneurs. Many of them are reluctant entrepreneurs' (Östling 2009: 78).

Out of the four musicians interviewed for this chapter, three regularly apply for grants. In Sweden there are many institutions that award grants and the main ones are Konstnärsnämnden (Arts Council), Statens Musikverk (Swedish Performing Arts Agency), Statens Kulturråd (Swedish Arts Council), and Vetenskapsrådet (Swedish Research Council). There are also many small private grants and scholarships, but these are usually tied to a region or a certain profile. The grants can range from approximately 4,000 to 10,000 Euros. A fortunate few music creators can in Sweden receive inkomstgaranti (guaranteed lowest income). Konstnärsnämnden currently supports 111 persons in the fields of art, music, form, theatre, dance and film with this guaranteed lowest income., which in 2016 was approximately 22,200 Euros. The income is reduced if the person earns money from their profession and falls to zero if their income is above 26,000 Euros (Konstnärsnämnden 2018). Another example of state support is Musikalliansen (funded by Staten Kulturråd[3]), which supports some 150 performing musicians (Musikalliansen 2017).

The interviews

I interviewed four Swedish composers about how they perceive their post-digital reality. The interviews were conducted separately via telephone. I selected the respondents with varied music backgrounds from pop, free improvization, electroacoustic music and sound design for computer games, to see if their experiences were similar or different. What they have in common is that they are independent composers and do not belong to a major label. They are small-scale entrepreneurs and they are all currently living and working in Sweden. Sten-Olof Hellström has been a professional composer and musician since the 1980s. He is now a part owner of the record company Schhh (schhh.se). He composes and performs contemporary music in the electroacoustic music genre. Lisa Ullén works with free form jazz and experimental improvized music, as a freelance musician/composer and with her own label, Disorder Production (http://www.disorder.se). Her work is also published on several smaller labels. Niklas Nähl is a sound designer for computer games. He has worked with companies such as Coilworks and is joint owner of Falling Tree Sound Studio (http://fallingtree.se). Erik Berntsson is an indie composer and musician who plays in several pop bands, such as Slowgold (http://slowgold.se) and Daniel Nordgren. He works mostly with music inspired by the 1970s, such as pop, psychedelics and blues.

The topics discussed in the interviews were marketing, the tools of music production, the economy, the community and the future of music in the post-digital era. For the question about how they market their music, it is interesting to note that there is a shift away from websites towards social media like Facebook and Twitter and other online resources, such as SoundCloud and Bandcamp. Ullén said she has not updated her website in years and Berntsson does not have a personal site any more. Nähl's studio Falling Tree uses a website as a portfolio, has a blog, and uses Soundcloud and pond5.com for sound clips, (sound) libraries and sample packets.

There was still a wish to market physical objects such as CDs, and LPs, but they all concurred that it probably never would regain more importance than that of curiosities. Berntsson seems to have more of a nostalgic image towards physical marketing with CDs and vinyl. He wished he could return to the analogue days and release music on vinyl: owning a vinyl engraver would enable him to do it his own way – to use different coloured vinyls and print in small series. Hellström was more positive and explained that digital technology has enabled his company to market their products globally with Facebook, Spotify and iTunes. According to Berntsson and Ullén, there is a growing counter movement against the digital music industry. An example of this is the return of cassette tapes and LPs, with some bands doing a small DIY release on cassette tapes and selling them at concerts and to friends. These analogue artefacts are often unique as they are individually made and sometimes the artists even fold their own covers. It is a return to a lo-fi medium with the aim of creating non-digital media as an opposition to digital media that can be duplicated endlessly.

Making cassette tapes is of course nothing new, for example Merzbow released noise recordings on cassette tapes in the 1980s on his own label and created his own home-made covers. However, the difference in cassette sales in the pre-digital era compared with today is that it is now more curiosities for marketing reasons than a source of income. The four composers expressed that marketing is a necessary evil in order to be able to make their music available.

The second topic discussed was whether the development of low cost digital tools is a blessing or a curse. The discussion touched on using digital versus analogue tools. Analogue equipment has made a comeback in recent years and is still considered by many as superior to digital equipment. The three composers corroborate this: Hellström, Ullén and Berntsson prefer to use analogue instruments, such as analogue synthesizers, acoustic pianos, drums, amplifiers, compressors, filters, distortion pedals etc. However, they also use digital technology for recording, editing and mastering (such as Pro Tools, Logic, Ableton Live and Max/MSP). Nähl often use a hybrid of analogue and digital technology when recording soundscapes and environmental sounds by using analogue microphones and processing them digitally. They all share the opinion that it is generally good that it is inexpensive to create music and that it is more democratic in the sense that most people now can afford to make music. Ullén said, 'it is in a way more democratic, but then one can discuss different qualities of what comes out of the noise?'

On the topic of economy all four composers explained that they have to rely on some way to supplement their income from music. This included working 'day jobs', such as teaching, and applying for grants. For example, Nähl works as a teacher to supplement his income. He spends a lot of time in the evenings, and at weekends and holidays composing sound design. Hellström's label *Schhh* does not generate enough revenue by just releasing music. They have many other projects that are related, for example sound excursions, concerts and workshops. The four interviewees concurred that it is almost necessary to run your own company for tax reasons, billing and so on. The composers that rely on grants also noted that there seems to be less money available – perhaps as a consequence of digital tools allowing for a growing number of composers/musicians. The grants level has not been adjusted accordingly either. Ullén expressed some frustration that musicians have to do everything themselves. She said: 'One wonders what kind of society we want. Should we have an artistic culture or is it going to be like in some other countries where you either have to be rich yourself to practice culture or have a rich sponsor?' Regarding the post-digital economy, all four agreed that independent composers receive hardly any money from music through sales. Berntsson suggested that there should be a system where internet users pay a fee (like public service television). Ullén also believed that a solution is needed and that it is not feasible that composers do not get paid. The main income for three of the composers comes from playing music live, but this does not generate enough money to live on. They all seemed to have the same issues and the post-digital music business presents the same problems and solutions. The economy is difficult to balance and they all had to multi-task: run their own companies, supplement income with other jobs, and apply for grants. It is interesting to note that the interviews show that the purpose of recorded music has shifted from being a way to generate income to a way to market themselves, for reviews and for grant applications.

The fourth topic was how the community has changed in the post-digital era. The four composers have experienced in some way the shift towards a more global community. The meeting place is to some extent on digital forums such as Facebook and Twitter, but mostly through physical networks such as music organizations, colleagues and friends. Ullén and Hellström belong to music organizations such as Fylkingen,[4] RANK[5] and EMS.[6] Ullén emphasized that it is important to have personal contacts and to work with musicians you really like. Berntsson points to the importance of building a circle of friends and like-minded people, and that is more conducive to take down the grand to the small and not fight against, or run after, the big companies. These music gatherings become, according to Berntsson, more intimate, almost 'like a ritual'. Nähl points out that for game music composers and sound designers there are also community meeting spaces such as game jams and discussion forums, and that the best way to make contacts is to socialize in person. In addition to the close 'physical' community the four composers also frequently use digital tools such as email, Facebook, Skype and Spotify to connect to the community on a global basis. Overall, there seems to be a need to meet outside the digital world and there still is a need for local community. In the best of worlds we can have both the small tight knit community as well as connections all around the world.

The final topic was how music will evolve in the post-digital era, which elicited similar replies from the four. They did not believe that they are going to be replaced by digital algorithms such as Hatsune Miku. They also felt that automated work and artificial intelligence will replace many of the traditional jobs and that we will have more leisure time, thus freeing up more time for the arts. Even though it is presently tough economically, none of the four interviewees would like to leave music as a profession in the future. They believed that there always are going to be ways for the musician to survive. Berntsson hoped that society will re-evaluate what employment is. For example, in Finland, there are trials running with a 'basic income',[7] where you have an income whether you work or not. This may enable the pursuit of dreams and ambitions without worrying about income from traditional employment. Hellström also added that sponsorship from the private sector will be more common in the future. Ullén responded that the next generation 'will continue our vision, even though it is a fringe that maybe only represents 1 per cent of the music market'. She added that 'the society can probably be evaluated by the art that is created and the effect it has on the society'. This is very much in line with Merriam's analysis of how musicians are defined in a society, as discussed previously. There is a curiosity amongst the younger composers interviewed about older technology. Nähl explained that there is a new retro movement where old games are re-released, for example 8-bit Nintendo and Commodore games. The two composers that lived through the period of vinyl LPs and cassette tapes did not seem very nostalgic. It is of course impossible to predict if the technology will shift back towards physical media again. There is a trend towards vinyl and cassette tapes but it is currently a niche activity. It is, however, interesting to note that new development seldom are clear-cut paradigm shifts, there is more likely to be two steps forward and one step back. None of the interviewees believed that music creation is going to be taken over by singing computer software like Hatsune Miku. There will always be a grass root resistance to the greater populistic forces. The torch of creative spirit will, as Lisa Ullén mused, 'be passed on to the next generation'. It is, as Merriam writes, something basically human to wish to create. Gibson's concept of affordances comes to mind: 'it is both physical and psychical, yet neither' (Gibson 1979: 129).

Conclusion

The opening quote by Merriam was that, 'who the musician is, how he behaves, what society thinks of him, and why these patterns emerge, are questions of vital importance to a thorough understanding of music as a human behavior' (Merriam 1964: 144). We certainly have a need to express ourselves and the possibilities are today in many respects better than previously. However, to make a living from music is harder, since music today is almost free for the consumer, and more people are fighting over a shrinking sum of money from grants and stipends. Even though there are signs of a return of material artefacts, such as LPs and cassettes, the music world has changed forever and will not return to the past. The interviews clearly show that the four musicians reveal aspects of a fractured lifestyle. The daily workload involves dealing with entrepreneurship, organizing events, applying for grants, communication, and the time devoted to practising music is shrinking. The financial burden also takes its toll according to the MusicTank study at the University of Westminster (Gross and Musgrave 2016) where they found that over 70 per cent of musicians suffer from depression. It is proper to reiterate Ullén's statement: 'The society probably can be evaluated by art and its effect it has on the society.' We are now well into the post-digital age – an age that offers little hope for music creators to regain decent revenues unless laws and regulations are imposed to make sure they are duly compensated. As stated earlier, Merriam wrote, 'What constitutes professionalism in given societies? . . . What is his social status?' (Merriam 1964: 144). One possible fallout from the post-digital economic hardship is that professional artists will be replaced by amateurs, who in turn may be replaced by digital algorithms. If we stop and take a minute to think and do not blindly rush into digitalization of all things man made, we may start to appreciate, empower and help fund the wondrous quirky and non-replicable unique art and music that only the 'analogue human' can express.

Notes

1 Piratbyrån, roughly translated as The Pirate Bureau, was an organization with the purpose to encourage file sharing and to be a counter movement towards the legal process suing file sharers: https://piratbyran.org

2 This was, according to Fleicher, stated by Monique Wadstedt at the trial against The Piratey Bay in March 2009. Original: En advokat slutpläderande: 'Det är som att ligga på rygg och låta stekta sparvar flyga in i munnen på dig, oavsett om du är hungrig eller inte. Sparvarna ligger också i drivor runt dig för att du ska kunna konsumera dem när du vill utan att det kräver någon som helst uppofring från din sida. Naturligtvis inträder en viss mättnadskänska.'

3 Swedish Arts Council

4 Fylkingen is an artist-run venue and association for experimental music and art: fylkingen.se

5   RANK is a Swedish Association of New Music Promoters: http://rankmusik.se/
info-english

6   EMS – Elektronmusikstudion is the centre for Swedish electroacoustic music and
sound-art: http://elektronmusikstudion.se/about/ems

7   See Henley's article about basic income: https://www.theguardian.com/world/2017/
jan/03/finland-trials-basic-income-for-unemployed

References

Apple Inc. (2002), Garageband. Available online: https://www.apple.com/lae/mac/
garageband/

Chalk, Andy (2014), 'BlizzCon 2014 Will Close with a Metallica Concert', *PC Gamer*,
21 October. Available online: https://www.pcgamer.com/blizzcon-2014-will-close-
with-a-metallica-concert/ (accessed 1 February 2018).

Dahlstrom, Dana, Nathan Farrington, Daniel Gobera, Ryan Roemer and Nabil Schear
(2010), *Piracy in the Digital Age*. University of California, San Diego, unpublished
paper.

Eno, Brian (2014), Lecture at Moderna Museet, Stockholm, 16 September.

Fleischer, Rasmus (2009), *Det Postdigitala Manifestet*, Ink Bokförlag, Sweden. Unofficial
draft. Translation to English by Johan Nyström Persson (2010).

Flores, Juan (2017), 'De tjänade mest 2017', *Dagens Nyheter*. Available online: https://
www.dn.se/ekonomi/de-tjanade-mest-2017/ (accessed 30 December 2017).

Gibson J.J. (1979), *The Ecological Approach to Visual Perception*. Boston, MA: Houghton
Mifflin Harcourt (HMH).

Gross, Sally Anne (2016), *Can Music Make You Sick?* MusicTank. London: University of
Westminster.

Grow, Kory (2014), 'Bono Apologizes for Forcing U2's Songs of Innocence on iTunes
Users', *Rolling Stone*. Available online: https://www.rollingstone.com/music/news/
bono-apologizes-for-forcing-u2s-songs-of-innocence-on-itunes-users-20141015
(accessed 9 February 2018).

Henley, Jon (2017), 'Finland Trials Basic Income for Unemployed', *Guardian*,
3 January. Available online: https://www.theguardian.com/world/2017/jan/03/
finland-trials-basic-income-for-unemployed (accessed 2018–02–27).

IFPI (2016), 'Facts and Stats'. Available online: http://www.ifpi.org/facts-and-stats.php
(accessed 15 February 2018).

Johansson, Ola (2010), 'Beyond ABBA: The Globalization of Swedish Popular Music',
Focus on Geography, 53: 134–41.

Karlsson, David and Lotta Lekvall (2002), *Den ofrivillige företagaren (rapport)*. Available
online: www.framtidenskultur (accessed 27 October 2014).

Koenig, Gottfried Michael (1970), *The Use of Computer Program in Creating Music*, UNESCO Rapport Music and Technology. Paris: La Revue Musicale.

Konstnärsnämnden (2017), Inkomstgarantier. Available online: http://www. konstnarsnamnden.se/konstnarsnamnden/stipendier_och_bidrag/inkomstgarantier (accessed 6 March 2018).

Landström, Rasmus (2010), 'Rasmus Fleicher Det Postdigitala Manifestet', *Dagens Bok*, 16 February. Available online: http://dagensbok.com/2010/02/16/rasmus-fleischer-det-postdigitala-manifestet/ (accessed 22 October 2014).

Merriam, Alan P. (1964), *The Anthropology of Man*. Evanston, IL: Northwestern University Press.

Musikalliansen. Available online: http://www.musikalliansen.org (accessed 13 February 2017).

Musikverket. Available online: http://musikverket.se (accessed 13 February 2018).

Östling, Fredrik (2009), *Komponistens villkor*. Stockholm: Konstnärsnämnden.

Peek, Hans B. (2010), 'The Emergence of the Compact Disc', *IEEE Communications Magazine*.

Schwartz, Barry (2005), *The Paradox of Choice*. TEDGlobal. Available online: https:// www.ted.com/talks/barry_schwartz_on_the_paradox_of_choice/transcript?share= 1ea6179d8f#t-1009194 (accessed 13 February 2018).

Seabrook, John (2014), 'Is Spotify the Music Industry's Friend or Its Foe?' *The New Yorker*, 24 November. Available online: https://www.newyorker.com/magazine/2014/ 11/24/revenue-streams (accessed 10 February 2018).

Statens Kulturråd. Available online: http://www.kulturradet.se/en/In-English/ (accessed 27 February 2018).

Statista, *Digital Music in the United States*. Available online: http://www.statista.com/ chart/2773/digital-music-in-the-united-states/ (accessed 27 October 2014).

Statista, *Music Album Sales in the US*. Available online: http://www.statista.com/ statistics/273308/music-album-sales-in-the-us/ (accessed 27 October 2014)

Statista, *Number of Apps Available in Leading App Stores*. Available online: https://www. statista.com/statistics/276623/number-of-apps-available-in-leading-app-stores/ (accessed 2 March 2018).

Sundberg, Sam and Anders Rydell (2009), *Piraterna, De svenska fildelarna som plundrade Hollywood*. Stockholm: Ordfront.

Vetenskapsrådet. Available online: https://www.vr.se.

Wikipedia, *Hatsune Miku*. Available online: http://en.wikipedia.org/wiki/Hatsune_Miku (accessed 27 October 2014)

8

Searching for International Success in Europe's Periphery: The Case of Gin Ga and Fran Palermo

Ewa Mazierska

This chapter considers the careers of two young indie bands, Gin Ga and Fran Palermo, operating on the peripheries of the pop music industry in Austria and Hungary, respectively. I am interested in establishing how wider circumstances, pertaining to the period of 'advanced convergent digitalization' (as explained in the introduction), when they began their career, the places in which they have operated and their specific career choices have affected their current standing and perspectives, in relation to their domestic and international careers. I also offer a hypothesis as to what the future holds for other bands who might follow in their footsteps.

My research is based on interviews with members of both bands and the manager of one of them, and textual analysis of their work from the years 2008–2017. As context, I will first sketch the history of pop-rock in the two countries and the existing research about the effect of convergent digitalization on the careers of upcoming musicians.

Popular music in Austria and Hungary

Much connects Austria and Hungary. These two countries once consituted one: Austro-Hungary, reigned over by the Habsburg family. Both countries also lost large chunks of their territory and population following the end of the First World War. Contemporary Austria has slightly less than 9 million people and is growing thanks to immigration, whilst Hungary has about 10 million people, but its population is falling due to a low birth rate and high levels of emigration.

Austria's capital, Vienna, is considered the capital of classical music. Here dwelt some of the most important composers of all time, such as Haydn, Mozart, Beethoven and Schubert, as well as creators of experimental music such as Arnold Schoenberg and Anton Webern. This classical musical heritage plays an important role in the way the country is perceived by foreigners and its inhabitants; every year millions of tourists visit Vienna to listen to the music of these composers and see places associated with their life and work. It is argued that the focus on classical music negatively affects the position of popular music in Austria. Not only is it disadvantaged by a low level of investment in popular music in comparison with that offered to classical music (Reitsamer 2011: 30), but also by a widespread perception that the country is locked in its past. Another specificity of Austria affecting its music is its physical and cultural proximity to Germany. This might be seen as an advantage, given that these two countries share the same language, which allows Austrian artists easy access to a much larger market. However, many Austrian artists believe that German listeners do not like Austrian accents, claiming that Austrian German is not really German and hence, to make pan-German careers, the performers have to conceal their national identity (Harauer 2001: 8–9).

Traditionally, the major music labels (the majors) were not interested in investing in the local talent, treating Austria merely as a market where they can sell large quantities of music produced in the 'centre', namely by Anglo-American artists (Harauer 2001: 16–17). The few international careers of Austrian pop-rock artists confirm this assessment. Those who managed to achieve international fame played down their Austrianness, either by singing in (non-Austrian) German or English, or by producing instrumental music. The latter is the case of Falco, the greatest postwar star from Austria, who mixed Austrian German with high German and English (Mazierska 2014: 33–42). Moreover, Falco attracted the attention of large record companies, such as AandM Records, which released his most popular record, *Falco 3* (1985), only after he proved to be a 'safe bet' by becoming the greatest star in Austria and a big star in Germany and many other European countries, hence virtually guaranteeing high returns to investors.

Another case in point is the international success of a group of electronic musicians who emerged in the early 1990s, such as Kruder and Dorfmeister, Patrick Pulsinger and Christian Fennesz. These artists played down their Austrianness by shunning lyrical content altogether, producing remixes of Anglo-American hits or composing instrumental music. They took advantage of technological changes and typically produced their own music and released it through local record companies, which they or their friends set up, and often sold their music by setting up online shops, being the first in Europe to do so. Electronic music is still the genre where Austrian pop-rock musicians receive most international recognition, as demonstrated by the success of Parov Stelar, Klangkarussel and HVOB. On some occasions the international success came at the same time or earlier than national fame. This is the case of Parov Stelar, who moved from his hometown of Linz almost straight to an international stage.

Austrian artists are not only disadvantaged by being treated as a colonial outpost of the global popular music industry, but also the relatively small size of the country, and especially the few large cities viable to hold concerts. As I was told by Falco's close collaborator, touring these cities takes less than a week and then one should wait at least half a year before visiting these places again, to give the audience a break and not look desperate for their attention. Aware of their provinciality, Austrians value most highly those artists with what can be termed 'international cultural capital', namely those that can prove they have achieved recognition beyond Austria's borders. For some time there was pressure to protect Austrian music on Austrian radio; for this purpose, some years ago the special interest group SOS Musikland was created. As a result, in 2009 the ORF (the Austrian national public service broadcaster) announced a voluntary regulation of 30 per cent Austrian music on its radio stations. However, in reality this quota was never achieved.

Hungary also has its fair share of important classical musicians, such as Franz Liszt, Béla Bartók and György Ligeti. Nevertheless, their importance does not overshadow pop-rock music in this country to such an extent as in its neighbour. Not unlike Austria, postwar Hungary can be seen as provincial in relation to an Anglo-American centre, but its situation was somewhat different due to being part of the Soviet Bloc. This meant that the cultural exchange with the West was made difficult not only due to the lack of interest of the West in the province, but also because the political authorities obstructed it by limiting opportunities for importing foreign records and local artists touring abroad. Despite these limitations and in part thanks to them, in the late 1960s and 1970s Hungary developed a strong pop-rock culture and within the Eastern Bloc it became a kind of rock empire, on a par with the larger countries of Yugoslavia and Poland. Many of its artists, such as Omega and Locomotiv GT, were fêted all over Eastern Europe. They benefited from staying on the 'wrong side' of the Iron Curtain because, in the domestic context and in Eastern Europe at large, they did not need to compete with Anglo-American rock to such an extent as pop-rock musicians in the other rock provinces, such as Austria, where access to Anglo-American music was not restricted by political factors. They were cheaper to book than British bands and their presence on the stages of countries such as Poland and the Soviet Union was less controversial. Moreover, despite their relative isolation, the local bands also managed to achieve success outside the Soviet Bloc (Csatári and Jávorszky 2016; Szemere 2017). This is especially the case with Omega, whose song 'Pearls In Her Hair' (1970) became an international hit, covered by many Western bands and in 2013 sampled by Kanye West in his track 'New Slaves'.

Paradoxically, after the fall of the Iron Curtain, Hungarian pop-rock enjoyed less international success, despite many of its artists switching to singing in English. This was a consequence of several factors. First, the connections with other Eastern European countries became weaker, because artists from 'friendly (ex-)socialist countries' receive no preferential treatment from music promoters and journalists, and thanks to platforms such as YouTube, Spotify and iTunes, Eastern European consumers now have access to the full range of western products. Second, for the global music industry, represented by the major record companies, Hungary, like the rest of Eastern Europe, has been predominantly a market to sell music from the Anglo-American centre rather than a place to invest and nurture local talent in the hope that it will become an international success. Such an approach became even stronger after the crisis of the record industry in the late 1990s. In this sense, the situation of popular music in post-1990s Hungary is no different from that in Austria during the whole postwar period. Also, in common with Austria, Hungary achieved greatest international success in electronic music in the last two decades or so, thanks to artists such as Yonderboi and Zagar, as in this type of music lyrics do not play as important a function as in (guitar) rock and pop, hence there is less risk of putting off the listener with poor English.

Anecdotal evidence suggests that Hungarians, more than Austrians, appreciate their own pop-rock. Budapest, in particular, has a vibrant music scene with numerous venues of different sizes, catering for diverse tastes. There are also many festivals scattered around the country's picturesque lakes, including several on Balaton, as well as Sziget Festival in Budapest (Szemere and Nagy 2017). Moreover, the openly nationalistic government of Viktor Orbán promotes protection of the domestic market for cultural goods against the influx of foreign products. This is reflected in the quota introduced in 2010 for Hungarian products in the media, which currently stands at 35 per cent and covers public service radio, as well as commercial radio, except for local/community radio stations (évi CLXXXV 2010).

Nevertheless, the relatively small size of Hungary and few large cities means that there are limited opportunities for musicians to make enough money from gigs to afford comfortable living. Another factor affecting income from live music is the relatively low wages and disposable income of Hungarians, which means that tickets for concerts must be cheap. That said, this problem is partly offset by a relatively low cost of living in Hungary and renders the country attractive to music-related tourism.

Making a career in music in the province during the period of advanced convergent digitization

Gin Ga and Fran Palermo started their activities in music during the period that the editors of this book label 'advanced convergent digitization' or 'post-digital'. It is worth reiterating briefly what this means for the upcoming musicians. In a nutshell, thanks to the increased access to studio technologies and software for producing music, the gap between professional and amateur musicians has significantly narrowed, in terms of equipment, knowledge, practice and sound. This has a democratizing effect on the career of musicians, who, at least in theory, can achieve the same level of proficiency as professionals without investing in expensive equipment and training. They can also sell their music directly to their fans, thanks to the infinite length of the 'digital shelf', on which the artists can place their products (Anderson 2006). As a result of this change, the pool of semi-professional musicians greatly increased, where a semi-professional musician: (a) has a self concept as musician, (b) strives for musical and organizational professionalism to enter the music market, and (c) already makes at least some money from musical activities (Marx 2017).

Whilst digital technologies have a democratizing effect on the production of music, they seem to have the opposite effect on distribution. As Gustavo Azenha pointed out as early as 2006:

> Just making music available on the internet does not mean it will be heard and consumed. Greater financial and technological resources allow major labels to more effectively promote and market online. For independent artists, the barriers to effectively promote and market music persist and are perhaps even greater

than in the past, despite examples of success stories that have been simplistically hyped as outcomes of internet empowerment.

Azenha 2006

Moreover, barriers to artistic success are especially high for those from the poorer classes and nations, which have more limited access to technological and financial resources and may also be limited by language barriers (ibid.), such as Eastern European countries and, albeit to a lesser extent, Austria. Andrew Leyshon goes as far as equating future opportunities for a musician's success with higher levels of education and wealth (Leyshom 2014). This opinion is confirmed by research concerning the politics of the majors in Eastern European countries. Michael Elavsky demonstrated in relation to the Czech Republic post-1990 that any attempts by the majors to market music from this country were nipped in the bud due to lack of faith on the part of the centre that the investment in the local product would pay off. The assumption of these powerful instititutions was that musicians from these countries should content themselves with success on the domestic market (Elavsky 2011).

The rational approach to such data for a young person from Austria and Hungary is to abandon their dream of success in popular music, especially international success, unless they are from a privileged background, similarly as the rational approach is not to spend money on buying lottery tickets. However, aspiring artists rarely believe statistics and, even if they do, most likely they discard them. This is partly because the need for self-expression is for many young people as great as the need to achieve a sustained income. Moreover, the media are filled with stories of individual success rather than collective failure. This is a part of neoliberal propaganda, which focuses on exceptional individuals, claiming – somewhat contradictorarily – that everybody can achieve comparable success if they try hard enough. Furthermore, the choice of a career in art or the creative industries in a wider sense comes across as less unsound if we take into account that many middle-class career paths, previously seen as sound (such as in academia), have become much more difficult.

The question is thus how to make money from music in this difficult climate, which largely translates into how to offset the decrease of income resulting from the 'triumph of free sharing'? The usual answer is to focus on selling live music. The increase in live events and ticket prices is presented by some authors as being more advantageous to the musicians as the decline in sales of records is disadvantageous. For example, Matthew David writes:

the rise of free sharing caused an increase in ticket prices and ticket volumes sold ... As artists receive payment for live performance rather than the promise of royalties that are almost entirely consumed by labels in the production of recorded works, artists are better off performing live than they are selling records. As the decline of the latter increased, the former artists benefitted from the decline in record sales.

David 2016: 59

This argument needs to be qualified, to take into account the position of different types of consumers and artists. In particular, David assumes that musicians' earnings is a matter of moving disposable income of consumers from one pocket (spent on records) to another (spent on concerts). This might be the case for some consumers, but not for all. In particular, many music fans tended to spend a large proportion of their income on records, but not on concerts, due to factors such as the lack of time, family situation, the distance from cultural centres or simply a preference for recorded music. When this group switched to services providing recorded music for free, their disposable income was not recuped by the music industry. Records can sell in very large numbers for a long time, providing sustainable income for artists, whilst concerts are ephemeral and can host a limited number of guests. What has not been earned in one gig will not be made up by another one. Even those musicians who enjoy playing live cannot do it continuously, as touring requires longer periods of rest or brings a distinct risk of physical and mental breakdown.

Furthermore, whilst the virtual shelf on which one can place records is practically unlimited, there in a limited space in which one can perform live. Austria and Hungary, including Vienna and Budapest, do not have many music clubs, and hence there is a queue of bands wanting to perform there. Similarly, there are only a few music festivals and they cannot host all bands operating in the country. Their choice is based on a number of factors, such as the band's reputation, as measured by critical recognition and the number of followers on social media, as well as personal connections with the artists, often facilitated by the band's management. The reliance on touring also points to the importance of continuously producing new material. This is because the audience wants to listen to new songs and festival organizers want to know that they invite a band with potential for development, as festivals tend to emphasize novelty. Moreover, being offered other opportunities to make money from music, such as composing music for films, television programmes and adverts, typically depends on having records that are commercially or critically successful. However, touring gives an opportunity to sell records and merchandise.

The model described above, in which live music is the main source of income for the artist, is regarded as a relatively new one in the western context, where recording constituted the foundation of the popular music industry for many decades (Marshall 2012). However, in Eastern Europe under state socialism, where royalties from selling records were low or an artist received a flat fee irrespective of the number of records sold, touring always constituted the core source of income and musicians were used to giving as many as 300 concerts per year and sometimes even more than one per day (Patton 2012; Ventsel 2016). Hence, it could be suggested that musicians in Hungary are better prepared to operate in such circumstances than those in the West, as they inherited this system and see it as natural.

Gin Ga: settling for semi-professionalism

I became interested in Gin Ga when listening to a box of CDs called 'Wien Musik', which included the best of Viennese music from specific years. I bought it in 2015, when visiting Vienna in relation to a project about Vienna electronica. I would like to emphasize this fact because, although I use YouTube, Spotify and Soundcloud, it is unlikely that I would have spotted Gin Ga on these platforms without any prior knowledge of their existence. Four other people whom I met who knew about Gin Ga – two Austrian and two Polish nationals – also learned about their productions through old-fashioned channels, namely Austrian and Polish radio, undermining the idea that social media is the main way to learn about newcomers.

The song on the CD was titled *Cinnamon* and to this day has remained one of my favourite tracks from Gin Ga. I liked its somewhat oriental melody and the extensive use of violin, untypical of mainstream rock music. In due course, I bought Gin Ga's records and was seeking direct contact with the band via email, in part to quench my fan curiosity but also to use them as a case study for this research. Consequently, in 2016 I met drummer Matias Meno twice, and on the second occasion I also met guitarist Klemens Wihidal, as well as their previous sound engineer. In this way, I learned about the band's history and their plans. Finally, in December 2017, I met the band's leader, Alex Konrad.

Gin Ga comprises four musicians: Alex Konrad, Emanuel Donner, Matias Meno and Klemens Wihidal, all born in the early 1980s. Konrad and Donner used to be close school friends, as were Meno and Wihidal. During this period they started to produce their own music, and eventually joined forces in 2003. They made two LP records – two versions of *They Should Have Told Us* produced in 2006 and 2008, and *Yes/No* produced in 2013 – and one EP, *10N1*, released in 2016. Since 2015, the musicians have also worked on solo projects: Meno as 'Meno', Donner as 'Eugene Delta' and Konrad and Wihidal as 'Mickey'. These works have been released or are to be released by summer 2018, first as videos on YouTube.

In interviews the band members admitted that from the beginning they saw themselves as an 'international' rather than 'national' (Austrian) band. Part of the reason for their cosmopolitan outlook resulted from specific personal circumstances: two members of the band, Konrad and Meno, have 'hyphenated' national identities. Alex Konrad's parents are Slovak and emigrated to Austria when Alex was two years old. At home the family communicated in Slovak rather than German. When Matias Meno was a child, he left Austria with his family to live in France. He spent his teenage years there and studied music, then returned to Vienna in his twenties. Konrad and Wihidal also spent part of their studies in London as Erasmus students. As a result of these experiences, their connection to Austrian culture is weaker than many of their peers and they prefer Anglo-American rock over Austrian and German music. When they started to make their own music the band's heroes were Radiohead rather than Falco or Kruder and Dorfmeister. Another sign of their cosmopolitan outlook is Matias changing his German name 'Lotsch' to 'Meno', as well as losing the 'h' in his first name, changing it from Mathias to Matias.

To realize their dream about international fame, the band, which was initially named Ginga, decided to sing all their productions in English. Their first record, *They Should Have Told Us*, was recorded in Vienna and paid for in part by the Österreichischer Musikfonds, an institution that supports the professional production of music in Austria. The record was greeted with positive reviews and interviews on radio and television and made some inroads into the Viennese alternative scene. There is no doubt that, apart from the music, one reason to attract attention to the band were its videos. These were relatively numerous and very effective, despite being made on a low budget, usually below €2,000. This was thanks to personal connections – their video director, Fanny Brunner, is a theatre director and real-life partner of the band's leader, Alex Konrad.

After the release of their first record, the band appointed two Belgian managers who worked for the label CNR Records Belgium, and one of whom,

Jeroen Siebens, worked with the four Austrian musicians in subsequent years. It is thanks to this connection that CNR showed interest in one of their songs, 'Fashion', but felt that to be successful for radio the song needed to be re-recorded. During the process, both the band and the label decided to re-record the whole of *They Should Have Told Us*, which took place in Belgium with remixing in London. Whether the whole operation ultimately paid sufficient financial dividend for the record company or themselves, the band was not sure, but it was worth doing from the perspective of personal satisfaction. Ginga felt that the new version sounded better and added to their self-perception as a cosmopolitan act. The 'Belgium connection' lasted until 2014. During this period, Ginga was renamed Gin Ga, to avoid being misspelt as 'ginger' – something the band has noticed when they spent more time in England.

Gin Ga's second album, *Yes/No*, was produced by Alex Beitzke, a successful Austrian producer based in London, who had worked with stars such as Ed Sheeran and Florence and the Machine. On this occasion the cost of production and of the accompanying videos were met by the band. Most of the work on the record took place in the North of England, where the band rented a house. Most likely, the effect of the collaboration with Beitzke and the context of the production resulted in a more mainstream 'English', as opposed to mildly oriental, sound of this record in comparison with the first one.

To some extent, the investment paid off, as the record contained Gin Ga's most successful song to date, 'Dancer', no doubt in part thanks to the simple, but effective video, shot on a staircase in an apartment block, where the band performs a type of acrobatic dance. The song was a success not only in Austria, but also in Poland, where it was played by Polish Radio 3 (Trójka), as well as receiving some airtime in countries such as Spain and Belgium. It also got over 220,000 views on YouTube and over 160,000 streams on Spotify. Following the recording, Gin Ga gave concerts in several European countries, such as Spain, Belgium, Estonia and on several occasions in Poland. However, their popularity in Poland, a country where they had the largest chance to make a mark, was not fully exploited by touring there or marketing in the media. The reason for this failure most likely lies in the lack of dynamism on the part of Gin Ga's management, as well as the members themselves. Konrad and Meno admitted that there were too many things to take care of: being a musician and cultural enterpreneur was at times an overwhelming task for the four members of the band.

Notwithstanding the above mentioned successes, even in their most prosperous period Gin Ga was never able to support themselves financially solely from their music. As a result, they had to combine producing music and touring with earning their living in a different way, and organized their lives so that these two activities were combined. In 2018, each of the members of the band is working in cultural industries or computer technologies and the bulk of their income comes from this activity, rather than music. In fact, they work outside the music industry partly to finance their music. Although their 'daytime' jobs involve a degree of flexibility – for example Konrad only works one week per month in film production, albeit very long hours – nevertheless it also reduces the time that can be devoted to music, forcing Gin Ga to prioritize certain aspects of their career.

The aspect they neglect is social media and marketing. For example, the band has its own website, but there is nothing there apart from its photograph. The site offers the option of signing up to the band's newsletter; I have done this but never received any newsletter. The band's Instagram account includes fewer than fifty photographs and more than a year has passed since a new one was posted. This also applied to the Twitter account as the band tweets rarely and the intervals between tweets sometimes approach a year. Neither does the band use direct-to-fan platforms such as Big Cartel, and confesses to being 'rather disorganized' in this respect. A sign of this was my own difficulty making contact with the band members. More activity can be observed on their Facebook page, but again it seems to me that they are less active than their competitors. Moreover, the way Facebook operates is also a source of frustration, because it charges users to deliver messages to the entire pool of their 'friends'. The neglect of their marketing side most likely reflects the lack of a local manager and a somewhat amateurish or romantic approach to their music, namely using it as a tool of self-expression rather than having a stable income. It might also reflect the fact that some of the social platforms that are widely used by musicians, such as Instagram, were introduced some years after they started their career, so they do not have 'social media in their blood', as do younger musicians.

Another sign of the band's leading towards 'romantic amateurism' is their approach to live music. Although they admit that this is the most viable way to have a stable income, this is not something to which they will commit, claiming that constant touring is exhausting. Moreover, they would not be able to choose such a lifestyle without neglecting their families and giving up their 'day' jobs, which are more lucrative. Furthermore, they rarely cover songs of other bands, focusing solely on their original repertoire. Ultimately, they are reconciled to their semi-professional position. This partly results from their recognition of and acceptance of the precarious work of young people. In their view, they have no straight choice between being a musician and a professional career, but between different precarious jobs, with music being the most attractive as it allows the higest degree of autonomy and self-expression. The internet allows them to continue in this capacity, rather than choosing between amateurism and professionalism.

As I mentioned earlier, since 2016 the members of Gin Ga have focused on different musical projects. I attempted to find out whether in these projects they have drawn on experience from their time in Gin Ga by, for example, investing more time and effort in marketing their music. I did not receive a clear answer, except from Meno and Konrad who mentioned that they now get more exposure on the radio. They also both admitted that it would now be wiser to sing in German, in light of the fact that Austria has become more inward-looking, but this will be difficult for them given their background, interests and general *Weltanschauung*.

Fran Palermo: diversified portfolio with a core

As with Gin Ga, my interest in Fran Palermo's artistic strategy followed my personal interest in the music. A journalist friend living in Budapest, Bence Kranicz, drew my attention to Fran Palermo after I told him about my trip to Vienna to interview Gin Ga and suggested that Fran Palermo could serve as a good comparator to the Austrian band. Kranicz arranged a meeting with the band's leader, Henri Gonzalez and another member, Dimitris Topuzidis, during my subsequent trip to Hungary in July 2016. Since then I also met the band's manager, Almos Galeotti, in May 2017 and invited Gonzalez and Galeotti to Preston in July 2017. I also attended a Fran Palermo concert and a solo concert by Gonzalez.

Henri Gonzalez (b. 1993) comes from a family of musicians. His father is a music teacher from Cuba and his mother is a Spanish-Hungarian ballerina, who met Gonzalez's father in Havana and returned to Hungary when pregnant with Henri. Gonzalez has four younger siblings, two of whom are also budding musicians. His father is currently living in Costa Rica, where he works in a music school, whilst his mother shares her residency between Hungary and Spain. Such mixed cultural, including linguistic, heritage, has influenced Fran Palermo's music, making it unique in the Hungarian context, but also affected Gonzalez's personal situation, not always in a positive way. He had to support himself

Figure 8.1 Fran Palermo. Photo courtesy of Henri Gonzalez and Almos Galeotti.

financially from a young age, balancing his need to develop as an artist with the necessity of earning his living.

Gonzalez set up Fran Palermo with school friends in 2011 and currently its members are in their early twenties. Initially it was a cover band, singing songs of bands such as Beirut, who also influenced its early productions. Their first original song, 'Arizona', is in the style of Beirut. It is a piece about desire for leaving and the difficulty of finding oneself in a new place – themes prevalent in many subsequent productions of the band. In due course, the proportion of cover songs in Fran Palermo's repertoire diminished and currently is less than 20 per cent. Since the band's inception, Gonzalez has written over 30 original songs and the band has released two albums, *Fran Palermo* (2015) and *Razzle Dazzle* (2016). A new EP, *Bonerider*, was released in October 2017.

The records received significant critical acclaim in Hungary, as reflected by a 2016 Petőfi Live Award for the best upcoming band, a prize given by the state-funded popular music radio channel. A sign of Fran Palermo's standing is their regular performances at the main music festivals in Hungary, such as the Sziget Festival, and at the largest music clubs in Budapest such as Akvarium and A38 Ship. Their most popular songs have over 100,000 views on YouTube and several have between 50,000 and 100,000 streams on Spotify. This might look like a modest achievement in comparison with mainstream British or American bands, but in Hungary they are amongst the most popular bands.

This success reflects not only the quality of their music, but also the efforts of the leader and the manager to make it well-known in Hungary. Galeotti told us that during a university placement at A38 Ship he met practically everybody who matters in the Hungarian music business: 'We hung out with a lot of people'. These local contacts pay off by allowing Fran Palermo access to the 'premium performance spaces' in Budapest.

Unlike with Gin Ga, which neglects its social media presence, Fran Palermo regularly updates its Instagram page where one can find information about its future and past concerts, records and other ventures. Gonzalez also has his own Instagram account, which serves to publicize his own and the band's activities, as well as to strengthen his image of a south-leaning and 'semi-exotic' artist with a penchant for modernist art, as reflected by frequent posts on artists such as Picasso and Miró as well as Gonzalez's own productions in their style.

Fran Palermo's presence on the international stage has so far been limited. The band performed several times in Transylvania, which is close to Hungary and has a large Hungarian minority, and at the festivals in Groningen in Holland in 2017 and Ljubljana in Slovenia in 2018. When writing this chapter, however, Galeotti was attempting to organize gigs in countries such as Austria and Poland. Both he and Gonzalez agree that only through performing abroad will they be able to gain international fandom, because putting songs in English on YouTube, Spotify and SoundCloud alone is not sufficient for this purpose.

Fran Palermo's line-up includes eight musicians, with Gonzalez as leader and the principal author of the lyrics and music. The line-up has changed many times, with several members leaving the band to study in Britain and Austria or to pursue a more stable occupation. Overall, there have been over thirty members of Fran Palermo up to this point, with Gonzalez and Galeotti as the only common denominator. This renders them less a band in the traditional, rock sense, which Gin Ga exemplifies, and more like a personal project for Gonzalez. The large number of musicians allows Fran Palermo to use a wide range of instruments, uncommon in rock bands, such as conga, trumpet, saxophone and rattles, as well as the traditional guitar, bass, drums and keyboard. This sets Fran Palermo apart from the majority of bands operating in a Hungarian context, which have a more traditional line-up, as well as from the popular 'Gypsy bands' whose music is based on traditional Roma motifs, even if repackaged for tourist consumption. Another reason for Fran Palermo's uniqueness is the large range of cultural influences from which the band draws, including Latino and African music. This is reflected in the titles of the songs, their lyrics, and the fact that Gonzalez sings in English and Spanish. However, there are also drawbacks to producing and performing such music in Hungary. The first is the sheer size of the band; this renders travelling expensive and uncomfortable as the band needs to rent a van to accommodate the members and their equipment. This is also reflected in the income from concerts. Even if it is sizeable, when divided between eight members it is reduced to pocket money. Consequently, apart from Gonzalez, the other members of the band have 'day jobs', such as working in a bar or as an assistant TV cameraman, or are students still living with their parents. Inevitably, the part-time character of their work does not incentivize them to devote their energy solely to Fran Palermo.

Another obstacle to achieving recognition in Hungary has been, until recently, their shunning of the Hungarian language. This has worked against the band in three interconnected ways. First, it alienated the part of the audience who does not know English (or Spanish) and cannot understand the lyrics. The advantage is that it might attract those who know these languages and get extra pleasure from understanding the songs. Anecdotal evidence confirms this opinion, as Fran Palermo is very popular with all my Hungarian academic colleagues, who appreciate the band's linguistic diversity. Not using the Hungarian language is also a factor of not being favoured by Hungarian state radio and other media, which are obliged to support national culture. Finally, shunning Hungarian is an obstacle to state support, which is typically directed towards national music. That said, as the band members and its manager admit, state grants are scarce anyway so are not factored into their career strategy. However, Gonzalez recently 'warmed up' to Hungarian. The band's last EP includes one song in Hungarian and this is the most-streamed track from the record. Moreover, at the end of 2017 Gonzalez started to perform a collection of Hungarian 'classics' of popular music merely with the accompaniment of a guitar. I attended one such concert in a club in Budapest and it was well attended, with the audience singing some of the songs along with Gonzalez.

The situation of Gonzalez is different from the rest of the band on a number of accounts. First, as leader of the band he receives a bigger chunk of income from gigs. He is also the sole beneficiary of the income from selling records, not least because he is the sole author of the songs and covers the costs of their production. Moreover, he is the only member of the band who combines playing in a band with a solo career. He frequently performs in Budapest clubs, singing and playing guitar, usually supported by his brother Daniel (also a member of Fran Palermo) on congas. Such performances are the main source of his income, largely because the fee does not need to be divided between eight people. Significantly, in these gigs the proportion of original songs of Fran Palermo is much lower; the majority are covers of popular songs, often Gonzalez's personal favourites from bands such as Foals, White Lies, Kasabian and the Doors. It is also possible that this choice reflects the type of audience he addresses, which is less focused and interested in the singer and just want to listen to something familiar. Gonzalez was also involved in the work of other artists, such as Péterfy Bori and Love Band from Budapest and a Spanish project called Music Madness Cash-Machine, which released its first LP in Budapest in 2017. He also performs with an electronic musician of Iraqi origin, Ramin Sayyah. As well as helping the artist to extend his audience and providing him with extra income, such guest appearances can be seen as a testing ground for his own work. Finally, Gonzalez has had some successes in selling his music to be used in commercials and films.

It is worth asking why Gonzalez does not give up on the band and focus on his solo career, or act as a guest artist on other musicians' projects and write 'commercial' music. Part of the answer is that his life (as those of the majority of artists) does not revolve around maximizing his income. Equally important is the sense of camaraderie from being in a band. Another factor is amassing a certain type of cultural capital thanks to playing in the band which furthers Gonzalez's solo career. He is a sought-after solo artist and guest performer because he is known as the leader of Fran Palermo. Finally, there is the hope that the band will achieve greater national and international popularity, which will allow its members to sustain themselves. This brings me to the question of the future of Fran Palermo and Gonzalez. Inevitably, there are three possible scenarios: sustainability, decline and greater success. It seems to me that the first would be relatively easy to achieve thanks to the high status of Fran Palermo on the Hungarian pop-rock scene and Gonzalez being perceived as not-quite Hungarian, which renders him unique in the Hungarian context. Of course, complacency and poor artistic choices might lead to decline. Some of Gonzalez's choices do strike me as poor, such as their first video to the song *Fritz Rock*, one of the band's most dynamic songs. The short film includes too many visual and filmic motifs and lacks a coherent narrative. Its 'visual diarrhoea' is also at odds with the aloof and ascetic image Gonzalez usually projects on stage. Given that the band has a limited budget for promotion, this video feels like a lost opportunity to present its work in an attractive way.

From talking to Gonzalez and Galeotti, it is clear that they strive for international success yet are aware of problems they have to overcome to achieve it. Some of these can be boiled down to financial investment, such as paying for transport and hotels abroad and marketing and 'smartening up' the band's productions. In particular, most likely it will pay off to produce more and better videos. Another way to widen the band's appeal is to produce new versions and remixes of their songs. This is important, as production of some of these songs leaves much to be desired, including their greatest hits, such as 'Am I Right, Boy?' and 'Monsoon', which enthuse audiences at concerts but sound flat when recorded. Furthermore, there is a need for Gonzales to work on his English pronunciation, which often betrays his Spanish heritage and leads to some phrases being difficult to understand. This problem is exacerbated by not including the lyrics on the record sleeves, or any information about the band except for titles of the songs. When discussing this issue with Gonzalez and Galeotti, they, not unlike the members of Gin Ga, argued that in songs music is more important than lyrics; hence not understanding the lyrics does not mean that the song will be rejected by the listener.

The question arises how these financial problems can be overcome. There are several possible scenarios. One is an increase in self-investment through channelling money earned elsewhere into music. This scenario is unlikely, given that practically all members of Fran Palermo treat their music as a way to make money rather than to lose it. The second scenario is finding music producers willing to invest in the band. Its corollary is that music labels in Hungary operate more as institutions offering services to artists rather than music producers in the old sense of investing in them in the expectation of multiplying their investment. A version of this scenario is using crowdfunding, but one cannot expect great investment this way, given the size of Hungary and the relatively low income of its population.

Conclusion

In this chapter I presented the careers of two bands, which although similar in some respects, most importantly in their desire to transcend the boundaries of a traditional rock and having an international outlook, also show differences in their career choices. Gin Ga privileged their international success from the beginning, as demonstrated by the type of work they produced and forging international links. They also settled for treating their music as semi-professional work. The strategy of Fran Palermo and especially band leader, Henri Gonzalez, is to create music that might appeal to foreign listeners, but build a sustained fan base at home and move towards increased professionalization by increasing the types of activities that bring income.

Although the sample on which I based my research is small, it confirms the view of Azenha (2006) that, paradoxically, in the era of 'convergent digitization' and globalization, investments in and support for artists from the peripheries will likely be less of a priority. Genres and artists from outside the USA, Western Europe and Japan, will continue to receive less serious support and attention from major labels. This continued marginalization will be especially salient for artists from non-English speaking countries with relatively small national markets (Azenha 2006). Accordingly, for provincials the local scene matters now more than ever before, because it is only in their own country or even their own city that they are able to compete with music coming from the Anglo-American centre.

References

Anderson, Chris (2006), *The Long Tail: Why the Future of Business Is Selling Less of More*. New York: Hyperion.

Azenha, Gustavo (2006), 'The Internet and the Decentralization of the Popular Music Industry: Critical reflections on technology, concentration and diversification', *Radical Musicology 1*. Available online: http://www.radical-musicology.org.uk/2006/Azenha.htm (accessed 29 November 2017).

Csatári, Bence and Béla Szilárd Jávorszky (2016), 'Omega: Red Star from Hungary', in Ewa Mazierska (ed.), *Popular Music in Eastern Europe: Breaking the Cold War Paradigm*, 265–82. London: Palgrave Macmillan.

David, Matthew (2016), 'The Legacy of Napster', in Raphaël Nowak and Andrew Whelan (eds), *Networked Music Cultures: Contemporary Approaches, Emerging Issues*, 49–65. London: Palgrave.

Elavsky, Michael C. (2011), 'Musically Mapped: Czech popular music as a second "world sound"', *European Journal of Cultural Studies*, 1: 3–24.

évi CLXXXV (2010), Törvény a médiaszolgáltatásokról és a tömegkommunikációról'. Available online: http://net.jogtar.hu/jr/gen/hjegy_doc.cgi?docid=A1000185.TV (accessed 20 December 2017).

Grőbchen, Walter, Thomas Miessgang, Florian Obkircherm and Gerhard Stőger (2013), *Wien Pop: Fűnf Jahrzehnte Musikgeschichte erzählt von 130 Protagonisten*. Vienna: Falter Verlag.

Harauer, Robert (2001), *Vienna Electronica; Die Szenen der Neuen Elekronischen Musik in Wien*. Vienna: Mediacult.

Haynes, Jo and Lee Marshall (2017), 'Beats and Tweets: Social media in the careers of independent musicians', *New Media and Society*, 20(5): 1973–93.

Leyshon, Andrew (2014), *Reformatted: Code, Networks, and Transformation of the Music Industry*. Oxford: Oxford University Press.

Marshall, Lee (2012), 'The 360 Deal and the "New" Music Industry', *European Journal of Cultural Studies*, 1: 77–99.

Marx, Tobias (2017), 'Musicians Among Themselves. Cohesion and performance of semi-professional bands'. Available online: https://www.researchgate.net/publication/317345883_Musicians_among_themselves_Cohesion_and_performance_of_semi-professional_bands (accessed 29 October 2017).

Mazierska, Ewa (2014), *Falco and Beyond: Neo Nothing Post of All*. Sheffield: Equinox.

Patton, Raymond (2012), 'The Communist Culture Industry: The music business in 1980s Poland', *Journal of Contemporary History*, 2: 427–49.

Reitsamer, Rosa (2011), 'The DIY Careers of Techno and Drum'n'Bass DJs in Vienna', *Dancecult*, 1: 28–43.

Szemere, Anna (2017), '"My Genes in My Suitcase, My Forehead in the Atmosphere": Perceptions of Hungarian popular music and its research abroad', in Emília Barna and Tamás Tófalvy (eds), *Made in Hungary: Studies in Popular Music*, 155–63. London: Routledge.

Szemere, Anna and Márta Kata Nagy (2017), 'Setting up a Tent in the "New Europe". The Sziget Festival of Budapest', in Emília Barna and Tamás Tófalvy (eds), *Made in Hungary: Studies in Popular Music*, 15–25. London: Routledge.

Ventsel, Aimar (2016), 'Estonian Invasion as Western Ersatz-pop', in Ewa Mazierska (ed.), *Popular Music in Eastern Europe: Breaking the Cold War Paradigm*, 69–88. London: Palgrave.

9

Electro Swing: Re-introducing the Sounds of the Past into the Music of the Future

Chris Inglis

As we are beginning to make headway into the twenty-first century, one of the most heavily used techniques in the production of popular music is the practice of sampling. This has become increasingly prevalent, particularly within contemporary electronic dance music, and now with more than 100 years of recorded popular music to pick and choose from, artists are beginning to look further and further into the past for inspiration. Perhaps counterintuitively, various pieces that make use of these 'vintage' samples now comprise some of the most forward-thinking and innovative instances of popular music, and this is no where more true than in the recently established genre of electro swing.

Of course, one may point out that artists have 'stolen' since time immemorial: 'Shakespeare from Ovid and Plutarch, Renaissance mass composers from Gregorian chants, Bartók from folk melodies, Bob Dylan from everyone, and blues singers from each other' (Williams 2014: 7). This is indeed true – but we have never quite seen a movement with such an outright emphasis on the stealing or borrowing of so-called vintage culture as electro swing. Through the practices of the various artists that will come to be discussed, it is demonstrable that EDM productions with an explicit focus on the past could well play a significant role in the music of the future.

It is important to establish first exactly what electro swing is. Of course, the terms 'electro', and 'swing' both represent specific genres – a simple fusion of which would not portray the genre entirely accurately. It is more useful to use Fikentscher's definition of the term electro: 'a commonly used label to market a variety of EDM styles' (2013: 139). Similarly, whilst the use of the term 'swing' may have proved useful during the early stages of the genre, it has since expanded to encompass a much wider degree of early styles. The unifying influence seems to be any dance-oriented style of popular music from roughly around 1900 to the early 1970s. It is for this reason that in recent years the genre has undergone a partial re-branding into what is now referred to as 'vintage remix'. In practice, both terms can be and are generally used to refer to the same thing, and I will use them interchangeably throughout this chapter.

A history of electro swing

There are varying accounts as to when the term 'electro swing' was first introduced. Michael Rack, the DJ behind the act Dutty Moonshine, argues that the term was first coined by the French label Wagram in 2009 to give a name to the collective sound of artists on the first of their *Electro Swing* compilations (Browne 2014). However, Marcus Füreder – who DJs under the name of Parov Stelar – claims to have invented the term long before this. In a 2012 interview, Füreder stated that 'I think it's seven years ago when I spoke to a French journalist. He asked me how I would describe the genre of some of my tracks and I said "electro swing"' (Bondy 2012). If we take Füreder's word, we can assume that the term was in circulation as early as 2005.

As with any style of music however, the roots of the genre go back much further than the introduction of any acknowledged term. It is impossible to pinpoint a precise moment to demonstrate the beginnings of the style, but an early example could be Herbie Hancock's *Future Shock*, released in 1983. Twenty years into his career as an accomplished jazz pianist, Hancock delved into the electro genre with this release with such enthusiasm that it has been described as 'this is where Hancock's restless creativity seems to find its main satisfaction – pioneering new electronic music' (Carr et al. 2000: 320).

The late 1980s would bring with them the arrival of jazz rap, primarily from artists coming out of New York. One of the first and most significant releases of this genre was Stetsasonic's 'Talkin' All That Jazz' (1988), which would set the scene for various emerging artists, including A Tribe Called Quest, De La Soul, Digable Planets, and the duo Gang Starr. Gang Starr's MC Guru was a particularly notable player with his solo release *Jazzmatazz* (1993), which as described in the liner notes, 'represents one of the very first full-fledged attempts to fuse rap and jazz'. And as with Herbie Hancock, Miles Davis would also begin to experiment with a fusion of jazz and electronic styles, working with hip-hop producer Easy Mo Bee for his final album, *Doo-Bop* (1992). Of course, Davis's involvement is unsurprising, considering his earlier so-called 'electric period'.

Alongside jazz rap, a number of other genres would begin to emerge around this time that would fuse jazz with electronic dance music. One of these was new jack swing, pioneered by producer Teddy Riley, who – in a play on Benny Goodman's title as the 'King of Swing' – came to be known as the 'King of New Jack Swing' (Hogan 2016). Working with artists such as Mary J. Blige and Michael Jackson, Riley would incorporate swing influences into their contemporary R&B sound. The genre of acid jazz would also play a part in the development of electro swing, where DJs such as Gilles Peterson would begin to mix jazz records with acid house, 'with its monotonous-yet-majestic, squelching analogue synthesizer basslines and melodies played over skeletal rhythm tracks – programmed on what sounds like cheap drum machines' (Cotgrove 2009: 58). Trip hop was yet another style to take influence from both EDM and jazz; first developed by Bristol-based acts such as Massive Attack and Portishead, the genre has been described as

> not 'real rap', not proper jazz, trip hop is in some ways a nineties update of fusion. But with a crucial difference; despite its fondness for jazzy flavours and blues keys, trip hop isn't based around real-time improvization but home-studio techniques like sampling and sequencing.
>
> Reynolds 2013: 396–97

The culmination of all these influences resulted in 'Lucas with the Lid Off' (1994) by the Danish rapper Lucas, which has been described as 'perhaps the earliest truly electro-swing record' (Hollywood 2010: 29). The track achieved some mainstream success (the music video was even nominated for a Grammy), although the evolution of the electro swing sound was still relatively slow. With the turn of the century came some one-off recordings such as Moby's 'Honey' (1999), Mr. Scruff's 'Get a Move On' (1999), and Jurassic 5's 'Swing Set' (2000), yet it wasn't until 2004 that 'a new genre as such really began to coalesce' (Hollywood 2010: 30). This year saw the release of Nicolas Repac's *Swing-Swing* (2004), and Parov Stelar's *Rough Cuts* (2004), the first examples of entire albums dedicated to the sound.

In the years following 2004, many acts would emerge who would play a significant role in the development of electro swing. Although most of the genre's development was occurring across mainland Europe, it is worth noting the formation of Goldfish, a South African duo who released their debut album, *Caught in the Loop*, in 2006. Back in Europe, the majority of the development was in France: in 2006 the turntablist group C2C won their fourth consecutive DMC team world champion title (DMC World DJ Championships 2015); the following year, Chinese Man released their debut album, *The Groove Sessions* (2007); and in 2008 Caravan Palace released their self-titled debut. As record labels caught onto the sound, compilation albums would also begin to emerge, including the aforementioned *Electro Swing* on Wagram, as well as *White Mink: Black Cotton* (2010), and *The Electro Swing Revolution Vol. 1* (2011).

A landmark moment came for the genre in 2010, with the release of Caro Emerald's *Deleted Scenes from the Cutting Room Floor* (2010). Released in her home country of the Netherlands, *Deleted Scenes* entered the Dutch charts at the number one spot, remaining there for 30 weeks, and breaking the record previously held by Michael Jackson's *Thriller* (NU.nl 2010). Emerald would later go on to experience similar success in the UK, with her second album, *The Shocking Miss Emerald* (2013) reaching the top of the British charts (Official Charts 2013) – the first electro swing album to do so.

The success of this album was perhaps due to its timing – 2013 was the year electro swing began to gain significant momentum in the UK. The clearest example of this is the launch of the Swingamajig festival, the world's first festival entirely dedicated to the genre. Headlined by the Correspondents, and featuring acts such as Lamuzgueule, Dutty Moonshine, and Mr Switch, this was a one-day event in the Digbeth area of Birmingham, which has continued annually since. Later on this year, electro swing would continue to entertain at British festivals. Winchester's annual BoomTown Fair for instance – set up as a mock city in which various districts are dedicated to specific styles of music – introduced the Mayfair Avenue district in 2013, focusing on the electro swing and vintage remix sound. Additionally, the first Maui Waui festival was held in 2013 in Suffolk. So, in the space of one year, three festivals with an explicit emphasis on electro swing had emerged in the UK.

Around this time, it would also become apparent that the genre was having an influence on mainstream culture, which is experiencing something of a vintage revival. One of the finest examples of this was the movie *The Great Gatsby* (2013), in which director Baz Luhrmann included an electro swing soundtrack. Making reference to this soundtrack, Luhrmann explains how this decision didn't come from 'Let's make a great soundtrack',

> it came from [F. Scott] Fitzgerald. When he wrote that book, he was a modernist, he was *in* the moment, and the music of the moment was African-American street music called Jazz, and when he put jazz music in Gatsby, everyone was like 'What are you crazy? It's a fad'. And then he put Hit Parade songs, pop songs, the

equivalent of Lana Del Rey singing a beautiful ballad. And [we tried to solve] the problem of 'How do you reveal the book, but how do you make it feel the way it felt to read it in 1925?' If Fitzgerald coined the phrase 'the Jazz Age', then I think we're living in 'The Hip Hop Age'.

Montgomery 2013

Buhrmann's description of his soundtrack sums up quite fittingly what the electro swing genre is intended to represent. Whilst the genre indeed takes influences from the music of the past, it also says just as much about how we are experiencing music in the present, and where the future is taking us. This point has been summed up by the electro swing artist Luca Gatti, who DJs under the name of Dr Cat: the genre 'not only [reconnects] with the past but springs out [into] the future' (Inglis 2017: 51).

Reconnecting with the past

Analysing Gatti's statement then, we may first look at the way in which the genre does indeed pay homage to the past. One could even say that electro swing features a degree of nostalgia, a suggestion that appears to be encouraged by its practitioners. An example of this can be demonstrated through Birmingham's Swingamajig festival, and specifically the 2014–15 New Year celebration event, as the poster for this featured the phrase 'party like it's 1929!' At events such as this one, and many other electro swing nights across Europe, not only do party-goers find themselves enjoying the music of the past, but often they will dress in vintage clothing, do vintage dances such as the lindy hop, and even drink vintage cocktails. It would seem that we have constructed a mythology around this particular era, in which revellers can experience the emotion of nostalgia to a considerable degree.

Nostalgia has been described as 'a mourning for the impossibility of mythical return' (Boym 2001: 8), and is a concept that can be found in many different musical genres, not just electro swing. Particularly in recent times, various genres have placed a great emphasis on the restoration and re-presentation of past sounds and styles, and can therefore be argued to encompass this nostalgic emotion almost self-evidently. This idea is certainly in contrast to the way in which popular music has traditionally been considered; Reynolds has made note of this, suggesting that 'pop ought to be all about the present tense, surely?' (2011: xviii), echoing the 'central tenet' of Strausbaugh's *Rock 'Til You Drop* that 'rock is youth music' (2002: 2). However, with the advent of such nostalgic genres,

Figure 9.1 Swingamajig, Birmingham, 31 December 2014.

including electro swing, Miller noted that 'rock now belongs to the past as much as to the future' (1999: 19), and Hogarty stated that 'popular music is simply not solely about youth anymore' (2017: 3).

Alex Rizzo, producer for the Brighton-based duo Skeewiff, has commented on these themes and discussed the reasons for the use of vintage music within his own productions:

> I also feel as if I am offering a service. An electro-swing track is part restoration, not just another remix. A lot of those incredible tracks could have been forgotten or disappeared over time as the masters were recorded in mono with a very limited frequency and dynamic range on shellac that degraded after the first few plays ... By refreshing old masterpieces, it gets the tracks out there and being enjoyed by a whole new generation ... and that is precisely what Skeewiff is all about.
>
> electro-swing.com 2012

It is essential to highlight the oft-forgotten point that early jazz would have been enjoyed in much the same way as we experience EDM today: 'jazz music began its life as dance music. Ragtime was used for cake-walking, New Orleans jazz was for street parades and swing-era jazz was for fox-trots and jitterbugs' (Thomas

2001: 166). This point has also been highlighted by Katz, who describes how 'early jazz was typically dance music, and bands were unlikely to cut a performance short if they sensed the audience would keep dancing, even if that meant playing for unusually long stretches' (2004: 74).

The type of music made by Rizzo, under the guise of Skeewiff, exemplifies this similarity. Drawing just as much influence from contemporary dance music as from jazz, Skeewiff do not appear to think either is superior, suggesting that they hold just as much affection towards the music of the past as the music of the present. Rizzo has commented on this too, explaining that 'there's a bit of everything we love I suppose . . . Hip hop, Exotica, Funk, Swing, Acid, Cha-Cha-Chas, Breaks, Spy Jazz, Soul . . . You name it – chances are there's a Skeewiff track that has a nod to it' (electro-swing.com 2012).

Another artist to have highlighted this connection is the Serbian DJ Marko Milicevic, who performs under the name of Gramophonedzie. Milicevic is notable for being one of the few artists to have had an electro swing track enter the mainstream, a feat he achieved with his single 'Why Don't You' (2010). In an interview with the *Telegraph*, Milicevic states that 'I realized swing was the club music of its time, similar in construction to modern dance music. There's build-ups, breakdowns, peak points, just put a beat and a groove underneath and it becomes familiar to today's clubbers' (Green 2010). He would later make a similar point in the *Independent*, arguing that 'swing and jazz is really fast, it was made for clubs and dancing, the only difference is it was made many years ago. There are songs by Judy Garland and Louis Armstrong you can play in clubs today with a slight tweak' (Verma 2011).

This brings about the suggestion that styles such as electro swing are simply the continuation of the original genre into the present day. Much like Baz Luhrmann's comments comparing the so-called 'Hip Hop Age' with the Jazz Age, many rappers such as Daddy-O of the group Stetsasonic have suggested that 'hip-hop is the jazz music of today' (McAdams and Nelson 1992: 24). As will be discussed below, music genres – particularly those such as jazz, in which experimentation is a key component – are expected to evolve, and a change in style does not necessarily constitute an entirely new genre.

This is not a new idea. In fact, some of the musicians of the original swing era made much the same points. To quote Louis Armstrong:

To me as far as I could see it all my life – Jazz and Swing is the same thing. . . In the good old days of Buddy Bolden. . . it was called Rag Time Music. . . Later on in the years it was called Jazz Music – Hot Music – Gut Bucket – and now they've poured a little gravy over it, called it Swing Music. . . Haw Haw haw. . . No matter how you slice it – it's still the same music.

McNally 2014: 246

Duke Ellington made this same point even more succinctly, simply stating that 'it's all music' (Luebbers 2008). Often, this lack of a strong distinction between various genres would actually be reflected in the music; Hustwitt points out that in the case of the Original Dixieland Jass Band, the 'song titles added to the confusion of terms: "Livery Stable *Blues*", "Tiger *Rag*", "Dixie *Jazz* One-Step"' (1983: 11). Through electro swing, this confusion has continued to the present day: one may cite various songs by Parov Stelar, including 'Dark *Jazz*' (2005), '*Ragtime* Cat' (2009), 'Booty *Swing*' (2012), and even '*Soul* Fever *Blues*' (2017), in which two supposedly distinct genres are referenced in the one song title.

It is undeniable that there are noticeable differences between the sounds of electro swing and the original music of the swing era, but when taking all of these points into account, this may only be due to a change in the era and to an extent the technology available. I would argue that – when ignoring the differences that unavoidably result from such music being produced in a different period – electro swing should be classified within the exact same genre boundaries as the original music on which it is based.

Building on this, it will prove useful to utilize Werner's idea of 'syndesis': a process that 'allows descendents to respond to previous works of art by incorporating elements of those works into their "new" creations' (1999: 334). Werner discusses how 'when a jazz trumpeter incorporates a Louis Armstrong riff into her solo or a hip-hop DJ samples James Brown, music transcends time' (1999: xii). This idea has also been mooted by Rietveld in relation to house music: the 'jazz attitude that plays with past and present forms of sounds in order to create a new form each time, thereby paying homage to a tradition and to a line-up of cultural ancestors' (1998: 17). This reference to a 'jazz attitude' within other styles of music is not uncommon; for instance, one may cite Thomas's analysis of MC Lyte's 1989 'Cha Cha Cha' (2001: 167), again reflecting the link between jazz and hip-hop.

As far as electro swing is concerned, I believe that one of the finest acts to demonstrate this idea of a 'jazz attitude' is the duo Goldfish. Whilst some of their songs, such as 'Wet Welly' (2008) and 'Get Busy Living' (2010) easily fit within the electro swing genre, others appear to sit within the realms of more established EDM genres, such as house and techno. However, even in cases such as these, I would argue that this 'jazz attitude' is still present. Band member Dominic Peters referred to this in discussing their track 'Drive Them Back to Darkness' (2013): 'we were jazz musicians so it's got that jazzy feel but then we kind of put like, almost like, rolling techno beats underneath it' (Goldfishlive 2013). What is possibly the best example of this comes in their single, 'Deep of the Night' (2016). To the untrained ear, this could easily be described as a purely EDM track, and it's true that the house influences are strong. Yet upon closer listening, a gypsy jazz guitar can be heard during the verses, reminiscent of Django Reinhardt's Quintette du Hot Club de France. Additionally, in live versions of the track (see GoldFish 2017: 11:10; Armada Music 2017; Expresso Show 2016), Peters regularly performs a piano solo in an explicitly jazz-like style, often featuring improvized interplaying with saxophonist David Poole. Examples like this can be found across the electro swing genre, where the jazz attitude is present even when the style of the song initially appears to be quite distinct from jazz.

As I have demonstrated, electro swing can certainly be shown to refer to, and to reconnect with the past. The more curious question emerges of what a genre that places such a high degree of importance on the idea of nostalgia can tell us about the music of our future.

Springing into the future

Given the previous points, we can conclude that electro swing may well be accepted as the jazz music of today, or at the very least, a descendent subgenre of jazz. The extent to which someone may agree with this statement likely comes down to their own personal definition of what it means for a piece of music to be considered jazz. It is worth spending some time analysing this idea, to demonstrate what this may mean for the future of the style.

A satisfactory definition of jazz is hard to come by. Attempts often point to some supposed key characteristics – such as a swung rhythm, or a degree of improvization – yet as argued by Harrison, jazz is far from this simple:

> Attempts at a definition of jazz have always failed, and this reveals something about its mixed origins and later stylistic diversity. Efforts to separate it from other, even related, types of music result in a false primacy of certain aspects, such as improvization. In fact improvization is sometimes absent from jazz, lengthy pieces such as Tadd Dameron's *Fontainebleau* having been fully composed on paper. Another supposed distinguishing feature is the type of

rhythmic momentum known as 'swing' (resulting from small departures from the regular pulse). But this, too, is absent from some authentic jazz, early and late.

Harrison 1986: 223

It is understandable why those who define jazz in such ways might object to the inclusion of electro swing under this banner. With the exception of certain practices common to DJing – such as improvized record selection – there is little-to-no improvization involved in electro swing. And ironically, despite the name, a lot of electro swing doesn't actually swing, preferring to take its beat from the standard 'four-to-the-floor' rhythm common to house music. Nevertheless, I don't believe that any of this should detract from its legitimacy as jazz music.

From the original days of ragtime, through early jazz, swing, bebop and the jazz fusion of the 1960s, the music that has historically been referred to as jazz has undergone many stylistic changes. The common thread that unites these various styles seems to be a level of experimentation, of pushing boundaries, and of breaking with tradition. Jazz musicians have regularly been at the forefront of cutting-edge music, and this appears to be far more of an essential characteristic than any specific stylistic technique. This is not to say that such stylistic techniques play no role, but simply not as definitive a role as a level of experimentation. And whilst jazz is not the only genre to feature this as a characteristic – some other notable examples being progressive rock and avant-garde music – I would argue that ensuring some degree of innovation draws us closer to a sufficient definition of jazz. As has been stated by DeVeaux, 'the essence of jazz is the process of change itself' (1998: 487).

Producer Hank Shocklee makes reference to this when comparing so-called 'trad jazz' acts with the jazz rap groups he was involved with:

the new guys who are coming up only mimic what they've heard in the past. And jazz was never like that. It was always an exploration music. It explored new levels, new sounds, new things. There was never a formula for jazz.

Dery 2004: 419

Shocklee's statement once again references this connection between hip-hop and jazz, a link that many hip-hop artists seem particularly eager to draw attention to. To quote jazz rap MC Guru, this movement is 'bringing jazz back where it belongs' (Smith 1994). It is possible to take Guru's statement as referencing the ghettoes in which jazz was born, the working-class cultures around which it developed, and an opposition to the type of elitism that jazz never originally exhibited; without detracting from these points, I believe there is more to his statement than just this.

As expressed by Nicholson, 'in the minds of many members of the public at large, and even some musicians, jazz today has come to represent the past rather than the present' (2005: x). It is undoubtedly true that – as discussed above – jazz is commonly thought of as a music associated with the past; a rather ironic idea when considering that this is a genre expected to experiment with new ideas. Thus, when Guru argues that the use of hip-hop brings jazz 'back where it belongs', he could easily be referring to the idea of belonging in the present, or even – the future. As a new experimental form (at least at the time of Guru's statement), hip-hop has brought new ideas to jazz, different and distinct to what had already been accomplished within the genre; and through the use of various styles of EDM, electro swing could be said to be doing very much the same thing. Indeed, it's been posited that 'perhaps more than anything, what defines the political character of dance culture is that it is not afraid of the future' (Gilbert and Pearson 1999: 184).

The electro swing DJ Richard Shawcross, who performs under the name of C@ in the H@, has commented on this suggestion that the genre is the future of jazz. Regarding how he would categorize electro swing, Shawcross states that 'if I had to define it under a broad umbrella genre, I would in fact call it Jazz, not Dance music' (Browne 2014). I have found that one of the most common criticisms that electro swing artists tend to make of others involved in the genre is that they have been lazy with the sound and haven't pushed it anywhere or tried anything new. A quote from the DJ Will Williamson, known as Father Funk, illustrates a typical response:

> so much jazz is just, like, amazing, and so much electro swing is wack – it's like, how can you get this, like, seven-minute beautiful jazz escapade and turn it into, like, this little loop and then put a house beat behind it and be like, 'it's done now'? It's like, fuck man, there's like this whole fucking journey you could have, like, gone on.
>
> Offbeat 2016

Whilst criticizing a large part of the electro swing genre, it's important to note that Williamson is not criticizing the genre itself. This is an important distinction to make as it demonstrates that he is indeed an admirer of the genre, just a rather selective one, and his own electro swing productions attest to this (see Tuxedo Junction 2016). And, once again, we have this acknowledgement of jazz.

Williamson's remarks are certainly emblematic of the stereotypical jazz aficionado, and his explicit references to jazz show that this is not merely coincidental. In cases such as this, electro swing is being judged as a distinct style of jazz, for the precise reason that it is being viewed as a distinct style of jazz.

Nicholson argues that 'it is vital for jazz musicians, as they have in the past, to keep their lines of input open to appropriate whatever is around them today . . . in order to continue the historic task of broadening the expressive base of the music' (2005: xi). As discussed earlier, jazz began its life as dance music, and I see no reason as to why the genre should choose to ignore the dance music of today. Through its fusion with electronic dance music, electro swing has not only brought about the potential to propel jazz music back into the present-day spotlight, but has also provided the opportunity for jazz to once again be at the forefront of future innovations.

Conclusion

Electro swing can already be seen to have developed into a considerably substantial music scene, with regular events being held across Europe, and to an extent, across the world. And, as exemplified by *The Great Gatsby*, it can have a considerable effect on mainstream culture, including popular music at large.

This can be demonstrated through a number of the more successful hit singles of the past few years, for instance Daft Punk's 'Get Lucky' (2013), which was co-written with Nile Rodgers of Chic fame, and incorporates various strong funk and disco elements. Other examples include Icona Pop's 'Emergency' (2015), which features a clear electro swing influence; and Galantis's 'Peanut Butter Jelly' (2015), which heavily samples the soul song 'Kiss My Love Goodbye' (1974) by Bettye Swann throughout. It is clear that some of the most successful singers of recent times are those who include an element of vintage influence across their music. Examples of this include Paloma Faith, Meghan Trainor, and Lady Gaga, who in 2014 released an album of jazz covers with famed crooner Tony Bennett (2014). One of the songs off this album, 'I Can't Give You Anything But Love', was even in fact given an official electro swing remix by Parov Stelar (LadyGagaVEVO 2014).

The genre's increasing popularity can be explained by the audience's desire for something new in the way they experience music, which electro swing arguably provides. There is a level of irony in the fact that this 'new' music is in fact 'vintage' music, yet a number of authors have pointed out that much of the audience could well be experiencing these styles for the first time. For instance, in speaking of the film *O Brother, Where Art Thou?* (2000), Holt argues that:

> the popularity of the film was conditioned by the fact that the majority of the audience was too young to have experienced its predecessors [...] like most revivals, the roots revival is fuelled by a strong sense of excitement about discovering a hitherto unknown past.
>
> 2007: 38

The idea is also discussed by Reynolds, who describes the way in which musicians may 'explore [the past] like an undiscovered land and bring back exotica to enrich the present' (2011: 229). Shipton also makes this point with specific reference to swing: 'the music may be well worn in the jazz community, but performing swing-era material for a young audience is introducing it to that listenership for the first time' (2007: 718). Thus, it is not surprising to see a vintage remix night, such as Itchy Feet, using the tagline 'hear something new'.

Across the popular music spectrum, the influence of 'vintage' or 'retro' culture is now widespread. We need only look at the bestselling singles of recent years

Figure 9.2 Itchy Feet, London, 7 July 2017.

for evidence of this (Official Charts 2016). Since 2013, they have been, respectively, 'Blurred Lines' by Robin Thicke (2013); 'Happy' by Pharrell Williams (2014); 'Uptown Funk' by Mark Ronson and Bruno Mars (2015), and 'One Dance' by Drake (2016). Whilst 'One Dance' does not have any obvious vintage element to it, of the remaining three, 'Blurred Lines' is heavily based upon the music of Marvin Gaye; 'Happy' would fall under the neo soul genre, and 'Uptown Funk', by its very title, demonstrates that it owes a large amount to the style of funk.

The rise of electro swing can be said to be both a cause and effect of popular culture's current obsession with vintage. Especially in the case of popular music, producers taking influence from the past truly are providing the audience with something new. It just so happens that the new music they are providing, is, well, old.

References

Armada Music (2017), 'GoldFish Feat. Diamond Thug – Deep Of The Night (Live Version) [Official Music Video]' *YouTube*. Available online: https://www.youtube.com/watch?v=y2qEPgK_jOE.

Bondy, Halley (2012), 'Parov Stelar Goes Beyond "Electro Swing"' *MTV Iggy*, 10 September. Available online: http://www.mtviggy.com/interviews/parov-stelar-goes-beyond-electro-swing/.

Boym, Svetlana (2001), *The Future of Nostalgia*. New York: Basic Books.

Browne, George (2014), 'The 3 Questions – Part 1', *Jack the Cad*, 25 March. Available online: http://jackthecad.blogspot.co.uk/2014/03/the-3-questions-part-1.html.

Carr, Ian, Digby Fairweather and Brian Priestley (2000), *Jazz: The Rough Guide*. London: Rough Guides Ltd.

Cotgrove, Mark (2009), *From Jazz Funk and Fusion to Acid Jazz: The History of the UK Jazz Dance Scene*. Milton Keynes: Chaser Publications and Authorhouse.

Dery, Mark (2004) 'Public Enemy Confrontation', in Murray Forman and Mark Anthony Neal (eds), *That's the Joint! The Hip-Hop Studies Reader*, 407–20. New York: Routledge.

DeVeaux, Scott (1998), 'Constructing the Jazz Tradition', in Robert G. O'Meally (ed.), *The Jazz Cadence of American Culture*, 484–514. New York: Columbia University Press.

DMC World DJ Championships (2015), 'DMC World Champions'. Available online: http://www.dmcdjchamps.com/champions.php.

electro-swing.com (2012), 'Skeewiff Interview'. Available online: http://electro-swing.com/2012/genre/electro-swing/interview-with-skeewiff-exclusive-download/.

Fikentscher, Kai (2013), '"It's Not the Mix, It's the Selection": Music programming in contemporary DJ culture', in Bernardo Attias, Anna Gavanas and Hillegonda

Rietveld (eds), *DJ Culture in the Mix: Power, Technology, and Social Change in Electronic Dance Music*, 123–50. London: Bloomsbury.

Gilbert, Jeremy and Ewan Pearson (1999), *Discographies: Dance Music, Culture and the Politics of Sound*. London: Routledge.

GoldFish (2017), 'ULTRA MIAMI SET 2017 LIVE STAGE – GoldFish' *SoundCloud*. Available online: https://soundcloud.com/goldfishlive/ultra-miami-set-2017-live-stage-goldfish.

Goldfishlive (2013), 'Goldfish Three-Second Memory-Track by Track interview (Part Four)' *YouTube*. Available online: https://www.youtube.com/watch?v=u6d1a_d9q_4.

Green, Thomas H. (2010), 'The new Jazz Age is upon us', *The Telegraph*, 9 December. Available online: http://www.telegraph.co.uk/culture/music/8189852/The-new-Jazz-Age-is-upon-us.html.

Harrison, Max (1986), 'Jazz', in Paul Oliver, Max Harrison and William Bolcom (eds), *The New Grove: Gospel, Blues and Jazz*, 223–356. London: W.W. Norton and Company.

Hogan, Ed (2016), 'Teddy Riley'. Available online: http://www.allmusic.com/artist/teddy-riley-mn0000018176/biography.

Hogarty, Jean (2017), *Popular Music and Retro Culture in the Digital Era*. New York: Routledge.

Hollywood, Nick (2010), 'Now That's What I Call Seriously Retro Electro', *Nude*, Summer.

Holt, Fabian (2007), *Genre in Popular Music*. Chicago, IL: University of Chicago Press.

Hustwitt, Mark (1987), '"Caught in a Whirlpool of Aching Sound": The production of dance music in Britain in the 1920s', *Popular Music*, 3: 7–31.

Inglis, Chris (2017), 'Sampling the Past: The role and function of vintage music within Electro Swing', in Haftor Medbøe, Zack Moir and Chris Atton (eds), *Continental Drift: 50 Years of Jazz from Europe*, 47–56. Edinburgh: Continental Drift Publishing.

Katz, Mark (2004), *Capturing Sound: How Technology Has Changed Music*. Berkeley, CA: University of California Press.

LadyGagaVEVO (2014), 'I Can't Give You Anything But Love – Parov Stelar Mix (Audio Video)' *YouTube*. Available online: https://www.youtube.com/watch?v=BVYfOwLqyck.

Luebbers, Johannes (2008), 'It's All Music', *Resonate Magazine*, 8 September. Available online: http://www.australianmusiccentre.com.au/article/it-s-all-music.

McAdams, Janine and Havelock Nelson (1992), 'Hip-Hop Puts Fresh Spin on Jazz', *Billboard*, 22 August.

McNally, Dennis (2014), *On Highway 61: Music, Race, and the Evolution of Cultural Freedom*. Berkeley, CA: Counterpoint.

Miller, James (1999), *Flowers in the Dustbin: The Rise of Rock and Roll, 1947–1977*. New York: Simon and Schuster.

Montgomery, James (2013), '"The Great Gatsby" Soundtrack: Jay-Z And Baz Luhrmann Re-Invent The Jazz Age', *MTV News*, 5 August. Available online: http://www.mtv.com/news/1707012/great-gatsby-soundtrack-jay-z-baz-luhrmann/.

Nicholson, Stuart (2005), *Is Jazz Dead? (Or has it moved to a new address?)*. New York: Routledge.

Offbeat (2016), 'Talking Shop Ep 006 – Father Funk (DJ/Producer)', *YouTube*. Available online: https://www.youtube.com/watch?v=Whx8F6lurF4.

Official Charts (2016), 'The Biggest Song of Every Year Revealed'. Available online: http://www.officialcharts.com/chart-news/the-biggest-song-of-every-year-revealed__2566/.

Reynolds, Simon (2011), *Retromania: Pop Culture's Addiction to Its Own Past*. London: Faber and Faber.

Reynolds, Simon (2013), *Energy Flash: A Journey through Rave Music and Dance Culture* rev. edn. London: Faber and Faber.

Rietveld, Hillegonda C. (1998), *This is Our House: House Music, Cultural Spaces and Technologies*. Aldershot: Ashgate.

Shipton, Alyn (2007), *A New History of Jazz*, 2nd edn. New York: Continuum.

Smith, Danyel (1994), 'Gang Starr: Jazzy Situation', *Vibe*, May.

Strausbaugh, John (2002), *Rock 'Til You Drop*, rev. edn. London: Verso.

Thomas, Reginald (2001), 'The Rhythm of Rhyme: A look at rap music as an art form from a jazz perspective', in James L. Conyers, Jr (ed.), *African American Jazz and Rap: Social and Philosophical Examinations of Black Expressive Behavior*, 163–69. Jefferson, NC: McFarland.

Tuxedo Junction (2016), *SoundCloud*. Available online: https://soundcloud.com/tuxedojunctionswing.

Verma, Rahul (2011), 'Electro-swing – Tonight we're going to party like it's 1929', *Independent*, April. Available online: http://www.independent.co.uk/arts-entertainment/music/features/electroswing-tonight-were-going-to-party-like-its-1929-2276174.html.

Werner, Craig (1999), *A Change Is Gonna Come: Music, Race and the Soul of America*. New York: Plume.

Williams, Justin (2014), *Rhymin' and Stealin': Musical Borrowing in Hip-Hop*. Ann Arbor, MI: University of Michigan Press.

Discography

Bennett, Tony and Lady Gaga (2014), *Cheek to Cheek*. Columbia.

Caravan Palace (2008), *Caravan Palace*. Wagram Music.

Chinese Man (2007), *The Groove Sessions volume 1: 2004–2007*. Chinese Man Records.

Daft Punk (2013), 'Get Lucky'. Columbia.

Davis, Miles (1992), *Doo-Bop*. Warner.

Drake (2016), 'One Dance'. OVO Sound.
Electro Swing (2009), Wagram Music.
The Electro Swing Revolution Vol. 1 (2011), Lola's World.
Emerald, Caro (2010), *Deleted Scenes from the Cutting Room Floor*. Grandmono Records.
Emerald, Caro (2013), *The Shocking Miss Emerald*. Grandmono Records.
Galantis (2015), 'Peanut Butter Jelly'. Big Beat Records.
Goldfish (2006), *Caught in the Loop*. Black Mango Music.
Goldfish (2008), *Perceptions Of Pacha*. Sony Music Entertainment Africa.
Goldfish (2010), *Get Busy Living*. Sony Music.
Goldfish (2013), *Three Second Memory*. Goldfish Music.
Goldfish (2016), 'Deep Of The Night'. Goldfish Music.
Gramophonedzie (2010), 'Why Don't You'. Positive Records.
Guru (1993), *Jazzmatazz Volume: 1*. Chrysalis Records.
Hancock, Herbie (1983), *Future Shock*. Columbia.
Icona Pop (2015), 'Emergency'. Atlantic.
Jurassic 5 (2000), *Quality Control*. Interscope Records.
Lucas (1994), *Lucacentric*. Big Beat.
MC Lyte (1989), *Eyes on This*. Atlantic Records.
Moby (1999), *Play*. EMI.
Mr. Scruff (1999), *Keep It Unreal*. Ninja Tune.
Repac, Nicolas (2004) *Swing-Swing*. No Format!
Ronson, Mark (2014), 'Uptown Funk'. RCA.
Stelar, Parov (2004) *Rough Cuts*. Etage Noir Recordings.
Stelar, Parov (2005) *Seven And Storm*. Etage Noir Recordings.
Stelar, Parov (2009), *Coco*. Etage Noir Recordings.
Stelar, Parov (2012), *The Princess*. Etage Noir Recordings.
Stelar, Parov (2017), *The Burning Spider*. Etage Noir Recordings.
Stetsasonic (1988), 'Talkin' All That Jazz'. Tommy Boy.
Swann, Bettye (1974), 'The Boy Next Door'/'Kiss My Love Goodbye'. Atlantic.
Thicke, Robin (2013), 'Blurred Lines'. Interscope Records.
White Mink: Black Cotton (2010), Freshly Squeezed Music.
Williams, Pharrell (2014), 'Happy'. Columbia.

Filmography

The Great Gatsby (2013), Directed by Baz Luhrmann. USA: Warner Bros. Pictures.
O Brother, Where Art Thou? (2000), Directed by the Coen Brothers. USA: Buena Vista Pictures.

Part Three

Music Consumption

Back to the Future: Proposing a Heuristic for Predicting the Future of Recorded Music Use

Mathew Flynn

On 28 February 2018, music streaming service Spotify filed papers to list as a public company on the New York Stock Exchange (Ingham 2018). Just ten years after its launch as a Swedish-based start-up, Spotify has grown to occupy a market-leading position in most western markets for audio streaming. The attitudes and actions of CEO Daniel Ek, and the other directors of the company, have attracted industry and academic plaudits and protests in equal measure. But who a decade earlier, other than possibly the owners and early investors, predicted Spotify's meteoric rise? Equally, whether Spotify succeeds in cementing its place as the music platform of choice in the next decade, and beyond, remains to be seen.

What this scenario illustrates is the fundamental and ongoing importance of prediction to the business processes and practices of the music industries. Given this book is concerned with music futures, this chapter tackles the general conservatism of music industry scholars when it comes to proposing predictions, by advocating a heuristic perspective of the music industries. To demonstrate this approach, the analysis seeks to address the limited recognition for the role that the music consumer plays in the production process. The opening section of the chapter summarizes the considerable contribution to music industry studies by the production of culture approach, but then seeks to highlight how the actions of consumers are often minimized within this theory. The remainder of the chapter uses examples of the parlour piano, phonograph and early radio to explore the importance of consumers' active participation in determining the success of mediums for music playback. The conclusion draws upon the numerous examples presented to establish a heuristic for the past, present and future of recorded music use. Essentially, that market-dominant music playback technologies increasingly improve situational control, personalize choice, but continually reduce the demands of knowledge, skill, labour and time on the part of consumers.

The problems with producing predictions

In a 2017 paper entitled 'What the digitalisation of music tells us about capitalism, culture and the power of the information technology sector', Hesmondhalgh and Meier chart the history of recording playback technologies. Their analysis of the impact of radio and record, cassette and CD players establishes the longstanding influence of the consumer electronics (CE) industry on music consumption. However, in line with many of the scholars they reference on how the contemporary music industries are configured (Burkart and McCourt 2006; Wikström 2009; Rogers 2013; Anderson 2014; Leyshon 2014; Marshall 2015; Morris 2015; Morris and Powers 2015; Mulligan 2015; Witt 2015), their perspective is predominantly rooted in a production of culture approach that minimizes the consumer's role in the process. As Hesmondhalgh and Meier state:

> Even if many consumers appreciated these changes, and believed they represented progress in terms of accessibility and so forth, it would be misleading to believe that they 'chose' them; new technologies were pushed onto the market by powerful corporations 'outside' the music industries (though often tied to them via ownership of record companies) and, in effect, imposed on consumers via marketing and the strategic withdrawal of 'outdated' goods. These dynamics were all to remain present in the twenty-first century, but in an intensified form.
>
> Hesmondhalgh and Meier 2017: 7

Whilst informative and insightful, the production perspective generally seeks to, either implicitly or explicitly, 'better understand contexts in which cultural symbols are consciously created for sale' (Peterson and Anand 2004: 324). This means that the frame of reference for assessing the viability of products is generally the industrial processes that supply music to consumers, not the consumers themselves. In many ways the approach has proved effective and efficient because, as Wikström states, understanding 'consumer behaviour dynamics simply is too complex' (2009: 151). However, this minimization of the significance of consumer choice usually reduces the discussion of future consumption trends to broad predictions. As Hesmondhalgh and Meier conclude, 'The dominance of the IT sector, if it continues to lead to constant turnovers in prevailing forms of consumption, will only contribute further to endless cycles of change, obsolescence and replacement' (2017: 12).

At the time of writing, the most up-to-date book-length analysis of the music industry is Tschmuck's (2017) *The Economics of Music*. In contrast to Hesmondhalgh and Meier's (2017) approach, Tschmuck argues that the digitalization of music was a symptom, not a cause, of the drop in record sales due to 'the conversion of an album market into a singles market' (2017). The basis for Tschmuck's analysis is that the products most effectively meeting consumer demands, irrespective of their technological design and status, are what drive market change. His argument implies significant questions about whether new technologies create new consumer demands or just more effectively meet existing, or even unrealized, wants and needs. In his analysis, what is implicit, but not explicitly stated, is that products and business models that increase consumer sovereignty, a theme he has addressed in a previous research (2012: 242), seemingly have the best chance of delivering market success. Tschmuck's research seems consistent with Voigt, Buliga and Michl's analysis of what drives the current success of Spotify's business model:

> What worked in favour of Spotify was Ek's principle that a successful business adapts to its customers, and does not urge them to change their own behaviour. He once noted that 'Spotify subscribers don't pay for content – they can get that for free through piracy – they pay for convenience'.
>
> Voigt, Buliga and Michl 2017: 145

Based upon this premise, Tschmuck's claim 'that the music-streaming business is the future of the recorded music industry' (2017) is unsurprising. More importantly, in 2018, when all global market indicators point in streaming's direction (IFPI 2017: 16), it is hardly predictive. Despite Tschmuck's greater emphasis on the significance of consumer behaviour, his analysis is equally as conservative when it comes to forecasting potential future developments.

In fact, there are very few contributions to music industry literature that are successful theorized attempts at prediction. The two notable exceptions are Attali's *Noise* ([1977] 1985) and Kusek and Leonhard's *The Future of Music* (2005). Both books propose and apply frameworks that have, since their respective publications, proved prescient. Yet, despite the continuous decade-long assessment and re-assessment of the record industry's plight and potential future, most scholars only offer broad predictions, such as the 'impact of new media technologies is better understood as part of a continuum of change' (Collins and Young 2014: 2). Evidently, most academics stop deliberately short of detailed prediction as to what technologies will drive the future direction of music. As Morris admits in his recent book *Selling Digital Music*, 'It is never a safe bet to finish a book on new media with predictions, so I'll refrain from doing so' (2015: 192). Similarly, when discussing the emergence of digital distribution, Tschmuck concluded, 'How these paths will look is impossible to predict at this moment' (2006: 223).

From a production of culture perspective, the decision to frame consumers as largely passive acceptors of the market manipulation of corporations and concede consumer behaviour as too complex to fathom, underrepresents consumers as a key link in the value chain. Even Tschmuck frames music use as 'reception' (2006: 210), a term that infers passivity in the consumer's engagement with the market. Although academics generally leave the forecasting of consumer demand and behaviour to corporations and entrepreneurs, evidently, in the music industries, prediction remains a fundamental part of the production process. As Marshall McLuhan, another scholar renowned for his prescience, observed, 'The owners of media always endeavour to give the public what it wants, because they sense that their power is in the medium and not in the message or programme' (1964: 235). Sterne's definition of a medium, as 'the social basis that allows a set of technologies to stand out as a unified thing with clearly defined functions' (2003: 182) suggests the power McLuhan refers to is somewhat dependent on the permission of the public. This notion is consistent with assertions by Tschmuck (2006, 2012, 2017) and Voigt, Buliga and Michl (2017) that digitized media companies adapt to existing consumer demands. Morris's observation about selling digital music that 'these economic models both foster and depend on various levels of audience labor' (2015: 84) supports this view. Therefore, there is a clear premise that consumer engagement does play an active role in determining the prevailing forms of consumption (Hesmondhalgh and Meier 2017: 12). In turn, exploring the function and process of predicting consumer attitudes and behaviour could be instructive in further developing music industries studies. Therefore, to explore the nature of audience labour, the next section of the chapter will consider different approaches to research on music use by music users.

The hard work of music consumption

Research on how music is used often focuses on the sociological, cultural, psychological and emotional impact of music on users, not the industrial or commercial significance of their use. This is evident from the more personalized accounts of the symbolic significance of music listening (DeNora 2000; Clarke 2005; Herbert 2011), to more specific theories on its taxonomy and psychology (Adorno 1962; Rösing 1984; Stockfelt 1997; Sloboda 1998, 2015; Huron 2002), to broader considerations of the attention paid to music (Kassabian 2013), and recent explorations on the interaction between music users and technologies (Nowak 2016; Nowak and Whelan 2016). However, recent examples of specific research on music use cohere around themes of how different music playback technologies and playlist choices are exercised in the digital age (Bull 2005, 2009; Kibby 2009; Avdeeff 2011; Bonnin and Jannach 2014; Bartmanski and Woodward 2015; Hagen 2015; Yang and Teng 2015; Kamalzadeh et al. 2016). As Krause, North and Hewitt propose:

> A general pattern was that experiences involving music that was chosen were more positive than were those involving music that was not chosen. For example, an MP3 player was associated with a very high degree of choice and also positive purposive consequences, whereas music heard in public was not associated with being liked or personally chosen and was negatively associated with actively engaged listening consequences.
>
> Krause et al. 2015: 166

This observation highlights the value consumers place on having playback and playlist control over their music listening. As Voigt, Buliga and Michl (2017) illustrated, Spotify's success is predicated on the fact they adapted to these positive purposive consequences. In turn, personally chosen and actively engaged listening places digitized music firmly in 'the realm of the experience economy rather than simply being a service or a product for consumption' (Pearce 2013:4). After the initial upfront cost of purchasing a smartphone or laptop as a playback device, through its free or paid subscribed access music streaming also epitomizes the post-object economy for recorded music (Anderson 2014: 9). There is no requirement on twenty-first century music consumers to 'devote their time to producing the means to buy recordings of other people's time' (Attali 1985: 101). Digital music consumers invest more in attention (Citton [2014] 2017; Davenport and Beck 2002; Kassabian 2013; Lanham 2006) than time or money in meeting their demands for recorded music experiences (Marshall 2014). In turn, the value of user attention is commodified as data by music streaming services to increase the value in their networks (Anderson 2014; McGuigan and Manzerolle 2014; Tschmuck 2017). This rivalry for the attention of music delivered across digital networks, which affords almost unlimited and ubiquitous access to recordings, has led Tschmuck to define music streaming as a (digital) common good (2017: 1269). Clearly, music streaming traverses a number of economies, but regardless of the outputs measured, consumers now 'purchase frequently, immediately and with a minimum effort' (Holton 1958: 53). Arguably, Holton's definition of a convenience good, with the most contentious element being 'purchase', best describes the consumer experience of music streaming. Daniel Ek's assertion that Spotify is selling convenience, not music, is consistent with this assessment.

When discussing the impact of music streaming on listening behaviour, Hagen observes a fundamental human–music–technology relationship and concludes, 'Music streaming contributes greatly to people's daily life management, as shaped by adaptations and user habits, and by the perceptual, conceptual and practical understanding of what the technology and the music are and do for the user' (2016: 243). Likewise, Radbourne says of audiences, 'The creative process is completed by a shared journey to market and aesthetic value which engages the individual consumer in the artistic idea, prototype testing, the production and the consumption. The term "consumer" may be more comfortably be "participant" or "partner"' (2013: 157). What Hagen observes and Radbourne argues is that the process of consumption requires a level of knowledge, skill and labour on the part of the consumer to complete the production cycle. Likewise, although not intended with the cultural labour of consumers in mind, Bank's assertion that 'it is crucial to our further understanding that academics pay more attention to the mutable conditions of cultural labour' (2010: 266) seems applicable in this context. Moreover, as Terranova observed very early in the development of the commercial internet, the provision of 'free labour' or 'playbour' as it is sometimes termed, 'is a fundamental moment in the creation of value in the digital economies' (2000: 36).

Hagen's (2016) summary of user adaptations, habits, and understandings is consistent with the concept of affordance (Norman 1988: 9), which considers the 'interactions between culturally situated humans and the culturally determined objects that they encounter in their environments' (Gjerdingen 2009: 124). In *The Audible Past*, Jonathan Sterne demonstrates the historical significance of music consumers having to develop the skills to effectively consume:

> Technique connotes practice, virtuosity, and the possibility of failure and accident, as in a musician's technique with a musical instrument. It is a learned skill, a set of repeatable activities within a limited number of framed contexts.
>
> Sterne 2003: 92

Throughout history then, playback devices can be seen to have afforded opportunities for modes of interaction to participant consumers. Therefore, considering the level of control a playback device affords over a situation, the choice it provides in terms of musical playlist and the range and level of playbour (skills developed and used towards instrumental ends) required to effectively produce that playlist, is one approach for assessing the significance of the part consumers play in the creation of demand for music playback.

The typical approach to this analysis would be either be through detailed historical accounts so effectively employed by many scholars (Barnard 1989; Millard 1995; Sterne 2003, 2012; Douglas 2004; Tschmuck 2006, 2012, 2017; Elborough 2008; Osborne 2013; Morris 2015; Taylor et al. 2012; Brackett 2016; Taylor 2016) or by using the compiled era-based analysis demonstrated by Hesmondhalgh and Meier (2017), Peterson and Berger ([1975] 1990) and Peterson (1990). However, histories are not without their limitations. Toynbee critiques the production perspective approach for 'backwardly' valorizing events (2000: 10). Likewise, Bradley views many historical accounts as 'composite' (1992: 9) and Keightley concurs with this notion of selectivity when he claims, historiographies often privilege 'rupture over continuity' (2004: 376). Moreover, as Bunzl asserts in his reflections on historical practice, 'foresight is not a condition required of a chronicler' (1997: 25). Furthermore, as Marwick argues, 'Systems and numbers should not be sneezed at. The historian's activities are closer to those of the scientist than those of the novelist or poet. However neat equations, still less general laws, do not figure in the historians work' (1998: 16).

These concerns provide a rationale and reason for the general reluctance of authors of historical accounts of the music industries to posit predictions. However, as Tschmuck has observed with the creativity and innovation of music companies:

> We can say that companies' future actions will correspond to the routines they applied in the past. Even under different circumstances, companies adapt their future behaviour as if it would develop according to old routines.
>
> Tschmuck 2006: 187

Therefore, by adopting and adapting Tschmuck's observation, is it possible to identify longstanding routines to make approximations about the direction of travel for how music users will adapt to playback technologies in the future? To attempt to answer this question, instead of presenting an historical analysis I will draw upon various composite histories of playback devices and backwardly valorize their development to unveil continuities in the old routines of participant consumption. Then, by viewing these selected histories through the prism of current concepts, this chapter will aim to facilitate some foresight through the application of a general law. Therefore, in uncovering a general law, what I am proposing is the development of a heuristic, as opposed to historic, approach. As Tschmuck has identified, 'heuristics essentially are rules of thumb' (2006: 189) that act as 'a simple procedure that helps find adequate, though often imperfect, answers to difficult questions' (Kahneman 2011: 97). The next section will explain the methodology behind this approach.

Presenting a heuristic instead of a history

In her summary of a comprehensive analysis of recorded music, Georgina Born highlights the process of the social-cultural needs of consumers preceding successful products:

> Broader cultural, social and economic conditions must be in place in order for a particular technology to become established as a mass medium. The social and cultural precedes the technology; just as, we might add, the aesthetic can precede the technology, prefiguring what is to come.
>
> Born 2009: 291

Essentially, Born's view is that historically established consumption heuristics prefigure the adoption of playback technologies.

Research in psychology and behavioural economics recognizes that consumers rely on simple heuristics instead of elaborate calculations in many everyday decisions, such as purchasing situations (Hauser 2011). This rule of thumb 'is based on experience, intuition, common sense' (Pinheiro and McNeill 2014: 46) and 'ignores part of the information, with the goal of making decisions more quickly, frugally and/or more accurately than more complex methods' (Gigerenzer and Gaissmaier 2011: 454). As del Campo et al. argue, 'a high amount of uncertainty present in the environment seems to increase reliance on heuristics' (2016: 393). Heuristics then, are an adequate but imperfect tool of prediction in complex markets. The question is, do music users apply a common and consistent heuristic when adapting to new music playback technologies?

Three concepts underpin my approach: playback, playlists and playbour. For the purposes of this chapter, I will elaborate on Krause, North and Hewitt's 'devices to access music' (2015: 157) to include the associated formats or platforms that work with the device for the definition of *playback*. I will expand Bonnin and Jannach's definition of *playlist* (2014: 2), which they limited to recordings, to mean any ordered sequence of music. Whereas the definition of *playbour* combines Terranova's concept of 'free labour' (2000: 36) that demonstrates Sterne's learned set of repeatable activities (2003: 92) within the context of the participant consumer completing a shared journey to market (Radbourne 2013: 157). In relation to the playbour definition, the term 'participant consumer' is employed to illustrate the action required to use music to facilitate or enhance desired experiences.

Contained within these core concepts are more nuanced choices that participant consumers make when using music. However, as opposed to considering *what* consumers listen to, the focus here is the preconditions for *how* they listen. Why consumers act the way they do in complex markets was the focus of *Competing Against Luck* (Christensen et al. 2016: 87): 'When we buy a product, we essentially "hire" it to make progress and get a job done. If it does the job well, we hire that same product again. If the product does a crummy job, we "fire" it and look around for something else'. Conversely, as Sterne explains about listening technologies, 'Each machine embodied a whole set of articulations; in turn, it was articulated to larger economic, technical, and social functions and relations among many other possible and actual uses' (Sterne 2003: 183). Therefore, between these two ideas and interactions exist sets of criteria, those implied by the device and those applied in the assessment of the devices adaptability to do the job by the consumer, both of which are set against the required level of playbour. Effectively cycles of replacement and obsolesce (Hesmondhalgh and Meier 2017: 12) are the hiring and firing of playback technologies by participant consumers, as new products on the market articulate improvements to getting the listening job done.

Although the piano predates consumer electronic technologies that grew to dominate the record industry, as Daub recounts, 'The standardisation and industrialisation of piano manufacturing in the first half of the nineteenth century made the instrument a "sonic hearth"' (Daub 2014: 37) of the middle-class homes of Europe and America. Therefore, the participant consumption explored here will predate the emergence of the record industry and will begin with an analysis of what the parlour piano afforded as a playback device.

Creating the criteria for consumption

The piano's installation into the affluent home was a consequence of the integral part performances and concerts had come to play in the leisure pursuits of the aristocracy and the bourgeoisie. The auditorium had become 'not only a musical but also a social and political space' (Müller 2010: 836). As Daub asserts, the piano 'made it possible to transfer this public music to the private sphere' (2014: 26) more than any other instrument had before that point. In current conceptions of popular media culture, this 'catering for ever smaller and specific audience groups' (Sandvoss et al. 2015: 57) would be defined as narrowcasting. As Botstein details, the cheap, sturdy, and standardized piano helped fuel the explosive growth in citizen participation (1992: 136–40) to satisfy the under-supply in demand for music. As Bailey observes, by the 1890s 'an increasing number of middle-class children were learning music hall songs from their nurses and nannies, and music hall song sheets were to be seen on drawing room pianos' (1986: 85). Botstein asserts that this 'newer piano-based standard of musical literacy made possible a profound democratization of musical culture' (1992: 137). This convergence of culture (Jenkins 2008) between both middle class children and their working-class nannies and music producers and users, through sheet music, enabled 'people to gain access to the musical canon, to experience and possess it' (Daub 2014: 38). This access and control of the playlists performed in homes meant 'amateur pianists provided an important customer base for nineteenth-century sheet music publishers' (Miller 2008: 429). And in terms of social status, 'It was worth a good deal to be able to show your neighbours that you could afford a piano and . . a collection of printed music to go with it' (Solie, 1994: 54). However, this democratization of access did not only come with a substantial financial cost, but a considerable playbour cost.

Although portrayed as a domestic leisure pursuit, the privatization and domestication of music use meant 'musical performance functioned as a form of labour' (Miller 2008: 432), with a great deal of compositions written for the relatively unskilled performer (Solie 1994: 54). Nevertheless, the 'attainment of music skill was far from effortless. It required dedication, discipline and physical exertion' (Miller 2008: 428). The role of pianist fell to predominantly young female members of the family; as Miller observes, 'She was an early home entertainment system broadcasting both femininity and music' (2008: 431). Solie's research looked at diaries of nineteenth-century women for accounts of feminine senses of duty associated with playing the piano. One account summarizes entries by Fanny Lewald who had, 'two piano lessons a week and practised for an hour every day for twenty-five years, despite the fact that she had no talent whatsoever and hated every moment of it' (1994: 54–55). Clearly, the work and skill required to use music in the home was considerable. For the more accomplished pianist there was opportunity (Miller 2008: 432), but for the majority with limited talent, both their capacity to reproduce repertoire and the fidelity in their reproduction of the sound limited the durability of the piano as a playback device.

The piano realized a domestic musical canon with the range and depth of the playlist dependent on the talent and commitment in the playbour of predominantly young women. In doing so, it also established the core criteria for why domestic playback devices are hired by music consumers to get a job done. Once beyond the obvious market access constraints of affordability, participant consumers essentially hired the piano based on criteria such as accessibility, reproducibility and popularity of the playlist, fidelity, personalization, durability, sociability and the cultural capital (Bourdieu 2010: 14) conferred by the status of ownership. These are all user experience criteria that continue to be applied when consumers consider hiring a playback device today. In applying Jenkins observation that 'convergence occurs within the brains of individual consumers and through their social interactions with others' (2008: 4), then the piano converged the public and the private music space, enabling one to inform the other and vice versa. Essentially, participant consumers bought the independence and convenience of control and choice over where, when and, to a performer capability extent, what type of music they wanted to play and hear. However, the home entertainment of the late nineteenth and early twentieth centuries required affluence to afford the technology and time, talent and tuition to be able to use it. Therefore, the adaptation of the existing piano technology to one that required less skill investment from the participant consumer meant that by 1919 the player piano[1] outnumbered straight pianos in sales (Carson 1990: 52). The shift in consumption from parlour to player piano was an early indication of the demand on producers to respond to participant consumer criteria in a shared journey to market. Then, as Scherer observes, the emergence of radio and the electronic phonograph in 1920s America caused the dramatic reduction in piano production rates, from a peak of 340,000 units per year between 1910 and 1920 to just 80,000 units by 1930 (2006: 140). Yet these 'turnovers in the prevailing forms of consumption' (Hesmondhalgh and Meier 2017: 12) were all based on the opportunity for the participant consumer to better meet the fundamental user criteria established by the parlour piano.

As Millard points out, between 1900 and 1920 the phonograph 'ushered in the age of mechanical entertainment' (1995: 65). In an article from 1924 entitled 'The Home Set to Music', Pauline Partridge states: 'Then along came the phonograph, or "talking machine", crowding the halfhearted amateur from the parlour floor perhaps, but putting music, real music, good music, into the American home for the first time in history' (Partridge cited in Katz 2012: 53). The power of this new playback medium was that it reconfigured playbour away from aptitudes that were relatively talent dependent, whilst affording the continuity of control over the playlist. As Taylor observes, 'the phonograph (preceded by the player piano) introduced a new mode in the commodification of music: it became something that one purchased as sound' (2012: 3). Albeit initially within the limitations of storage and playback capacities, effectively the phonograph was a device that fitted into the same user criteria for narrowcasting as the piano. Again, as Partridge observes, 'Indeed, the record takes the place of the printed music which perhaps nobody in the household could play' (Partridge, cited in Katz 2012: 55). Partridge's observation is apt in illustrating how the medium gained its power by adapting to the demands of the consumer to improve playlist choice and quality, whilst also reducing the level of participation in playback generation. As the numerous format histories already cited will attest, whilst the transition phases between recorded music playback technologies is a history of evolved changes over time, what has remained largely consistent is the user criteria applied by participant consumers when hiring and firing devices. To produce competitive advantage and create customers (Drucker 1955: 29), playback device manufacturers had to continually meet, largely unchanged, demands for performance quality, playback fidelity and playlist capacity.

Highlighting the shared journey to market, the early phonograph demanded the participant consumer develop the skill of listening. As Sterne observes, 'Listening becomes a technical skill, a skill that can be developed and used toward instrumental ends' (2003: 93). The transferability of the listening skill from the phonograph to the radio, coupled with the opportunity to place the actual broadcast sounds of the concert hall in the parlour, may in some small way account for the fact that, 'The recording boom was diminished by a separate CE led boom that was to have a huge influence on the music industries: radio' (Hesmondhalgh and Meier 2017: 5). By its very nature of broadcasting, radio also offered a different shared journey to market for the participant consumer as they entered 'a world of mass culture' (Taylor 2012: 2). Unlike the one-to-few narrowcasting afforded by the piano or the phonograph, radio afforded a one-to-many shared mass media experience.

Decreasing the work required to be content with content

The process of displacement of the piano by radio was summarized by Scherer: 'A new different way of consuming music in the home had appeared, changing radically the character of American family life and making music available every day to families that otherwise would have attended public concerts only rarely' (2006: 140). Although technology for wireless telegraphy had been in existence since the 1890s, in the USA, 'The rapidity with which the radio craze swept the country between 1920 and 1924 prompted analogies to tidal waves and highly contagious diseases' (Douglas 2004: 52). The rapid rise of radio in America was quantified by Slotten: 'At the beginning of 1921, 28 licensed stations were operating in the United States; by the end of the year, there were more than 550' (2003: ix).

Despite the 1920s frenzy for radio, 'even after radio became popular, one still had to purchase components and assemble them into a set' (Taylor 2012: 241). In particular, young men gained a solid grasp of electronics through tinkering with their own sets (Douglas 2004: 53). These early adopting (Rogers 1962: 19) radio hams, as they became known, not only demonstrated the purpose and function of radio to the emerging mass market, but, in doing so, demonstrated the significance of participant consumption in the proliferation of broadcast radio. This level of consumption activity has led Douglas to argue that the exploratory listening the tinkering facilitated was important in helping redefine masculinity in the rapidly modernizing 1920s (2004: 66). However, more broadly, as Warren asserts, 'without the successful cultivation of some measurable and proactive listenership, radio fails' (2005: 1). In turn, Sterne acknowledges the role of women:

> The listening white woman thus supplanted the image of the Victorian woman expressing herself and entertaining the family at the piano. This change was as much a result of real participation of women in emerging networks of sociability – including the networks of sound reproduction – as it was a result of the 'image' of mass culture and new media as somehow feminized.
>
> 2003: 228

Ranging from technical contribution to socially and symbolically significant listening participation, the differently assumed roles (although not necessarily always gender defined) illustrate how the types of playbour afforded by the same playback device could operate and fluctuate on a continuum of participant consumption.

Russo claims, 'Radio's position as the premier domestic mass entertainment medium of the 1920s, 1930s, and 1940s occupies a central place in the historical understanding of its position as a cultural form and the role of listening in that process' (2010: 153). Likewise, Goodman (2016) argues for more historical prominence to be given to group radio listening in the interwar period. The group listening broadcast was programmed to foster discussion amongst the coordinated group of listeners with the expressed intention 'that serious, active listening needed to be deliberately fostered in conscious opposition to the distracted or passive listening of the radio age' (2016: 438). Whilst not as proactive as the self-assembling radio hams, group listening practices certainly demonstrated the shared journey to market that Radbourne (2013: 157) marks out. However, coordinated group listening events were short lived and by the '1930s and 1940s distracted listening shifted from being viewed as a threat to being seen as a complementary practice, and then finally to being understood as a normative model in its own right' (Russo 2010: 154).

The commercialization and corporatization of American radio, with advances in technology and formalization of regulation (see Peterson 1990; Slotten 2003), meant that by 1954 there were two or more radios in 70 per cent of American households (Douglas 2004: 225). The opportunity to listen to different programmes concurrently within the same household meant that although distinctions in taste had first appeared in the 1920s, personalized listening became commonplace for Americans by the 1940s (Russo 2010: 182). The exercising of station selection between demographics goes some way to contradicting the notion that listening was generally distracted. Participant consumption was also evident in other ways. As Frith suggests, it was only the success of the jukebox that enabled the record industry to survive the 1930s depression era (2003: 96). In turn, the jukebox played a pivotal role in the formatting of mass market radio: allegedly, Top Forty radio programming was inspired by an observation in 1955 by New Orleans commercial radio station owner Todd Storz that consumers repeatedly played the same song on the jukebox (Gelatt 1977: 306). The concept and architecture of what was to become known as the playlist – a rotation system of new record releases that ensured 'the biggest current sellers were played at set intervals' (Barnard 1989: 41) – was the innovation of commercial radio, but it derived from the inspiration of participant consumption.

Evidently, the power of mediums for the public playback of recorded music, as we conceive of them now, are in some way attributable to the influence of the participant consumer. From the radio hams who built sets, to the early proactive listener, up to the users of jukeboxes that sustained the record industry and influenced the playlist format, participant consumers heuristically imposed their user criteria on the consumer electronic, record and radio industries to direct the owners of media towards what they wanted. Far from demonstrating complex behaviour dynamics, the basic demands of convenient control of the playback device and playlist choice were sufficient to produce progress in new technologies designed to better meet music user demands.

Radio's golden era charts a journey of consumer participation from one of engaged technical contribution to one of more socially and commercially significant participation. Whereas radio passivity is usually in reference to the mode of listening (Adorno 1962; Rösing 1984), what radio also afforded listeners was an increasing passivity in their interaction with the playback device. Negus's concise summary in *Popular Music in Theory* (1996: 74–85) accounts for how developments in radio technology from headphones to speakers to portable sets and eventual installation in cars, modified the focus of broadcasters from initially appealing to headphone wearing individuals, to group audiences and eventually individual mobile listeners. By the time the transistor and car radio were commonplace in the mid-1960s (Douglas 2004: 219–55) consumer levels of participation had been largely reduced to being able to turn on the device and tune the dial. In exchange for individuated access and the lessening demand of labour, knowledge and skill to engage with radio, consumers conceded control of the playlist to a rudimentary decision between the genre conventions and record promotions of competing radio stations (Rossman 2013: 100). However, by individualizing, personalizing and most significantly making music portable, radio significantly improved consumer's reasons to hire music playback as both a leisure, and significantly, as a supporting secondary activity. In doing so, radio also extended the user criteria applied by participant consumers. In addition to the user criteria established by the piano, radio added portability and constancy and consistency of the playlist. I will conclude the chapter by using heuristics to summarize this combination of user criteria.

What the participant consumer really, really wants – proposing a heuristic of record music use

Between the narrowcast playback of the piano and its displacement by the broadcast playback of radio, the core user criteria for participant consumption in shared journeys to market were established. Obviously this is not necessarily an either or situation, with many households owning pianos, phonographs and radios concurrently and employing them in different contexts. However, radio's continued resilience as a medium of playlist consumption, compared to the displacement of the piano by the phonograph and, in turn, the record, cassette, CD and MP3 player by the streaming platform, is sufficiently instructive to establish a rule of thumb that remains equally applicable to historic, current and future music playback technologies. Regardless of the fluctuations of the priority in which participant consumers order user criteria when selecting and using a playback device, essentially they are balancing the affordances of the device in a given situation against the level of playbour required to exert control over the playlist. Therefore, a heuristic for assessing the future cultural and commercial viability of playback technologies is:

> Music playback devices that improve situational control and playlist choice whilst, at the same time, becoming less reliant on the skill, knowledge and ability (playbour) of the participant consumer, will displace, replace and surpass incumbent technologies in the mass market.

Essentially, as Daniel Ek has successfully demonstrated, selling music playback formats, services and technologies was, is and will continue to be about adapting to the convenience of the consumer.

If this were a historiography, then a much fuller analysis of the fluctuations in appropriations of playback devices would be necessary. For example, as the device that pioneered the mobile private consumption of music in a public space (DuGay et al. 1997), the Sony Walkman certainly afforded a reconsideration of the priority order of user criteria that privileged portability and privacy over playlist choice and fidelity. In a 2018 article in the *New York Times*, Tim Wu argues, 'With the Walkman we can see a subtle but fundamental shift in the ideology of convenience. If the first convenience revolution promised to make life and work easier for you, the second promised to make it easier to be you.' O'Hara and Brown offer an apt description of both the practical and symbolic values of the appeal of the personal listening experience in the public domain: 'Not only does this change listening behaviour and circumstances, it also affords the social value of the portable device as a projection of a person's musical identity' (2010: 4). However, O'Hara and Brown are describing the iPod. This illustrates, as with the piano and the phonograph, that even though the playback devices and formats evolve, the user criteria that consumers apply when hiring a listening experience remain consistent.

As O'Hara and Brown (ibid.) recognize, what the iPod did typify was an increasing shift towards intangible MP3 formats that, once again, traded the criteria of storage capacity and playlist choice for sonic fidelity. As Shuker observes of the convenience of intangibility, for many 'the dematerialization of music is a positive development, and their music is acquired primarily in digital form' (Shuker 2010: 69). Essentially, digitization ended playlist choice as a user criterion, a situation that has triggered the battle for the convenience of curation between competing streaming platforms (Morris and Powers 2015). Likewise, in an interesting recent reordering of user criteria, the market resurgence of vinyl in the 2010s can be understood as a demonstration of resistance by those music users who are less than enamoured with the cult of convenience (Wu 2018). The desire to draw a distinction in the symbolic values perceived between types of consumer participation has led Bartmanski and Woodward to define vinyl as a 'product that does not absolutely rule the market through economic dimensions, but reigns as a material condensation of quality, ritual, distinction, effort, and competence in music' (2018: 176). Despite Bartmanski and Woodward's celebration of the cultural capital attributed to vinyl in the digital age, the fact that 'music-streaming services encompass aggregative features that invite participation and enable listeners to perform as content curators of their music consumption' (Hagen 2015: 643) means, more effectively than with any previous playback medium, that streaming reduces the demands of playbour whilst expanding participant consumer playback and playlist control. It is this level of convenience that ensures Tschmuck's (2017) prediction that 'the music streaming business is the future of the recorded music industry' certainly holds for now.

Conclusion

As with much of this analysis that has retrofitted current concepts over selected histories the conclusion offers one final example. Although referring to the malleability of music's form under digitization, Morris's assertion that 'user experiences of music are highly dependent on and mediated by music's commodity form' (2015: 193) is just as apt to describe music playback choice in the early twentieth century, or indeed any historical period of music selected for scrutiny. Conversely, what I have argued is the success of the commodity form through which music is mediated is equally as highly dependent on the user experience, or more definitively participant consumption. Through an analysis of the establishment of user criteria at the formation of markets for recorded music consumption, my aim here has been to tease out the rules of thumb participant consumers apply when engaged in the playbour required to use playback devices and control playlist choices. I have deliberately stepped back from a detailed assessment of the more recent analogue and digital music devices and formats. Apart from being far beyond the scope of a single book chapter, what I hope my look at the piano, phonograph and radio have illustrated is, by taking a long-view of playback devices, it is feasible to extrapolate how participant consumers apply consistent criteria to simplify complex market choices, irrespective of the constant turnovers in prevailing forms of consumption (Hesmondhalgh and Meier 2017: 12). My proposed heuristic certainly demands greater scrutiny in its applicability to many of the excellent histories and analyses by the authors cited here, the many more referred to within the book, and the multitude not referenced who have shaped thinking about the music industries. And whilst establishing the historical credibility of the heuristic may be something others or I may take on in the future, its true test is in addressing the problem with prediction. Therefore, unlike Morris (2015), it would be remiss of me to play it safe and renege on the opportunity for a prediction. Heuristically viewed, the emergence of home-based voice activation devices that act as controllers and conduits for music playback are consistent with technologies that reduce playbour (the level of literacy and skill needed to type to search) and improve playback situation control. A pre-schooler who cannot yet use the typed search function on Spotify can voice command a device such as Amazon's Alexa to play nursery rhymes. By broadening the demographic, this device expands the participation of consumers and in turn makes listening more convenient. Therefore, the heuristic predicts that voice recognition devices, or similar technology converged within other mediums for playback, will become as ubiquitous in the home as radio did. It remains to be seen if the heuristic is correct.

Note

1 Player Piano: a piano fitted with a pneumatic apparatus enabling it to be played automatically by means of a rotating perforated roll signalling the notes to be played. (Oxford Dictionaries definition)

References

Adorno, Theodor W. (1962), *Introduction to the Sociology of Music*. London: Continuum International Publishing.

Anderson, Tim J. (2014), *Popular Music in a Digital Music Economy: Problems and Practices for an Emerging Service Industry*. New York: Routledge.

Attali, Jacques ([1977] 1985), *Noise: The Political Economy of Music*, trans. B. Massumi. London: University of Minnesota Press.

Avdeeff, Melissa (2011), 'Challenges Facing Musical Engagement and Taste in Digitality', IASPM 2011 conference proceedings. Available online: http://www.google.co.uk/url?s a=tandrct=jandq=andesrc=sandsource=webandcd=3andved=0ahUKEwju1pGF0LbN AhUJJMAKHXl2D9gQFggkMAIandurl=http per cent3A per cent2F per cent2Fwww. iaspm.net per cent2Fproceedings per cent2Findex.php per cent2Fiaspm2011 per cent2Fiaspm2011 per cent2Fpaper per cent2Fdownload per cent2F11 per cent2F4andusg=AFQjCNFRoS-tPvO6J1y8YksQZKFl1LjbIQandsig2=fI8-qxia99gjpii wtmdBvgandbvm=bv.124817099,d.ZGg (accessed 13 March 2018).

Bailey, Peter (1986), *Music Hall: The Business of Pleasure*. Milton Keynes: Open University Press.

Banks, Mark (2010), 'Autonomy Guaranteed? Cultural work and the "art–commerce relation"', *Journal for Cultural Research*, 14(3): 251–69.

Barnard, Stephen (1989), *On the Radio: Music Radio in Britain*. Milton Keynes: Open University Press.

Bartmanski, Dominik and Ian Woodward (2015), 'The Vinyl: The analogue medium in the age of digital reproduction', *Journal of Consumer Culture*, 15(1): 3–27.

Bartmanski, Dominik and Ian Woodward (2018), 'Vinyl Record: A cultural icon', *Consumption Markets and Culture*, 21(2): 171–77.

Bonnin, Geoffray and Dietmar Jannach (2014), 'Automated Generation of Music Playlists: Survey and experiments 26:3', *ACM Computing Surveys*, 47(2) Article 26.

Born, Georgina (2009), 'Afterword: Recording: From reproduction to representation to remediation', in N. Cook, E. Clarke, D. Leech-Wilkinson and J. Rink (eds), *The Cambridge Companion to Record Music*. Cambridge: Cambridge University Press.

Botstein, Leon (1992), 'Listening through Reading: Musical literacy and the concert audience', *19th-Century Music*, 16(2): 129–45.

Bourdieu, Pierre ([1984] 2010), *Distinction: A Social Critique of the Judgement of Taste*, trans. Abingdon: Routledge.

Brackett, David (2016), *Categorizing Sound: Genre and Twentieth-century Popular Music*, Berkeley: University of California Press.

Bradley, Dick (1992), *Understanding Rock 'n' Roll: Popular Music in Britain 1955–1964*. Buckingham: Open University Press

Bull, Michael (2005), 'No Dead Air! The iPod and the culture of mobile listening', *Leisure Studies*, 24(4): 343–55.

Bull, Michael (2009), 'The Auditory Nostalgia of iPod Culture', in K. Bisterveld and J. van Dijck (eds), *Sound Souvenirs. Audio Technologies, Memory and Cultural Practices*, 83–93. Amsterdam: Amsterdam University Press.

Bunzl, Martin (1997), *Real History: Reflections on Historical Practice*. London: Routledge.

Burkart, Patrick and Tom McCourt (2006), *Digital Music Wars: Ownership and Control of the Celestial Jukebox*. Lanham, MD: Rowman and Littlefield.

Carson, Gerald (1990), 'The Piano in the Parlor: When there was a parlor', *Timeline*, 7(6): 42–54.

Christensen, Clayton M., Taddy Hall, Karen Dillon and David S. Duncan (2016), *Competing against luck: The Story of Innovation and Customer Choice*, e-book, New York: Harper Business.

Citton, Yves ([2014] 2017), *The Ecology of Attention*, trans. B. Norman. Cambridge: Polity.

Clarke, Eric (2005), *Ways of Listening: An Ecological Approach to the Perception of Musical Meaning*. Oxford: Oxford University Press.

Collins, Steve and Sherman Young (2014), *Beyond 2.0: The Future of Music*. Sheffield: Equinox.

Daub, Adrian (2014), *Four-handed Monsters: Four-handed Piano Playing and Nineteenth Century Culture*. Oxford: Oxford University Press.

Davenport, Thomas H. and John C. Beck (2001), *The Attention Economy: Understanding the New Currency of Business*. Boston, MA: Harvard Business School Press.

del Campo, Cristina, Sandra Pauser, Elisabeth Steiner and Rudolf Vetschera (2016), 'Decision Making Styles and the Use of Heuristics in Decision Making', *Journal of Business Economics*, 86(4): 389–412.

DeNora, Tia (2000), *Music in Everyday Life*. Cambridge: Cambridge University Press.

Douglas, Susan J. (2004), *Listening In: Radio and the American Imagination*. Minneapolis: University of Minnesota Press.

Drucker, Peter F. (1955), *The Practice of Management*. London: Heinemann.

Du Gay, Paul, Stuart Hall, Linda James, Hugh Mackay and Keith Negus (1997), *Doing Cultural Studies: The Story of the Sony Walkman*. London: Sage.

Elborough, Travis (2008), *The Long-player Goodbye: The Album from Vinyl to iPod and Back Again*. London: Hodder and Stoughton.

Frith, Simon (2003), 'Music and Everyday Life', in M. Clayton, T. Herbert and R. Middleton (eds), *The Cultural Study of Music: A Critical Introduction*, 92–101 London: Routledge.

Gelatt, Roland (1977), *The Fabulous Phonograph: From 1877–1977*. London: Macmillan.

Gigerenzer, Gerd and Wolfgang Gaissmaier (2011), 'Heuristic Decision Making', *Annual Review of Psychology*, 62(1): 451–82.

Gjerdingen, Robert (2009), 'The Price of Perceived Affordance: Commentary for Huron and Berec', *Empirical Musicology Review*, 4(3): 123–25.

Goodman, David (2016), 'A Transnational History of Radio Listening Groups I: The United Kingdom and United States', *Historical Journal of Film, Radio and Television*, 36(3): 436–65.

Hagen, Anja Nylund (2015), 'The Playlist Experience: Personal playlists in music streaming services', *Popular Music and Society*, 38(5): 625–45.

Hagen, Anja Nylund (2016), 'Music Streaming the Everyday Life', in R. Nowak and
A. Whelan (eds), *Networked Music Cultures: Contemporary Approaches, Emerging Issues*. London: Palgrave Macmillan.

Hauser, John (2011), 'A Marketing Science Perspective on Recognition-based Heuristics (and the Fast-and-Frugal Paradigm)', *Judgement and Decision Making*, 6(5): 396–408.

Herbert, Ruth (2011), *Everyday Music Listening: Absorption, Dissociation and Trancing*. Farnham: Routledge.

Hesmondhalgh, David and Leslie M. Meier (2017), 'What the Digitalisation of Music Tells us about Capitalism, Culture and the Power of the Information Technology Sector', *Information, Communication and Society*, 20: 1–16.

Holton, Richard (1958), 'The Distinction between Convenience Goods, Shopping Goods, and Speciality Goods', *Journal of Marketing*, 23(1): 53–56.

Huron, David (2002), 'Listening Styles and Listening Strategies', Society for Music Theory 2002 Conference, Columbus, Ohio. Available online: http://www.musiccog. ohio-state.edu/Huron/Talks/SMT.2002/handout.html.

IFPI (2017), 'Global Music Report 2017: Annual state of the industry', IFPI. Available online: http://www.ifpi.org/downloads/GMR2017.pdf (accessed 8 March 2018).

Ingham, Tim (2018), 'Spotify Lost $1.4bn Last Year – and it's just filed to go public', Music Business Worldwide, 28 February. Available online: https://www. musicbusinessworldwide.com/spotify-lost-1-4bn-last-year-and-its-just-filed-to-go-public (accessed 8 March 2018).

Jenkins, Henry (2008), *Convergence Culture: Where Old and New Media Collide*. New York: New York University Press.

Kamalzadeh, Mohsen, Dominikus Baur and Torsten Möller (2016), 'Listen or Interact? A large-scale survey on music listening and management behaviours', *Journal of New Music Research*, 45(1): 42–67.

Kahneman, Daniel (2011), *Thinking Fast and Slow*. London: Penguin.

Kassabian, Anahid (2013), *Ubiquitous Listening: Affect, Attention and Distributed Subjectivity*. London: University of California Press.

Katz, Mark (2012), 'The Listener and the Phonograph', in T.D. Taylor, M. Katz and T. Grajeda (eds), *Music, Sound, and Technology in America: A Documentary History of Early Phonograph, Cinema and Radio*. Durham, NC: Duke University Press.

Keightley, Keir (2004), 'Long Play: Adult-oriented popular music and the temporal logics of the post-war sound recording industry in the USA', *Media, Culture and Society*, 26(3): 375–91.

Kibby, Marjorie (2009), 'Collect Yourself: Negotiating personal music archives', *Information, Communication and Society*, 12(3): 428–43.

Krause, Amanda E., Adrian C. North and Lauren Y. Hewitt (2015), 'Music-listening in Everyday Life: Devices and choice', *Psychology of Music*, 2: 155–70.

Kusek, David and Gerd Leonhard (2005), *The Future of Music: Manifesto for the Digital Music Revolution*. Boston, MA: Berklee Press.

Lanham, Richard A. (2006), *The Economics of Attention: Style and Substance in the Age of Information*. Chicago, IL: Chicago University Press.

Leyshon, Andrew (2014), *Reformatted: Code, Networks, and the Transformation of the Music Industry*. Oxford: Oxford University Press.

Marshall, Lee (2014), 'Whither Now? Music collecting in the age of the cloud', in D. Laing and L. Marshall (eds), *Popular Music Matters: Essays in Honour of Simon Frith*, 61–72. Farnham: Ashgate,.

Marshall, Lee (2015), '"Let's Keep Music Special. F–Spotify": On-demand streaming and the controversy over artist royalties', *Creative Industries Journal*, 8(2): 177–89.

Marwick, Arthur (1999), *The Sixties: Cultural Revolution in Britain, France, Italy, and the United States, c.1958–c.1974*. Oxford: Oxford University Press.

McGuigan, Lee and Vincent Manzerolle (2014), *The Audience Commodity in the Digital Age*. New York: Peter Lang.

McLuhan, Marshall ([1964] 2001), *Understanding Media*. Oxford: Routledge.

Millard, Andre (1995), *America on Record: A History of Recorded Sound*. Cambridge: Cambridge University Press.

Miller, Karl Hagstrom (2008), 'Working Musicians: Exploring the rhetorical ties between musical labour and leisure', *Leisure Studies*, 27(4): 427–41.

Morris, Jeremy Wade (2015), *Selling Digital Music, Formatting Culture*. Oakland: University of California Press.

Morris, Jeremy Wade and Devon Powers (2015), 'Control, Curation and Musical Experience in Streaming Music Services', *Creative Industries Journal*, 8(2): 106–22.

Müller, Sven Oliver (2010), 'Analysing Musical Culture in Nineteenth-century Europe: Towards a musical turn?', *European Review of History*, 17(6): 835–59.

Mulligan, Mark (2015), *Awakening: The Music Industry in the Digital Age*. London: MIDIA Research.

Negus, Keith (1996), *Popular Music in Theory: An Introduction*. Cambridge: Polity.

Norman, Donald A. (1988), *The Psychology of Everyday Things*. New York: Basic Books.

Nowak, Raphaël (2016), *Consuming Music in the Digital Age: Technologies, Roles and Everyday Life*. Basingstoke: Palgrave Macmillan.

Nowak, Raphaël and Whelan, Andrew (2016), *Networked Music Cultures: Contemporary Approaches, Emerging Issues*. London: Palgrave Macmillan.

O'Hara, Kenton and Barry Brown (2006), *Consuming Music Together: Social and Collaborative Aspects of Music Consumption Technologies*. Dordrecht: Springer

Osborne, Richard (2013), *Vinyl: A History of the Analogue Record*. Farnham: Ashgate.

Pearce, Philip, L. (2013) 'From Discord to Harmony: Connecting Australian music and business through the experience economy', in P. Tschmuck, P.L. Pearce and

S. Campbell (eds), *Business and the Experience Economy: The Australian Case*. New York: Springer.

Peterson, Richard A. (1990), 'Why 1955? Explaining the advent of rock music', *Popular Music*, 9(1): 97–116.

Peterson, Richard A. and David Berger ([1975] 1990), 'Cycles in Symbol Production', in S. Frith and A. Goodwin (eds), *On Record*, 117–133. London: Routledge

Peterson, Richard A. and N. Anand (2004), 'The Production of Culture Perspective', *Annual Review of Sociology*, 30: 311–34.

Pinheiro, Carlos Andre Reis and Fiona McNeill (2014), *Heuristics in Analytics. A Practical Perspective of What Influences Our Analytical World*. New Jersey: John Wiley and Sons.

Radbourne, Jennifer (2013), 'Converging with Audiences', in J. Radbourne, H. Glow and K. Johanson (eds), *The Audience Experience: A Critical Analysis of Audiences in the Performing Arts*. Bristol: Intellect.

Rogers, Everett M. (1962), *Diffusion of Innovations*. New York: Free Press.

Rogers, Jim (2013), *The Death and Life of the Music Industry in the Digital Age*. London: Bloomsbury.

Rösing, Helmut (1984), 'Listening Behaviour and Musical Preference in the Age of "Transmitted Music"', *Popular Music*, 4: 119–49.

Rossman, Gabriel (2012), *Climbing the Charts: What Radio Airplay Tells us About the Diffusion of Innovation*. Oxford: Princeton University Press.

Russo, Alexander (2010), *Points on the Dial: Golden Age Radio beyond the Networks*. Durham, NC: Duke University Press.

Sandvoss, Cornel, Kelly Youngs and Joanne Hobbs (2015), 'Television Fandom in the Age of Narrowcasting: The politics of proximity in regional scripted reality dramas *The Only Way is Essex* and *Made in Chelsea*', in L. Geraghty (eds), *Popular Media Cultures*. London: Palgrave Macmillan.

Scherer, F.M. (2006), 'The Evolution of Music Markets', in V.A. Ginsburgh and D. Throsby (eds), *Handbook of the Economics of Art and Culture*. Oxford: Elsevier.

Shuker, Roy (2010), *Wax Trash and Vinyl Treasures: Record Collecting as a Social Practice*. Farnham: Ashgate.

Sloboda, John (1998), 'Does Music Mean Anything?' *Musicae Scientiae*, 1(1): 21–31.

Sloboda, John (2015), 'How Does Music Trigger and Influence Our Emotions?' BBC Radio 3, 25 September. Available online at http://www.bbc.co.uk/programmes/p033hq6q (accessed 8 March 2018).

Slotten, Hugh R. (2003), *Radio and Television Regulation: Broadcast Technology in the United States, 1920–1960*. Baltimore, MD: Johns Hopkins University Press.

Sterne, Jonathan (2003), *The Audible Past: Cultural Origins of Sound Reproduction*. Durham, NC: Duke University Press.

Sterne, Jonathan (2012), *MP3: The Meaning of a Format*. Durham, NC: Duke University Press.

Stockfelt, Ola (1997), 'Adequate Modes of Listening', in D. Schwarz, A. Kasabian and L. Siegel (eds), *Keeping Score*, 129–146. London: University Press of Virginia.

Solie, Ruth A. (1994) 'Gender, Genre, and the Parlour Piano', *The Wordsworth Circle*, 25(1): 53–56.

Taylor, Timothy D. (2016), *Music and Capitalism: A History of the Present*. London: University of Chicago Press.

Taylor, Timothy D., Mark Katz and Tony Grajeda (2012), *Music, Sound, and Technology in America: A Documentary History of Early Phonograph, Cinema, and Radio*. Durham, NC: Duke University Press.

Terranova, Tiziana (2000), 'Free Labor: Producing culture for the digital economy', *Social Text*, 18(2): 33–58.

Toynbee, Jason (2000), *Making Popular Music: Musicians, Creativity and Institutions*. London: Bloomsbury.

Tschmuck, Peter (2006), *Creativity and Innovation in the Music Industry*. Heidelberg: Springer.

Tschmuck, Peter (2012), *Creativity and Innovation in the Music Industry*, 2nd edn. Heidelberg: Springer.

Tschmuck, Peter (2017), *The Economics of Music*, E-book. Newcastle: Agenda.

Voigt, Kai-Ingo, Oana Buliga and Kathrin Michl (2017), *Business Model Pioneers: How Innovators Successfully Implement New Business Models*. Switzerland: Springer.

Warren, Steve (2005), *Radio: The Book*, 4th edn. Abingdon: Taylor and Francis.

Wikström, Patrik (2009), *The Music Industry: Music in the Cloud*. Cambridge: Polity.

Witt, Stephen F. (2015), *How Music Got Free: What Happens When an Entire Generation Commits the Same Crime?* London: The Bodley Head.

Wu, Tim (2018), 'The Tyranny of Convenience', *New York Times*, 16 February. Available online: https://www.nytimes.com/2018/02/16/opinion/sunday/tyranny-convenience.html (accessed 14 March 2018).

Yang, Yi-Hsuan and Yuan-Ching Teng (2015), 'Quantitative Study of Music Listening Behaviour in a Smartphone Context', *ACM Transactions on Interactive Intelligent Systems*, 5(3): Article 14.

11

Current Music and Media Use of Young People in Austria: The Musical Practice of the Future?[1]

Michael Huber

New conditions

It is hard to see where the future of music listening lies. A hallmark of reliable research is its tendency to remain very reserved in its predictions. The 'momentary' aspect is down to the fact that we can only draw reliable conclusions from facts we can perceive *today*. However, these facts may look different a year from now, at which point we would have to check, expand and correct the results. The history of music consumption, in particular, has repeatedly shown that in times of technological evolution, people's behaviour regarding music can change rapidly. The phonographic industry knows this only too well. EMI Music, the record company of the Beatles, is no longer with us, as it totally underestimated how the internet would affect its core business. On the other hand, Apple Inc. spent many years producing hardware for a loyal following of music makers, with relatively modest annual profits in the tens or hundreds of millions. Only in 2003 did this music industry outsider finally create something that the established industry leaders had been incapable of: a central, widely accepted legal platform for downloads. At the same time, Apple's lifestyle products – its iPod and iPhone – provided the right hardware for enjoying the now-legal MP3 music, and Apple's profits rose almost continuously from then on. Its 2016 profit of US$45.7 billion was 800 times that of the pre-iTunes era.

Due to technical, economic, and social developments in society, the conditions for dealing with music have radically changed in the past twenty years. The Austrian music sociologist Kurt Blaukopf called this the 'mediamorphosis of music' (Blaukopf 1992). Subsequently, referring to Max Weber, Blaukopf argued that the goal of music sociology research is 'the compilation of all social data relevant to musical practice, the classification of this data according to its

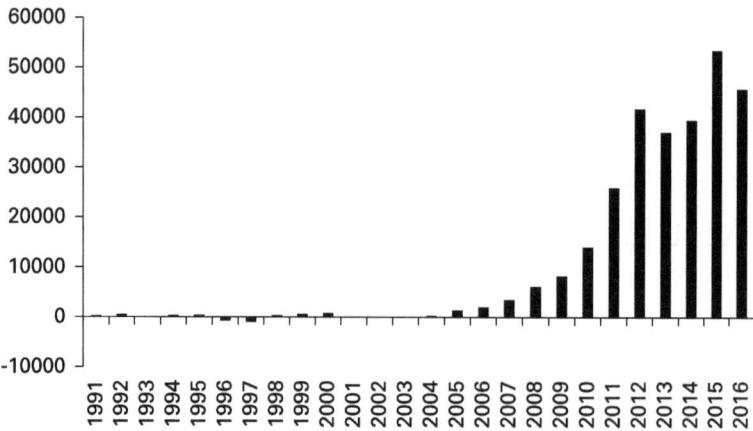

Figure 11.1 Apple Inc. annual net profit (millions of US$).[2]

importance for musical practice, and the recording of data of crucial significance
in altering practices' (1992: 5). This means that what we can do to bring clarity to
the cloudy waters of music listening in the digital era is to record data of crucial
significance in altering music-listening practices. Blaukopf applies the term
'musical practice' far more broadly than just the playing/creation of music: he
extended its meaning to cover '*types* of musical behaviour, *patterns* of musical
behaviour (i.e., rules of behaviour), and musical behaviour *expectations*' (1992: 5).
Through all this, music sociology research must also observe and address social
change; and thus we come to the future of music listening. To be able to speak
with authority, we must turn our attention to the group that most strongly brings
about social change, to those who most clearly demonstrate new musical
behaviours, that is, teenagers and young adults.

As far back as the early 1970s – when it was not yet at all clear that a scientific
approach could be applied to youth culture or popular music – Vienna's Institute
for Music Sociology already had its eye on 'New Patterns of Musical Behaviour
of the Young Generation in Industrial Societies' (Bontinck 1974). The main focus
was a previously unseen intensity in the musical activities of young people, as
they emulated the example of popular beat and rock bands. In the postwar
period, listening to music had played a key role in the developmental steps every
young person must take (leaving the parental nest, creating their own identity),
and had become a key activity in youth culture. For decades, young people's
enthusiasm for consuming music made them the core target group for the global
music industry, but the ability to distribute music digitally has changed this

situation considerably. The free use of music via the internet is a problem that threatens the very existence of the recording industry, whose principal business in the German-speaking countries remains the sale of music recorded on physical media. In Austria, 56 per cent of the recording industry's turnover in 2016 was generated by CDs (with vinyl at 7 per cent and DVDs at 5 per cent); in Germany 54 per cent was generated by CDs (with vinyl at 4.4 per cent and DVDs at 3.4 per cent) (Bundesverband Musikindustrie 2017; IFPI Austria 2017). Any music sociological research programme following Blaukopf now needs to examine the extent to which the new conditions manifest themselves through changed practices regarding music. The research findings presented here show the example of Austria. This small country, with its population of around nine million is unlikely to represent the global trend in music reception. But the fact is that there *is* no (longer any) *global* trend, as the differing significance of music streaming in different music markets shows. Whilst music streaming in vanguard countries such as Sweden (the home of Spotify) or South Korea is highly developed – with a share of the digital market of over 90 per cent – Japan, Austria, Germany and the UK trail far behind, at around 40 per cent (Tschmuck 2016). So, at least as regards the future of the music streaming market, it may be useful to take the similar current status of these four countries as our starting point, and to assume that our knowledge of the attitudes and behaviours of people in Austria regarding music may also be of interest at least to the world's second-, third- and fourth-largest phonographic markets.

For fifty years now, the empirical surveys carried out by Vienna's Institute for Music Sociology have been marked by their firm theoretical basis. In contrast to the major national surveys,[3] here the processes of societal change and structural inequalities hiding behind the raw data are addressed on a socio-theoretical level. What role does music play in people's lives today (and tomorrow)? Which socio-structural features have a decisive influence on music reception? Here, it is interesting to ask not only *what* music people are listening to and *how*, but also *why*.

The theoretical positions on the new possibilities and challenges of music reception essentially fall into two ideological camps. Music pedagogical research in Germany identified a tendency towards a 'musical self-socialisation of adolescents' (Müller and Rhein 2005) as a consequence of the new technical conditions. From this perspective, the internet not only plays a big role as a communication tool and a source of information, but is also established as the most powerful competitor to music socialization authorities such as radio, TV, magazines, parents or friends. This seems to refute the findings of Pierre Bourdieu (1979), who claimed that we are irretrievably informed by primary socialization and family background. As with any sociological 'why' question, this can only be partially answered through *quantitative* methods. However, with *qualitative* methods we can provide a sound basis for further research, which may in turn enrich our representative data through case studies. It is clear, however, that those who have grown up with the internet and mobile phones show considerably different approaches and listening habits than the well-explored audiences of the analogue era. At the same time, many people's musical behaviour might be hardly influenced by digitalization. How strong are the effects of mass media and peer groups in establishing new ways of music reception?

To answer these questions, in 2010 the Institute for Music Sociology in Vienna conducted a survey on the musical attitudes and behaviour of the Austrian population. A rerun was completed in the summer of 2015. More than 1,000 face-to-face interviews in each survey (of representative samples regarding age, gender, education, income, regional affiliation) allow us to present valid data on current and possibly future music listening in the digital mediamorphosis.

The best way to make predictions about the possible future of music listening is to observe young people, so to create with a meaningful comparison this chapter presents two perspectives of the Austrian survey of musical behaviours: young people and older people. This not only shows the relative significance of new approaches to music listening; but also makes clear the extent to which they represent a break with established habits.

As a result of the technological developments of the past twenty years, the Austrain population appears, in its music reception, to be divided into onliner and offliner. There were different musical behaviours before – especially in conjunction with the attributes age and education – but with digitization the differences got stronger and were nourished by a new facet that is yet to be answered by educational and cultural policy. In 1993, the internet became an everyday search and communication platform through its interactive and user friendly visualization in a web browser. Within two decades, the handling of information and the framework for everyone handling information had changed dramatically. Today's possibilities of music reception have little in common with the situation in the 1990s, when the recording industry controlled production, promotion and distribution of music in segmented mass markets. Digitization, broadband internet, high transfer rates as well as cheap and convenient platforms transferred the authority to dispose from the recording industry to the consumers. The attendant conflict between the recording industry and those who liked to download music for free has lost most of its explosiveness in the last few years, which mainly results from the new possibilities of Web 2.0. At this developmental stage of the internet, the network participants become 'prosumers' (Toffler 1981) with various possibilities to change the shape of the internet by adding words, pictures and sounds. Young users especially like to comment, rate and share content. Naturally, those who now have to adjust are not as comfortable as those known as the Web 2.0 generation, who grew up with this situation.

Since the Web 2.0 generation stands out so strongly as a discrete listener group, the 2015 survey had to cover a greater number of young people so as to provide a large enough sample for particular evaluation. Thus the under-30s are over-represented here (33 per cent), and were then weighted accordingly when the total sample was analysed, allowing reliable calculations to be made concerning the real 'digital natives', the age 16–25s.[4] Statistical correlations between variables or indices (dimensions of measure) were computed using Cramer's V, Spearman or Pearson correlations, according to the quality of data. All correlations described and interpreted here are significant. The most significant correlations are shown on the graphs in capitals on the *y*-axis (e.g., 'INTERNET' in Figure 11.4).

Empirical findings

Compared to other leisure activities, the Web 2.0 generation and the over-26s differ relatively little in *how often* they listen to music. Whilst young people in Austria spend a lot more of their free time with friends or at the cinema, and spend far less time reading or watching television, they are only slightly more likely to listen attentively to music. As for the *total number of concerts attended*, and *incidental music listening*, we see virtually no difference between the age groups.

The picture is very different, however, when it comes to a pragmatic approach to music, whereby the Web 2.0 generation demonstrates far greater awareness of how they *use* music. Although older people do appreciate music's ability to create the right atmosphere, only slightly over one-third rate this as 'very important'; amongst young people, this is almost two-thirds. Equally clear are the differences concerning music as an atmospheric background for parties and get-togethers, music as a subject of discussion, music as a reminder of experiences or people, and music as a means to bond with friends. The question of 'why?' was not on the agenda of the study, as that would have been met inadequately by quantitative methods. Nevertheless, we can hypothesize that the availability of music everywhere and at any time, leading some researchers to compare music to utility (Kusek and Leonard 2005), has fostered a pragmatic approach by the Web 2.0 generation, whereas this attitude has still to be learned by the older generations.

Music is chiefly a companion through day-to-day life. Whilst already over half of over-26s say they enjoy listening to music while on the move (in the car, on the train or bus etc.), fully three-quarters of young people say the same. Although neither younger nor older respondents claim to particularly enjoy listening to music while eating or working, in all other day-to-day situations the under-26s take far greater pleasure in music as an accompaniment. The differences are most marked as regards music during sport, for evenings out, and when with friends. This shows the different requirements from music listening. Is music something to address in an attentive manner in an appropriate surrounding? Or is it merely a tool to facilitate the arrangement of everyday life, more a means to an end than an end in itself?

As to the question of how much money is spent on music, there are significant but not great differences between spending on music downloads and streaming.

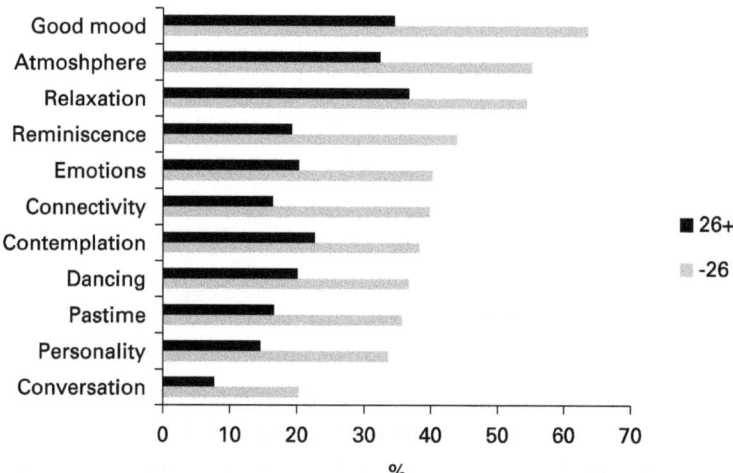

Figure 11.2 Very important functions of music.

However, the two age groups spend very similar amounts on musical performances and physical media. It is notable that even young people are not overly keen to spend money on downloads or streaming as opposed to spending on concerts.

When asked which music styles they preferred, both age groups said they enjoyed jazz, rock and world music. By contrast, pop/hits, techno/house and hip-hop are very clearly music styles for the young, with classical, Austrian folk and 'Schlager' music finding far more fans amongst the over-26s. How *often* music is listened to also shows marked differences between the generations, with young people listening to techno/house and hip-hop very much more often than the older group. The contrasts are less marked for folk and Schlager music, but still relatively large when compared to the pop/hits and rock styles, although the two age groups do also show significant differences in how often they listen to these styles. The over-26s do not listen to classical music significantly more often, despite the claimed preference for it. Apparently daily life in Austria exposes one to a certain amount of classical music – somewhat more, indeed, than one may actually set out to hear. This might be due to the relatively strong presence of classical music in the old mass media, reflecting its extraordinary social valuation in Austria owed to educational and cultural policy from after the Second World War until today. In schools, the works of the great composers are communicated as important part of the Austrian identity, and public authorities use 90 per cent of their financial cultural aid to promote classical music (Huber, Leitich and Fürnkranz 2014).

Bringing together the central perspectives of social change and social inequality raises the question of the extent to which the music tastes of the Web 2.0 generation have been influenced by other socialization factors as compared to the older generation. It may be that it is more difficult for today's young people to develop their own music tastes in isolation from their parents, given that the parents themselves grew up with music that was (back then) part of a rebellious youth culture, such as rock, hip-hop or techno, whereas now there is no comparable socializing music culture. This is to be recognized not least in the dwindled prominence of Cultural Studies, known for focusing especially on music-related youth cultures. If we are aware of the goal-oriented music approach of young people using smartphones, YouTube and Musical.ly for communication and impression management, we must realize that the culture central to today's young people is not one of music consumption – rather, it is a mass social movement based on communication (including about music).

Long-term youth studies increasingly transferred the main focus of their analyses from the use of music to the use of media (Deutsche Shell 2002; Albert, Hurrelmann and Quentzel 2015; Medienpädagogischer Forschungsverbund Südwest 2017). Significantly, young people in Germany today are more likely to become addicted to the internet than the 'good old' drugs of the twentieth century's music cultures (Mortler 2016). The ability to see and be seen, and to comment and to be commented upon via social media, has overshadowed any preoccupation with music. Music has been re-evaluated, from a core interest to a welcome tool for impression management. So what we have here is not merely a new way of listening to music, but a change in the overall role that music is playing in the life of the listeners. Music lost its dominance as an identification object to meet development tasks of the adolescence. Today music is just one of several potential communication topics offered through the internet. In contrast to the twentieth century when the core target consumer of the music industry was the young, today it is the 30–50-year-olds (Huber 2018). The Web 2.0 generation's attitude to music is thus very different to that of anyone who was socialized through analogue music. And this development seems to be unstoppable and irreversible.

For a clearer understanding of this new characteristic, respondents' music tastes were compared with those of their parents. To avoid comparisons based falsely on age, the music styles were compared according to what all respondents' preferences had been when they were 14. This involved, for example, initially examining how many (young) respondents preferred rock music during their teens, then finding what proportion of parents had also preferred rock music at that age. The difference between these two values then represents the level of musical emancipation, which is then used as a basis for comparing the 16–25 and 26+ age groups. The results confirmed the theory mentioned above, that the music choices of the teen members of the Web 2.0 generation do indeed position them in some ways closer to their parents' music tastes than is the case with the over-26s. Overall the highest levels of musical emancipation[5] here are seen in world music (amongst the young) and Austrian folk music (amongst the older respondents). The lowest level of emancipation is seen in both groups where the parents were fans of jazz. Figure 11.3 shows the deviation from parents' tastes, but not the direction (stronger or weaker presence). Long bars represent greater differences between respondents' music tastes at 14 and those of their parents at 14. The sequence from top to bottom reflects the size of the difference in emancipation between the age groups (Austrian folk, 17 per cent; hip-hop, 12 per cent etc.).

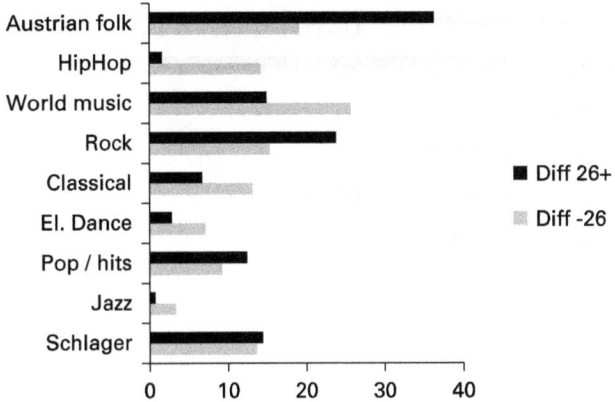

Figure 11.3 Deviation in respondents' preferences from those of their parents.

We see that amongst the over-26s the strongest emancipation of young people's tastes from those of their parents is (was) in Austrian folk music. Similarly strong emancipation is seen in rock, but in the other direction – that is, towards the style.[6] Obviously in the second half of the twentieth century it was a popular act of youth insurgence to dislike Austrian folk and to like rock music. The isolation strategy of the Web 2.0 generation is shown further by the fact that their emancipation no longer shifts from Austrian folk to rock music, but from world music to hip-hop, reflecting the global rise of this genre (Hooton 2015). Incidentally, the relationship to parents' attitudes towards Schlager music demonstrates no cohort effect; here the Web 2.0 generation scarcely differs at all from the over-26s.

In response to the related question on what had most strongly influenced respondents' music tastes, relatively few members of the Web 2.0 generation mentioned their parents, whereas amongst the over-26s their parents were identified as far more important: the third-strongest influence. The perceived influence of the internet as a socialization factor showed a particularly strong contrast between the generations: deemed the strongest influence by 21 per cent of young people but only 2.4 per cent of the over-26s. Regarding the socialization question, the internet is the only influence with a significant variation in estimated importance, meaning that the difference here is correspondingly greater.

There is general agreement across the generations that the most important factors overall in the creation of music tastes were friends and the (old) mass media of radio and television. So, there still seems to be a need for moderated

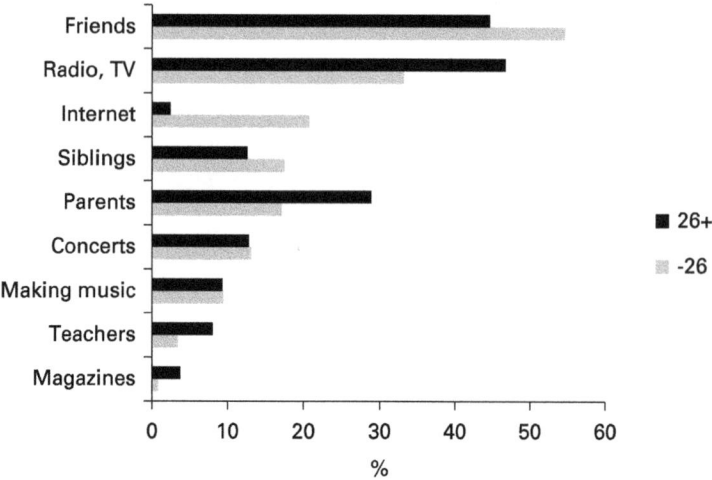

Figure 11.4 Estimated importance of socialization factors.

music programmes, and a need for opinion, assessment, and attitude. All this is delivered more credibly and reliably by pre-internet channels, as they are based on editorial responsibility; in other words, verifiable expertise.

The great variation between the different generations in the importance of the internet for enjoying music is echoed in the frequency with which they use various devices for music playback. Whilst for the over-26s the radio remains unchallenged at number one, the last few years have seen young people shifting *en masse* to the smartphone. In the entire special analysis of the Web 2.0 generation, the greatest difference of all between the age groups is the frequency of smartphone use for music. Mobile MP3 devices (e.g., iPods) and computers are also more important sources of music for younger people, who tend to turn to radio and television far less often than older people.

The dramatic shift that has taken place here over just a few years is very clear when compared with the surveys from 2010 and 2015. In 2010, mobile phones with an internet connection were still luxury items, and were thus the least important music players for all groups, even the young. By 2015, almost every teenager in Austria had one of these pocket computers with an internet connection, bringing the smartphone to the top spot for young people wanting to listen to music.

How does the Web 2.0 generation differ from older people in how they use the internet for music? Neither generation is particularly ready to actually buy

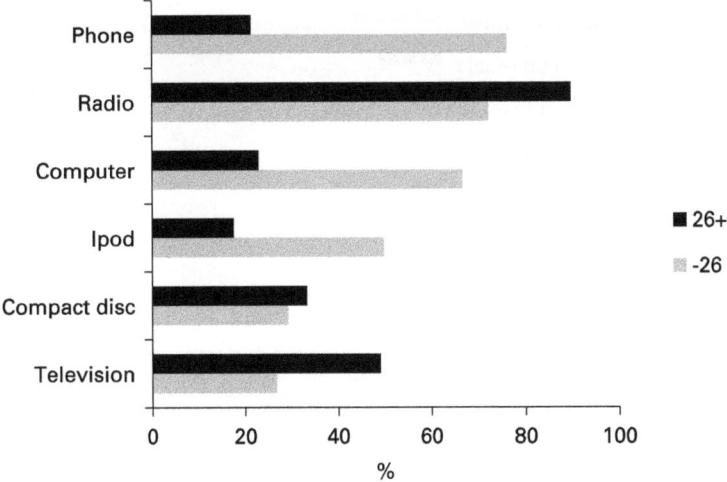

Figure 11.5 Devices used for listening to music (at least several times per week).

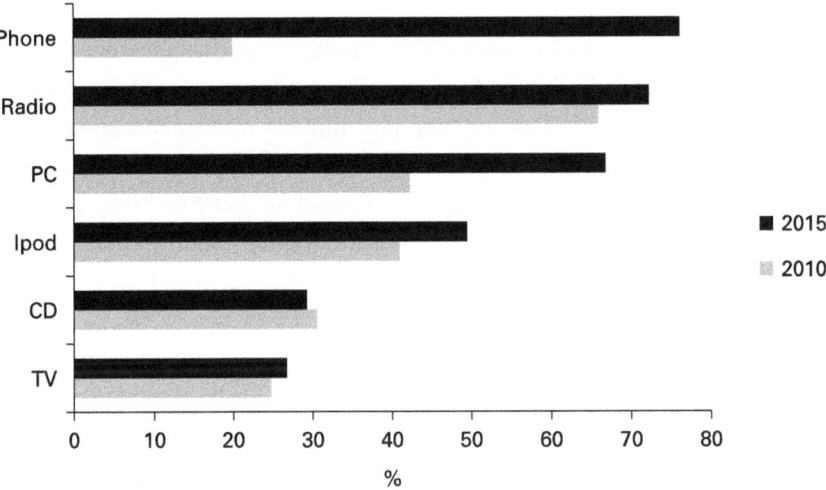

Figure 11.6 Media that young people frequently use for listening to music (2010 vs. 2015).

music via the internet, with the over-26s being even less willing to do so. There are highly significant differences in how often the internet is used for listening to music, for obtaining information on music, for free downloads, to express enjoyment of music, and as a platform for communication. For many young people, internet platforms like YouTube, WhatsApp or Musical.ly are the drop-in centre for music. And there is also room for discussing, sharing and rating of

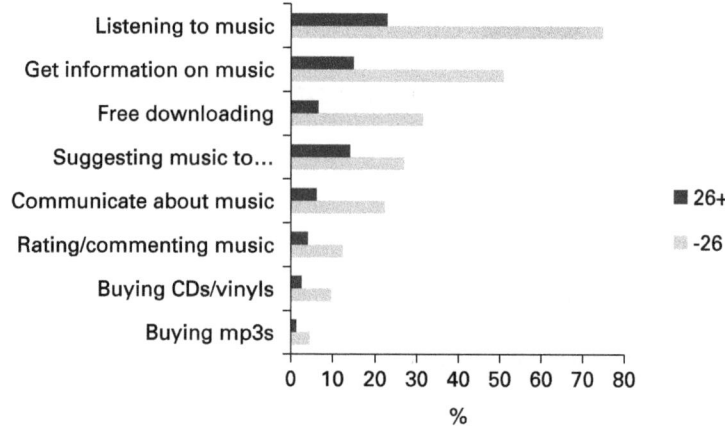

Figure 11.7 The use of the internet for music (at least several times per week).

music, which is important for the Web 2.0 generation but yet to be adopted by the elder generations.

If one were to come to the conclusion that today's young people were obsessed with computers and the internet for enjoying music, one would, however, be mistaken. The under-26s also sing and play musical instruments significantly more often than older people, even though they are no more likely to have had musical parents as role models. One reason might be that youngsters generally have more free time than their parents. Furthermore, this could point to an Austrian peculiarity of making music as a very popular leisure-time pursuit for young people.

The question regarding parents as role models was a notable one during the surveys. Pierre Bourdieu's conclusion that primary socialization is decisive for one's later approach to music has also been empirically confirmed more recently, several times (Nagel et al. 1997; Nagel and Ganzeboom 2002; Nagel 2010). Opponents of this view point to their observation of musical self-socialization, whereby the decisive role of old institutions such as the family is in fact diminished, and the individual is now called on – alone, open to ideas and with the help of music and media – to establish their own allegiances and demarcations (Müller and Rhein 2005). The study presented here applied higher statistical analysis processes to examine the influence of various socialization determinants and other factors on attitudes and behaviours regarding music; demonstrating that the question of parents' influence on preferred music styles of their children does not have a clear answer.

Whilst an attachment to pop/rock or regionally/traditionally oriented music may be seen as being culturally inherited, frequent enjoyment of jazz, classical or electronic music tends to stand more for emancipation. 'Omnivores' (Peterson 1992) who are interested in all kinds of music maintain the highbrow tastes they have inherited, but display a form of emancipation through their readiness to also go lowbrow. On the one hand, this may be because today it is more frowned-upon to look down on socially weaker citizens. On the other hand, due to the globalized social and cultural life, national highbrow cultures lost their binding character as legitimate culture. An examination of respondents' own estimations of the importance of various musical influences reveals clear differences according to age and level of formal education. Whilst 46 per cent of the over-75s cite their parents/grandparents as the most important factor in their musical socialization, only 17 per cent of under-26s do so. And while the internet is not even mentioned by the over-45s, it is given as an answer by 20 per cent of under-26s. With regard to the highest level of formal education achieved, parents and the internet have the greatest influence on those with the lowest levels of education, whereas for those with lower–middle levels of education, radio and television have the greatest influence.

An interesting concurrence of age and education as influencing factors to music reception is to be observed by looking at the cultural omnivores.[7] By recovering tolerant taste as a new distinction strategy of the cultured class in the 1990s, Richard A. Peterson brought new dynamics to research into social inequality and cultural reception (Peterson 1992). Through secondary analyses of the surveys of public participation in the arts, he was able to show that in the USA Bourdieu's predicated distinction strategies of neglecting popular music styles were marginal: rather, the acceptance of popular music styles, especially by younger respondents, had risen between 1982 and 1992. These highly educated people with high incomes, who liked classical music and opera or even called these their favourites strikingly often, also showed a liking for inferior 'lowbrow' music styles. Subsequently, Peterson's findings were discussed intensively and surveyed globally, resulting in a dilution of the 'omnivores' definition (Peterson and Kern 1996; Bryson 1996; Emmison 2003; Peterson 2007). In German-speaking countries, the quest for musical omnivores provided inconsistent results due to the lack of reliable characteristics and a predominance of theoretical approaches. The present report (Huber 2018) can put things right with significant findings. Around one-sixth of the Austrian population can be described as musical 'omnivores'. These highly educated and comparatively young listeners prefer the highbrow music styles of jazz and classical, but they also show an explicit appreciation of popular and folk styles, which is a distinctive contrasting feature to highly educated elderly Austrians who often show strict denial of 'lowbrow' music. In some respects, this cultural openness can be seen as emancipation of the young cultural elite from their parents' generation.

Conclusion

Does the present status of music listening in the Web 2.0 generation represent the future of music listening in society as a whole? We do not know. But it may well be that many of these new patterns of musical behaviour, like music reception through smartphones and the internet, or creative and down-to-earth use of music for communication and impression management, will become central to society. Our empirical survey shows one thing very clearly: the future of music listening in the digital era hinges on the internet and how people use it for information, communication and receiving music. The extent to which this already applies to the Web 2.0 generation allows us to surmise that what we are seeing here is more than just a group trend. On the other hand, experience shows us that established music reception channels are not completely sidelined by new technology. In western industrialized countries, CDs are a well-rooted cultural technology, and are likely to persist for decades as a way of listening to music. It will be interesting to see if listening to music via older, slower, more awkward, and more expensive media, such as CDs or vinyl records, will continue to survive as a contrast to the more convenient ways of consuming music. Spontaneous decisions for a variety of approaches are likely to be a characteristic of how we enjoy music in the future. We choose between streaming, physical media and live performance according to the situation and what we want from our music at a given moment. Here we can imagine parallels to our eating habits: microwave frozen pizza when time is of the essence; freshly made food from ingredients specifically bought for the purpose when we want something special; and on special occasions, fine dining in a restaurant. Through all this it is vital to emphasize that blanket judgements concerning music reception have little value, as the influence of cultural capital is hard at work here. A high level of education can only compensate, to a limited extent, for potential biases or lack of parental influence. But musical education in school can bring an individual into contact with a variety of musical characters and practices. And that might foster a competent and autonomous approach to music as soon as it becomes a theme with and in the new media.

Notes

1   This paper is an updated and improved version of Huber 2016.
2   Apple Annual Report 1991–2016 (http://investor.apple.com/financials.cfm).
3   See Donnat 2011, ICPSR 2012, European Commission 2013.
4   n = 292; for practical reasons it was not possible to survey people under 16, as permission would have had to be obtained from parents/legal guardians.
5   Musical emacipation here is understood as choosing something different from what parents liked.
6   From the Web 2.0 generation, only 19 per cent fewer respondents gave Austrian folk music as their favourite music than their parents had stated it to be. Among older repondents, this was 36 per cent fewer. Fifteen per cent more young people gave rock as their favourite music than did their parents; among older people this figure was 23 per cent.
7   See also Emília Barna's contribution to this book.

References

Albert, Mathias, Klaus Hurrelmann and Gudrun Quenzel (eds) (2015), *17. Shell Jugendstudie. Jugend (2015).* Frankfurt/Main: Fischer.

Blaukopf, Kurt (1992), *Musical Life in a Changing Society: Aspects of Music Sociology.* Portland, OR: Amadeus Press.

Bontinck, Irmgard (ed.) (1974), *New Patterns of Musical Behaviour: A Survey of Youth Activities in 18 Countries.* Vienna: Universal Edition.

Bourdieu, Pierre (1979), *La distinction: critique sociale du jugement.* Paris: Editions de Minuit.

Bryson, Bethany (1996), 'Anything but Heavy Metal: Symbolic exclusion and musical dislikes', *American Sociological Review*, 61: 884–99.

Bundesverband Musikindustrie (ed.) (2017), *Musikindustrie in Zahlen.* Berlin: self-published.

Collopy, Dennis and David Bahanovic (2008), *Music Experience and Behaviour in Young People: Main Findings and Conclusions.* London: British Music Rights.

Deutsche Shell (ed.) (2002), *50 Jahre Shell Jugendstudie.* Berlin: Ullstein.

Donnat, Olivier (2011), *Pratiques culturelles, 1973–2008. Dynamiques générationelles et pesanteurs sociales.* Paris: Ministère de la Culture et de la Communication.

Elvers, Paul et al. (2015), 'Exploring the Musical Taste of Expert Listeners: Musicology students reveal tendency toward omnivorous taste', *Frontiers in Psychology*, 6, article 1252.

Emmison, Michael (2003), 'Social Class and Cultural Mobility: Reconfiguring the cultural omnivore thesis', *Journal of Sociology*, 39: 211–30.

Hooton, Christopher (2015), 'Hip-hop is the Most Listened to Genre in the World, According to Spotify Analysis of 20 Billion Tracks', *Independent*, 14 July. Available at: http://www.independent.co.uk/arts-entertainment/music/news/hip-hop-is-the-most-listened-to-genre-in-the-world-according-to-spotify-analysis-of-20-billion-10388091.html (accessed 14 January 2018).

Huber, Harald, Lisa Leitich and Magdalena Fürnkranz (2014), *Austrian Report on Musical Diversity. Österreichischer Bericht zur Vielfalt der Musik 2000–2010*. Vienna: Universität für Musik und darstellende Kunst Wien.

Huber, Michael (2016), 'Salle de concert ou Internet?', in *Où va la musique? Numérimorphose et nouvelles expériences d'écoute*, ed. Philippe Le Guern, 93–108. Paris: Presses des Mines.

Huber, Michael (2018), *Musikhören im Zeitalter Web 2.0 – Theoretische Grundlagen und empirische Befunde*. Wiesbaden: Springer VS.

IFPI Austria (ed.) (2017), *Österreichischer Musikmarkt 2016*. Vienna: self-published.

Inter-University Consortium for Political and Social Research (ICPSR) (ed.) (2012), *Survey of Public Participation in the Arts (SPPA) 2012*. Washington, DC: National Endowment for the Arts.

Ipsos/IFPI (ed.) (2016), *Music Consumer Insight Report* 2016. Available online: www.ifpi. org/downloads/Music-Consumer-Insight-Report–2016.pdf (accessed 7 January 2017).

Kusek, David and Gerd Leonhard (2006), *The Future of Music: Manifesto for the Digital Music Revolution*. Boston, MA: Berklee Press.

Medienpädagogischer Forschungsverbund Südwest (ed.) (2017), *JIM-Studie 2017. Jugend, Information, (Multi-)Media*. Stuttgart: mpfs.

Mortler, Marlene (ed.) (2016), *Drogen- und Suchtbericht der Bundesregierung 2016*. Berlin: Bundesministerium für Gesundheit.

Müller, Renate and Stefanie Rhein (2005) 'Musical Self-socialisation of Adolescents: Theoretical perspectives and empirical findings', in Noraldine Bailer and Michael Huber (eds), *Youth – Music – Socialisation*, 11–28. Vienna: Institut für Musiksoziologie.

Nagel, Ineke (2010), 'Cultural Participation between the Ages of 14 and 24. Intergenerational Transmission or Cultural Mobility?', *European Sociological Review*, 26(5): 541–56.

Nagel, Ineke et al. (1997), 'Effects of Art Education in Secondary Schools on Cultural Participation in Later Life', *Journal of Art and Design Education*, 16(3): 325–31.

Nagel, Ineke and Harry B.G Ganzeboom (2002), 'Participation in Legitimate Culture: Family and School Effects from Adolescence to Adulthood', *The Netherlands' Journal of Social Sciences*, 38(2): 102–20.

Peterson, Richard (1992), 'Understanding Audience Segmentation: From elite and mass to omnivore and univore', *Poetics*, 21: 243–58.

Peterson, Richard (2007), 'Comment on Chan and Goldthorpe: Omnivore, what's in a name, what's in a measure?', *Poetics*, 35: 301–5.

Peterson, Richard and Roger Kern (1996), 'Changing Highbrow Taste: From snob to omnivore', *American Sociological Review*, 61: 900–7.

Ter Bogt, F.M. Tom et al. (2011), 'Moved by Music. A typology of music listeners', *Psychology of Music*, 39: 147–63.

Toffler, Alvin (1981), *The Third Wave. The Classic Study of Tomorrow*. Toronto: Bantam.

Tschmuck, Peter (2016), 'Der Boom des internationalen Musikstreaming-Marktes, 2011–2015'. Available online: https://musikwirtschaftsforschung.wordpress.com/2016/07/25/der-boom-des-internationalen-musikstreaming-marktes-2011-2015 (accessed 7 January 2017).

Weber, Max (1995), *Wissenschaft als Beruf*. Stuttgart: Reclam.

12

Curators as Taste Entrepreneurs in the Digital Music Industries

Emília Barna

The power of lists

On 22 November 2017, online electronic music magazine and community platform *Resident Advisor*, established in 2001, published a feature article explaining why the team had decided to stop publishing their annual 'RA polls', a standard feature of the platform since 2006.[1] Here they explain how their mission has always been 'to support local electronic music scenes and to connect the larger electronic music community', yet since their position in the digitized music industry shifted, the role of the polls in relation to this mission has arguably also become problematic. The article discusses three particular issues. The first is the gatekeeping position that *Resident Advisor* has come to occupy, manifested in the symbolic power of the end-of-the-year lists. As the article explains, *Resident Advisor* has grown from a local, Sydney-focused website, to a global one, and reflecting on this significant growth in influence, they realize that '[t]oday, the decisions [they] make can affect club culture and electronic music, a world [they] love and where [they] hope to be a force for good'. An artist being named in the *Resident Advisor* polls could directly be translated into recognition, an increase in reputation, as well as economic capital through subsequently receiving invitations or being able to negotiate a higher fee. *Resident Advisor* are aware that influence comes with responsibility:

> [w]hat began as a lighthearted way to praise our favourite artists and toast the year gone by had become something of more serious consequence: an industry index influencing many different parts of club culture, from event lineups to artist fees to the atmosphere of the scene in general.
>
> Resident Advisor 2017

Responsibility in its turn necessitates a strategy with regard to representation, which is the second issue addressed. The article argues that 'the homogeneity of the results didn't represent the diversity of the scene', either with regard to gender, or to geography: 'the DJ and Live Act lists were overwhelmingly dominated by men, mostly from the US and Europe', while the electronic music scene of 2016 includes 'countless incredibly talented women play[ing] to packed clubs each weekend'. The team feels that the polls treat the contribution of these women – and, presumably, under-represented geographical areas – unfairly.

The third issue addressed is ranking and the implicated competition: '[they] decided that they don't want to rank artists in this way', as 'to put artists in a list in descending order of perceived quality does a disservice to them, even the ones at the top, and creates an atmosphere of self-interested competition'. Rating and ranking are certainly also established practices in the traditional mainstream music industry in the form of record charts such as Billboard and awards such as the Grammys. Nevertheless, they have become a ubiquitous feature of the digital sphere, extended from the original more centralized and formalized forms to peer ranking and giving stars, votes, 'likes' and 'dislikes' to services, as well as all kinds of content and the creators of content (Hearn 2010; see also Suhr 2012). The constant quantification in which internet users are encouraged to engage reinforces an individualistic spirit of competition, not only amongst more traditional providers of services, such as hotels or restaurants, but also artists and other creators.

I want to draw a parallel between the self-reflexive statement of *Resident Advisor* and the following opinion from a DJ, or curator, who worked for the former music playlist platform and 'music discovery service' 22tracks. 22tracks was a free online 'music discovery service' based in Amsterdam and active between 2009 and 2017. The platform offered playlists of twenty-two relatively new music tracks – usually from the past six to twelve months – curated by DJs based in a variety of cities, with twenty-two DJs or DJ teams in each city. At the time of my research in 2014, playlists from Amsterdam, Paris, Brussels and London were featured, and in 2016, Berlin, Dubai, Haarlem, Marseille, New York, Tel Aviv, Vilnius were added to these. The playlists in each city corresponded to twenty-two different genres or styles, such as alternative, beats, contemporary, disco, hip-hop, indie/rock, jazz, Latin, or tropical. The playlists therefore aimed to represent the respective cities as localities, and different styles and genres at the same time. They were all updated weekly with a number of new tracks.

In the quote below, the DJ compares the practices of online music blogs such as Pitchfork with 22tracks' own methods of showcasing music:

> I was never a fan of blogs because blogs have something really arrogant about them … to be honest, I don't like people who write about music. I don't like reviews of albums, I think it's really weird to put sound into text and especially when they add a personal touch to it, which is totally the blogging thing, because it's not good journalism … when you just say your opinion about it … and 22tracks just puts online music and there is like no info to it, just there. With blogs … people, who like … the *Wire* or … *Pitchfork* and shit like that and then they think they're relevant, but it's also curated, it's also picked from the internet. So if you're like a band and you don't have contact with *Pitchfork*, or one stupid guy from *Pitchfork* thinks you're not good enough, then 3000 other people will think you're not good enough, because [the review]'s out there. And that's [what I don't like about] the blogs and curating. But when it comes to radio shows or 22tracks it's different, because there are no words written. If you don't like it you just don't upload it or you don't say anything about it.
>
> M3[2]

Whilst it seems problematic to posit a sharp distinction between showcasing pure music, which, as we will see, is itself always a selective representation following a particular logic, and the evaluating practices of the music blogs and other online platforms that have come to serve as important reference points within music culture, the marked annoyance of the DJ with the power of these evaluations over musicians' reputations is illustrative of the significance of gatekeeping and representation. In addition, the DJ questions the reasonableness of the power attached to the personal tastes of music bloggers or reviewers in deciding which artist gets (positive) coverage and which one does not, or whose career is put in danger by a negative review. He also highlights the importance of connections – social capital – for securing presence and good reviews on Pitchfork.

But how exactly should we conceive of the relationship between 'curating', the primary function of 22tracks, and displaying personal taste? And how are the debates around gatekeeping, representation and diversity, and competition, related to the restructuring of the music industries along with digitization, in particular to the emergence of new intermediaries between producer and consumer? Here I will explore these questions with the help of interviews conducted in 2014 with the DJs or curators (they frequently used both terms) of the former music platform 22tracks. The interviews explored their work, the way they viewed and made sense of this work, and of 22tracks itself, in the context of the changing technological environment of online music and the gradual restructuring of the music industries.

Legitimate omnivorousness: taste, society and neoliberalism

In today's capitalist societies, we increasingly define ourselves, and our relations to other people, through acts and choices of consumption. Consumption has emerged as a structuring force in society, not only in the sense that our preferences for consumer products – whether furniture, clothes, mobile phones, or music, that is, our tastes – are determined by, and in their turn reproduce our social class positions (Bourdieu 1984 [1979]), but also in the sense that our participation in society is increasingly only possible through our fulfilling roles as consumers (Simányi 2005; Bauman 2001). It is difficult therefore to overestimate the stakes in articulating taste, and the power of shaping taste.

Various authors (e.g., Thornton 1995; Hennion 2001) have shown that forming and expressing taste functions as (sub)cultural capital in the fields of cultural production (Bourdieu 1993), including more formal art worlds as well as informal music scenes and subcultures. It is even possible to demonstrate how taste judgements are rooted in global power hierarchies (Taylor 2004). In the field of popular music, digitization has marked a rupture in the old order through the reordering of the structure of the music industries,[3] with an upheaval followed by an elongated period with increasingly sharp competition for positions in which stakes become higher. Culturally, this struggle is manifested in hopes (such as the democratic promise of the internet) and fears (such as regarding the impact of file-sharing on the part of established actors of the industry), 'freedom fights' (such as innovative business strategies relying on new technology used by independent artists) as well as instances of backlash (such as regulations supporting the interests of traditional record labels). Can this period therefore be described as one characterized by a struggle for positions, including legitimate taste-making positions?

In his book *Distinction*, based on an empirical study conducted in France in the 1960s, Bourdieu (1984 [1979]) distinguishes between *legitimate* taste, defined by those in possession of high levels of cultural capital, *middle-brow* taste, and *popular* taste. Works and artists belonging to the legitimate category do so because, due to the symbolic power of the dominant class, they are acknowledged as 'good' by the whole of society, even by those social classes that do not consume them, since they do not have access, cognitive and/or material, to highbrow works. Bourdieu's well-known findings have been empirically tested more recently within a US context, resulting in Peterson's theory of the *cultural omnivore* (Peterson and Simkus 1992; Peterson and Kern 1996), according to which a consumption pattern characterized by choices from a variety of cultural domains – cultural omnivorousness – is gradually replacing the univore 'snob' pattern of highbrow consumption. For instance, instead of only listening to classical music and opera, people with high cultural capital may choose to enjoy works of classical music alongside jazz and rock. The explanations behind this shift are primarily sociological, including social and geographical mobility, and the 'baby boom' generation not turning away from popular culture in adulthood (van Eijck 2000: 214). DiMaggio identifies 'a large, well-educated, geographically mobile' elite whose typically multi-sited occupational environment also 'reward[s] participation in multiple cultural traditions' (DiMaggio 1991: 144, quoted in van Eijck 2000: 221). Bryson (1996) complements this analysis by introducing a structurally determined tolerance, or 'multi-cultural capital', as an explanatory factor for cultural omnivorousness, demonstrating through the distribution of musical dislikes that musical exclusivity decreases as we ascend the social ladder (and besides class, gender and age have also been shown to be determining factors in the degree of mixing).

It is important to stress that the cultural omnivore thesis does not negate the continuing importance of distinction (Coulangeon and Lemel 2007). Rather, omnivorous behaviour, along with the (multi-)cultural capital it requires, becomes the marker of high-class status itself. Or, as van Eijck puts it, '[c]ontrary to "omnivore taste" signifying a transcendence of class, consumption choices continue to be expressive of, and in their turn (re)produce class boundaries' (van Eijck 2000: 211). Today, the cultural omnivore thesis is so widely acknowledged that it is directly applied in advertising by music streaming services. According to the anthropologist Nick Seaver, Pandora[4] applies a diversity metric to rank the range of a particular listener's music taste: 'A higher diversity score should indicate a higher social status, which means that these listeners can have more expensive ads sold against them' (as cited in Harvey 2014; *see also* Prey 2016).

Whilst in this instance diversity in itself is taken to represent higher social status, legitimate eclecticism has its own logic, which is embedded into social relations: for instance, consuming genres coded as articulating subaltern voices, such as hip-hop or ethnic music, is regarded as 'cool' by the cultural elite in western societies, whilst a markedly aspiring lower–middle class articulation – such as Céline Dion, whose voice is described by Wilson as *nouveau riche* itself (Wilson 2014: 72) – is amongst the most widely renounced.

The increasing dominance of cultural omnivorousness as legitimate taste is accompanied by a tendency of cultural hybridity, or 'cross-cultural products' (van Eijck 2000: 208), yet the relationship between the increasing hybridity of cultural forms and social structure remains undertheorized. What is apparent is that the distinct discourses and the attached value regimes that govern music, identified by Frith (2002 [1996]) as the discourses of *art, commercial,* and *folk* music, whilst still relevant (Taylor 2004), can no longer be so clearly attached to cultural forms. The theorization of this increasing cultural hybridity and social structure could begin with an analysis of the so-called 'poptimism' discourse that has emerged in popular music journalism as a counter-discourse and critique of 'rockism' and its authenticity seeking. Saul Austerlitz is broadly cited as the defining article detecting this tendency in music journalism:

> Poptimism wants to be in touch with the taste of average music fans, to speak to the rush that comes from hearing a great single on the radio, or YouTube, and to value it no differently from a song with more 'serious' artistic intent. It's a laudable goal, emerging in part from the identity politics of the 1990s and in part from a desire to undo the original sin of rock 'n' roll: white male performers' co-opting of established styles and undeservedly receiving credit as musical innovators.
>
> Austerlitz 2014

Whilst the 'poptimist' discourse has indeed directly addressed structural issues such as the white and masculine bias of 'rockist' writing, at the same time, with a gesture that in Mark Fisher's (2009) term may be called 'capitalist realism', it knowingly embraces the commercial logic of pop. Its emphasis on the dismissal of the guilt in 'guilty pleasures' (Broyles 2010) serves to justify an uninhibited enjoyment and celebration of the products of the music industries, in line with the dominant neoliberal capitalist ideology. This is the discursive environment in which a new, young elite of 'taste entrepreneurs', emerging with the digital transformation of the music industries, are situated.

Intermediaries: taste, technology and control

In techno-optimistic narratives, cultural diversification, democratization, and industry deconcentration have been named as the most important promises of the internet in general, as well as, in particular, the digitization of the music industries. Whether musicians – or cultural creators – are able to gain more control, and whether music consumers around the world have easier access to a more diverse set of cultural goods, have therefore been amongst the central questions of analyses of the shift. Azenha (2006) provided an exceptionally helpful exploration of the decentralization and the diversification hypotheses in a music industries context. He demonstrated early on what other authors (e.g., Collins and Young 2014) have since increasingly confirmed: that online distribution would be key in determining the extent to which the internet reduces barriers of entry to musicians seeking alternative pathways independent of record labels. Secondly, he argued that contrary to the general assumption, deconcentration does not automatically equal cultural – in this case, musical – diversification (par. 83), moreover, that cultural diversification does not automatically equal social democratization. For instance, the decentralization of the 1950s, which had been enabled by cheaper recording technology, and was characterized by the proliferation of independent studios and the localization of radio in the US, contributed to the popularity of such genres as jazz, rhythm 'n' blues, and rock 'n' roll. It thus created more opportunities for more black artists. Nevertheless, it was largely white people – through record labels and studios – that were able to capitalize on these trends by incorporating stylistic innovations (par. 29). In addition, in the history of the recording industry, periods of deconcentration have always been followed by processes of reconsolidation and the reinforcing of major label control. '[T]he privileged access of established actors in the music industry to capital, social networks, technology and knowledge allows them to most adeptly acclimatize to new forms of distribution, licensing, promotion and marketing' (par. 36). Currently, so-called 360-degree record deals are also an industry innovation, allowing record labels to potentially regain some of the power lost in part to file-sharing and in part to companies such as Apple or Google (cf. Marshall 2012). Access to opportunities opened up by new technology similarly tends to follow existing social structures.

> Because access to technologies and the knowledge to use them most effectively are conditioned by existing socio-economic disparities, they tend to facilitate the reproduction of the multiple and overlapping centre-periphery relations (i.e., between classes, races, ethnicities, genders, nations, regions, neighbourhoods, etc.) that colour the music industry and its broader societal context. Those within the established (social, economic and geographical) centres of the music industry are best poised to capitalize on new opportunities facilitated by new technologies.
>
> Azenha 2006: par. 38

Placing curation in a social and a geographical perspective, as I discuss below, demonstrates that these points are valid today, even if the commodification of digital music has taken place much faster than anticipated by Azenha.

In response to those who claimed that the internet would lead the cultural industries towards a process of disintermediation, the necessity of intermediation is also underlined by Azenha: '[j]ust making music available on the Internet does not mean it will be heard and consumed' (par. 49; cf. Collins and Young 2014: 63–66). Traditionally, intermediary roles have been fulfilled by record labels, A&R people, managers, distributors, touring companies, radio, publishers – as well as business affairs people such as accountants and lawyers. As Negus observes, whilst 'A&R staff may provide a hip face, may hang out in the mythical "street" or club', accountants and lawyers 'are the ones drawing up the finer details of any contract and negotiating with performers and their representatives' (Negus 2002: 506). Some authors, like Mark Mulligan, assume a conservative view and lament the loss of the expertise of these traditional actors: 'Record label A&R teams filter the best from the rest, whilst in DIY there is a risk of the self-congratulatory echo chamber, of friends, family and uber fans perpetually praising rather providing tough love' (Mulligan 2014: 10). Nevertheless, traditional actors have not disappeared, rather, they in part have succeeded in making use of new intermediaries: 'major labels', for instance, 'can more easily leverage popular music downloading services to have their music and advertisements featured on their websites' (Azenha 2006: par. 49). This process can be described as reintermediation.

New intermediaries, on the other hand, include digital retailers, digital distributors, aggregators, online independent labels, as well as streaming services. So far, I have used 'intermediaries' in an industry sense, to refer to actors fulfilling the function of mediating between producer and consumer. Yet 'intermediary' may also refer to cultural intermediaries as understood by Bourdieu and used somewhat differently later on – as Hesmondhalgh (2006) points out – by other authors such as Featherstone (1991) or Negus (2002). It is worthwhile revisiting this meaning. As Hesmondhalgh summarizes:

> Bourdieu seems to have intended the term 'new cultural intermediaries' to refer to a particular type of new petit-bourgeois profession, associated with cultural commentary in the mass media, 'the most typical of whom are the producers of cultural programmes on TV and radio or the critics of "quality" newspapers and magazines and all the writer-journalists and journalist-writers' (1984/1979: 325). Presumably, the 'old' cultural intermediaries were those who

acted as critics and as experts on serious, legitimate culture in the pre-mass media age.

Hesmondhalgh 2006: 226

Negus, also drawing on Bourdieu (and critiquing his concept), understands cultural intermediaries as intermediaries between producers and consumers,[5] but he also stresses the

> growth of a cluster of 'cultural industries' dependent upon advertising imagery, promotional techniques and marketing methods have 'widened the distance ... between producers and consumers' (Garnham 2000: 162). The increasing use of publicity, public relations and marketing, and other symbolic intermediary activity, has not necessarily resulted in production and consumption being brought closer together. Instead, it has exaggerated the space between the product (or performer) and the public.

Negus 2002: 508

When asked who the primary tastemakers are in the music industries today, the interviewed DJ-curators mentioned both traditional and new intermediaries. The traditional ones included A&R people and other label employees or record companies themselves, radio (and well-known radio personalities), music magazines and journalists, as well as record stores. The new intermediaries included 22tracks itself, as well as DJs, blogs such as *Hypemachine* or *Stereogum*, online magazines, YouTube, the simultaneously online and offline event Boiler Room, as well as festivals. An increasing percentage of music industry revenue is from live music, and festivals such as All Tomorrow's Parties are now also often 'curated' by well-known artists, as well as artists and producers. Based on this, it indeed seems that in the digitized music industries we can also observe a broadening of the space between producer and consumer, occupied by a multitude of various actors, new entrepreneurs as well as old functions, and an overlap of a variety of functions, as in the case of influential top artists who are also regarded as tastemakers (e.g., Beyoncé Knowles or Jay-Z).

Digitization has been leading the music industries towards the solidification of a bifurcated structure (Collins and Young 2014: 85). On the one hand, despite the democratic promises, concentration has increased not only through the newly strengthening power of major record companies, but even more so through the growing power of large IT companies Apple and Google (the latter is present mostly through YouTube). Parallel to this, the already layered independent sector is becoming increasingly multi-layered, and independence is becoming an even more complicated stance than before. Collins and Young describe the emergence of a new 'middle class' of artists managing to pursue relatively lucrative careers in the new online and digital environment by developing the right technological skills and strategies (2014: 112–13) – even if these careers are not necessarily comparable to those of the top artists represented by majors. Hesmondhalgh and Meier speak of 'fairly well-established large independents ... many of them with close financing, distribution and other connections to the majors', coexisting with 'a world of amateur and precarious semi-professional musical production, including the continuing world of underground scenes and micro-independent institutions' (Hesmondhalgh and Meier 2015: 102).

The DJs of 22tracks generally spoke of 'a more linear structure' replaced by a more complex, 'intertwined' one (M1), but they differed in their evaluation of what this meant with regard to two of the mentioned three promises of the internet: diversification and democratization. An optimistic reading of how this structure has enabled new pathways and more people independent of the traditional major label structure to become 'decision makers' (M1) coexisted with a nuanced view of an emerging bifurcated structure:

> I'm almost sure that there will be just one record company, just one major company, and a constellation of small record companies, small structures, and some way it's a good thing because usually in each aspect of life it's good to have a big structure and a lot of small structures because it is creative, there is a lot of energy in the small circles so maybe in the future there will be a big big big record company with artists like Lady Gaga, Justin Bieber and stuff like that, and a lot of small companies or no companies at all, people with their own small companies at home, working in their own studio, putting songs on the internet, using 22tracks to broadcast music.
>
> M5

Another DJ alluded to the way new releases on majors can be pushed to the starting page of streaming platforms – the leverage mentioned by Azenha:

> You get music around you all the time and the company who has the biggest money in their campaigns to get their music to most people [will do so], and people like what they hear a lot, so in a way music is chosen for you.
>
> M2

22tracks itself decided to partner with streaming platform Spotify in 2016 after seven years as an independent platform.

Curators as 'taste entrepreneurs'

'22tracks.com is all about curating' – this is how the 'music discovery service' defined itself. Curating, however, certainly remains 'a fuzzy concept' (Jansson and Hracs 2017). It comes with high cultural connotations, as the profession of curator is traditionally associated with museums and galleries. Nevertheless, I want to argue that its prevalent use in a much broader cultural context (which, besides music, includes food and fashion; Jansson and Hracs 2017: 2–3) to refer to the functions of taste-making, gatekeeping, selection and distinction is in line with cultural hybridization and the expansion of cultural omnivorousness. The increased reference to, and (self-)identification as, curators can be understood as part of a strategy of legitimation in the cultural field, in a similar manner to the cultural intermediaries described by Bourdieu.

In a popular music context, curation has been used in its more traditional sense in relation to popular music-themed museums and exhibitions (Leonard and Knifton 2012). It has also been used, as mentioned, to refer to events – the programmes of festivals in particular, curated by artists to reflect their own tastes. Festivals themselves have also been interpreted as tastemakers:

> In Belgium we have Tomorrowland, when it comes to the EDM genre, I think Tomorrowland is really a tastemaker because the big names are created on Tomorrowland, like with the managements and the Live Nations and the bookings agents.
>
> M3

Music bloggers, as well as DJs have also been referred to as curators, most typically in relation to the compilation of playlists. Music playlists may be curated by humans or algorithms,[6] and human curators may be professional playlist curators – there are professionalized playlist provider services such as Songza or Soundiiz – or regular users such as music fans, or, as in the case of 22tracks, people involved in the music industries in various ways. Even pop stars have been called curators: Kheraj (2017) refers to Selena Gomez as a curator in order to emphasize the fact that the production of the pop text has become a highly professionalized cooperative enterprise, where the 'conductor' of the process may no longer be the producer, the A&R person or the manager, as in the old model, but rather the pop star themselves. Moreover, Kheraj's argument is made explicitly in defence of pop stars, who are criticized for not writing their own songs, thus his employment of the term may be understood as a legitimizing gesture.

We can see that the above uses in part overlap with the 'tastemakers' identified by the interviewed DJs. In an attempt to clarify, to a possible extent, the meaning of curation, elsewhere I gave two definitions, a weak and a strong one. In a weak sense, it has been defined as 'the ability to spot things' (Josh Spear, quoted in Dumenco 2011), or, in the words of a 22tracks DJ, 'curating is about seeing a bigger picture and trying to get some parts out of it' (M3). In a strong sense:

> All interviewees agreed upon the fact that 22tracks playlists represented (their) personal tastes – for them, individual taste appears to be the central organizing principle. Some of the DJs specifically stated that they only select what they like ... this may override the principle of representing a particular genre. The importance of taste in the sense of value judgment, that is, the ability to distinguish between 'good' and 'bad', is necessarily overall implied. According to the Brussels city manager, the DJs have to be the best in their genre or style. This requires experience – implicitly, the knowledge necessary to make apt value judgments. 'Good selections' is a criterion for a good DJ, where 'good' refers not only to the perceived quality, novelty and engagingness of the tracks, but also the extent to which they can be perceived as showcasing a musical personality and individual style with their own unique taste. The compiling of playlists thus constitutes a kind of creative contribution, and the playlists themselves the creative outlet of DJ-curators. We may call this a strong notion of curation.
>
> Barna 2017

In other words, a (professional) curator employs their taste as a creative tool:

> A personal taste [is] what makes your style as a DJ or as a selector or as a curator or as a journalist or blogger, the things that you curate, that's the only weapon you have as a DJ, it's what you select.
>
> M2

Or:

> Our DJs are the best curators or one of the best curators in their musical style, living their lives to select the best in a certain genre ... for you. ... I do like to watch movies, but I'm not the movie enthusiast to watch 100 movies to be able to know which are the 20 best. ... I am very happy that there are ... journalists who do that job for me and then I can select the 20 best movies out of the 100 that were made this year. And the same with the DJs ... they make a selection for many other people ... they make the life of other people easier.
>
> M1

The DJ-curators of 22tracks can thus be called taste entrepreneurs – they form part of a group of music professionals who function as cultural intermediaries. They hold positions in which they are able to tell 'good' from 'bad', 'cool' or 'trendy' from 'outdated', and distinguish between what is legitimate and what is not. They are both top consumers, connoisseurs with a high level of (sub)cultural capital, and cultural producers who think of playlists as their own personal creative outlets in which they invest and which they approach methodologically. For example, one of the DJs detailed the steps he always takes when selecting the five new tracks for the playlist each week, from looking at particular magazines and listening to demo tapes sent to him to the principles he applies with regard to selecting local artists: 'I will choose one big artist . . . One more alternative artist, but who people know. One completely unknown artist. One electronic track, one . . . little bit e-pop oriented' (M5).

They build careers, their own brands, through showcasing their taste through their repertoire: 'I'm a brand on the internet or something, a music connotation or something' (M3). They refer to autonomy and freedom in expression of their tastes: 'In 22tracks I only play music that I like. And it's also one of the reasons I like this tool, because I can play everything I want' (M5), as well as the stressing importance of control:

> If you click on it, you click Moody, then you don't know what it is, it's not a genre, it more a kind of vibe . . . so yeah, I always hope that people listen to it at night or when they are sick . . . Sometimes people come to me, people I know or people who know me from the club things, and they're like, yeah, I checked out your radio show and it was . . . I don't know, it was weird and then I ask, when did you check it, and they're like, at my job, like two in the afternoon. I won't check it either at that time. That's the bad thing about internet, it's total[ly] free. You can't control the situation, you can't control it. Actually, I would like to go back to the old days when it was on radio, strictly radio.
>
> M3

Conclusions

Curators can therefore be viewed as a group of new music professionals carving out positions in the expanding intermediary space between producers and consumers identified by Negus (2002: 508). Even if they are amateur curators – which they often are – and they are typically at least partly independent music industry people, there is a professional ethic and method that characterizes their work. They possess symbolic power through their compiled playlists, they are in gatekeeping positions from where they are able, for instance, in the case of 22tracks DJs, to assist artists in their local networks and grant representation to local 'sounds'. Returning to the last issue raised by *Resident Advisor*, responsibility in terms of representation and cultural diversity, it is important to observe that in the case of 22tracks at least, at the time of my research, out of the eighty-eight DJs, only five were female, and in the DJ teams overall, only three teams included female members. This raises important questions with regard to the distribution of symbolic power in society, which we cannot, and should not, avoid addressing in the future.

Notes

1   I wish to thank M A student Mihály Fazekas for bringing this example to my attention during our 2017 Autumn 'Digital music industries' module at the Budapest University of Technology and Economics.
2   I will refer to my seven interview subjects anonymously throughout the text. 'M' refers to male and the subjects are numbered.
3   The history of the music industry, as has been shown by, among others, Azenha (2006), can be described as a history of ruptures and reorderings.
4   Pandora is a recommendation-based music streaming service operating in the US.
5   As does Hesmondhalgh (2006). Yet in *Distinction*, Bourdieu makes it quite clear that first and foremost, they mediate between *classes*, by creating and channelling – interpreting – an accessible 'version' of legitimate culture – this is what he calls middle-brow.
6   Even though understanding algorithm as *non-human* is a problematic simplification, as algorithms are designed by humans based on measurements of human choices.

References

Austerlitz, Saul (2014), 'The Pernicious Rise of Poptimism', *New York Times*, 4 April. Available online: https://www.nytimes.com/2014/04/06/magazine/the-pernicious-rise-of-poptimism.html?_r=1 (accessed 1 January 2018).
Azenha, Gustavo (2006), 'The Internet and the Decentralization of the Popular Music Industry: Critical reflections on technology, concentration and diversification', *Radical Musicology 1*. Available online: http://www.radical-musicology.org.uk/2006/Azenha.htm (accessed 1 January 2018).

Barna, Emília (2017), 'The Perfect Guide in a Crowded Musical Landscape': Online music platforms and curatorship', *First Monday,* 22(4): 3 April. Available online: http://firstmonday.org/ojs/index.php/fm/article/view/6914/6086 (accessed 1 January 2018).

Bauman, Zygmunt (2001), 'From Work Ethic to the Aesthetic of Consumption', in P. Beilharz (ed.), *The Bauman Reader*, 311–33. Malden: Blackwell Publishers.

Bourdieu, Pierre (1984 [1979]), *Distinction*, trans. Richard Nice. Cambridge, MA: Harvard University Press.

Bourdieu, Pierre (1993), *The Field of Cultural Production.* Cambridge: Polity Press.

Broyles, Susan Elizabeth (2010), *No End in Sight: A Critique of Poptimism's Counter-Hegemonic Aesthetics.* MA Thesis, University of Texas.

Bryson, Bethany (1996), '"Anything but Heavy Metal": Symbolic Exclusion and Musical Dislikes', *American Sociological Review,* 61(5): 884–99.

Collins, Steve and Sherman Young (2014), *Beyond 2.0: The Future of Music.* Sheffield: Equinox.

Coulangeon, Philippe and Yannick Lemel (2007), 'Is "distinction" really outdated? Questioning the meaning of the omnivorization of musical taste in contemporary France', *Poetics,* 33(2–3): 93–111.

DiMaggio, Paul (1991), 'Social Structure, Institutions, and Cultural Goods: The case of the United States', in Pierre Bourdieu and James S. Coleman (eds), *Social Theory for a Changing Society.* Boulder, CO: Westview Press.

Dumenco, Simon (2011), 'Why Calling Yourself a Curator is the New Power Move'. *Details,* 29(5): 82.

Featherstone, Michael (1991), *Consumer Culture and Postmodernism.* London: Sage.

Fisher, Mark (2009), *Capitalist Realism.* London: Zero Books.

Frith, Simon (2002 [1996]), *Performing Rites: On the Value of Popular Music.* Oxford: Oxford University Press.

Garnham, Nicholas (2000), *Emancipation, the Media and Modernity.* Oxford: Oxford University Press.

Harvey, Eric (2014), 'Station to Station: The past, present, and future of streaming music'. *Pitchfork.com.* 16 April. Available online: https:/pitchfork.com/features/cover-story/reader/streaming/ (accessed 1 January 2018).

Hearn, Alison (2010), 'Structuring Feeling: Web 2.0, online ranking and rating, and the digital "reputation" economy', *Ephemera,* 10(3/4): 421–38.

Hennion, Antoine (2001), 'Music Lovers: Taste as performance', *Theory, Culture and Society,* 18(5): 1–22.

Hesmondhalgh, David (2006), 'Bourdieu, the Media and Cultural Production', *Media, Culture and Society,* 28(2): 211–31.

Hesmondhalgh, David and Leslie Meier (2015), 'Popular Music, Independence and the Concept of the Alternative in Contemporary Capitalism', in James Bennett and Niki Strange (eds), *Media Independence: Working with Freedom or Working for Free?*, 94–116, New York: Routledge.

Jansson, Johan and Brian J. Hracs (2017), 'Curating Music in the Digital Age', *Economy, Governance, Culture 1/2017*. Southampton: University of Southampton.

Kheraj, Alim (2017), 'Why Do We Look Down on Pop Stars Who Don't Write Their Own Songs?' *Noisey.vice.com*, 27 March. Available online: https://noisey.vice.com/en_us/article/pgw8j9/pop-stars-curation-songwriters-selena-gomez-beyonce-drake (accessed 1 January 2018).

Leonard, Marion and Robert Knifton (2012), '"Museums of Sound": Collecting and Curating Everyday Popular Music Experiences', in Robert Snape, Helen Pussard and Michael Constantine (eds), *Recording Leisure Lives: Everyday Leisure in Twentieth Century Britain*, 67–83. Eastbourne: Leisure Studies Association.

Marshall, Lee (2012), 'The 360 Deal and the "New" Music Industry', *European Journal of Cultural Studies*, 16(1): 77–99.

Mulligan, Mark (2014), 'The Death of the Long Tail: The superstar music economy', *Music Industry Blog*, 4 March. Available online: https://musicindustryblog.wordpress.com/2014/03/04/the-death-of-the-long-tail/ (accessed 1 January 2018).

Negus, Keith (2002), 'The Work of Cultural Intermediaries and the Enduring Distance between Production and Consumption', *Cultural Studies*, 16(4): 501–15.

Peterson, Richard A. and Roger M. Kern (1996), 'Changing Highbrow Taste: From snob to omnivore', *American Sociological Review*, 61(5): 900–7.

Peterson, Richard A. and Albert Simkus (1992), 'How Musical Taste Groups Mark Occupational Status Groups', in Michél Lamont and Marcel Fournier (eds), *Cultivating Differences: Symbolic Boundaries and the Making of Inequality*, 152–68. Chicago, IL: University of Chicago Press.

Prey, Robert (2016), 'Nothing Personal: Algorithmic individuation on music streaming platforms', *Media, Culture and Society*, November 30: 1–15.

Resident Advisor (2017), 'Opinion: Why we're stopping the RA polls', *Residentadvisor.net*, 22 November. Available online: https://www.residentadvisor.net/features/3105 (accessed 15 December 2017).

Simányi, Léna (2005), 'Bevezetés a fogyasztói társadalom elméletébe' [Introduction to the theory of consumer society], *Replika 51–52*, 165–95.

Suhr, Cecilia. H. (2012), *Social Media and Music: The Digital Field of Cultural Production*. Bern: Peter Lang.

Taylor, Timothy D. (2004), 'Bad World Music', in Christopher J. Washburne and Maiken Derno (eds), *Bad Music: The Music We Love to Hate*, 65–81. New York and London: Routledge.

Thornton, Sarah (1995), *Club Cultures: Music, Media and Subcultural Capital*. Cambridge: Polity Press.

van Eijck, Koen (2000), 'Richard A. Peterson and the Cultural Consumption', *Poetics*, 28: 207–24.

Wilson, Carl (2014), *Let's Talk About Love. Why Other People Have Such Bad Taste*. New York, London, Delhi, Sydney: Bloomsbury.

13

An Echoic Chamber: Algorithmic Curation and Personalized Listening

Andrew Fry

Which song next? A question faced by every listener. With growing choice, selecting the next song has never been more complex. Businesses have turned to digital solutions to solve this problem, applying the same tools and techniques used within high-frequency trading in financial markets, and terrorist surveillance by government intelligence agencies – a persistent attempt to quantify both music and human behaviour. Strategies to answer this question continue to develop, continue to shape listener's experiences, and continue to exert power over listeners: these strategies will be investigated here.

Data-driven personalization

The catalogues provided by music streaming services have expanded – Apple Music currently claim to provide 45 million songs (Apple Inc. 2017a). On-demand music consumption has exploded, for example Spotify now has 70 million paying subscribers [Stutz 2018]). A comprehensive market now exists with Amazon Prime Music, Apple Music, Deezer, Google Play Music, Pandora, Spotify, and TIDAL. These competitors are no longer impeded by restrictive data transfer speeds or storage, and increased processing power allows advanced tools. These tools enable machine learning, 'a branch of artificial intelligence based on the idea that machines should be able to learn and adapt through experience' (SAS 2017a); and the analysis of big data, the 'large volume of data – both structured and unstructured – that inundates a business on a day-to-day basis' (SAS 2017b). This opens up new possibilities for managing the catalogues, better understanding the songs, the users, how they interact with one another, and how to improve this interaction – making it easier for users to find the music they want to listen to.

Vast catalogues of songs need to be filtered, and these evolving tools are the current weapons in the fight for market domination. The quicker songs are found, the more likely users are to pay for the service.

Filtering data is fundamental to many online services – Amazon products, Facebook profiles, Google web pages – their databases are simply too vast for the individual human user to navigate. This filtering was initially broad, a search resulting in products, profiles or pages listed in a rudimentary order: alphabetical, price or popularity. However, as the databases grew, and new tools and techniques developed, results became increasingly personalized, displayed and ordered depending on the individual user – as understood by the service. This personalization process is an attempt to give the customer what they want, at least what the service determines they want, as quickly as possible. To inform this personalized ordering, companies develop taste profiles for their users, recording and analysing the behaviour of individuals, and comparing this to databases of others. Using these taste profiles for personalization is increasingly ubiquitous. The adverts, films, images, news, prices, products, and social media updates displayed may be curated around an individual's taste profile (Tufekci 2015). This could be Google returning search results that they 'believe are the most relevant to the user' (Google 2017), Netflix recommending particular films (Vanderbilt 2016: 69), or advertisers on Facebook being able to target users by gender, age, location, those who have referenced 'Jew hater' (ProPublica 2017), or even exclude specific races (ProPublica 2016). Digital algorithms perform this filtering, and are 'a set of guidelines that describe how to perform a task' (Brogan 2016) such as how the data is used. In 2005, Eric Schmidt, then CEO of Google, stated that providing more than one search result should be considered a systemic bug:

> We should be able to give you the right answer just once. We should know what you meant. You should look for information. We should get it exactly right and we should give it to you in your language and we should never be wrong.
>
> Charlie Rose 2005

Three years after Googlewhacking entered the lexicon (Unblinking 2002), this idea still remains the utopian vision: to provide a single, perfect result, be it product, profile, web page or song. A filter that provides more than one result is a filter that can be improved.

Music streaming services face similar challenges to other online services. The large databases, of up to 40 million songs, need to be filtered and structured for the user, thus curation has emerged as the key to market competition (Popper 2015; Rundle 2015). This curation has also evolved from a simple order to individually personalized results. To curate tens of millions of songs, for tens of millions of listeners, digital tools are required. Digital tools require data, therefore collecting and analysing data has become the fulcrum of the curatorial process. Digital music catalogues are populated with songs and data provided by record labels and artists (via aggregators and distributors), therefore streaming services can immediately build a fundamental understanding of each song, for example, artist name, song title, song length, song genre, associated album title, associated album genre, release date. This data allows the catalogues to be filtered (searched) and sorted, for example by song title or genre. These primary data points are important, yet insufficient for personalization. With the initial data alone, curation is limited, and songs arranged by album, genre, decade or alphabetically. Additionally, it generally requires the listener to know precisely what they were looking for; for example, searching for the name of a song. With 40 million songs to choose from, human users are unlikely to remember every one. This rudimentary curation has therefore been deemed by the market as inadequate (Popper 2015; Rundle 2015). Furthermore, a song is not simply a digital file, but an experience. Emotion, memory and mood all infiltrate this experience. Songs that conjure feelings of love, recall summer, or suit the early morning commute are not necessarily titled as such. As profit-centred businesses, the objective of music streaming services is to retain users by providing them with the next song that they want to hear. To better provide this song, more data is needed.

Different companies have sought to address the challenge of data-gathering in different ways. Online radio service Pandora, within their *Music Genome Project*, relies on musicologists to analyse their catalogue (Pandora 2017), noting around 450 characteristics for each song: 'a detailed analysis that describes what kind of instruments are in the song, what those instruments are doing ... harmony, melody, rhythm, what the voices sound like' (Popper 2015). This data is also shown to the listeners, an explanation of why the current song is playing: 'we're playing this track because it features mellow rock instrumentation, demanding vocal performances, interweaving vocal harmony, mixed minor and major tonality, and melodic songwriting' (Knight 2015). This project has been running for over a decade using human musicologists, who are neither fast nor cheap. Although some services have opted for this human-driven approach, many now employ digital tools wherever they can – big data analysis, machine learning, algorithms – both within curation and to acquire new data on their catalogues. YouTube's curatorial system is self-described as 'one of the largest scale and most sophisticated industrial recommendation systems in existence' (Covington et al. 2016). It utilizes deep learning, 'a type of machine learning that trains a computer to perform human-like tasks, such as recognizing [*sic*] speech, identifying images or making predictions' (SAS 2017c), with models that learn 'approximately one billion parameters and are trained on hundreds of billions of examples' (Covington et al. 2016), to manage and curate the 1 billion hours of video watched daily on the service by over 1 billion users (YouTube 2017). In 2014, Spotify acquired The Echo Nest (Popper 2015), a company that 'gathers information about new music posted to blogs, news websites, and social media' (Knight 2015), as well as using acoustic analysis, collaborative filtering (Popper 2015), and other techniques to power their recommendation system, a system that, aside from Spotify, is used by over 430 other music applications (The Echo Nest 2017). Different methods, but all aimed at gathering as much data as possible on every song, and building a profile for each.

There are therefore two databases built simultaneously by the given service – one for the songs, and one for the users. With regard to the users, taste profiles are developed using recorded behaviour and personal details:

–   Who the user is: Name? Location? Gender? Email address?
–   Listening habits: What (artists, genres, songs)? Where (geographical location)? When (time of day, frequency)?
–   Interaction: Which devices are used? How often are songs skipped? If so, which songs? Are albums preferred over singles? Are songs played on repeat? Are there preferred genres?

This data is the starting point when developing a user's taste profile. In developing an understanding of how the user has historically behaved, services hope to better predict their future interaction. If this can be predicted, users' experience of the service can be adjusted and personalized, showing users what they are predicted to want, and concealing what they are predicted to not want. Through analysing these big data sets – all personal information and recorded behaviour held on all users – and applying machine learning, services can develop a greater understanding of their users. The biggest services such as Spotify and Apple Music have tens of millions of users, and the data on an individual user can be analysed against all others. Increasingly granular queries can be raised, further informing taste profiles, fine-tuning them, improving their accuracy, and therefore becoming more representative of the user(s). For example:

–   If a user regularly listens when connected via Bluetooth to a car during weekdays between 8–9am and 5–6pm, is this a driving commuter?
–   If a user listens through a desktop computer at the same location during weekdays between 9am and 5pm, are they working in an office?

This becomes a continual process. The resulting data furnishing new queries, exponentially producing more data and hypotheses on each user:

–   If a user regularly listens when connected via Bluetooth to a car, what kind of phone is it? What kind of car is it? How much do these products cost? How often do they update their products? Can this knowledge determine their wealth? What do other wealthy driving commuters listen to?
–   If a user works in an office, and rarely skips songs when playing an entire album, what should the service suggest next? Which albums do similar office workers listen to?

These same processes can be applied to every other node in the database, with relevant queries raised for each song, artist, genre and album:

–   How do listeners interact with a specific song? Does it get skipped more than other songs? Do users turn the volume up for this song more than others? Is it shared on Facebook more than others?
–   Do commuters prefer a specific album? Or a specific genre? Are certain genres played more at certain times of the year?

The vast quantities of data regarding the content and the users can then be synthesized, raising additional queries to further develop understanding of both:

–   Do other 30-year-old, female, Portland-based, driving commuters enjoy ambient music by Samson Stilwell in the morning during December?
–   If Bob Marley streams increase by 50 per cent during June to September in North America, can this be considered summer music? And do 50-year-old, liberal, male, New York users prefer listening to this or Laurel Halo in the summer?

And so it continues. This level of understanding is the result of many layers of data, gradually and continually fused to develop more detailed user taste profiles, and synthesising this knowledge with the profiles of each song, artist, album and genre.

The motive behind the data collection and analysis is to personalize the streaming service, something previously impossible due to lesser processing capabilities. In the past, services may have displayed varying albums in different territories, or at different times of the year, however nowadays, individual customization is increasingly prevalent. Two of the largest streaming services, Spotify and Apple Music, personalize their users' experience in similar ways. Both interfaces allow users to navigate pre-programmed playlists based on genre (*Pop, Latin*), activity (*Backyard BBQ, Morning Commute*), and mood (*Good Vibes, Down In The Dumps*). Although humans oversee much of this curation – Zane Lowe and Julie Adenuga produce conventional radio shows for Apple Music (Apple, Inc. 2015), and Tuma Basa (former programmer at MTV and BET) curates Spotify's RapCaviar playlist (Knopper 2017) – elsewhere, services utilize data. On Spotify, each artist, song, and album can be used as the basis of a 'radio' station, a continual playlist of similar (as judged by the service) songs. Every user is also shown six playlists ('Your Daily Mix') providing continually playing songs based on certain clandestine themes, and the 'Discover Weekly' playlist is updated every Monday with thirty songs, selected by algorithm, specifically for the individual listener. Additional personalization is increasingly pervasive and obscure. Spotify search results now differ user-to-user – typing in *p* in the search shows *Philip Glass* to one user, and *Paramore* to another. Gradually everything can become structured and designed around the individual user. The absolutely personalized streaming service is here, and it's only going to evolve.

Within every curatorial method there will be a ratio between human and algorithm, however, all will be somewhat driven by data. As a rule, in the new streaming landscape, the more personalized the listening experience, the more data-driven it will be. As with the understanding of songs and users, the curatorial algorithms are also continually updated through deductive techniques: feedback loops driving the users' experience. For example:

–   Discover Weekly: The number of songs skipped in a user's playlist may refine the selection for the next week. If a user regularly skips songs they haven't heard before, the number of previously unheard songs may decrease the following week.

- Radio: Two songs regularly included by listeners in the same personal playlist may be considered evidence of song similarity, therefore they may become more likely to be included in the same 'radio' station as each other.

The fuel that drives the algorithmic personalization of individual users' playlists is data. Every click, skip, or volume adjustment can be recorded and used as evidence of a certain predilection, appending the individual's taste profile. What the user experiences, sees, and hears, becomes dependent on their own interaction. Every listener's experience is disparate.

These processes of personalization may have ulterior motives, particularly as regards relationships with content providers – record labels and artists. Many industry qualms around the business model of streaming have been overcome, but ongoing business relationships are never guaranteed and services need to continually work to maintain them. The more songs are streamed, the more providers are paid, the better the working relationship. These conditions may somewhat influence song suggestion, for example:

- By increasing the use of certain labels' content in playlists when a new licensing deal is approaching, more income can be generated, possibly giving the service a better negotiating position.
- Conversely, reducing the use of certain content if the provider is not offering favourable terms, supplying exclusive albums to competing services (Ingham 2016), making critical statements to the press about the service, or about high-paying advertisers.
- Guaranteeing positioning in playlists, particularly to those artists currently touring, or with upcoming marketing campaigns, in exchange for better deal terms, or other financial incentives.
- Improved playlist placement based on personal relationships, for example, an artist playing an executive's wedding (Johnson 2016).

The better that playlists are curated – providing listeners with songs they actually want to hear – the more listeners will rely on them. According to Spotify, in the first year of 'Discover Weekly', 40 million users streamed nearly 5 billion songs (Spotify 2016). Thus the playlists will become more powerful, and progressively more important for both services and content providers. If the majority of listeners rely on pre-programmed or algorithmically generated playlists, placement becomes financially incredibly important to labels and artists. Within this curation, there are clear benefits to the users – ideally enjoying more music – however, understanding the additional financial motives behind personalization is important as we consider the consequences of these curatorial processes.

As the user-base of these services grows (Spotify is currently projected to end 2017 with 70 million paying subscribers and around 160 million total active users [Ingham 2017b]), so too will pressure from financial stakeholders, including advertisers and content providers. Services will be seeking new strategies to obtain, retain and commercialize users. With curation emerging as a key differentiation between competing services (Popper 2015), a great deal of focus will fall on improving algorithmic recommendations. As curatorial algorithms are steadily deemed obsolete, following either customer feedback or competitor advances, additional data sources on the users may be incorporated to improve them. To some degree it is unclear as to what data is currently collected, and how the data that is currently collected is being used, however the natural progression of services trying to understand user behaviour is to seek more data. Monitoring, recording, and analysing data is widely viewed as vital to the understanding, and prediction, of human behaviour, whether it is the NSA monitoring in-flight cellphone calls (Follorou 2016), webcam streams (Ackerman and Ball 2014), and text messages (Cooney 2014); Google monitoring email content (Gibbs 2014) and search results (Eckersley et al. 2006); or political campaigns using the Polis canvassing app to document face-to-face encounters with voters (Shieber 2017). For example, future song suggestions could be informed by:

– Broader behavioural habits: internet browsing, past Amazon purchases, weekly time spent on social media. These may suggest particular listening proclivities, particularly when compared with other users showing similar behavioural characteristics. Perhaps time spent viewing Arca's Instagram profile would increase the likelihood of more Arca tracks being suggested. Perhaps user preference with regards artwork imagery, colours, or fonts used in album descriptions can be determined.
– Social connections: members from a device's contact list, number of Facebook connections, how often a user calls their parents. This knowledge about social interactions may inform future influencer marketing, highlighting particular individuals who are more susceptible, or more helpful when promoting new releases, products or playlists.

- Local conditions: weather, ambient sound levels, physical movement, physical location. These services could suggest songs better suited to loud environments, song tempos matched to the user's jogging speed, or peaceful music when at a library.
- Political allegiance or financial status: andy@goldmansachs.com may correspond to different preferences than andy@wearethe99percent.us; libertarians may prefer less-personalized playlists.

With personalization of music streaming services increasingly pervasive, and data-gathering likely to intensify, it is important to consider the consequences of these processes to better understand the new reality of music consumption.

The filter bubble

The term *filter bubble*, depicted by Eli Pariser (2011: 9), describes an outcome of the personalization of online services. As the experience of the user is specifically personalized, with different products, profiles, web pages or songs, visible and invisible, the individual may become intellectually unaware of their wider environment, isolating them within a bubble controlled and designed by an algorithmic filter. Since the election of Donald Trump to the US Presidency (along with the UK's Brexit vote), the term filter bubble has been increasingly used to explain the widely (at least in some parts of society) unexpected results (El-Bermawy 2016; Tait 2016; Jackson 2017). The argument follows that with large portions of American (and British) voters obtaining their news through personalized services (Google, Facebook), alternative viewpoints were kept hidden by the service's filters, leading to total shock when the results were announced. Liberals were blissfully unaware of dissenting opinions, not shown conservative search results, updates, or news on social media that would have suggested there were more pro-Trump or pro-Brexit voters – kept away from opinions different to their own. Exacerbating this is the increased use of data analysis by political candidates during campaigns. Hillary Clinton worked with 'cutting-edge big data analysts from BlueLabs and received support from Google and DreamWorks' (Hannes and Krogerus 2017), and Donald Trump and Ted Cruz worked with Cambridge Analytica, a data analysis and communication company, reportedly paying $15 million and $5.8 million, respectively, for their support (Hannes and Krogerus 2017). Cambridge Analytica received particular attention, having stated that they 'were able to form a model to predict the personality of every single adult in the United States of America' (Hannes and Krogerus 2017), and utilized data-mining and psychometrics to build an enormous database of 220 million people (Hannes and Krogerus 2017). Their work, allegedly, allowed candidates to target individual voters with individually curated messages. Donald Trump's 'striking inconsistencies, his much-criticized fickleness, and the resulting array of contradictory messages' (Hannes and Krogerus 2017) was in fact described by data scientist Cathy O'Neil as him acting 'like a perfectly opportunistic algorithm' (O'Neil 2017a). Alexander Nix, Cambridge Analytica CEO, said that 'Pretty much every message that Trump put out was data-driven' (Hannes and Krogerus 2017). Data-driven personalization, in the media, politics, and music, is increasingly prevalent, and the individual may be slowly inhabiting a bubble generated by the filtering process.

A fundamental problem with users' experience of music being controlled by algorithm, is that the algorithm may simply not be working particularly well: not developing a realistic understanding of users, not suggesting songs that listeners especially enjoy, or not unearthing new music for the listeners. The discovery of new music is not categorically positive, however, services are often advertised with terms suggesting otherwise, and their ability to provide successful discovery is marketed as unalloyed truth. Spotify promotes its service as a way to 'discover new tracks, and build the perfect collection' (Spotify 2017), and Apple Music describes itself as 'always bringing you content that's new and noteworthy' (Apple, Inc. 2017b). The purpose of this chapter is not to investigate the wording of advertising material, however these controlling algorithms are generally considered trade secrets (Feldman 2017), thus opaque, therefore in relying on their suggestions the user has to blindly (or perhaps deafly) trust them. The means in which services describe themselves indicate that their systems are successful at providing discovery and the ability to find what the user wants, but this is not necessarily true. As with other digital technology, the algorithms and processes will be continually tweaked and updated, however many commentators do not place much trust in them at present: 'there is still no algorithm that can account for human taste' (Knight 2015). In their analysis of music recommendation systems, Thite et al. argue that music suggestion is very different to other products: if Amazon finds that two products are regularly bought together, each can 'be recommended to a user if she already bought one of them before', however 'two songs being frequently listened to together doesn't imply that a new user would like the other song if she has already listened to one of the songs' (Thite et al. 2013). In addition, Will Knight, senior editor for AI at *MIT Technology Review*, asserts that 'algorithms cannot arrange songs in a creative way', and they cannot 'distinguish between a truly original piece and yet another me-too imitation of a popular sound' (Knight 2015). Songs that do not follow existing structural, tonal, or genre rules may simply be missed, or ignored by the algorithm. If listeners increasingly rely on them, services need to ensure that they work successfully. Digital tools may continue to be used in curating music streaming, however Spotify's Chris Johnson (who leads one of Spotify's data science teams in New York) recognizes these problems, and accepts that 'human expertise will remain a key part of Spotify's algorithms for the foreseeable future' (Knight 2015).

The reliance on algorithmic curation may restrict new discovery, and although discovering new music may not be categorically good for listeners, as Eli Pariser highlights in his book *The Filter Bubble*, there are still significant consequences of the individual being separated from new experiences. Exposure to alternative and conflicting perspectives helps society better examine and understand itself, and John Stuart Mill's notion was that 'even if all were agreed on an essential proposition it would be essential to give an ear to the one person who did not, lest people forget how to justify their original agreement' (Mill n.d., cited in Hitchens 2001: 29). Only when exposed to a range of different ideas does progressive understanding, consideration, and opinion occur: 'a world constructed from the familiar is a world in which there's nothing to learn' (Pariser 2011: 15). Music is no different. If new discovery is controlled, the serendipitous hearing of something new becomes impossible: serendipity being, by definition, unprogrammable. The algorithmic system will axiomatically never play an unpredictable song, and will never be able to astonish the listener with the unexpected, as 'it's nearly impossible to sort the usefully serendipitous and randomly provocative from the just plain irrelevant' (Pariser 2011: 97). With serendipity removed, curiosity becomes crucial. If the algorithm cannot provide unexpected music, the listener has to go looking for themselves. Proactive curiosity, however, may also decline as users become accustomed to a passive approach when looking for the next song: 'when your doorstep is crowded with salient content, there's little reason to travel any farther' (Pariser 2011: 94). Furthermore, if each user is faced with an individually personalized experience, vaguely different to everyone else's, they may become increasingly unaware of what is being hidden – Donald Rumsfeld's 'unknown unknowns' (Rumsfeld

2002). As Pariser notes, 'to feel curiosity, we have to be conscious that something's being hidden' (Pariser 2011: 91).

In *Blink*, Malcolm Gladwell writes that 'when we become expert in something, our tastes grow more esoteric and complex' (Gladwell 2005: 179), however within the filter bubble, algorithmically created through taste profiles and recorded data, we are unlikely to become expert in anything other than ourselves, or worse, the approximation of ourselves that the data predicts. The filter bubble in which the listener may experience music removes serendipity and risks reducing the desire for new discovery, and as long as the algorithm works well enough – not absolutely inappropriate suggestions – the pressure is further reduced to search for something better. The next song simply becomes that which the listener is predicted not to skip.

A feedback loop is built if the listener reacts positively to the algorithmic recommendations – listening, saving, looping. This behaviour is also recorded, seemingly turning the initial prediction into an accurate prophecy: *we thought you'd like this, and you did.* The feedback loop continues with prediction, behaviour confirming the prediction, another prediction, then more behaviour confirming the second prediction. This process continually builds more affirming data reinforcing the initial predictions: *we thought you'd like this, you did, and when we kept giving it to you, you kept liking it, therefore our model and predictions are working.* Not only could these self-fulfilling prophecies lead to a mundane experience for the listener, but over time the limited experience can shape the listener's preferences: 'these services may end up creating a good fit between you and your media by changing ... you' (Pariser 2011: 112). Within online media, the limited, filtered system is known as an echo chamber – it does not matter how much you might be posting about a political issue, Facebook's algorithms still control who sees the posts. Music curatorial algorithms may have a similar effect, the listener inhabiting an environment in which they hear what they are predicted to enjoy, and are kept unaware of everything they may not. A song that is prominent on one user's service may be obscured on another's. Feedback loops encouraging an unsurprising experience, a system that values consumption over stimulation, passive acceptance over active curiosity.

There are positive outcomes to personalized curation. The techniques have been developed to allow users to more easily navigate vast catalogues. Less time searching, more time listening. As long as the processes of data collection, analysis, and suggestion are working successfully, this may in fact be a better overall experience for the listener. Eli Pariser, however, suggests that although filter bubbles may 'act like a magnifying glass, helpfully expanding our view of a niche area of knowledge' (Pariser 2011: 83), and this may also 'limit what we are exposed to and therefore affect the way we think and learn' (Pariser 2011: 83). Efficient navigation of catalogues, and keeping the customer happy, are both sound business objectives. If the tools and techniques can be further improved, in time they may also grow into business advantages – services standing out due to their algorithmic suggestion capabilities.

One often unacknowledged issue around music personalization is the financial incentive at the core of algorithm design. As highlighted by Celma and Cano (2008), Kay, Matuszek and Munson (2015), and Friedman and Nissenbaum (1992), bias within algorithms is already widely recognized, however the commercial influence upon algorithm design should be explored further. Although user experience is important to these services, the algorithms are primarily designed to generate more revenue, through both maintaining corporate relationships, and obtaining and retaining customers. Financial objectives do not require algorithms to be perfect for the user, simply good enough. The predicted song does not need to be exactly what the listener wants, just sufficient to retain them as a paying customer. Aside from their customer relationships, services also need to retain strong relationships with content suppliers (artists, labels, distributors), advertisers (on ad-supported services), and in some cases, shareholders. Hypothetically, these other relationships may distinctly inform the development of curatorial algorithms. For example, increased use of:

–   The roster of artists from a particular major label (i.e., an important content supplier) within curated playlists, increasing the label's revenue, maintaining and improving the relationship.
–   Songs featuring keywords (Frank Ocean's *Nikes*), artists being used on wider marketing campaigns (Taylor Swift featuring in a Coke commercial for the Super Bowl), or just songs that are inherently connected to brands (Justin Timberlake's *I'm Lovin' It*).
–   Songs that are more likely to be enjoyed by the listener. There is less risk of them leaving the service, more likely to stay a paying customer.

Strong financial pressures may ensure that the algorithmically suggested songs are better for the service financially, rather than ideal for the customer. The services design the algorithm, therefore have ultimate control over which songs are pushed towards the user. A conflict therefore develops between providing listeners with the perfect music experience and generating revenue. Services must consider both sides of this conflict when designing their recommendation algorithms. Users have to enjoy their experience: otherwise they can take their subscriptions elsewhere, yet corporate partners, content providers, advertisers, shareholders, and other financial stakeholders must also be appeased. The opaque nature of these algorithm's design makes it impossible to analyse any inherent bias, therefore the customer has to be particularly wary of placing absolute trust in the service's recommendations. These recommendations may be regulated by a number of influences, many ultimately not be in the interest of the listening user, but the profit-focused corporation. There are many who feel the negative effects of filter bubbles are overstated. In 2015, Facebook published an in-depth study into the phenomena, broadly concluding that although their algorithms do enforce some level of control over the user's experience, specifically within news coverage, the main bias comes from user's own interaction – their friends, and what they interact with. This is summed up in an article by Adi Robertson in online magazine *The Verge*: 'it's not your feed that's primarily stopping you from reading opposing viewpoints – it's you' (2015).

Although algorithms may produce an isolated listening environment, there is an argument that this is nothing new. Media curation is as old as media itself. Editors select news stories, radio DJs choose songs, stores only stock certain albums – the consumer has never had complete access through a single source. However, Tufekci (2015) does note that algorithmic curation is significantly less transparent, thus less accountable. There are other factors that control what the listener hears: economic factors control what they can afford to consume as premium subscriptions are not necessarily cost-effective for everyone; legal and contractual issues, for example The Beatles catalogue only arrived on iTunes in 2010 after years of negotiation; and exclusive content, as artists such as Frank Ocean, Kanye West and Drake have all released service-exclusive albums, restricting who can listen to them. Individuals' isolation is also prevalent elsewhere: noise-cancelling headphones isolate the listener from local environmental sounds; self-service checkouts isolate the shopper from staff; and personal cars isolate the traveller from public transport. Many decisions in an individual's life are curatorial – which sounds not to hear, whom to interact with – and many of these choices involve giving up the curation to other people or services. Digital algorithms, although biased and controlling, are not necessarily unique in this practice.

What lies ahead

The use of behavioural data for personalization seems likely to continue. Cathy O'Neil says, 'It's safe to say that most important moments where people interact with large bureaucratic systems now involve an algorithm in the form of a scoring system' (O'Neil 2017b). O'Neil believes this will be increasingly true in many aspects of life: 'getting into college, getting a job, being assessed as a worker, getting a credit card or insurance, voting, and even policing' (O'Neil 2017b), as is currently true when consuming media such as news, social media, movie streaming.

As previously described, various problems may arise from this system; however, the potential of an improved user experience, plus enormous financial incentives, will ensure that online services, including music streaming services, will continue to develop their methods. As highlighted with media reports surrounding Cambridge Analytica in the 2016 US Presidential Election, vast quantities of personal information and behavioural data, when combined with machine learning, psychometric analysis techniques, and continual feedback, can, at least theoretically, be used to shape the individual's knowledge and experience of the wider world. Within politics this may be through adjusting particular campaign messages. For example, Grassegger and Krogerus (2017) suggest that when discussing the second amendment (protecting the 'right of the people to keep and bear arms' [National Archives 1789]), one campaign image may be aimed at individuals 'concerned with the threat of burglary', which emphasizes the 'insurance policy of a gun' and perhaps a photograph showing 'the hand of an intruder smashing a window', whereas another image, aimed at those who 'care about tradition, and habits, and family' (Grassegger and Krogerus 2017) may emphasize sport and family bonding. Both messages are striving for the same result, but using different imagery depending on the targeted individual. This therefore entrusts enormous power to the services that develop, update, and control the tools that support personalization – the curatorial algorithms and databases on individuals. This power may not provide thorough benefits to the individual, but still incentivizes companies to continue using these tools, gather more data, and to further refine the algorithms, effectively guaranteeing that personalization continues.

If data gathering and service personalization are likely to become universal, regardless of any negative, if unintended consequences, the focus should be ensuring that these systems are beneficial to the users. By engaging with a diverse range of news sources, the media consumer can synthesize differing reports and opinions, and develop a broader comprehension of a topic, lessening the impact of bias from a single source. The same is true for music consumption. To avoid the possible negative side effects of personalization – financially motivated reduced exposure to a wide range of music, curtailed new opinion and understanding, and curiosity weakened through passive listening experiences – the discerning listener needs to both recognize that biased curation is occurring, and actively work against being constrained within a filter bubble. As with news, this may be achieved by using multiple services – different algorithms with different suggestions. However, these algorithms may have very similar goals, ensuring customer retention through suggesting songs that are more likely to be listened to, and therefore using competing services may simply produce broadly similar outcomes. Although the algorithmic curation promotes a passive approach to listening, proactively changing behaviour will broaden the scope of the algorithmic filter. By not listening to the same artists, albums and genres, the individual user can wider the filter's parameters, allowing more variation into future suggestions, and keeping their own musical horizons broad. Passive listening may be easier, but by actively listening to music, personally exploring the enormous catalogues available, the limitations of algorithmic curation may be stemmed. Recorded behaviour can lead to a controlled, narrow experience, yet it can also do the opposite. By listening to particular songs, artists and genres, they become more likely to be suggested in the future; therefore by listening to a more eclectic range of music, the individual user can widen the algorithm's future suggestions.

The second approach is to focus on the algorithms. For such a powerful tool, algorithms are not particularly tightly regulated. O'Neil notes that 'in the US, a disparate group of federal agencies is in charge of enforcing laws in their industry or domain, none of which is particularly on top of the complex world of big data algorithms' (O'Neil 2017b). This leaves many organizations and areas 'untouched by scrutiny' (O'Neil 2017b). Although there are proposals towards avoiding algorithmic harm, extensive governmental control is currently far off. The effects within music may be subtle and less dangerous than other algorithms, for example those used for political campaigning, therefore higher control is unlikely, and also perhaps unnecessary. The leadership therefore falls to the developers of the algorithms themselves. The pressure to improve the algorithms for the users must come from both user feedback, and the company's desire for better services. If ubiquitous personalized curation is inevitable, the goal must be providing better suggestions, ensuring that users are not cocooned into limited (and limiting) environments, but are exposed to a diverse range of music; albeit music that still engages the listener. In *The Filter Bubble*, Pariser emphasizes work by David Hume, and the subsequent influence upon Karl Popper, around the philosophical problem of induction (Pariser 2011: 133). '"Falsifiability", Popper argued, was the key to the search for truth' (Pariser 2011: 134). Rather than a given theory being considered accurate until proved otherwise, for example, a user wants more folk music suggestions as they have listened to that previously, the system should continually try to disprove (i.e., falsify) the theory, to push closer to the truth: a user has listened to folk previously, so let's suggest hip-hop to better ensure our understanding of them. Services should consider this falsifiability when developing algorithms, continually providing songs that the data suggests the users may not like, to prove their initial predictions correct. Clearly this could be a risk to services: to retain a user's subscription the predictions do not necessarily need to be perfect just sufficiently acceptable. This process will however provide a better understanding of users, therefore will still be beneficial to services. Perhaps this process already occurs, however the current design of recommendation algorithms is sufficiently private that this cannot be confirmed.

Both users and services must take an active role in improving the algorithmic suggestions. Users should understandthe systems more, check their behaviour with the algorithm in mind, and ensure that they broaden their listening habits as much as possible. For the user's benefit, the services also need to consider how the algorithms are designed, and through continual improvement; not simply by increasing the data points of recorded behaviour, but by providing wide-ranging suggestions and continually using techniques to improve the algorithms, using the feedback loop for improvement rather than just increased precision. Looking ahead, Pariser suggests that 'the technology of the future will work about as well as the technology of the past – which is to say, well enough, but not perfectly' (Pariser 2011: 214). Both the users and the services should proceed with caution, remaining as objective as possible about the technologies' effectiveness and continually questioning the successes and failures, both intended and unintended.

Conclusion

Algorithmic curation is increasingly ubiquitous, and practically necessary. The consequences of passive listening and algorithmic curation are potentially invasive and detrimental to listeners, yet the secretive design of these algorithms does not currently allow the situation to be satisfactorily evaluated. At present however, the most dubious aspect of these systems is the insidious pressure of various stakeholders, including content providers and advertisers. The scale of influence that financial relationships have upon suggestions is unclear, but is likely to compel recommendation systems to be structured not for listener enjoyment, but financial gain for both services and their associates. Digital algorithms increasingly exert power over music listeners and therefore must be examined. Understanding these systems is the first step towards improvement. Within this area, many processes appear new – instant access to recorded music, absolutely personalized suggestions, vast and detailed databases on millions of users – however, the issues faced by contemporary listeners are not. There are covert business relationships controlling media, multinational corporations exerting power over customers for financial gain, and individuals and groups isolated from differing ideas. Algorithmic control is a reductive system, an attempt to quantify art, the audience, and the subjective nature of enjoyment. Rather than being captivated by apparent innovation, we – the listeners of today – need to proactively assert control over our own experience in order to form a more perfect soundscape of our lives.

References

Ackerman, Spencer and James Ball (2014), 'Optic Nerve: Millions of Yahoo webcam images intercepted by GCHQ', *Guardian*, 28 February. Available online: https://www.theguardian.com/world/2014/feb/27/gchq-nsa-webcam-images-internet-yahoo (accessed 3 April 2017).

Apple, Inc. (2015), 'Introducing Apple Music – All The Ways You Love Music. All in one place', *Apple, Inc.*, 8 June. Available online: https://www.apple.com/newsroom/2015/06/08Introducing-Apple-Music-All-The-Ways-You-Love-Music-All-in-One-Place-/ (accessed 10 December 2017).

Apple, Inc. (2017a), 'HomePod Reinvents Music in the Home', *Apple, Inc.*, 5 June. Available online: https://www.apple.com/newsroom/2017/06/homepod-reinvents-music-in-the-home/ (accessed 10 December 2017).

Apple, Inc. (2017b), 'Discover More Music in More Ways', *Apple, Inc.*, n.d. Available online: https://www.apple.com/apple-music/ (accessed 10 December 2017).

Brogan, Jacob (2016), 'What's the Deal With Algorithms?', *Slate*, 2 February. Available online: http://www.slate.com/articles/technology/future_tense/2016/02/what_is_an_algorithm_an_explainer.html (accessed 10 December 2017).

Celma, Òscar and Pedro Cano (2008), 'From Hits to Niches? or How Popular Artists can Bias Music Recommendation and Discovery'. Barcelona: Universitat Pompeu Fabra.

Charlie Rose (2005), [TV programme] Bloomberg Television, 3 May, 21.00.

Cooney, Peter (2014), 'NSA Collects Nearly 200 Million Global Text Messages Every Day [Report]', *Business Insider*, 16 January. Available online: http://www.businessinsider.com/nsa-collects-text-messages-2014-1 (accessed 3 April 2017).

Covington, Paul, Jay Adams and Emre Sargin (2016), 'Deep Neural Networks for YouTube Recommendations', *Google*, 15 September. Available online: https://static.googleusercontent.com/media/research.google.com/en//pubs/archive/45530.pdf (accessed 10 December 2017).

The Echo Nest (2017), 'We Know Music . . ', The Echo Nest, n.d. Available online: http://the.echonest.com/ (accessed 10 December 2017).

Eckersley, Peter, Seth Schoen, Kevin Bankston and Derek Slater (2006), 'Six Tips to Protect Your Search Privacy', *Electronic Frontier Foundation*, 14 September. Available online: https://www.eff.org/wp/six-tips-protect-your-search-privacy (accessed 1 December 2017).

El-Bermawy, Mostafa (2016), 'Your Filter Bubble is Destroying Democracy', *Wired*, 18 November. Available online: https://www.wired.com/2016/11/filter-bubble-destroying-democracy/ (accessed 3 April 2017).

Feldman, Brian (2017), 'Spotify Has the Only Algorithms I Don't Fear', *Yahoo Finance*, 29 September. Available online: https://finance.yahoo.com/news/spotify-only-algorithms-don-t-211457426.html (accessed 8 December 2017).

Follorou, Jacques (2016), 'American and British Spy Agencies Targeted in-Flight Mobile Phone Use', *The Intercept*, 7 December. Available online: https://theintercept.com/2016/12/07/american-and-british-spy-agencies-targeted-in-flight-mobile-phone-use/ (accessed 3 April 2017).

Friedman, Batya and Helen Nissenbaum (1992), 'Bias in Computer Systems', Clare Boothe Luce Foundation.

Gibbs, Samuel (2014), 'Gmail Does Scan All Emails, New Google Terms Clarify', *Guardian*, 15 April. Available online: https://www.theguardian.com/technology/2014/apr/15/gmail-scans-all-emails-new-google-terms-clarify (accessed 15 November 2017).

Gladwell, Malcolm (2005), *blink*. New York: Little, Brown and Company.

Google (2017), 'How Google Search Works', *Google*, n.d. Available online: https://support.google.com/webmasters/answer/70897?hl=en (accessed 10 December 2017).

Grassegger, Hannes and Mikael Krogerus (2017), 'The Data That Turned the World Upside Down', *Motherboard*, 28 January. Available online: https://motherboard.vice.com/en_us/article/mg9vvn/how-our-likes-helped-trump-win (accessed 3 April 2017).

Hitchens, Christopher (2001), *Letters to a Young Contrarian*. New York: Basic Books.

Ingham, Tim (2016), 'Katy Perry Knows Exactly How Much Spotify is Punishing Apple Exclusive Artists . . ', *Music Business Worldwide*, 29 August. Available online: https://

www.musicbusinessworldwide.com/katy-perry-knows-exactly-how-much-spotify-is-punishing-apple-exclusive-artists/ (accessed 10 December 2017).

Ingham, Tim (2017b), 'Spotify is Set to End 2017 with 70m Subscribers and $5bn in Revenue, but How Much Money Will It Lose?', *Music Business Worldwide*, 3 August. Available online: https://www.musicbusinessworldwide.com/spotify-is-set-to-end-2017-with-70m-subscribers-and-5bn-in-revenue-but-how-much-money-will-it-lose/ (accessed 29 September 2017).

Jackson, Jasper (2017), 'Eli Pariser: Activist whose filter bubble warnings presaged Trump and Brexit', *Guardian*, 8 January. Available online: https://www.theguardian.com/media/2017/jan/08/eli-pariser-activist-whose-filter-bubble-warnings-presaged-trump-and-brexit (accessed 3 April 2017).

Johnson, Eric (2016), 'Bruno Mars and Mark Zuckerberg Showed up at Spotify CEO Daniel Ek's Wedding', *recode*, 28 August. Available online: https://www.recode.net/2016/8/28/12681664/bruno-mars-mark-zuckerberg-daniel-ek-spotify-wedding (accessed 9 December 2017).

Kay, Matthew, Cynthia Matuszek and Sean A. Munson (2015), 'Unequal Representation and Gender Stereotypes in Image Search Results for Occupations'. Washington, DC: University of Washington.

Knight, Will (2015), 'The Hit Charade', *MIT Technology Review*, 22 September. Available online: https://www.technologyreview.com/s/541471/the-hit-charade/ (accessed 10 December 2017).

Knopper, Steve (2017), 'How Spotify Playlists Create Hits', 15 August. Available online: http://www.rollingstone.com/music/news/inside-spotifys-playlists-curators-and-fake-artists-w497702 (accessed 10 December 2017).

National Archives (1789), 'Transcription of the 1789 Joint Resolution of Congress Proposing 12 Amendments to the U.S. Constitution: Amendment II', 25 September. Available online: https://www.archives.gov/founding-docs/bill-of-rights-transcript (accessed 19 November 2017).

O'Neil, Cathy (2017a), 'Donald Trump Is the Singularity', *Bloomberg*, 6 February. Available online: https://www.bloomberg.com/view/articles/2017-02-06/donald-trump-is-the-singularity (accessed 4 April 2017).

O'Neil, Cathy (2017b). 'How Can We Stop Algorithms Telling Lies?', 16 July. Available online: https://www.theguardian.com/technology/2017/jul/16/how-can-we-stop-algorithms-telling-lies (accessed 19 November 2017).

Pandora (2017), 'About the Music Genome Project', *Pandora*, n.d. Available online: https://www.pandora.com/about/mgp (accessed 10 December 2017).

Pariser, Eli (2011), *The Filter Bubble: How The New Personalized Web Is Changing What We Read And How We Think*. London: Penguin Books.

Popper, Ben (2015), 'How Spotify's Discover Weekly Cracked Human Curation at Internet Scale', *The Verge*, 30 September. Available online: https://www.theverge.com/2015/9/30/9416579/spotify-discover-weekly-online-music-curation-interview (accessed 10 December 2017).

ProPublica (2016), 'Facebook Lets Advertisers Exclude Users by Race', *ProPublica*, 28
    October. Available online: https://www.propublica.org/article/facebook-lets-
    advertisers-exclude-users-by-race (accessed 10 December 2017).

ProPublica (2017), 'Facebook Enabled Advertisers to Reach Jew Haters', *ProPublica*, 14
    September. Available online: https://www.propublica.org/article/facebook-enabled-
    advertisers-to-reach-jew-haters (accessed 10 December 2017).

Robertson, Adi (2015), 'Facebook Says its Algorithms Aren't Responsible for Your Online
    Echo Chamber', 7 May. Available online: https://www.theverge.com/2015/5/7/8564795/
    facebook-online-opinion-filter-bubble-news-feed-study (accessed 2 December 2015).

Rumsfeld, Donald (2002), 'DoD News Briefing – Secretary Rumsfeld and Gen. Myers',
    U.S. Department of Defense, 12 February. Available online: http://archive.defense.
    gov/Transcripts/Transcript.aspx?TranscriptID=2636 (accessed 15 September
    2017).

Rundle, Michael (2015), 'Apple Music's Jimmy Lovine: No one will be able to catch us',
    Wired, 7 August. Available online: http://www.wired.co.uk/article/apple-music-
    jimmy-iovine-interview (accessed 10 December 2017)

SAS (2017a), 'Machine Learning', *SAS*, n.d. Available online: https://www.sas.com/
    en_us/insights/analytics/machine-learning.html (accessed 10 December 2017).

SAS (2017b), 'Big Data', *SAS*, n.d. Available online: https://www.sas.com/en_us/insights/
    big-data/what-is-big-data.html# (accessed 10 December 2017).

SAS (2017c), 'Deep Learning', *SAS*, n.d. Available online: https://www.sas.com/en_us/
    insights/analytics/deep-learning.html (accessed 10 December 2017).

Shieber, Jonathan (2017), 'Polis is reinventing the door-to-door salesman', *TechCrunch*,
    24 March. Available online: https://techcrunch.com/2017/03/24/polis-is-reinventing-
    the-door-to-door-salesman/ (accessed 2 December 2017).

Spotify (2016), 'Discover Weekly Reaches Nearly 5 Billion Tracks Streamed Since
    Launch', 25 May. Available online: https://press.spotify.com/us/2016/05/25/discover-
    weekly-reaches-nearly-5-billion-tracks-streamed-since-launch/ (accessed 29
    November 2017).

Spotify (2017), 'What's on Spotify?', n.d. Available online: https://www.spotify.com/us/
    (accessed 12 December 2017).

Stutz, Colin (2018), 'Spotify Hits 70M Subscribers', *Billboard*, 4 January. Available online:
    https://www.billboard.com/articles/business/8092645/spotify-hits-70-million-
    subscribers (accessed 15 March 2018).

Tait, Amelia (2016), 'How to Burst Your Social Media Bubble', *New Statesman*, 11
    November. Available online: https://www.newstatesman.com/science-tech/social-
    media/2016/11/how-burst-your-social-media-bubble (accessed 3 April 2017).

Thite, Aashish, Prakhar Panwaria and Shishir Prasad (2013), 'Music Recommendation
    System: Offline evaluation of learning methodologies', Wisconsin: University of
    Wisconsin.

Turfekci, Zeynep (2015), 'Algorithmic Harms beyond Facebook and Google: Emergent
    challenges of computational agency'. Colorado: Colorado Technology Law Journal.

Unblinking (2002), 'Googlewhacking: The Search for the One True Googlewhack',
   Unblinking, 13 March. Available online: http://unblinking.com/heh/googlewhack.
   htm (accessed 10 December 2017).

Vanderbilt, Tom (2016), *You May Also Like: Taste in an Age of Endless Choice*. New York:
   Vintage Books.

YouTube (2017), 'YouTube for Press', *YouTube*, 1 December. Available online: https://
   www.youtube.com/yt/about/press/ (accessed 10 December 2017).

Index

22tracks 254, 263–65
50 Cent 63
808 State 22, 139, 148–50, 153

ABBA 80, 162, 169
algorithms 2, 18, 24–25, 155, 159–61, 166, 168,
    263, 266, 269–90
    algorithmic curation 16–17, 269–90
alternative alternative 74–78
Amazon 4, 6, 9, 58, 228, 269–70, 276, 278
Aphex Twin 149
Apple 4, 10, 16, 52, 58, 76, 156–57, 162,
    235–36, 259, 261, 272, 274, 278, 286
Accept 98
Avery, Daniel 124

Bartók, Béla 17 3
Beatles, the 136, 235, 282
Bearded Youth 69
Beethoven, Ludwig van 172
Beitzke, Alex 180
Berghain 113
Berntsson, Erik 164–67
Biting Tongues 147–48
Bjork 63, 150
blockchain technology 20–21, 51–68, 127–28
Blair, Tony 26
'Blue Monday' 138, 153
Bourdieu, Pierre 1, 27, 37, 47, 86, 88, 120, 221,
    229, 238, 246, 249, 256, 260–61, 263,
    266–67
Buzzcocks, the 76, 147–48

Cabello, Camila 7–8
capital, cultural 256
Caravan Palace 194
clubs, clubbing 21, 70, 78, 85–87, 111–31
cultural intermediaries 260–61
cultural omnivore 257
curating 255, 263–65
Curtis, Ian 140–42

digitization 2–6, 10–11, 18, 24, 188, 227, 238,
    255, 258, 261
    convergent digitization 3–6, 10, 188

DIY (Do-It-Yourself) 35, 37, 42, 147–48
Donner, Emanuel 178–79
Drake 204, 282
Dry Bar 117
Dutty Moonshine 192, 194

Eastern Bloc 123, 124
Ek, Daniel 6, 211, 213, 216, 226
electro swing 191–207
Elrow 112
Eno, Brian 73, 146, 148, 160, 169
Explosions in the Sky 76, 78

Fabric 114
Factory Club 137, 146
Factory Records 116, 138–39, 144, 148,
    152
Falco 172–73, 179
Fennesz, Christian 172
Florence and the Machine 180
Fran Palermo 23, 171, 175, 182–88

gatekeeping, gatekeepers 10, 16, 24, 57, 253,
    255, 263, 266
Gin Ga 23, 171, 175, 178–84, 187
Glass, Philip 274
Gonzalez, Henri 182–88
Grainge, Lucian 6
Guča Trumpet Festival 99
Guru 192, 200–1

Haçienda 111, 114, 116, 137, 145–46
Haydn, Joseph 173
Heap, Imogen 58, 61–62, 66
Hellström, Sten-Olof 164–67
Hidden 118–23
Hook, Peter 22, 135, 139–45, 151–53
HVOB 173

independent artists 33, 38
independent record labels 34–39, 41–46
Iron Maiden 98
Islington Mill 117, 118
iTunes 6, 16, 34, 44, 56, 58, 155, 162, 164, 169,
    174, 235, 282

Jarocin Rock Festival 93, 99–100, 103, 105–6
Jobs, Steve 6, 58
Joy Division 22, 72, 139–44, 152–53

Klangkarussel 173
Konrad, Alex 178–82
Kraftwerk 63
Kruder and Dorfmeister 172, 179

Ligeti, György 173
Lipa, Dua 8
Liszt, Franz 173
Locomotiv GT 173

Madchester 116, 123, 138
major record labels 7, 10–11, 20, 29, 33–43,
    45, 48, 58, 75, 76, 148–49, 162–63, 172,
    174–76, 188, 259–62, 281
Marx, Karl 4, 12
Massey, Graham 22, 135, 139, 145–53
Massive Attack 193
Meno, Matias 178–82
Metallica 162
Miku, Hatsune 159, 166, 167
minor record labels 39–41
Mozart, Wolfgang Amadeus 172

Nähl, Niklas 164–67
neoliberalism 2, 4–5, 9–11, 13–15, 19, 21–22,
    27, 30, 33, 65, 76, 111, 119, 121, 123–27,
    136, 138–39, 142, 148, 150, 162, 176,
    256, 258
New Order 22, 138–39, 142–45, 152–53
Niemen, Czesław 106
Night and Day 117

Ocean, Frank 281, 282
Omega 173–74
Orban, Viktor 174
Orbison, Roy 15
O.Z.O.R.A. Festival 93, 100–1, 104–6

Palmer, Amanda 12
Parov Stelar 173, 192, 198
Partisan Collective 123–27
Pitchfork 255
playback 211–12, 215–19, 221–28
playbour 216, 218–23, 226–28
post-internet 2–3, 5, 26, 30
post-rock 11, 21, 69–92
Prince 161, 162
Pulsinger, Patrick 172

remix 1, 8, 26, 150, 172, 180, 187, 192, 194, 196,
    202–3, 214
Resident Advisor 253–56
Ronson, Mark 204

sample, sampling 8, 11, 23, 26, 73–4, 88, 159,
    164, 174, 188, 191, 193, 198, 202, 205,
    238–39
Sankeys 116, 118
Schoenberg, Arnold 172
Schubert, Franz 172
Sex Pistols 137, 139–40
Sheeran, Ed 8, 180
Slowgold 164
Spotify 34, 44–45, 47, 211, 213, 215–16,
    228, 231–32, 237, 250, 262, 269, 272,
    274–76, 278–79, 287–89
Springsteen, Bruce 97
Strauss, Richard 12
streaming 4–6, 9–10, 14, 16–17, 23–25, 29, 51,
    56–57, 60, 65, 67, 123–24, 126,
    155, 160, 162, 211, 213, 215–16,
    226–27, 237, 240–41, 248, 258,
    260, 262, 266, 269–70, 274–75, 277,
    279, 283
Sumner, Bernard 140, 142
Swift, Taylor 281

taste 255–58
    taste entrepreneurs 258
    taste, legitimate 256–58
Timberlake, Justin 281
Thatcher, Margaret 4, 136, 146

Ullén, Lisa 164, 165, 166, 167, 168,
U2 161, 162

Warehouse Project, the 116, 118, 122
Webern, Anton 172
West, Kanye 124, 174, 282
Wilson, Tony 22, 113, 116, 137, 138, 140, 146,
    149
White Hotel, the 118–23
Wihidal, Klemens 178–79

Yonderboi 174
YouTube 4, 6, 9–11, 14–16, 47, 52, 58, 62, 156,
    161, 174, 178–80, 183–84, 204, 241,
    245, 258, 261, 272

Zagar 174
ZTT Records 149–50

Lightning Source UK Ltd.
Milton Keynes UK
UKHW040651311218
334517UK00003B/68/P